MILLER'S
COLLECTORS CARS
PRICE GUIDE

1992-1993
(Volume II)

Compiled and Edited by

Judith and Martin Miller

General Editor: Robert Murfin

Foreword by Lord Montagu of Beaulieu

BCA
LONDON · NEW YORK · SYDNEY · TORONTO

MILLER'S COLLECTORS CARS PRICE GUIDE 1992-1993

Created and designed by
Millers Publications
The Cellars, High Street
Tenterden, Kent TN30 6BN
Telephone: (058 06) 6411

Part of Reed International Books Limited

This edition published 1992 by
BCA by arrangement
with Millers Publications
CN 5631

Compiled and edited by
Judith and Martin Miller

General Editor: Robert Murfin
Production Team: Sue Boyd
Marion Rickman, Jo Wood
Jody Taylor, Stephen Parry
Advertising Executive: Elizabeth Smith
Display Advertisements: Trudi Hinkley, Elizabeth Warwick
Index compiled by: DD Editorial Services, Beccles

Copyright © 1992 Millers Publications

A CIP catalogue record for this book is
available from the British Library

Typeset by Mainline Typesetters Ltd, St. Leonards-on-Sea
Illustrations by G.H. Graphics, St. Leonards-on-Sea
Colour origination by Scantrans, Singapore.
Printed and bound in England by William Clowes Ltd.,
Beccles and London

Introduction

Let me start by thanking you all for your helpful comments and suggestions on our first Miller's Collectors Cars Price Guide. It has been very well received and, I am delighted to say, has in fact virtually sold out.

I should like to introduce this, our second volume. It runs along the same lines as our other Price Guides – every entry is different from previous years and thus grows into a complete visual reference work for all our readers, regardless of the level of interest.

The past year has seen a levelling off and steadying of prices in the collectors car market. This has meant that the over-hyped and over-speculated vehicles are now selling at realistic prices, while good, honest, clean cars have shown increases in both interest and value.

Our aim in this book is to provide you, the reader, with an overview of the collectors car marketplace. In order to achieve this we have, in conjunction with private collectors, car clubs and our panel of experts, prepared what we hope is a comprehensive listing of collectors vehicles, priced according to condition. We have illustrated the list with examples supplied to us for publication; please study the code at the end of each caption – this will tell you the source of that particular entry.

Finally, I should like to thank all the car clubs, individuals and our team of experts, especially Peter Card and Malcolm Welford at ADT Auctions, for all their help with this second edition and thank you all for your comments and suggestions, many of which we have incorporated into this edition.

Acknowledgements

The publishers would like to acknowledge the great assistance given by our consultants.

Peter Card — ADT Auctions Ltd, *Classic & Historic Car Division, Blackbushe Airport,*

Malcolm Welford — *Blackwater, Camberley, Surrey*

Malcolm Barber — Sotheby's, *34-35 New Bond Street, London W1*

Tony Leslie — Holmesdale Sevens, *Fareham, Chilsham Lane Herstmonceux, East Sussex*

Derek Green — Cedar Classic Cars, *Hartley Witney, Hants*

David Baldock — Chequers Garage, *North Road, Goudhurst, Kent*

Adrian Hamilton — Duncan Hamilton & Co Ltd, *The Square, Bagshot, Surrey*

1956 Ford Thunderbird.   £12,000-15,000   *AUT*

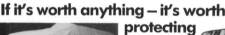

Foreword

I am delighted to write this foreword to Miller's Collectors Cars Price Guide 1992-93. For the enthusiast this book provides a pictorial history of the car, from the steam powered horseless carriage to the Ferrari F.40 – a splendid photographic record – and in addition, for the collector, provides an overview of the marketplace.

The National Motor Museum at Beaulieu, which I founded 40 years ago, is now one of the largest automobile collections in the world and its comprehensive libraries of books, photographs and film provide a service for motoring enthusiasts all over the world. As hosts to many motor-related sales ourselves, including Europe's largest auto-jumble event, and Christie's historic vehicle sales, we at the National Motor Museum have witnessed at first hand the tremendous popularity of motoring memorabilia that has grown up over the last 20 years, alongside interest in the cars themselves.

I am convinced that this, the second edition of Miller's Collectors Cars Price Guide, will become a must for collectors of classic cars.

Montagu of Beaulieu

1992

Key to Illustrations

Each illustration and descriptive caption is accompanied by a letter-code. By reference to the following list of Auctioneers (denoted by *) and Dealers (•), the source of any item may be immediately determined. In no way does this constitute or imply a contract or binding offer on the part of any of our contributors to supply or sell the goods illustrated, or similar articles, at the prices stated. Advertisers in this year's directory are denoted by †.

AC   • American Connection. Tel: (0803) 606989

ADT   †* ADT Auctions Ltd, Classic & Historic Car Division, Blackbushe Airport, Blackwater, Camberley, Surrey. Tel: (0252) 878555

APP   †• Richard Appleyard, Sunderland House, Sunderland Street, Tickhill, Doncaster, S. Yorks. Tel: (0302) 743782

AUT   †• Autodrome, Omega Place, Caledonian Road, London N1. Tel: 071-833 2076

BA   †• Balmoral Automobile Co Ltd, 260 Knights Hill, West Norwood, London SE27. Tel: 081-761 1155

BC   • Beaulieu Cars Ltd, Beaulieu, Hants. Tel: (0590) 612444

BHM   †• Brands Hatch Morgans, Brands Hatch Circuit, Fawkham, Kent. Tel: (0474) 874147

BLE   †• Ivor Bleaney, PO Box 60, Salisbury, Wilts. Tel: (0794) 390895

BS   • Below Stairs, 103 High Street, Hungerford, Berks. Tel: (0488) 682317

C   * Christie's, 8 King Street, St James's, London SW1. Tel: 071-839 9060

CA   †• Chris Alford Racing & Sports Cars, Newland Cottage, Hassocks, W. Sussex. Tel: (0273) 845966

C.A.R.S.   †• Classic Automobilia & Regalia Specialists, Prinny's Antiques Gallery, 3 Meeting House Lane, The Lanes, Brighton, E. Sussex. Tel: (0273) 204554/601960 (24-hour answerphone)

CB   • Cropredy Bridge Garage Ltd (Exclusively Jensen), Riverside Works, Cropredy, Banbury, Oxon. Tel: (0295) 758444

CC   • Collectors Cars (Mr D. Connell), Drakeshill, Birmingham Road, Kenilworth, Warwicks. Tel: (0926) 57705

CCTC   • Classic Car Trade Centre, 47 Ash Grove, Chelmsford, Essex. Tel: (0245) 358028

Cen   * Central Motor Auctions PLC, Central House, Pontefract Road, Rothwell, Leeds. Tel: (0532) 820707

CGB   †• Cars Gone By, Maidstone, Kent. Tel: (0622) 630220/630110

CH   †• Chestnut House Sports Cars, Tydd St Giles, Wisbech, Cambs. Tel: (0945) 870833

CLC   • Country Lane Classics, The Barn, Macclesfield, Cheshire. Tel: (0625) 860149

C(M)   * Christie's (Monaco), S.A.M., Park Palace, 98000, Monte Carlo. Tel: 010 339 325 1933

A Rolls-Royce Phantom I nickel radiator, with shutters, 33in (84cm) high.   Est. **£1,800-2,500**   S

CMA   * Classic Motor Auctions Ltd, PO Box 20, Fishponds, Bristol. Tel: (0272) 710370

CNY   * Christie, Manson & Woods International Inc, 502 Park Avenue, New York, NY 10022. Tel 0101 212 546 1000

CR   †• Classic Restorations, Arch 124, Cornwall Road, Waterloo, London SE1. Tel: 071-928 6613

DB   †• David Baldock, North Road, Goudhurst, Kent. Tel: (0580) 211326

DDM   * Dickinson, Davy and Markham, Wrawby Street, Brigg, S. Humberside. Tel: (0652) 53666

DF   • David Foster, 87 Foxley Lane, Purley, Surrey. Tel: 081-668 1246

DG   †• Cedar Classic Cars (Derek Green), Hartley Witney, Hants. Tel: (0734) 326628

DHA   • Duncan Hamilton & Co (Byfleet) Ltd, The Square, Bagshot, Surrey. Tel: (0276) 71010

DL   • Dunsfold Land Rovers Ltd, Dunsfold, Surrey. Tel: (0483) 200567

ESM   †• East Sussex Minors, Bearhurst Farm, Stonegate, Wadhurst, E. Sussex. Tel: (0580) 200203

FCV   • Forge Classic & Vintage Vehicles, St Michael's, Tenterden, Kent. Tel: (05806) 6446

FFA   • Finesse Fine Art, 9 Coniston Crescent, Weymouth, Dorset. Tel: (0305) 770463

FM   • Franco Macri. Tel: (0797) 253252

FOR   †• Fortescue Garages Ltd, 2A Luther Road, Winton, Bournemouth, Dorset. Tel: (0202) 529929

GH Gawsworth Hall. Tel: (0260) 223456

HA * Hampson Auctions, Road Four, Winsford Industrial Estate, Winsford, Cheshire. Tel: (0606) 559054

HCI †● Harvey Classic Investments, Egham, Surrey. Tel: (0784) 434063

HS ● Holmesdale Sevens, Fareham, Chilsham Lane, Herstmonceux, E. Sussex. Tel: (0323) 833603

HSS * Henry Spencer & Sons, 20 The Square, Retford, Notts. Tel: (0777) 708633

HWA ● Harry Woodnorth Automobiles, 1650 North Bosworth Avenue, Chicago, Illinois 60622, USA. Tel: 0101 312 227 1340

JB ● J & B Car Sales, Fina Service Station, Hale Street, East Peckham, Tonbridge, Kent. Tel: (0622) 872819

JC ● Japanese Classics. Tel: 061-707 3795

KI * Kruse International, PO Box 190, Auburn, Indiana 46706, USA. Tel: 0101 219 925 5600

KSC †● Kent Sports Cars, Nonington, Dover, Kent. Tel: (0304) 840878

LAR * Leigh Auction Rooms, John Stacey & Sons (Leigh-on-Sea) Ltd, 88-90 Pall Mall, Leigh-on-Sea, Essex. Tel: (0702) 77051

LF * Lambert & Foster, 77 Commercial Road, Paddock Wood, Kent. Tel: (0892) 832325

MC ● Manor Classics. Tel: (0295) 758355

MM †● The Morgan Model Co, Mill Lane, Bulkeley, Malpas, Cheshire. Tel: (0829) 720514

Mot ● Motospot, North Kilworth, Lutterworth, Leics. Tel: (0455) 552548 or (0831) 120498

MSMP ● Mike Smith's Motoring Past, Chiltern House, Ashendon, Aylesbury, Bucks. Tel: (0296) 651283

MSN ● Murray Scott-Nelson, Beaconsfield Street, Scarborough, N. Yorks. Tel: (0723) 361227

O * Orion Auction House, Victoria Building, 13 Bld Princesse Charlotte, Monte Carlo, MC98000, Monaco. Tel: 93 301669

OBA †● Outback Autos, Windy Ridge, Walcups Lane, Great Massingham, Norfolk. Tel: (0485) 520394

OC ● Orchid Cars. Tel: (0980) 623805

ONS * Onslows, Metrostore, Townmead Road, London SW6. Tel: 071-793 0240.

1923 Triumph 550cc Solo Motorcycle, £2,000-2,250 *S*

Chevy 350 Late Model Sprint Car. £2,000-2,500 *PMc*

PA †● Pioneer Automobiles, Andover Road, Whitchurch, Hants. Tel: (0256) 896483

PC Private Collection

PiK †● Porters in Kensington, 11-14 Atherstone Mews, S. Kensington, London SW7. Tel: 071-584 7458

PJF ● P. J. Fischer Classic Automobiles, Dyers Lane, Upper Richmond Road, Putney, London SW15. Tel: 081-785 6633

PMc * Paul McInnis Inc, Auction Gallery, Route 88, 356 Exeter Road, Hampton Falls, New Hampshire 03844, USA. Tel: 0101 603 778 8989

RBB * Russell, Baldwin and Bright, Ryelands Road, Leominster, Herefordshire. Tel: (0568) 611166

RCC †● The Real Car Co, Snowdonia Business Park, Coed y Parc, Bethesda, Gwynedd. Tel: (0248) 602649

RE ● Rons Emporium, 98 Church Lane, Sholden, Deal, Kent. Tel: (0304) 374784

Ree †● Rees Bros. Tel: (0252) 23038

RTC ● Red Triangle Classic Cars, Cherry Street, Warwick. Tel: (0926) 410176

S †* Sotheby's, 34-35 New Bond Street, London W1. Tel: 071-493 8080

SC ● Sporting Classics, Phil Hacker, The Oast, Shears Farm, North Road, Goudhurst, Kent. Tel: (0580) 211275

SCC †● Simon Copsey Classic Cars, Sparrowes Nest, Henley Road, Ipswich, Suffolk. Tel: (0473) 256936

SL †● Stephen Langton Ltd, Blindley Heath, Surrey. Tel: (0342) 833732

S(M) * Sotheby's, B.P. 45 Le Sporting Hiver, Place du Casino, MC 98001, Monaco Cedex. Tel: 33 (93) 30 88 80

S(NY) * Sotheby's, 1334 York Avenue, New York, NY 10021, USA. Tel: 0101 212 606 7000

S8 †● Straight Eight Ltd, 152-160 Goldhawk Road, London W12. Tel: 081-743 1599

WCC †● Worthing Carriage Company, 3 Littlehampton Road, Worthing, W. Sussex. Tel: (0903) 830314

WH * Walton & Hipkiss, 111 Worcester Road, Hagley, Nr Stourbridge, W. Midlands

INDEX TO ADVERTISERS

STATE OF THE MARKET

The golden days of 1989 now seem long past and the excitement and frantic purchasing power of the populace has been reduced at the expense of world inflation, interest rates and redundancy. Cars that were perceived to be 'good news' and, in consequence, fetching high sums at the end of the 1980s, have dropped in value dramatically and I am sorry to say some investors have, with astonishing ease, lost an appreciable amount of money!

While these words may appear to be pessimistic, is this really the current state of the marketplace? Are classic and historic cars now considered to be 'bad news'?

I am delighted to say that in my view this is not the case. Certainly no one can doubt that values are lower than they were in 1989, but the one word I have yet to use and that transcends all of the current doom and gloom is enthusiasm. Enthusiasm continues to be a thread of stimulus that has always been associated with motoring and, I am delighted to say, is alive and kicking and, if anything, on the ascendancy.

Everything moves in cycles so they say, and this is no more true than it is in the collectors' market today. In the 1960s prices of veteran and vintage vehicles increased steadily, but by the early 1970s and again in the early 1980s prices levelled off. That same levelling is taking place ten years later, albeit rather more dramatically because of the golden days of 1989. However, we can take comfort from the knowledge that the long term collector can rest assured that the real investment in his vehicle is the joy of ownership which is multiplied significantly by its use.

The Classic and Historic Division of ADT Auctions is often asked some important but simple questions about the purchasing of a classic car. These not unreasonable questions usually fall into four categories and, for the purpose of this introduction, we will label them the WHY, WHAT, WHEN and WHERE of buying a collectors vehicle.

It has been said in the past, and there may be some truth in the statement, that if an aspiring collector has to ask 'why' he should collect something, then the answer is that he probably should not. Unfortunately this answer is too simple for our purposes. My belief is that at various times in our lives we have gained pleasure in the remembrance of incidents and experiences of long ago, and in all probability the most significant catalyst for nostalgia has been the motor industry in all its forms.

In later life and with a disposable income, we now find that we are able to afford such luxuries and, in consequence, gain pleasure from the ownership of these vehicles.

To answer 'what' to collect poses a far more difficult question and is not easily answered. Notwithstanding my comments above, careful consideration needs to be given to the choice of vehicle purchased. It is important that you should buy the best you can afford, taking care to leave some money aside for those irritating incidentals that will need addressing once in possession of a newly acquired car. Perhaps a supplementary question should be what is the car going to be used for? If family motoring is envisaged, then a four seat (or larger) vehicle is essential and if a family mutiny is to be avoided, then make sure the vehicle is reasonably draught proofed if you intend using the vehicle all year round. Sports cars in their various forms are great fun, particularly if that excellent MG maxim, 'Safety First', is adhered to.

It is also true that many people forget how much time is taken up looking after a veteran, vintage or classic car. For the man who has little time to spare on garage duty, it is perhaps unwise to buy a vintage-thoroughbred like, for example, a Vauxhall, Invicta or Bentley. Pre-war cars need constant adjustment and servicing and it is quite wrong to believe that a vehicle will look after itself. Not only is this true for older vehicles – for example Aston Martin cars of the 1960s encompassed factory instructions for service every 2,000 miles, a schedule which I doubt few owners have adhered to, either today or when new.

On the other hand, the servicing and maintenance of vintage and classic cars is surprisingly easy and well within the ability of most enthusiasts.

When buying an imported car, if possible, always try to purchase right hand drive because insurance companies will usually charge a higher premium for LHD vehicles. These cars will probably have been imported from either South Africa or Australia, but do make sure that if the car has not yet been UK registered at the DVLA, that a Customs and Excise form 386, confirming that all duties have been paid, comes with the vehicle's purchase.

In short, out of the very wide choice of vehicles available today, make sure you find a car that not only matches your pocket, but also enhances your family circumstances.

Having dealt with the what and why of purchasing a collectors car, the 'when' is very much a matter of personal timing. It could be said that 1992 is a buyer's market, particularly bearing in mind the variety available in all categories.

The marketplace has always favoured long term ownership where the vehicle's investment potential, whilst important, has always taken second place to what I call 'investment in enjoyment'. Always buy to please rather than for investment and I will guarantee peace of mind. Finally, where do you buy your classic or vintage car? There are three very distinct sources for car purchase. The first of these is to buy the car privately from an individual who is just simply transferring title.

Always ask to see what documentation comes with the car, check that the engine and chassis number match up to the logbooks, but more importantly, never be in a hurry to purchase.

The second method of buying a car is to purchase through one of the many and well-respected car dealers. As above, the dealer will not mind you asking pertinent questions about the car, looking at the service history and old MOT certificates and allowing a third party to inspect the mechanical serviceability of the vehicle. The dealer will hold his reputation dear, particularly if he has been in business for many years and, in consequence, will not mind telling you about past satisfied purchasers. Remember a dealer is also human and if treated with respect will reward with open handed honesty.

The third and perhaps most interesting method of purchase is through one of the many auction houses who specialise in the selling of veteran, vintage and classic cars.

Peter W. Card

CONTENTS

AC

Make: **AC**
Model: Cobra
Type: 289
Years Manufactured: 1962-69
Quantity: 560
Price when new: Mk III, £2,573
Engine Type: Ford V8, front engine/rear drive
Size: 4260/4727cc
Max Power: 164-197 bhp
Max Torque: 269-314 ft/lb @ 4800/3400 rpm
Transmission: 4 speed
Wheelbase: 90in
Performance: Max speed: 138 mph; 0-60: 5.5 secs. Mpg: 17.

1926 AC Royal, 2 seater with dickey, 4 cylinder, condition 1.
£15,000-16,000 *Mot*

A 6 cylinder would probably fetch £20,000+ today.

Make the Most of Miller's

Price ranges in this book reflect what one should expect to pay for a similar example. When selling, however, one should expect to receive a lower figure. This will fluctuate according to a dealer's stock, saleability at a particular time, etc. It is always advisable, when selling, to approach a reputable specialist dealer or an auction house which has specialist sales

1965 AC Cobra 289 Sports Two Seater Roadster, coachwork by AC Cars, front engine, Ford V8 cylinder, 90° cast iron block and cylinder heads, 2 overhead valves per cylinder operated by pushrods and rockers from single block- 4727cc, mounted camshaft in centre of V, 289cu in, bore 101.6mm, stroke 73mm, compression ratio 8.6:1, 260bhp at 4,800rpm, single Holley carburettor, single dry-plate clutch with Borg Warner 4 speed gearbox, open propeller shaft to Salisbury limited slip final drive rear axle, tubular chassis frame with two 4in longitudinal tubes and front and rear subframes with alloy 2 seater roadster bodywork, independent suspension front and rear, by transverse leaf springs and lower wishbones and hydraulic shock absorbers, 4 wheel Girling disc brakes and calipers, 15in wire spoke centre lock wheels with 185 x 15in tyres, wheelbase 90in left hand drive.   Est. **£95,000-100,000** *CNY*

Make: **AC**
Model: Cobra
Type: 427
Years Manufactured: 1965-68
Quantity: 510
Price when new: £2,951
Engine Type: V8, front engine/rear drive
Size: 6998cc
Max Power: 390 bhp @ 5200 rpm
Max Torque: 475 ft/lb @ 3700 rpm
Transmission: 4 speed
Wheelbase: 90in
Performance: Max speed: 143 mph; 0-60: 4.8 secs. Mpg: 12.

1966 AC Cobra 427, 427cid, V8 overhead valve, 425hp at 3,700rpm, 4 speed, 90in wheelbase, full restoration, complete and original car, original 428 engine replaced with a more valuable and more powerful 427, with a Shelby signature in the boot.
Est.   **£218,000-230,000** *S(NY)*

MAKE	ENGINE	DATES	CONDITION		
AC	cc/cyl		1	2	3
Sociable	636/1	1907-12	£11,000	£9,000	£5,000
12/24 (Anzani)	1498/4	1919-27	£17,000	£13,000	£8,000
16/40	1991/6	1920-28	£21,000	£16,000	£12,000
16/60 Drophead/					
Saloon	1991/6	1937-40	£30,000	£23,000	£16,000
16/70 Sports Tourer	1991/6	1937-40	£43,000	£30,000	£21,000
16/80 Competition					
2 seater	1991/6	1937-40	£75,000	£50,000	£42,000
16/90 Blown					
Competition 2 seater	1991/6	1937-40	£95,000	£70,000	£50,000

1965/69 AC Cobra 427.
£120,000-140,000   *AUT*

Make: **AC**
Model: 428
Type: Convertible or Coupé
Years Manufactured: 1965-73
Quantity: Coupé, 58; Conv, 28
Price when new: Coupé, £5,573;
Conv, £5,324
Engine Type: Ford US overhead
valve V8
Size: 7014cc
Max Power: 345 bhp @ 4600
rpm
Max Torque: 462 ft/lb @ 2800
rpm
Transmission: 4 speed or auto
Wheelbase: 96in
Performance: Max speed: 140
mph; 0-60: 5.9-6.2 secs.

1973 AC 428 Convertible, bodywork by Frua.
S8   *Very Rare.*

1980 AC 3000 ME.
£13,000-15,000   *PC*

1970 AC 428 Fastback Sports Coupé, coachwork by
Frua, engine V8 cylinder in 90° formation, pushrod
operated overhead valves, bore 104.9mm, stroke
101.1mm, 7016cc, 3 speed automatic transmission,
hypoid bevel rear axle, independent front and rear
suspension by coil springs and wishbones, 4 wheel
disc brakes, wheelbase 96in, tyres 205 x 15in.
£23,000-24,000   *S*

MAKE AC	ENGINE cc/cyl	DATES	CONDITION 1	2	3
2-litre	1991/6	1947-55	£5,000	£3,000	£350
Buckland	1991/6	1949-54	£6,000	£5,000	£1,250
Ace	1991/6	1953-63	£42,000	£26,000	£18,000
Ace Bristol	1971/6	1954-63	£50,000	£37,000	£26,000
Ace 2.6	1553/6	1961-62	£55,000	£40,000	£29,000
Aceca	1991/6	1954-63	£26,000	£21,000	£15,000
Aceca Bristol	1971/6	1956-63	£30,000	£23,000	£19,000
Greyhound Bristol	1971/6	1961-63	£16,000	£13,000	£8,500
Cobra Mk II 289	4735/8	1963-64	£95,000	£85,000	£80,000
Cobra Mk III 427	6998/8	1965-67	£115,000	£100,000	£95,000
428 Frua	7014/8	1967-73	£35,000	£26,000	£17,000
428 Frua Convertible	7014/8	1967-73	£48,000	£38,000	£30,000
3000 ME	2994/6	1976-84	£17,000	£12,000	£10,000

Alfa Romeo

1947 Alfa Romeo 6C 2500cc Cabriolet, coachwork by Pinin Farina, 6 cylinder in line, water-cooled monobloc, double overhead camshafts, bore 72mm, stroke 100mm, 2443cc, 4 speed column change gearbox with synchromesh on third and top, single dry plate clutch, hypoid bevel rear axle, wheelbase 118in, independent front and rear suspension by coil springs. **£27,500-29,000** *S*

After the close of WWII Alfa Romeo overcame immediate post-war production difficulties by manufacturing a range of 2500cc cars developed from the pre-war 2300cc range, using a similar chassis and re-worked engine. A variety of coachwork styles was offered, and the Pinin Farina workshops were commissioned to execute a series of more individual designs on the quite sporting chassis. The cabriolet version was capable of a maximum speed close to 100mph.

1958/61 Alfa Romeo 2000 Spider. £9,000-14,000 *AUT*

1964 Alfa Romeo Giulia Sprint Speciale, coachwork by Bertone, 4 cylinder in line engine, twin overhead camshaft, 1570cc, bore 78mm, stroke 82mm, compression ratio 9.7:1, 125bhp at 6,500rpm, twin sidedraught Weber carburettors, 5 speed Porsche type gearbox with synchromesh with single dry plate clutch, axle ratio 4.56, disc brakes at front and aluminium finned drum at rear, front suspension lower A-arm with upper transverse and longitudinal links, roll bar, hydraulic shock absorbers, rear solid axle with longitudinal radius arms and T bar locators, 15in perforated disc wheels with 155 x 15in tyres, left hand drive. **£27,500-29,000** *C*

MAKE Alfa Romeo	ENGINE cc/cyl	DATES	CONDITION 1	2	3
24HP	4084/4	1910-11	£25,000	£20,000	£15,000
12HP	2413/4	1910-11	£20,000	£13,000	£9,000
40-60	6028/4	1913-15	£38,000	£25,000	£18,000
RL	2916/6	1921-22	£35,000	£25,000	£18,000
RM	1944/4	1924-25	£33,000	£20,000	£18,000
6C 1500	1487/6	1927-28	£14,000	£10,000	£8,000
6C 1750	1752/6	1923-33	£100,000+		
8C 2300	2336/8	1931-34	£300,000+		
6C 1900	1917/6	1933	£18,000	£15,000	£12,000
6C 2300	2309/6	1934	£22,000	£18,000	£15,000
8C 2900	2905/8	1935-39	£500,000+		
6C 2500 SS	2443/6	1939-45	£30,000+		

The variety of Alfa Romeos is endless! Value is very dependent on sporting history, body style and engine type.

1958 Alfa Romeo Giulietta 750 E Series Sprint Veloce Coupé, 4 cylinder in line, water-cooled, overhead camshaft, 90.6hp, bore 74mm, stroke 75mm, 1290cc, 2 twin choke horizontal carburettors, 4 speed manual gearbox, hypoid bevel final drive, independent front suspension, drum brakes, wheelbase 2,380mm, 5.00 x 16in tyres.
Est. £15,500-17,000   *S*

1962/68 Alfa Romeo Giulia Sprint GT.
£20,000-25,000   *AUT*

Make: **Alfa Romeo**
Model: Giulietta
Type: Saloon/Coupé/Sports
Years Manufactured: 1954-63
Quantity: 45,814 all types
Price when new: Saloon, £2,191; Coupé, £2,315
Engine Type: Double overhead camshaft 4 cyl
Size: 1290cc
Max Power: 80 bhp @ 6300 rpm; 90 bhp @ 6500 rpm (Veloce); 115 bhp @ 6500 (Sprint Speciale and Zagato)
Max Torque: 86.8 ft/lb @ 4500 rpm (Veloce)
Transmission: 4 speed, 5 speed on Sprint Speciale and Zagato
Wheelbase: 93.7in; Spider, SS and SZ, 88.6in
Performance: Max speed: 103 mph (Sprint, Spider); 112 mph (Spider Veloce); 124 mph (SS and SZ); 0-60: 11.0 secs (Spider Veloce).

Make: **Alfa Romeo**
Model: Giulia Spider
Type: Sports Car
Years Manufactured: 1966-date
Price when new: 1962-65, 1570cc, £1,499
Engine Type: Front engine, rear drive, 4 cyl
Size: 1290-1962cc
Max Power: 132 bhp @ 5500 rpm
Max Torque: 132 ft/lb @ 2900 rpm
Transmission: 5 speed
Wheelbase: 88.6in
Performance: Max speed: 116 mph (2000 Spider Veloce); 0-60: 9.8 secs; Mpg: 27.

1963 Alfa Romeo Giulia Spider, rust free, USA import, left hand drive, good running condition, original with some cosmetic restoration required.   **£6,500-7,500**   *CCTC*

Make: **Alfa Romeo**
Model: 2000 and 2600
Type: Saloon/Spider/Sprint Coupé
Years Manufactured: 1958-68
Quantity: 13,502 all types
Engine Type: Double overhead camshaft 4 cyl
Size: 1975cc (2000); 1997.4cc Volante/Sportiva); 2854cc (2600)
Max Power: 115 bhp @ 5700-5900 rpm (2000); 158/138 @ bhp 6500 rpm (Disco Volante/Sportiva); 145 bhp @ 5900 rpm (2600)
Transmission: 5 speed, 4 speed on Disco Volante
Wheelbase: 101.6in, Sprint; 98.4in, Spider
Performance: Max speed: 109 mph (2000); 137 mph (Sportiva); 135-140 mph (Disco Volante); 125 mph (2600).

1966/67 Alfa Romeo Duetto.
£6,000-12,000
AUT

1962/65 Alfa Romeo 2600 Spider.
£14,000-20,000
AUT

1957/62 Alfa Romeo Giulietta SS. £20,000-25,000 *AUT*

1966 Alfa Romeo Duetto, left hand drive. £10,500-11,500 *WCC*

1970 Alfa Romeo Junior Zagato, 1300cc, outstanding condition. £16,500-17,000 *FM*

Originality is the key point when it comes to any Zagato car. Only 1,108 Junior Zagato 1300cc cars were manufactured.

1967 Alfa Romeo Junior GT Mk I, left hand drive, one owner, mint condition, original, 40,000km from new, original tyres. £7,500-8,000 *FM*

1967 Alfa Romeo GTA, totally unrestored, perfect original condition, correct twinspark 1300cc engine, Campagnolo wheels, left hand drive. £28,500-30,000 *FM*

1970 Alfa Romeo Junior Z, 1750cc. Est. £10,000-11,500 *ADT*

1970 Alfa Romeo Giulia Junior Zagato Coupé, coachwork by Zagato, 4 cylinder in line engine, twin overhead camshafts, 2 valves per cylinder, 1962cc, bore 84mm, stroke 88.5mm, compression ratio 9:1, 132bhp at 5,500rpm, twin Weber carburettors, single dry plate clutch with 5 speed all synchromesh gearbox, unit construction chassis with steel panels, 2 door Kamm tailed 2 + 2 seater coupé bodywork with full width plexiglas front cover over headlights and front grille opening, front suspension coil springs, wishbones, torsion bars, anti-roll bar, telescopic shock absorbers, rear rigid axle, coil springs trailing lower radius arms, transverse V radius arms, power assisted disc brakes, 5½ x 14in disc wheels with 165 x 14in tyres, 2,250mm wheelbase, 1,324mm front track, 1,274mm rear track, overall length 3,900mm, left hand drive. £9,750-11,000 *C*

MAKE Alfa Romeo	ENGINE cc/cyl	DATES	CONDITION 1	2	3
2000 Spider	1974/4	1958-61	£16,000	£10,000	£4,000
2600 Sprint	2584/6	1962-66	£12,000	£8,000	£4,000
2600 Spider	2584/6	1962-65	£25,000	£17,000	£12,000
Giulietta Sprint	1290/4	1955-62	£15,000	£8,000	£4,000
Giulietta Spider	1290/4	1956-62	£13,000	£7,000	£3,500
Giulia Saloon	1570/4	1962-72	£4,000	£2,500	£300
Giulia Sprint (rhd)	1570/4	1962-68	£15,000	£6,500	£2,000
Giulia Spider (rhd)	1570/4	1962-65	£14,000	£7,500	£2,500
Giulia SS	1570/4	1962-66	£35,000	£25,000	£18,000
GT 1300 Junior	1290/4	1966-72	£7,500	£5,500	£4,000
1300GT Junior	1290/4	1973-75	£4,000	£2,000	£750
Giulia Sprint GT (105)	1570/4	1962-68	£9,500	£5,000	£3,000
1600GT Junior	1570/4	1972-75	£7,500	£4,000	£1,400
1750/2000 Berlina	1779/ 1962/4	1967-77	£2,750	£1,700	£1,000
1750GTV	1779/4	1967-72	£12,000	£7,500	£3,000
2000GTV	1962/4	1971-77	£12,000	£7,500	£3,000
1600/1750 (Duetto)	1570/ 1779/4	1966-67	£14,000	£9,000	£6,000
1750/2000 Spider (Kamm)	1779/ 1962/4	1967-78	£10,000	£7,000	£3,500
Montreal	2593/8	1970-77	£16,000	£12,000	£7,000
Junior Zagato 1290	1290/4	1968-74	£18,000	£15,000	£6,000
Junior Zagato 1600	1570/4	1968-74	£22,000	£17,000	£6,500
Alfetta GT/GTV (chrome)	1962/4	1974-84	£3,000	£1,500	£500
Alfasud	1186/ 1490/4	1972-83	£1,500	£600	£250
Alfasud ti	1186/ 1490/4	1974-81	£2,500	£1,000	£500
Alfasud Sprint	1284/ 1490/4	1976-85	£4,000	£2,000	£500
GTV6	2492/6	1981-	£4,000	£2,000	£500

1972 Alfa Romeo GT Junior, 1570cc, 4 cylinders. £3,300-3,500 *AUT*

1970 Alfa Romeo 1750 GTV Bertone, unused for many years, 65,000km, resprayed, left hand drive. £7,250-7,500 *FM*

1970 Alfa Romeo 1300 Spider, original throughout in very good condition. £8,000-10,000 *DG*

1976 Alfa Romeo Junior 1.6 litre GT Saloon, flat 4 cylinder, horizontally opposed overhead valve, water-cooled engine, 1570cc, 5 speed gearbox, independent suspension, live rear axle, wheelbase 92½in. Est. £6,500-8,000 *S*

Miller's is a price GUIDE not a price LIST

1967/72 Alfa Romeo 1750 GTV.
£2,000-5,000   *AUT*

1978 Alfa Romeo
2000 Spider
Veloce, 1962cc,
4 cylinders.
Est. £7,000-9,000
PC

1975 Alfa Romeo
GT 1600 Junior,
1570cc, 4 cylinders.
Est. £5,500-6,500
ADT

1970-77 Alfa Romeo
2000 Spider
Veloce, right hand
drive.
£4,000- 7,000
AUT

1974 Alfa Romeo GTV, 2 litre, low
mileage, condition 1.
£5,500-6,000   *PA*

1973 Alfa Romeo
Spider Veloce,
1962cc, 4 cylinders.
£7,500-8,500   *ADT*

1975 Alfa Romeo 2000 Veloce Spider, coachwork by Pininfarina, 4 cylinder in line engine, water-cooled monobloc, twin overhead camshaft, bore 84mm, stroke 88.5mm, 1962cc, 5 speed gearbox, bevel rear axle, independent front and rear suspension, wheelbase 88in, tyres 165 x 14in.
£8,000-9,000   *S*

Alfa Romeo's 2000 cars introduced in 1971 were developed from the 1300cc Giuletta engine which was progressively developed through 1600cc to 1750cc and finally, in a slightly elongated engine, to 1962cc. The new 2 litre engine developed some 132bhp at 5,500rpm and propelled the elegant Pininfarina Spider bodied cars at a top speed of 121mph. The Spider weighed only 19½cwt and borrowed much of its design from the earlier Duetto although the rear end treatment was updated with a Kamm tail.

1975 Alfa Romeo 1600 Junior Z, 1570cc, 4 cylinders.
£10,000-12,000   *ADT*

Shown initially at the Turin Motor Show in late 1969, the Junior Z had a 1300cc engine and it was not until 1972/73 that the 1600cc engine became available. The cars were all left hand drive with typically Italian styling and performance. The 1600s carried the same bodywork with a few changes to the bumpers and rear light clusters.

1977 Alfa Romeo Montreal, 2589cc, 8 cylinders.
Est.   £13,000-14,000   *ADT*

1974 Alfa Romeo Montreal. Est. £12,000-18,000   *LF*

The engine was a road tuned version of the Type 33 racing V8 until with twin overhead camshafts, 2.6 litres and fuel injection, 5 speed ZF gearbox with 200bhp, 137mph and 0-60 in 7.6 seconds.

1989 Alfa Romeo Spider 2.0, converted to right hand drive, suspension modified to accommodate wide wheels, hard and soft tops, 10,000km.
Est. £10,000-14,000   *LF*

Did you know
MILLER'S Collectors Cars Price Guide builds up year by year to form the most comprehensive photo-reference system available

Make: **Alfa Romeo**
Model: Alfasud
Type: Saloon/Coupé/
Years Manufactured: 1972-83
Quantity: 1,008,787 (all)
Engine Type: Front engine/front drive, ohc flat 4
Size: 1186-1490cc
Max Power: 63-105 bhp @ 6000/5800 rpm
Transmission: 4 speed/5 speed
Performance: Max speed: 90-106 mph; 0-60: 10-15 secs; Mpg: 28-40.

1981 Alfa Romeo Sud 1.3 Hatchback, 14,000 miles and full service history. £2,800-3,000 *LF*

Allard

1952 Allard K2 Roadster, Cadillac Competition V8 cylinder, 5424cc, bore 97mm, stroke 92mm, forged steel crankshaft, hydraulic Isky race cams, compression ratio 9:1, 300bhp at 6,000rpm, 4 twin choked Stromberg 97A carburettors, single dry plate clutch with La Salle 3 speed manual gearbox, box steel channel-type chassis frame with X cross members and 2 door, 2 seater roadster bodywork, front independent suspension with coil springs, swinging half axles, radius arms, hydraulic shock absorbers, rear transverse leaf springs, rigid axle, hydraulic shock absorbers, 4 wheel hydraulic drum brakes, 16in pressed steel type wheels with chrome embellishers and 16 x 6.00in tyres, wheelbase 106in, left hand drive.
£38,000-45,000 *CNY*

Sydney Allard's name has been synonymous with various forms of motor sport since the mid 1930s when he dominated trials and hillclimbs with his Ford V8 Specials. The basis of these was to form the new range of Allards that was introduced in 1946 with their box section rigid frame chassis and Ford V8 engines. In the beginning there were touring and competition two seaters, touring and drophead four seaters and in 1948 there was a two door P1 Saloon, the type that provided Sydney Allard with his 1952 Monte Carlo Rally win. The export market to America was their future aim and various tuned V8 powered engine options were available ranging from the 3.6 litre Ford or 3.9 Mercury to the fearsome 5.4 litre Cadillac. Many cars were exported without engines and

transmission, enabling the owners to install their own preference and state of tune units.

The two most popular sports models were the famous K2 and subsequent J2 models. They shared the same chassis configuration but the K2 has the all-enveloping bodywork compared with the cycle wing-type of the J2. The K2 was introduced in late 1951 to provide a more modern style two seater sports roadster comparable with the Jaguar XK 120. It was an immediate success providing the best of both worlds in being a more comfortable and usable road car, but at weekends could be an effective competitor in sports car events. Very few remain and it has become one of the most desirable Allards.

1947 Allard K1 Sports, 3.9 litre, Mercury engine, good continuous history, restored 10 years ago.
£24,500-25,500 *MC*

MAKE Allard	ENGINE cc/cyl	DATES	CONDITION 1	2	3
K/K2/L/M/M2X	3622/8	1947-54	£17,000	£9,000	£5,500
K3	var/8	1953-54	£22,000	£13,000	£10,000
P1	3622/8	1949-52	£16,000	£10,000	£5,500
P2	3622/8	1952-54	£25,000	£18,000	£11,000
J2/J2X	var/8	1950-54	£70,000	£60,000	£55,000
Palm Beach	1508/4, 2262/6	1952-55	£10,000	£7,500	£4,500
Palm Beach II	2252/ 3442/6	1956-60	£27,500	£18,000	£13,000

Alvis

1931 12/50 Alvis, 1645cc straight 4 overhead valve engine with a separate 4 speed right hand change gearbox, and both hand and foot brakes work on all 4 wheels, some body parts are available for restoration, the wheels have been rebuilt and have new tyres, and the engine and gearbox have been rebuilt.
Est. **£5,000-7,000**   *LF*

1933 Alvis Firefly, 4 seater tourer by Cross and Ellis, condition 2.
£18,000-20,000   *PA*

1934 Alvis Firebird 14hp 4 door Saloon, 4 cylinder, water-cooled, overhead valve, monobloc engine, 1842cc, 4 speed gearbox, single dry plate clutch, spiral bevel rear axle, wheelbase 118½in, 3.00 x 20in tyres.
£8,750-9,750   *S*

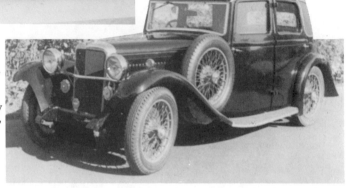

MAKE	ENGINE	DATES	CONDITION		
Alvis	cc/cyl		1	2	3
10/30	1460/4	1920-22	£7,000	£5,000	£3,000
12/50	1496/4	1923-32	£12,000	£8,000	£5,000
Firefly	1496/4	1932-34	£14,000	£10,000	£6,000
Speed 20 (tourer)	2511/6	1932-36	£35,000	£28,000	£18,000
Speed 20 (closed)	2511/6	1932-36	£22,000	£15,000	£11,000
Crested eagle	3571/6	1933-39	£10,000	£7,000	£4,000
Firebird (tourer)	1842/4	1934-39	£13,000	£10,000	£6,000
Firebird (closed)	1842/4	1934-39	£7,000	£5,000	£4,000
Speed 25 (tourer)	3571/6	1936-40	£40,000	£30,000	£20,000
Speed 25 (closed)	3571/6	1936-40	£20,000	£15,000	£12,000
3.5 litre	3571/6	1935-36	£35,000	£25,000	£18,000
4.3 litre	4387/6	1936-40	£44,000	£30,000	£22,000
Silver Crest	2362/6	1936-40	£14,000	£10,000	£7,000
TA	3571/6	1936-39	£18,000	£12,000	£8,000
12/70	1842/4	1937-40	£15,000	£10,000	£7,000

1934 Alvis Speed 20 Tourer, re-bodied from a saloon, condition 2.
£26,500-27,500   *Mot*

> **Miller's is a price GUIDE not a price LIST**

1936 Alvis Speed 25 Three Position Drophead, coachwork by Charlesworth Bodies Ltd, Coventry, 6 cylinder in line, water-cooled monobloc, pushrod operated, overhead valves, bore 83mm, stroke 110mm, 3571cc, 3 SU carburettors, 4 speed gearbox, all synchromesh and reverse, single plate clutch, full floating rear axle with spiral bevel final drive, independent front suspension, semi-elliptic leaf spring rear, wheelbase 88in, 5.50 x 19in tyres, a sound original car requiring attention to bring it into excellent condition.   Est. **£28,000-32,000**   S

The Type SC Speed 25 was exhibited at the Olympia Motor Show in October 1938 and incorporated a number of improvements. Even greater engine smoothness was obtained by alterations to the cam profiles and a dual exhaust system with six expansion chambers was fitted.

1934 Alvis Speed 20 Saloon, by Charlesworth, condition 1. **£21,000-23,000**   *PA*

1932 Alvis 12/50 DHC, in excellent condition. **£18,000-21,000**   *RTC*

1936 Alvis 3½ litre Mk VI, Charlesworth body, with many unusual features, as a special order for Sydney Guy. **£30,000-40,000**   *MC*

1933 Alvis Silver Eagle, good condition. **£14,000-16,000**   *RTC*

1936 Alvis Speed 20 Convertible, 4 door body by King & Son, Sydney. **£50,000-60,000**   *BLE*

1936 Alvis Speed 20 Three Position Drophead Coupé, coachwork by Charlesworth Bodies (1931) Ltd, 6 cylinder in line, water-cooled engine, pushrod operated, overhead valves, bore 83mm, stroke 110mm, 3571cc, 4 speed synchromesh gearbox, single dry plate clutch, open shaft, spiral bevel rear axle, transverse independent front suspension, semi-elliptic leaf rear springs, wheelbase 88in, 19in tyres, louvred bonnet and scuttle, side mounted spare, pram-iron hood, knock on wire wheels, P100 headlamps. **£38,000-43,000**   *DG*

A 3571cc engine from a Crested Eagle is fitted, considered by Alvis cognoscenti to be an acceptable and indeed desirable modification.

Alvis Ltd began motor car production in Coventry in 1919 and during the pre-war years built up a strong sporting car reputation. Since the last war and prior to their closure of the car division, two distinctive models were produced – the Fourteen and Three Litre. The former was announced in 1945, finally appearing in 1946 and was seen as a modified version of the pre-war 12/70. The engine and chassis were of that vintage, but the beautifully built bodies were very well equipped with full leather interior. The car provided effortless cruising at 70mph with good fuel consumption, and top gear performance was brisk for a long stroke pushrod engine of 1.9 litres.

1949 Alvis TA14 Drophead Coupé, 4 cylinder, overhead valve, bore 74mm, stroke 110mm, 1892cc, 4 speed manual gearbox, 4 wheel drum brakes, semi-elliptic front and rear suspension, right hand drive. Est. **£17,000-20,000**   *C*

This Alvis was the property of one family for in excess of 20 years, and from the service records was maintained meticulously during this period. In 1988 and 1989 the owners undertook a comprehensive body restoration and there are bills in the region of £12,000 to support this.

1939 Alvis Speed 25 Sports Saloon, coachwork by Charlesworth. Est. **£23,000-28,000**   *S*

1952 Alvis TA21 Drop Head Coupé, by Tickford, 2993cc, 6 cylinder, compression ratio 7.25:1, overhead valves, Solex dual downdraught carburettor with air silencer fed by an AC mechanical fuel pump, 4 speed gearbox with reverse, 15in tyres. Est. **£10,000-13,000**   *ADT*

1949 Alvis TA14, with Duncan body, in excellent condition. **£8,000-10,000**   *RTC*

1940 Alvis Speed 25 Type SC Sports Saloon, coachwork by Charlesworth Bodies Ltd, Coventry. Est. **£25,000-27,000**   *S*

Locate the source

The source of each illustration in Miller's can be found by checking the code letters below each caption with the list of contributors

ALVIS

Locate the source

The source of each illustration in Miller's can be found by checking the code letters below each caption with the list of contributors

1949 Alvis TA14 Four Door Saloon, 1892cc.
Est. £7,000-9,000   *ADT*

1953 Alvis TC21/100 Grey Lady,
in excellent condition.
£15,000-17,000   *RTC*

1951 Alvis TA21 Drop Head Coupé, excellent condition.
£15,000-17,000   *RTC*

Make: **Alvis**
Model: TC/TD/TE/TF
Type: Saloon/Convertible
Years Manufactured: 1953-67
Price when new: TD21 Saloon, 1958-62, £2,827
Engine Type: Overhead valve 6 cyl
Size: 2993cc
Max Power: 115 bhp @ 4000 rpm
Transmission: 4 speed
Performance: Max speed: 104 mph; 0-60: 14 secs; Mpg: 18-20.

1954 Alvis TC21/100 Grey Lady,
in good overall condition.
£14,000-16,000   *RTC*

1962 Alvis TD21 Drop Head Coupé, totally restored.
£65,000+   *RTC*

1956/63 Alvis TD21.
£6,000-12,000   *AUT*

MAKE	ENGINE	DATES	CONDITION		
Alvis	cc/cyl		1	2	3
TA14	1892/4	1946-50	£10,000	£7,000	£3,000
TA14 DHC	1892/4	1946-50	£15,000	£12,000	£5,000
TB14	1892/4	1949-50	£15,000	£9,000	£7,000
TB21	2993/6	1951	£15,000	£9,000	£6,000
TA21/TC21	2993/6	1950-55	£15,500	£9,500	£4,000
TA21/TC21 DHC	2993/6	1950-55	£20,000	£15,000	£11,500
TC21/100	2993/6	1953-56	£17,000	£11,000	£4,500
TC21/100 DHC	2993/6	1954-56	£25,000	£21,000	£14,000
TD21	2993/6	1956-62	£15,000	£12,000	£7,000
TD21 DHC	2993/6	1956-62	£25,000	£20,000	£12,000
TE21	2993/6	1963-67	£18,000	£15,000	£12,000
TE21 DHC	2993/6	1963-67	£28,000	£23,000	£15,000
TF21	2993/6	1966-67	£18,000	£15,000	£10,000
TF21 DHC	2993/6	1966-67	£25,000	£18,000	£12,000

1963 Alvis TD21 Series II Two Door Saloon, coachwork by Park Ward, 6 cylinder overhead valve, water-cooled monobloc, 2993cc, bore 84mm, stroke 90mm, 5 speed all synchromesh gearbox, front suspension by coil and wishbone, semi-elliptic rear, hypoid bevel live rear axle, 6.00 x 15in tyres.
Est. **£7,000-9,000** *S*

Miller's is a price GUIDE not a price LIST

Originally styled by Graber of Switzerland the TD21 was evolved from TC108/G of the mid-1950s. Park Ward successfully produced lighter weight panels and together with minor restyling reducing body weight helped Alvis achieve the height of its post-war reputation in the beginning of the 1960s. The final Alvis car was produced in 1967 following the acquisition of the company by Rover.

1960 Alvis TD21 Drop Head Coupé, totally restored.
£65,000+ *RTC*

1962 Alvis TD21 Drop Head Coupé, built for James Mason, excellent original condition, left hand drive.
£43,000-45,000 *RTC*

Did you know
MILLER'S Collectors Cars Price Guide builds up year by year to form the most comprehensive photo-reference system available

1960 Alvis TD21, 2993cc, 6 cylinders.
Est. **£9,000-11,000** *ADT*

1964 Alvis TE Saloon, in good condition.
£12,000-14,000   *RTC*

1965 Alvis TE Drop Head Coupé, in excellent condition.
£40,000-42,000   *RTC*

1964 Alvis TE21 Two Door Saloon.
£7,500-8,000   *DB*

1966 Alvis TE21 Series III Drop Head Coupé, 6 cylinder in line, water-cooled monobloc, pushrod operated, overhead valve, bore 84mm, stroke 90mm, 2993cc, 5 speed ZF gearbox, single dry plate clutch, independent coil spring front suspension, semi-elliptic leaf rear springs, wheelbase 111½in, 185 x 15in tyres.
£14,750-15,750   *S*

Amphicar

1965 Amphicar.
£6,000-6,500   *S8*

Probably the only real amphibious vehicle ever available to the public. Built in Germany, Amphicars were made between 1961-68 and could achieve over 60mph on the road and 6½ knots in the water. In 1965 two Amphicars crossed the English Channel between Dover and Calais (it took 7 hours 20 minutes and cost £4 in petrol).

About 800 were built with over 600 going to the U.S.A.

Use the Index!

Because certain items might fit easily into any of a number of categories, the quickest and surest method of locating any entry is by reference to the index at the back of the book.

This has been fully cross-referenced for absolute simplicity

Armstrong Siddeley

1949 Armstrong Siddeley Hurricane Drop Head Coupé, 1991cc, 6 cylinders.
£5,500-6,000   *ADT*

The new post-war design was announced by Armstrong Siddeley in May 1945. The Hurricane used the pre-war 16hp 2 litre engine in a new independent front suspension chassis, with advanced and attractive body styling with a sliding type gearbox with synchromesh available as an alternative to the Wilson pre-select. Due to its Hawker Siddeley heritage, the company named their cars after famous aircraft of the war, so models such as Hurricane, Lancaster, Typhoon and Whitley graced the advertisements of the post-war boom.

MAKE Armstrong Siddeley	ENGINE cc/cyl	DATES	CONDITION		
			1	2	3
Hurricane	1991/6	1945-53	£9,500	£5,500	£2,500
Typhoon	1991/6	1946-50	£7,000	£3,000	£1,000
Lancaster/Whitley	1991/ 2306/6	1946-53	£7,500	£3,500	£1,250
Sapphire 234/236	2290/4, 2309/6	1955-58	£5,000	£3,500	£2,500
Sapphire 346	3440/6	1953-58	£8,500	£5,000	£2,500
Star Sapphire	3990/6	1958-60	£8,000	£5,000	£2,500

Arnolt Bristol

Few cars have such diverse lineage as the Arnolt Bristol. The sleek roadster body, built by Bertone, was Italian, the engine had its origins in Germany, the chassis and suspension were built in England, and the whole package was conceived by an American for the American sports car market. Introduced in 1957, the Arnolt Bristol became an immediate success with its class win at Sebring, a victory which it duplicated in 1958. Of 140 Arnolt Bristols produced, including 12 last year models that were destroyed in a factory fire in 1961, it is estimated that only 92 still remain.

1957 Arnolt Bristol, coachwork by Bertone, 6 cylinder, 2 litre.   Est. **£22,500-28,500**   *S(NY)*

Aston Martin

1954 Aston Martin DB2/4 Drop Head Coupé, 2995cc.
£33,000-34,000   *HA*

The vast majority of DB2/4s built were saloons, only 73 being drop head coupés. Performance was lively for the early 50s, Autocar magazine recording 0-60 in 12.6 seconds and a maximum speed of 120mph.

1938 Aston Martin 2 litre Speed Model Sports Two Seater, 4 cylinder in line, water-cooled monobloc, overhead valves, bore 78mm, stroke 102mm, 1949cc, 4 speed gearbox with central remote control, single dry plate clutch, open shaft, spiral bevel final drive, semi-elliptic leaf springs front and rear, wheelbase 100in, 5.25/5.50 x 17in tyres.
Est. **£55,000-65,000**   *S*

Built in 1938, originally with drop head coupé coachwork by E. D. Abbott, and has now been fitted with two seater sports coachwork.

1958/63 Aston Martin DB4, left hand drive.
£35,000-40,000   *AUT*

1957 Aston Martin DB Mk III, 6 cylinder, twin overhead camshaft, 2922cc, 4 speed manual with overdrive, right hand drive, in running order, the chassis may need cleaning and the water pump needs replacing, the body and interior are scruffy.
Est. £15,000-18,000   *C*

The final refinement of the early Feltham DB cars was the excellent Mk III. After the first 100 cars, of which this is the 114th, Girling front brakes were standardised. These superb brakes were also used on the DB4GT and later V8s. The Mk III was faster than the Mk II and 0-60 fell below 10 seconds.

1955 Aston Martin DB2/4 Drop Head Coupé.
£65,000-75,000   *PiK*

MAKE	ENGINE	DATES	CONDITION		
Aston Martin	cc/cyl		1	2	3
Lionel Martin Cars	1486/4	1921-25	£30,000	£20,000	£18,000
International	1486/4	1927-32	£33,000	£20,000	£18,000
Le Mans	1486/4	1932-33	£65,000	£45,000	£38,000
Mk II	1486/4	1934-36	£45,000	£35,000	£30,000
Ulster	1486/4	1934-36	£85,000	£65,000	—
2 litre	1950/4	1936-40	£21,000	£16,000	£14,000

Value is dependent upon racing history, originality and completeness.
Add 40% if a competition winner.

1959 Aston Martin DB2/4 Convertible Mk III, overdrive, 4 wheel disc brakes, very good condition.
£60,000-70,000   *S8*

1953/55 Aston Martin DB2/4 Mk I.
£15,000-25,000   *AUT*

1953 Aston Martin DB2/4, fully restored and condition 1.
£25,000-35,000
PA

1965/71 Aston Martin DB6 Automatic.
£15,000-28,000   *AUT*

According to the original build sheet, this 1960 Series Two DB4 spent its early life in Jersey, Channel Islands. It then went to the USA and was brought back and registered in England in 1988. At this time the car had a great deal of money spent on it, including new running gear, inner panels and exterior paintwork. New chrome wire wheels and the correct Avon Turbospeed tyres are fitted.

1960 Aston Martin DB4 Mk II,
3.7 litres.
Est. **£24,000-26,000**   *HA*

1955 Aston Martin DB2/4 Mk II,
2922cc, 6 cylinders.
Est. **£30,000-33,000**
ADT

1962 Aston Martin DB4 Sports Saloon, 6 cylinder in line, water-cooled monobloc engine, twin overhead camshaft, bore 92mm, stroke 92mm, 3670cc, 4 speed synchromesh gearbox, Borg and Beck twin plate clutch, hypoid bevel final drive, independent coil spring front and rear suspension, wheelbase 98in, 15in tyres.
£22,000-23,500   *S*

Make: **Aston Martin**
Model: DB5
Type: Saloon/Convertible/Estate
Years Manufactured: 1963-65
Quantity: 1,050
Price when new: £4,248
Engine Type: Front engine, rear drive, in-line 6 cyl
Size: 3995cc
Max Power: 282 bhp @ 5500 rpm; Vantage option, 325 bhp @ 5750 rpm
Max Torque: 288 ft/lb @ 3850 rpm
Transmission: 4 or 5 speed, optional overdrive on 4 speed, or automatic
Wheelbase: 98in
Performance: Max speed: 141 mph; 0-60: 8.1 secs; Mpg: 15.

1963 Aston Martin DB5 Standard, non Vantage, 5 speed manual gearbox, right hand drive.   **£27,000-32,000**   *PC*

1963 Aston Martin DB4 Series V Vantage.
£36,000-38,000   *AUT*

1964 Aston Martin DB4 Series V Vantage.
£35,000-37,000   *PiK*

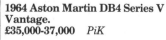

Miller's is a price GUIDE not a price LIST

ASTON MARTIN

1969 Aston Martin DB6 Mk I,
3994cc, 6 cylinders.
Est. £27,000-31,000   *ADT*

Although the DB6 of 1965 may have appeared to be similar in looks to the earlier cars in the same family it was, in fact, quite a different vehicle. Using the same chassis layout as its predecessor, the DB5, the wheelbase was lengthened to give extra space to the rear seat area. To increase the head room inside the car, the profile of the roof was changed to give a squarer look, ending in an upturned tail and boot lid. Mechanically the DB6 was unchanged from the DB5, being a straight six of 3995cc capacity

Make: **Aston Martin**
Model: DB6
Type: Saloon/Volante
Years Manufactured: 1965-71
Quantity: 1,753
Price when new: Mk I, £5,084; Mk II, £5,501
Engine Type: Front engine, rear drive, in-line 6 cyl
Size: 3995cc
Max Power: 282 bhp @ 5500 rpm; Vantage option, 325 bhp @ 5750 rpm
Max Torque: 288 ft/lb @ 3850 rpm
Transmission: 5 speed overdrive or 3 speed auto
Wheelbase: 101.7in
Performance: Max speed: 148 mph; 0-60: 6.5 secs; Mpg: 15.

1966 Aston Martin DB6 Mk I, 3995cc, 6 cylinders.
Est.   £26,000-28,000   *ADT*

1970 Aston Martin DBS6 2+2 Coupé, 6 cylinder in line, overhead camshaft, water-cooled monobloc engine, bore 96mm, stroke 92mm, 3995cc, automatic transmission, power steering, De Dion rear axle and suspension, independent front suspension, wheelbase 102¾in, 225/70VR 15in tyres.
£9,000-10,000   *S*
Introduced in 1968 the DBS combined exciting new coachwork with the tried and tested twin overhead camshaft 6 cylinder engine, and power steering came with the Mk II in 1970.

1970 Aston Martin DB6 Mk II Sports Saloon, 6 cylinder in line, water-cooled monobloc engine, bore 96mm, stroke 92mm, 3995cc, 3 speed automatic gearbox, hypoid rear axle, independent front suspension with transverse wishbones and coil springs, parallel trailing link and coil spring rear suspension, wheelbase 101¾in, 8.15 x 15in tyres, converted from manual to automatic transmission, restored.   Est. £35,000-45,000   *S*

1967/71 Aston Martin DB6 Volante.
£50,000-70,000   *AUT*

1967/72 Aston Martin DBS.
£6,000-12,000   *AUT*

MAKE Aston Martin	ENGINE cc/cyl	DATES	CONDITION 1	2	3
DB1	1970/4	1948-50	£26,000	£14,500	£13,000
DB2	2580/6	1950-53	£28,000	£16,000	£14,500
DB2 Conv	2580/6	1951-53	£30,000	£21,000	£17,500
DB2/4 Mk I/II	2580/ 2922/6	1953-57	£26,000	£15,500	£14,000
DB2/4 Mk II Conv	2580/ 2922/6	1953-57	£34,000	£25,000	£18,500
DB2/4 Mk III	2580/ 2922/6	1957-59	£25,000	£19,000	£17,500
DB2/4 Mk III Conv	2922/6	1957-59	£34,500	£25,500	£20,000
DB Mk III	2922/6	1957-59	£33,000	£24,000	£17,500
DB Mk III Conv	2922/6	1957-59	£35,000	£28,000	£24,000
DB4	3670/6	1959-63	£32,000	£24,000	£16,500
DB4 Conv	3670/6	1961-63	£52,000	£35,000	—
DB4 GT	3670/6	1961-63	£95,000	£80,000	—
DB5	3995/6	1964-65	£35,000	£28,000	£20,000
DB5 Conv	3995/6	1964-65	£46,000	£30,000	—
DB6	3995/6	1965-69	£26,000	£24,000	£20,000
DB6 Mk I auto	3995/6	1965-69	£22,000	£18,000	£15,500
DB6 Mk I Volante	3995/6	1965-71	£38,000	£32,000	£28,000
DB6 Mk II Volante	3995/6	1969-70	£40,000	£36,000	£30,000
DBS	3995/6	1967-72	£12,000	£9,500	£6,500
AM Vantage	3995/6	1972-73	£16,000	£11,000	£8,000

1974 Aston Martin V8, the only hand built model left in the world. **£45,000-50,000** *FOR*

1970 Aston Martin DB6. £25,000-30,000 *S8*

Did you know

MILLER'S Collectors Cars Price Guide builds up year by year to form the most comprehensive photo-reference system available

1974 Aston Martin DBS V8, 5340cc, 8 cylinders. Est. **£20,000-22,000** *ADT*

1973 Aston Martin V8, 5340cc engine, 5 speed manual gearbox, light alloy bodywork mounted on a steel platform chassis. **£28,000-30,000** *HA*

Constructed at the Newport Pagnell factory, the Aston Martin V8 Coupé was initially the fastest British sports car of its day being capable of over 140mph.

Make: **Aston Martin**
Model: DBS V8
Type: Saloon/Convertible
Years Manufactured: 1969-date
Quantity: Still in production
Price when new: £7,501
Engine Type: Front engine, rear drive, V8
Size: 5340cc
Max Power: 350-375 bhp (estimated)
Transmission: 5 speed or auto
Wheelbase: 102.8in
Performance: Max speed: 145 mph; 0-60: 6.2 secs; Mpg: 13.

ASTON MARTIN

1978 to date Aston Martin V8 Volante.   £50,000-80,000   *AUT*

Condition Guide

1. *A vehicle in top class condition but not 'concours d'elegance' standard, either fully restored or in very good original condition*
2. *A good, clean, roadworthy vehicle, both mechanically and bodily sound*
3. *A runner, but in need of attention, probably both to bodywork and mechanics. Must have current MOT*

1985 Aston Martin V8 Saloon.
£38,000-40,000   *AUT*

1979 Aston Martin V8 Volante,
V8 cylinder, 2 overhead camshafts
per bank, 5340cc, automatic
transmission, right hand drive.
£50,000-52,000   *C*

1979 Aston Martin V8 Volante,
V8 cylinder, alloy block and
cylinder heads, 2 valves per cylinder
operated by 2 overhead camshafts
per bank, 5340cc, bore 100mm,
stroke 85mm, compression ratio
9.3:1, 330bhp at 6,000rpm, 4 Weber
42 DGNF carburettors, single dry
plate clutch transmission,
ZF 5 speed manual gearbox, hypoid
bevel with limited slip differential
final drive, steel sheet box type
platform chassis with 2 door,
4 seater convertible, electric hood,
coachwork, front independent
suspension with double wishbones,
coil springs and anti-roll bar,
telescopic shock absorbers, De Dion
rear axle, parallel trailing arms,
transverse Watts linkage, 4 wheel
disc brakes, dual circuit, 15 x 8in
wide alloy wheels with 235/
70 x 15in tyres, wheelbase
2,610mm, right hand drive.
£53,000-55,000   *C*

*Aston Martin launched their new V8
Convertible, known as the Volante
and the Vantage improved
performance version in 1977, and
within a further year introduced a
completely revised V8 Saloon, code
named Oscar India. This car had a
new broader dome-shaped bonnet
revised rear end treatment
incorporating a spoiler on the boot
lid. The fascia was redesigned with
wood trim as was the centre console
and the air conditioning was
upgraded together with many other
smaller items. These revisions
brought about a greater feeling of
luxury and updated the car amongst
its competitors.*

1977 Aston Martin V8.
£20,000-25,000 *S8*

**1977/89 Aston Martin V8
Vantage.**
£35,000-40,000 *AUT*

Make: **Aston Martin**
Model: Vantage
Type: Saloon/Convertible
Years Manufactured: 1977-date
Quantity: Still in production
Price when new: £6,949
Engine Type: Front engine, rear
drive, V8
Size: 5340cc
Max Power: 406 bhp (estimated)
Transmission: 5 speed or auto
Wheelbase: 102.8in
Performance: Max speed: 170
mph; 0-60: 5.4 secs; Mpg: 14.

**1986/90 Aston Martin V8 Volante
Vantage.**
£90,000-100,000 *AUT*

Make: **Aston Martin**
Model: Lagonda
Type: Saloon
Years Manufactured: 1976-date
Quantity: Still in production
Engine Type: Front engine, rear
drive, V8
Size: 5340cc
Transmission: Auto
Performance: Max speed: 143
mph; 0-60: 8.8 secs; Mpg: 14.

1983 Aston Martin V8 Lagonda,
excellent condition throughout,
24,000km.
£24,000-26,000 *HWA*

1980 Aston Martin Lagonda.
£20,000-25,000 *S8*

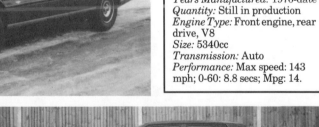

1985 Aston Martin Lagonda. **£28,000-30,000** *AUT*

Auburn

The Auburn Automobile Company of Auburn, Indiana, pioneers of the American automobile industry, built their first cars in 1900. In 1924, however, the dynamic E. L. Cord took over the company and from that time onwards the company took a leading position in the industry. Auburns were among the best looking cars on the American market, and both in styling and technical innovation were well in advance of most of their competitors from 1925 onwards.

1934 Auburn Four Door Phaeton, new restoration. **£34,000-38,000** *HWA*

Austin

1921 Austin 20hp Four Seater Tourer, 4 cylinder in line, water-cooled monobloc engine, side valve, bore 95mm, stroke 127mm, 3600cc, 4 speed gearbox, single plate clutch, shaft and bevel final drive, semi-elliptic leaf spring suspension, wheelbase 129in, 820 x 120mm tyres. **£21,000-22,000** *S*

In 1914 no less than 1,500 Austin cars left the Longbridge works. However, the outbreak of war that year saw production switch to munitions, resulting in a trebling of size by 1917. The end of the year saw Herbert Austin embark on a one model policy with the announcement of the Austin 20 first unveiled to the press late in 1918. Herbert's new car was probably influenced by the Hudson Super 6 used by Austin towards the end of the war. It was a no frills car with a simple chassis design, monobloc engine, centre change 4 speed gearbox and plenty of litres to give the new car excellent performance and remarkably smooth motoring. The new cars were offered at the notably cheap price of £495 which compared with £700 or so for the pre-war equivalent. A bold marketing decision indeed at a time when the Official Receiver was never far from Austin's door, and a commercial decision the dire consequences of which were saved only by the arrival of the 12hp and 7hp cars in 1921 and 1922 respectively.

1907 Austin Cabriolet, 4 cylinder, 18/24hp, 6 seater, 3 position hood. **£48,000-50,000** *SL*

1927 Austin 20hp Five Seater Tourer, 4 cylinder in line, water-cooled, monobloc engine, side valve, bore 95mm, stroke 127mm, 3600cc, treasury rating 22.4hp, 4 speed central gate change gearbox, single dry plate clutch, helical bevel rear axle, semi-elliptic leaf springs front and rear, wheelbase 130in, 6.00 x 21in tyres. **£9,500-10,000** *S*

MAKE Austin	ENGINE cc/cyl	DATES	CONDITION 1	2	3
25/30	4900/4	1906	£35,000	£25,000	£20,000
20	3600/4	1919-27	£22,000	£14,000	£8,000
12	1661/4	1922-26	£8,000	£5,000	£2,000
7	747/4	1924-39	£8,000	£4,000	£1,500
7 Coachbuilt	747/4	1924-39	£10,000	£9,000	£7,000
12/4	1861/4	1927-35	£5,500	£4,000	£2,000
16	2249/6	1928-36	£9,000	£7,000	£4,000
20/6	3400/6	1928-38	£15,000	£10,000	£8,000
12/6	1496/6	1932-37	£6,000	£4,000	£1,500
12/4	1535/4	1933-39	£5,000	£3,500	£1,500
10/4	1125/4	1933-47	£4,000	£3,000	£1,000
18	2510/6	1934-39	£8,000	£5,000	£3,000
14	1711/6	1937-39	£6,000	£4,000	£2,000
Big Seven	900/4	1938-39	£3,500	£2,500	£1,500
8	900/4	1939-47	£3,000	£2,000	£1,000
28	4016/6	1939	£6,000	£4,000	£2,000

1928 Austin 7 Top Hat, the body and mechanics are very good and the interior has been completely renovated.
£5,500-6,000 *LF*

1928 Austin 7 Chummy, very good condition.
£7,000-8,000 *PA*

1928 Austin 7 Chummy Tourer, very fine and original example.
£6,500-7,000 *C*

1927 Austin 7hp Chummy Tourer, 4 cylinder in line, water-cooled monobloc engine, side valve, bore 56mm, stroke 76mm, 747cc, 3 speed gate change gearbox, single dry plate clutch, spiral bevel rear axle, transverse semi-elliptic leaf front springs, quarter-elliptic leaf rear springs, wheelbase 75in, 3.50 x 19in tyres.
£6,900-7,500 *S*

The Chummy, or Occasional Four, was the most common of the early production models and offered accommodation for 3 adults or 2 adults and 2-3 children. In 1927 this well-equipped little car was offered for a very modest £135.

Make the Most of Miller's

Price ranges in this book reflect what one should expect to pay for a similar example. When selling, however, one should expect to receive a lower figure. This will fluctuate according to a dealer's stock, saleability at a particular time, etc. It is always advisable, when selling, to approach a reputable specialist dealer or an auction house which has specialist sales

1928 Austin 7 Top Hat, the original magneto engine and 3 speed gearbox replaced by a slightly later 750cc coil engine and 4 speed synchromesh box when the car was rebuilt some 2 years ago, also with the original type magneto engine with magneto and dynamo and the 3 speed crash box.
£5,400-5,800 *LF*

AUSTIN

1932 Austin 7hp Box Saloon,
4 cylinder in line, water-cooled
monobloc engine, side valve, bore
56mm, stroke 76mm, 747cc, 3 speed
ball change gearbox, single dry
plate clutch, spiral bevel rear axle,
transverse semi-elliptic leaf front
spring, quarter-elliptic rear springs,
wheelbase 81in, 19in tyres.
Est. **£4,500-5,000** *S*

*This is an early 1932 example and
has the correct 3 speed gearbox and
scuttle mounted petrol tank.*

1933 Austin 7 Saloon, fully
restored with some history.
£6,000-6,500 *ADT*

1932 Austin 7hp Box Saloon.
£5,500-6,000 *S*

1932 Austin 7,
condition 1.
£4,900-5,300 *CC*

*The Austin 7 first appeared in 1922,
the product of an 18-year-old
draughtsman, Stanley Edge, and
reputedly designed by him in the
billiard room at Austin's home,
Lickey Grange. The announcement
of the Austin 7 led to the decline in
popularity of the motorcycle
combination. With 45mph economy
and 50mph performance, it was very
popular with many early motorists.
By 1932 the Austin 7 had grown in
size and reputation and the larger
81in wheelbase made the box saloon
a spacious family car and offered at a
price of only £125.*

**1935 Austin 7 Four
Seater Open Tourer
Model AK,**
4 cylinder, 748cc,
4 speed, synchromesh
on 2nd, 3rd and 4th
gears, right hand
drive.
Est. **£5,500-6,000** *C*

1933 Austin 7 Two Seater, condition 2.
£3,800-4,200 *HS*

*At first glance this Austin appears to
be a Ruby Tourer. In fact it is a
development of the Ruby, introduced
in 1934 and known as the AK which
was produced for 2 years. The AK
comprises mainly Ruby mechanics
and also parts from earlier models,
e.g. the dash assembly and the
battery under the driver's seat. The
total production of this model is
unknown, but they seem to be very
rare today and in 1985 only
11 appeared on the register.*

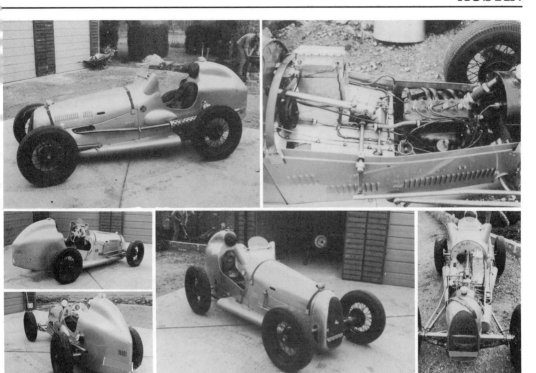

1928/1980 Austin 7 Wragg Single Seat Replica, one of 7 built and accepted by the VSCC for racing, in good condition, with supercharger.
£10,000-20,000   *DG*

1938 Austin 7 Ruby Saloon,
original and condition 2.
£3,500-4,000   *PA*

1934 Austin 7 Ruby.
£8,000-10,000   *ADT*

This Ruby was ordered by a lady who intended to use the car to the full but in fact stored it in her country house garage and covered it with rugs. Seventeen years ago the vehicle was purchased by its current owner, again a lady, who has only taken it to the local garage for servicing. Amazingly it has covered little more than 50 miles since 1974, and is believed to have done only 2,322 miles from new – a fact which is reflected in this price.

1927 Austin 7 Special, aluminium body.
£6,000-6,500   *CA*

1935 Austin 7 Special, restored, with new battery, exhaust, aeroscreens and wiring.
Est. **£2,000-3,000**   *LF*

1935 Austin 7 Ruby Tourer, condition 2.
£3,800-4,000 *HS*

1937 Austin 7 Ruby, condition B.
£3,000-3,200 *CC*

1936 Austin 7 Nippy, condition A.
£7,300-7,500 *CC*

1937 Austin Big 7, original condition.
£3,500-4,250 *FCV*

This is an early model without running boards.

1934 Austin 10/4 Cabriolet, condition 1.
£7,000-7,250 *CC*

1932 Austin 10/4.
£5,000-5,500 *LF*

1933 Austin 10/4, 1125cc, side valve engine, only 4 owners up until 1967.
£5,000-5,500 *Cen*

1937 Austin Big 7, condition 2.
£3,500-4,000 *PA*

c1934 Austin 7hp Two Seater Special.
£4,750-5,250 *S*

This aluminium bodied car is built on the lines of a Cambridge Special. The engine dates from 1929 and is fitted with a Zenith side draught carburettor. An early 3 speed gearbox is fitted and the car has the dropped sports front axle. Early Chummy style headlamps are fitted and the car sports 15in wheels and a Bluemels Brooklands steering wheel.

Austin Big 7 Six Lite,
4 door model.
£5,000-6,000 *PC*

1933 Austin 10/4, condition 1.
£4,500-5,500 *PA*

1933 Austin 10 Cabriolet, original, condition 2.
£5,500-6,000 *Mot*

1934 Austin 10/4.
Est. **£3,800-4,400** *LF*

1936 Austin 10 Clifton Two Seater and Dickey Convertible,
original condition.
£6,000-7,500 *FCV*

Following the success of the Austin 7, other manufacturers followed the trend towards small car production and when Ford introduced their 8hp car in 1932 this was a clear challenge to the Austin/Morris supremacy in this field. With almost 200cc more than the Austin 7 it was a clear threat to that model, however in April 1932 the Austin 10hp was to appear to bridge the gap between the 7hp and 12hp models. By 1934 the Austin 10 production was exceeding that of the 7hp car, with 24,149 cars leaving the Austin production line that year out of a total production of 68,291 units. The new car was well built and sold for a competitive £172 10s 0d.

1934 Austin 10hp Four Door Saloon, 4 cylinder in line, water-cooled monobloc, side valve engine, bore 63.5mm, stroke 89mm, 1125cc, 4 speed gearbox with synchromesh on third and top, single dry plate clutch, spiral bevel rear axle, semi-elliptic leaf springs front and rear, wheelbase 93in, 4.50 x 18in tyres.
£4,500-5,500 *S*

1929 Austin 16/6, condition 1.
£13,000-14,000 *CC*

Austin 16/6 Harrow, 6 cylinder engine, 2249cc.
£9,000-11,000 *ADT*

1931 Austin 16/6 Harrow, 2 seater tourer with dickey, condition 2.
£8,000-9,500 *PA*

1937 Austin 10 Cambridge, condition 2.
£3,500-4,000 *PA*

> **Miller's is a price GUIDE not a price LIST**

1935 Austin 12/4 Ascot, condition 1.
£6,000-7,000 *PA*

1939 Austin 8, 900cc, 4 cylinders, approximately 17,000 miles from new.
£4,000-4,500 *ADT*

1938 Austin Windsor Saloon, 2510cc, 6 cylinders, long wheelbase type 18, good condition.
£5,500-6,000 *ADT*

Models with the long wheelbase type 18 chassis were priced at £258 and in completed form cost over £400. The strength of the Austin 123in chassis lent itself to the building of limousine coachwork, as in the case of this most rare Windsor saloon.

1955 Austin A30 Four Door Saloon, excellent original condition.
£700-900   *Cen*

1957 Austin A35 Pick-up.
£1,750-2,500   *PC*

Introduced at the 1951 Motor Show the A30 was Austin's first post-war small car. Powered by an 803cc engine it featured unitary construction and independent front suspension.

1957 Austin A35 Saloon, 948cc, 4 cylinders.
£3,850-4,100   *ADT*

This vehicle was purchased in 1957 by a non car driving aunt for her nephew who had agreed to pay for the upkeep of the car and its free use, by the nephew, so long as he chauffeured his aunt at weekends. The shame is, however, that the aunt and nephew had a disagreement and in consequence the car laid in dry store for a number of years and would only appear to have been moved once a year for its annual service, clean and, in later years, MOT. In consequence the car today has only completed 751 miles.

| MAKE | ENGINE | DATES | CONDITION | | |
Austin	cc/cyl		1	2	3
16	2199/4	1945-49	£3,000	£2,000	£1,000
A40 Devon	1200/4	1947-52	£1,500	£1,000	£750
A40 Sports	1200/4	1950-53	£6,000	£4,000	£2,000
A40 Somerset	1200/4	1952-54	£2,000	£1,500	£750
A40 Somerset DHC	1200/4	1954	£5,000	£4,000	£2,500
A40 Dorset 2 door	1200/4	1947-48	£2,000	£1,500	£1,000
A70 Hampshire	2199/4	1948-50	£1,750	£1,500	£1,000
A70 Hereford	2199/4	1950-54	£1,850	£1,500	£1,000
A90 Atlantic DHC	2660/4	1949-52	£8,000	£6,000	£3,000
A90 Atlantic	2660/4	1949-52	£5,000	£3,000	£2,000
A40/A50 Cambridge	1200/4	1954-57	£1,200	£750	£500
A55 Mk I Cambridge	1489/4	1957-59	£1,000	£750	£500
A55 Mk II	1489/4	1959-61	£1,000	£750	£500
A60 Cambridge	1622/4	1961-69	£1,000	£750	£500
A90/95 Westminster	2639/6	1954-59	£2,000	£1,500	£750
A99 Westminster	2912/6	1959-61	£1,500	£1,000	£500
A105 Westminster	2639/6	1956-59	£2,000	£1,500	£750
A110 Mk I/II	2912/6	1961-68	£2,000	£1,500	£750
Nash Metropolitan	1489/4	1957-61	£2,500	£1,500	£750
Nash Metropolitan DHC	1489/4	1957-61	£4,000	£3,000	£1,500
A30	803/4	1952-56	£1,000	£500	—
A30 Countryman	803/4	1954-56	£1,500	£1,000	—
A35	948/4	1956-59	£1,000	£500	—
A35 Countryman	948/4	1956-62	£1,500	£1,000	—
A40 Farina Mk I	948/4	1958-62	£1,250	£750	£200
A40 Mk I Countryman	948/4	1959-62	£1,500	£1,000	£400
A40 Farina Mk II	1098/4	1962-67	£1,000	£750	—
A40 Mk II Countryman	1098/4	1962-67	£1,200	£750	£300
1100	1098/4	1963-73	£1,000	£750	—
1300 Mk I/II	1275/4	1967-74	£750	£500	—
1300GT	1275/4	1969-74	£1,250	£1,000	£750
1800/2200		1964-75	£1,500	£900	£600
3 litre	2912/6	1968-71	£3,000	£1,500	£500

1958 Austin A35 Van.
£1,500-2,000   *WCC*

1955 Austin A90 Saloon, 2639cc, 6 cylinders, original and unrestored, 5,000 miles from new.
£3,500-3,750   *WH*

1956 Austin A40 Cambridge, 1200cc, 4 cylinders.
£2,250-2,750   *ADT*

Make: **Austin**
Model: A40 Farina
Type: Saloon
Years Manufactured: Mk I, 1958-61; Mk II, 1961-67
Price when new: Mk I, £651; Mk II, £617
Engine Type: Overhead valve 4 cyl
Size: Mk I and early Mk II, 948cc; Mk II from 1962, 1098cc
Max Power: 948cc, 37 bhp @ 5000 rpm; 1098cc, 48 bhp @ 5100 rpm
Transmission: 4 speed
Performance: Max speed: 948cc, 75 mph; 1098cc, 80 mph; 0-60: 948cc, 29 secs; 1098cc, 23 secs; Mpg: 38-42.

1963 Austin A40, good condition, reconditioned engine.
£300-400   *ADT*

1966 Austin Mini Cooper S, 1275cc, Mk I.
£3,500-4,000   *DB*

Cross Reference
Morris Mini

1968 Austin Cambridge Estate.
£500-1,500   *PC*

Turkish-born Alec Issigonis followed a family tradition as an engineer, in his early days concentrating on suspension development and after a brief sojourn at Humber he moved to Morris where he designed the Morris Minor – a car initially described by Lord Nuffield as a 'poached egg' but later acknowledged by Nuffield as 'the golden egg'. After a brief time with Alvis in the mid-50s, Issigonis returned to BMC as Technical Director and was to develop the Mini, announced in 1959.

1961 Austin 7 Mini Saloon, 4 cylinder in line, water-cooled monobloc engine, overhead valve, bore 62.9mm, stroke 68.26mm, 848cc, transverse mounted engine, 4 speed gearbox, front wheel drive via helical spur gears, independent front and rear suspension, wheelbase 80in, 10in tyres, museum stored.
£1,350-1,500 *S*

1966 Austin Mini Cooper Mk I, 998cc, 4 cylinders, restored 1988/89, 3,000 miles since rebuild.
£900-1,000 *ADT*

A great number of Minis have received the faker's attention – BEWARE! The only certain check is the chassis number which must be verified.

1968 Austin Mini Cooper S Mk II, 1293cc, 4 cylinders.
Est. **£6,000-7,000** *ADT*

1969 Austin Mini Cooper Mk II Saloon, 998cc, transverse front mounted, 4 cylinder overhead valve, water-cooled monobloc engine, 4 speed gearbox in sump, driving front wheels, hydromatic suspension front and rear, wheelbase 80in.
Est. **£5,500-6,000** *S*

Available in either Morris Mini Minor or Austin 7 Mini forms, to cater for established marque loyalties, the Mini, with its 848cc transverse engine, was an instant success. Early teething troubles, particularly from water-logged engines, were soon overcome and the genius of the designer is reflected in the car's longevity.

1971 Austin Mini Cooper S, 1275cc, 4 cylinders.
Est. **£4,000-5,000** *ADT*

Austin Nash Metropolitan

Make: **Austin**
Model: Nash Metropolitan
Type: Fixed Head Coupé or Convertible
Years Manufactured: (UK) 1957-61
Price when new: Coupé, £713; Convertible, £725
Engine Type: Overhead valve 4 cyl
Size: 1200cc, later 1489cc
Max Power: 1489cc, 51 bhp @ 4250 rpm
Transmission: 3 speed manual
Performance: Max speed: 1489cc, 80+ mph; 0-60: 1489cc, 25 secs; Mpg: 1489cc, 28-32.

1958 Austin Nash Metropolitan, 1498cc, 4 cylinders. Est. **£4,000-4,500**   *ADT*

Austin Healey

1959 Austin Healey Sprite, totally restored to high specification. **£10,500-11,000**   *CLC*

1958 Austin Healey Sprite.
£6,000-7,000   *SC*

1960 Austin Healey Sprite Mk I, left hand drive, USA import. **£3,250-3,500**   *CCTC*

Make: **Austin-Healey**
Model: Sprite
Type: Sports
Years Manufactured: 1958-71
Quantity: 129,359
Price when new: £612-703
Engine Type: Overhead valve 4 cyl
Size: 948/1098/1275cc
Max Power: 43/56/65 bhp @ 5000 rpm
Max Torque: 948cc, 52 ft/lb @ 3300 rpm
Transmission: 4 speed
Wheelbase: 80in
Performance: Max speed: 85/90/93 mph; 0-60: 23/18/15 secs; Mpg: 35-45.

1960 Austin Healey Sprite, totally restored to high specification. **£13,000-14,000**   *CLC*

1959 Austin Healey Mk I Sprite, racing trim in club racing specification.
£5,500-6,000   *CA*

> **Cross Reference**
> Race Cars

1955 Austin Healey 100/4, 2660cc, 4 cylinders.
£9,000-10,000   *ADT*

1954 Austin Healey 100/4, 2600cc, good original condition, not yet registered in the UK.
Est. **£9,000-11,000**   *LF*

1955 Austin Healey 100/4, 4 cylinders, overhead valve, 2.6 litres, 4 speed transmission, wheelbase 90in, a race car since new, in good cosmetic condition with a new engine.
£9,500-10,500   *S(NY)*

1954 Austin Healey BN1, 2660cc, 4 cylinders.
Est. **£16,000-18,000**   *ADT*

MAKE	ENGINE	DATES	CONDITION		
Austin-Healey	cc/cyl		1	2	3
100 BN 1/2	2660/4	1953-56	£20,000	£15,000	£8,000
100/6, BN4/BN6	2639/6	1956-59	£21,000	£15,000	£8,000
3000 Mk I	2912/6	1959-61	£22,000	£14,000	£9,000
3000 Mk II	2912/6	1961-62	£22,000	£15,000	£9,000
3000 Mk IIA	2912/6	1962-64	£22,000	£15,000	£11,000
3000 Mk III	2912/6	1964-68	£22,000	£16,000	£12,000
Sprite Mk I	948/4	1958-61	£6,000	£4,000	£2,000
Sprite Mk II	948/4	1961-64	£3,000	£2,000	£500
Sprite Mk III	1098/4	1964-66	£3,000	£2,000	£500
Sprite Mk IV	1275/4	1966-71	£3,000	£2,000	£500

1956 Austin Healey 100/6, fully restored, with factory hardtop.
£10,000-14,000   *DG*

1957 Austin Healey 100/6 BN4, open 2+2 seater, 6 cylinder pushrod engine, 2639cc, twin 1½in SU carburettors, 102bhp at 4,600rpm, fully restored to a high specification.
£26,000-26,500   *MSN*

1958 Austin Healey 100/6, wire wheels, overdrive, left hand drive.
£11,000-13,000   *BA*

1954 Austin Healey 100, left hand drive, needs restoration, USA import.
£5,500-5,750   *CCTC*

1959 Austin Healey 100/6, 2639cc, 6 cylinders.
£9,000-11,000   *ADT*

1959 Austin Healey 3000 Mk I, original condition, resprayed.
£20,000-25,000   *DG*

1959 Austin Healey 3000 Mk I BT7, fully restored to a high specification.
£25,000-25,500   *MSN*

1961 Austin Healey 3000 Mk II BN7, 2912cc, triple 1½in SU carburettors, 132bhp at 4,750rpm.
£25,000-26,000   *MSN*

1964 Austin Healey 3000 Mk II, 2912cc, totally rebuilt engine, new brakes, new chrome, new wings and bumpers, stainless steel exhaust, 5 new chrome wire wheels and tyres. Est. **£20,000-25,000** *LF*

1966 Austin Healey 3000 Mk III Phase 2 BJ8, restyled interior and revised exhaust system, 6 cylinder pushrod engine, 2912cc, twin 2in SU carburettors, 150bhp at 5,250rpm. **£25,000-25,500** *MSN*

1962 Austin Healey 3000 Mk I, USA import, left hand drive, needs restoration. **£4,500-5,000** *CCTC*

1966 Austin Healey 3000 Mk III, 2912cc, 6 cylinders. Est. **£22,000-23,000** *ADT*

Austin Healey Mk II, triple carburettors, original 27,000 miles. **£22,000-25,000** *FOR*

1959 Austin Healey 3000 Mk I. **£18,000-20,000** *WCC*

Austin Healey 3000 Mk III, 2912cc, totally rebuilt. Est. **£16,000-20,000** *LF*

Autobianchi

1970 Autobianchi Eden Rock Cabriolet.
£3,000-5,000 *AUT*

Bayliss-Thomas

1925 Bayliss-Thomas 12/27hp Four Seater Open Tourer, coachwork by Mulliners of Birmingham, Meadows 4 cylinder, overhead valve, water-cooled monobloc engine, bore 69mm, stroke 100mm, 1496cc, Meadows 3 speed crash gearbox, semi-elliptic springs front and rear, high tension magneto ignition, thermo syphon cooling, spiral bevel rear axle, wheelbase 108in, 4.50 x 19in tyres.
£10,000-11,000 *S*

Bean

1928 Bean 14/45 Four Seater Tourer, 2297cc, 4 cylinders.
£11,000-12,000 *ADT*

Harper Sons & Bean, who had been motor component manufacturers, took over the manufacture of the pedestrian Perry light car in 1919. The company's 11.9hp single model policy never really did succeed. However, in a short time, the company carried out a cost cutting exercise which meant that a 4 seater tourer could be purchased for £80. 1924 saw the introduction of the 2.3 litre 14, a far better designed machine with a sound, reliable engine and gearbox of unit construction.

Bentley

1926 Bentley 3 Litre Speed Model by Vanden Plas.
£85,000-95,000 *PiK*

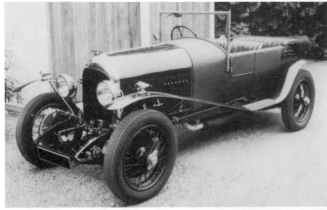

1924 Bentley 3 Litre, 3000cc, originally a 1924 Blue Label 3 litre with a Gurney Nutting saloon body on the 130in chassis. c1981 the chassis was shortened to the 117in short chassis Red Label specification and was also fitted with an A gearbox and Smiths Sloper carburettors also to Red Label specification. During the period from 1987 to 1989 the car underwent a complete rebuild and the Vanden Plas replica body was fitted.
Est. **£70,000-80,000** *LF*

1926 Bentley Blue Label 3 Litre Two Seater Sports with Dickey Seat, 4 cylinder, water-cooled monobloc engine with bevel driven single overhead camshaft, bore 80mm, stroke 149mm, 2996cc, 4 speed gearbox with right hand change, inverted cone clutch, spiral bevel rear axle, wheelbase 132in, 33 x 6.75in beaded edge tyres.
£50,000-55,000 *S*

A most original example of the 3 litre, mounted on a Light Touring chassis, is still fitted with its original engine, and still with the original 2 seater Vanden Plas body.

1927 Bentley 3 Litre Red Label, Short Chassis Speed Model by Vanden Plas.
£100,000-150,000 *BLE*

c1928 Bentley 4½ Litre Two Seater Tourer, 4500cc, 4 cylinders, originally fitted with Gurney Nutting coachwork, rebuilt in 1948 and fitted an HM Bentley styled 2 seater body with racing style 50 gallon petrol tank.
Est. **£70,000-90,000** *ADT*

The 4½ litre Bentley was produced at Cricklewood from 1927 following the prototype of the model's gallant efforts at Le Mans the same year. They had proved themselves to be reliable and fast cars, lapping easily at 80mph. The 4½ litre showed longevity in competition and the works continued to enter cars until 1931.

1935 Bentley 3½ Litre Drophead by Park Ward.
£55,000-60,000 *PiK*

BENTLEY

1934 Bentley 3½ Litre Vanden Plas Style Replica Tourer, condition 1.
£35,000-38,000   *PA*

1936 Bentley 3½ Litre Drophead Coupé by Mayfair, one owner since the mid-50s, stored since the 60s, now back on the road, in very original condition.
£46,000-48,000   *RCC*

1935 Bentley 3½ Litre Park Ward Saloon.
£19,500-22,000   *DB*

1935 Bentley 3½ Litre Park Ward Drophead Coupé, original condition throughout.
£60,000-65,000   *DG*

1936 Bentley 4¼ Litre Sports Saloon, 6 cylinder in line, water-cooled monobloc engine, pushrod operated overhead valves, bore 3½in, stroke 4½in, 4257cc, 4 speed gearbox, reverse right hand change, single dry plate clutch, spiral bevel rear axle, semi-elliptic spring suspension, wheelbase 126in, 17in tyres.
Est. £40,000-45,000   *S*

MAKE **Bentley**	ENGINE cc/cyl	DATES	CONDITION 1	2	3
3 litre	2996/4	1920-27	£70,000	£60,000	£40,000
Speed Six	6597/6	1926-32	£110,000	£75,000	£50,000
4.5 litre	4398/4	1928-32	£100,000	£70,000	£50,000
8 litre	7983/6	1930-32	£250,000	200,000	£100,000
3.5 litre	3699/6	1934-37	£65,000	£30,000	£15,000
4.25 litre	4257/6	1937-39	£70,000	£35,000	£20,000
Mark V	4257/6	1939-41	£45,000	£25,000	£20,000

Prices are very dependent on engine type, body style and extras like supercharger, gearbox ratio, history and originality.

1936 Bentley 3½ Litre Derby Drophead.
£45,000-55,000   *BLE*

1936 Bentley 4¼ Litre 3 Position Drophead Bentley by Hooper, the only 4¼ litre Bentley by Hooper.
£65,000-85,000   *BLE*

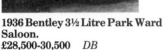

1936 Bentley 3½ Litre Park Ward Saloon.
£28,500-30,500   *DB*

1937 Bentley 4¼ Litre Thrupp & Maberly Sports Saloon, just out of long term storage and in need of total restoration, but complete and original.
£13,000-14,000   *RCC*

Following the acquisition by Rolls-Royce Ltd in 1931 the first new car to bear the Bentley label was the all new 'Silent Sportscar', the 3½ litre introduced to the public in August 1933 at Ascot. It grew out of the development of the Peregrine chassis, a Rolls-Royce project, and the all new 3½ litre engine gave the car performance previously associated with the marque but with a new silence bred from Rolls-Royce engineering.

1937 Bentley 4¼ Litre Sports Saloon, coachwork by Mann Egerton & Co. Ltd., 6 cylinder in line engine, water-cooled monobloc, pushrod operated overhead valves, bore 3½in, stroke 4½in, 4257cc, 4 speed gearbox, right hand change, disc clutch, open shaft, spiral bevel rear axle, semi-elliptic leaf springs front and rear, wheelbase 126in, 18in tyres, sunroof professionally sealed but otherwise original specification.
Est. £22,000-25,000   *S*

1937 Bentley 4¼ Litre Four Door Park Ward Saloon, original vehicle.
£24,000-25,000   *BA*

1938 Bentley 4¼ litre Sports Saloon, coachwork by James Young.
£24,200-26,000   S

1948 Bentley Mk VI, 4257cc, 6 cylinders.
Est. £14,000-18,000   ADT

The Bentley Mk VI was the first Crewe-built car to be offered complete with both chassis and body, a departure from the pre-war days.

1948 Bentley Mk VI Two Door Four Seater Tourer, coachwork by Saoutchik, Neuilly, Paris, 6 cylinder in line, cast iron monobloc, alloy cylinder head, overhead inlet valves by pushrods, side exhaust valves, single camshaft, 4257cc, bore 89mm, stroke 114mm, compression ratio 6.4:1, 135bhp at 4,000rpm, twin SU H4 carburettors, twin SU petrol pumps, single dry plate clutch with 4 speed manual gearbox, right hand gear change, synchromesh on 2nd, 3rd and 4th, semi-floating hypoid bevel final drive, deep channel section steel chassis with cruciform bracing and 2 door, 4 seater Saoutchik open touring sports bodywork, front independent suspension, coil springs, wishbones, hydraulic shock absorbers, anti-roll bar, rear semi-elliptic leaf springs, 4 wheel drum brakes, mechanical at rear, hydraulic at front assisted by mechanical friction disc servo, 16in pressed steel disc type wheels with 6.40 x 16in tyres, wheelbase 120in, right hand drive.
Est. £82,000-90,000   CNY

Two major developments accompanied Rolls-Royce and Bentley Motors' return to car production in 1946. Firstly, all car manufacturing was transferred from Derby to Crewe, and secondly the decision to supply complete cars with standardised bodywork, made to the Company's specification and finished in their own workshops.

1949 Bentley Mk VI, 4257cc, 6 cylinders.
Est. £9,000-11,000   ADT

1949 Bentley Mk VI DHC, by Park Ward, 4257cc, 6 cylinders.
£35,000-38,000   ADT

1949 Bentley Mk VI Standard Steel Saloon, 6 cylinder in line engine, water-cooled monobloc, pushrod operated overhead inlet valves, side exhaust valves, bore 3½in, stroke 4½in, 4257cc, 4 speed right hand change gearbox, single dry plate clutch, hypoid bevel rear axle, independent front suspension, semi-elliptic leaf rear springs, wheelbase 120in, 16in tyres. Est. £15,000-17,000   *S*

1948 Bentley Mk VI, by H. J. Mulliner, sports saloon. £30,000-45,000   *PJF*

1950 Bentley Mallileau Mk VI Tourer, Est. £10,000-15,000   *ADT*

Because of the durability of the ever-popular Bentley Mk VI, and in particular the chassis and engine, the Mallileau company purchased the older Mk VI Bentleys, stripped them down to their bare component parts, and used the chassis and engine as a base for 4 seater tourers.

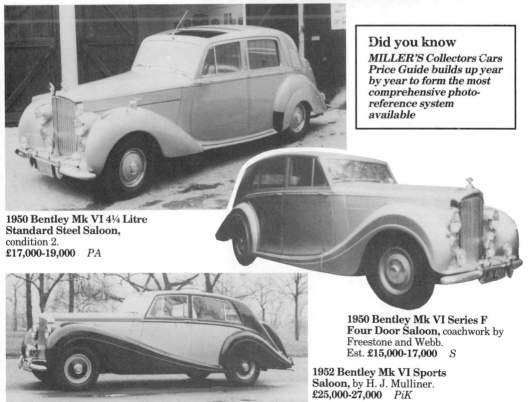

> **Did you know**
>
> *MILLER'S Collectors Cars Price Guide builds up year by year to form the most comprehensive photo-reference system available*

1950 Bentley Mk VI 4¼ Litre Standard Steel Saloon, condition 2. £17,000-19,000   *PA*

1950 Bentley Mk VI Series F Four Door Saloon, coachwork by Freestone and Webb. Est. £15,000-17,000   *S*

1952 Bentley Mk VI Sports Saloon, by H. J. Mulliner. £25,000-27,000   *PiK*

1953 Bentley R Type Four Door Saloon, coachwork by James Young.
Est. **£13,000-17,000** *C*

The Bentleys of the post-war years commenced with the Mk VI, which featured the well-known Rolls-Royce inlet over exhaust valve engine. The Mk VI was succeeded by the R Type in 1952, which had the more powerful engine available in the final versions of the Mk VI. The great majority of R Types continued to be built with factory bodywork, whilst a few featured specialist coachwork.

1952 Bentley R Type Series S Standard Steel Saloon, sound condition, seats retrimmed, requires cosmetic work.
Est. **£13,000-14,000** *S*

The new R Type was launched in the autumn of 1952 featuring the larger engine that had been offered in its predecessor the Mk VI. The chassis was slightly longer giving more luggage capacity although otherwise it retained many of the best features of the previous model in true Bentley tradition. Hydramatic transmission was also available as an option and this was initially only available in left hand drive for the overseas market, needless to say it was an immediate success in the United States.

A rebuilt car is not necessarily of more value than a car in good original condition, even if the restoration has cost thousands of pounds.

1952 R Type Bentley Continental, by H. J. Mulliner.
£100,000-175,000 *PJF*

1955 Bentley S1 Continental, by Park Ward, condition 1.
£60,000-70,000 *BLE*

1956 Bentley Fastback, by H. J. Mulliner.
£75,000-125,000 *PJF*

1956 Bentley S1 Continental Two Door Saloon, by James Young.
£90,000-95,000 *S8*

The S1 Bentley introduced in 1955 was the last model to outsell its companion Rolls-Royce, the Silver Cloud 1. They took over from the R Type and Silver Dawn although the Silver Wraith continued to be made in declining numbers for a further 4 years. This is the last of the 6 cylinder models and utilises what is in effect a bored out version of the 20hp engine introduced as far back as 1922.

1956 Bentley S1 Sports Saloon, coachwork by Freestone & Webb. This body may well be unique on a Bentley.
£15,000-16,000 *S*

1956 Bentley S1 Convertible, by H. J. Mulliner.
£120,000-175,000 *PJF*

1957 Bentley S1 Continental Drophead Coupé, coachwork by Park Ward, very original and solid car throughout, electric hood motor missing.
£280,000-300,000 *CNY*

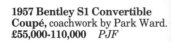

Bentley S1 Four Door Saloon, coachwork by James Young.
£35,000-45,000 *PJF*

1957 Bentley S1 Convertible Coupé, coachwork by Park Ward.
£55,000-110,000 *PJF*

1957 Bentley S1 Four Door Continental, coachwork by James Young, only 17 cars made.
£55,000-110,000 *PJF*

1958 Bentley S1 Continental Convertible, coachwork by Park Ward.
£125,000-200,000 *PJF*

1958 Bentley S1.
£9,000-10,000 *BA*

1958 Bentley S1 Series D Continental Two Door Fastback, coachwork by H. J. Mulliner, 6 cylinder water-cooled monobloc engine with pushrod operated overhead inlet valves and side exhaust valves, bore 3.75in, stroke 4.5in, 4887cc, hydramatic automatic gearbox, independent front suspension by coil spring, wishbone and hydraulic damper, rear suspension, half-elliptic with hydraulic damper and live axle, wheelbase 123in, 8.20 x 15in tyres.
Est. £68,000-75,000 *S*

1959 Bentley S1 Two Door Coupé, prototype H. J. Mulliner model. Later this body was fitted to the S2 chassis.
£110,000-120,000 *PJF*

MAKE Bentley	ENGINE cc/cyl	DATES	CONDITION		
			1	2	3
Abbreviations: HJM = H J Mulliner; PW = Park Ward; M/PW = Mulliner/Park Ward					
Mk VI Standard Steel	4257/ 4566/6	1946-52	£20,000	£12,000	£7,000
Mk VI Coachbuilt	4257/ 4566/6	1946-52	£27,500	£19,000	£15,000
Mk VI Coachbuilt DHC	4566/6	1946-52	£48,000	£33,000	£24,000
R Type Standard Steel	4566/6	1952-55	£22,000	£12,000	£7,000
R Type Coachbuilt	4566/6	1952-55	£32,000	£20,000	£15,000
R Type Coachbuilt DHC	4566/ 4887/6	1952-55	£50,000	£35,000	£25,000
R Type Cont (HJM)	4887/6	1952-55	£70,000	£40,000	£29,000
S1 Standard Steel	4887/6	1955-59	£20,000	£12,000	£7,000
S1 Cont 2 door (PW)	4877/6	1955-59	£50,000	£35,000	£25,000
S1 Cont Drop Head	4877/6	1955-59	£90,000	£75,000	£50,000
S1 Cont F'back (HJM)	4877/6	1955-58	£60,000	£35,000	£25,000
S2 Standard Steel	6230/8	1959-62	£18,000	£12,000	£8,000
S2 Cont 2 door (HJM)	6230/8	1959-62	£50,000	£40,000	£30,000
S2 Flying Spur (HJM)	6230/8	1959-62	£45,000	£33,000	£22,000
S2 Conv (PW)	6230/8	1959-62	£85,000	£70,000	£50,000
S3 Standard Steel	6230/8	1962-65	£24,000	£15,000	£12,000
S3 Cont/Flying Spur	6230/8	1962-65	£45,000	£38,000	£30,000
S3 2 door (PW)	6230/8	1962-65	£35,000	£30,000	£22,000
S3 Conv (PW)	6230/8	1962-65	£50,000	£40,000	£32,000
T1	6230/6, 6750/8	1965-77	£15,000	£10,000	£6,000
T1 door (M/PW)	6230/6, 6750/8	1965-70	£21,000	£18,000	£12,000
T1 Drop Head (M/PW)	6230/6, 6750/8	1965-70	£30,000	£25,000	£18,000

1959 Bentley S2, fair condition.
£5,000-5,500 *LF*

The S2 Bentley was introduced with a V8 6230cc engine in place of the 4.8 litre straight 6 engine in the Series 1.

1958 Bentley S1 Flying Spur Four Door Saloon, by H. J. Mulliner.
£55,000-110,000 *PJF*

1960 Bentley S2 Two Door Flying Spur.
£50,000-55,000 *S8*

1959 Bentley S1 Four-Light Flying Spur, by H. J. Mulliner.
£65,000-115,000 *PJF*

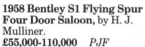

Make: **Bentley**
Model: Continental S2/S3
Type: Saloon/Convertible
Years Manufactured: 1959-66
Quantity: 700
Price when new: £5,661-£8,945
Engine Type: V8
Size: 6230cc
Transmission: Auto
Performance: Max speed: 113 mph; 0-60: 8.9 secs; Mpg: 14.

1960 Bentley S2 Continental, 6230cc, 8 cylinders, recently re-imported.
£18,000-20,000 *ADT*

The basic price for a standard steel Silver Cloud II in 1960 was £3,995 while that of the Continental was nearer £6,000.

1960 Bentley S2 Drophead Coupé, coachwork by Park Ward, V8 cylinder, water-cooled pushrod operated overhead valve, bore 104.14mm, stroke 91.44mm, 6230cc, automatic 4 speed transmission, semi-floating hypoid spiral rear axle, independent coil spring and unequal wishbone front suspension, semi-elliptic leaf spring rear suspension, wheelbase 123in, 15in tyres.
Est. **£45,000-55,000** *S(M)*

1960 Bentley S2 Standard Steel Sports Saloon, in sound and original condition.
Est. £14,500-15,500   *S*

1962 Bentley S3 Saloon, 6230cc, full service history, recorded mileage 130,000.
£13,500-15,000   *HA*

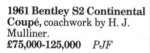

1962 Bentley S2 Continental Flying Spur, coachwork by H. J. Mulliner.
Est. £60,000-65,000   *C*

1961 Bentley S2 Continental Coupé, coachwork by H. J. Mulliner.
£75,000-125,000   *PJF*

1962 Bentley S2.
£15,000-30,000   *PJF*

Condition Guide

1. *A vehicle in top class condition but not 'concours d'elegance' standard, either fully restored or in very good original condition*
2. *A good, clean, roadworthy vehicle, both mechanically and bodily sound*
3. *A runner, but in need of attention, probably both to bodywork and mechanics. Must have current MOT*

1964 Bentley S3 long wheel base, by H. J. Mulliner.
£35,000-50,000   *PJF*

1962 Bentley S2 Continental Convertible, by Park Ward. £75,000-130,000 *PJF*

1962 Bentley Continental Flying Spur, coachwork by H. J. Mulliner. £54,000-58,000 *CNY*

1964 Bentley S3 Continental Flying Spur Sports Saloon, coachwork by Park Ward, 90° V8 cylinder engine, water-cooled, overhead valves, bore 4.1in , stroke 3.6in, 6230cc, aluminium cylinder heads, 4 speed automatic transmission, shaft drive to live rear axle, independent front suspension and semi-elliptic rear leaf springs, power assisted steering, wheelbase 123in.
Est. £55,000-75,000 *S*

1964 Bentley S3, 6230cc, 8 cylinders.
Est. £9,000-10,000 *ADT*

1965 Bentley S3 Standard Steel. £25,000-45,000 *PJF*

1966 Bentley T Type Four Door Saloon, V8 cylinder engine, water-cooled, pushrod operated overhead valves, bore 4.1in, stroke 3.6in, 6230cc, 4 speed automatic gearbox, hypoid bevel final drive, independent front and rear suspension, wheelbase 119½in, 8.1 x 15in tyres, for restoration and is at present a non-runner.
£5,000-6,000 *S*

BENZ

1966 Bentley S3 Continental Flying Spur Sports Saloon, coachwork by H. J. Mulliner.
Est. £47,000-50,000   *S*

1965 Bentley S3 Continental Flying Spur, by H. J. Mulliner.
£60,000-120,000   *PJF*

1971/84 Bentley Corniche.
£30,000-32,000   *AUT*

1971 Bentley T Type, in good condition throughout.
£8,000-11,000   *PC*

Benz

1897 Benz Velo, 1 cylinder, 3½hp.
£60,000-63,000   *SL*

Cross Reference
Liver Benz

1957 Berkeley, twin cylinder 2 stroke engine, 328cc, 4 wheeler version.
£2,250-2,750   *DB*

1985 Bentley 8.
£25,000-30,000   *S8*

Berkeley

MAKE	ENGINE	DATES	CONDITION		
Berkeley	cc/cyl		1	2	3
B60	322/2	1956-57	£2,000	£1,000	£500
B65	328/2	1957-60	£2,500	£1,500	£850
B90	492/3	1957-59	£2,500	£1,500	£850
B95/105	692/2	1959-61	£3,000	£2,250	£1,000

Bizzarrini

Make: **Bizzarrini**
Model: GT Strada 5300
Type: Sports/Coupé
Years Manufactured: 1963-69
Engine Type: Chevrolet overhead valve V8
Size: 5354cc
Max Power: 365 bhp @ 6000 rpm
Max Torque: 376 ft/lb @ 3500 rpm
Transmission: 4 speed manual
Wheelbase: 96.5in
Performance: Max speed: 145 mph; 0-60: 6.4 secs.

1968 Bizzarrini GT Strada 5300 Coupé, coachwork by BBM, Modena (Bertone styled), Chevrolet V8 cylinder, overhead valves, pushrods and rockers from single camshaft, 5354cc, bore 101.6mm, stroke 82.6mm, 365bhp at 6,200rpm, single four-choke downdraught Holley carburettor, single dry plate clutch, 4 speed manual all synchromesh gearbox, hypoid-drive rear axle with limited slip-differential, platform type steel frame chassis with Bertone styled 2 seater, 2 door coupé body, front independent suspension by coil springs, wishbones and anti-roll bar, rear De Dion suspension with coil springs, longitudinal and transverse Watts linkage, telescopic shock absorbers, 4 wheel disc brakes with vacuum servo, 15in Borrani centre lock cast alloy wheels with 205 x 15in tyres, wheelbase 2,460mm, 160+mph, left hand drive.
Est. **£95,000-120,000** *C(M)*

BMW

1940 BMW 327 Coupé, 6 cylinder, overhead valve, 1971cc, 4 speed manual transmission, 4 wheel hydraulic brakes, left hand drive.
£5,500-6,500 *C*

1941 BMW 321 Coupé, 1971cc, 6 cylinders. Est.
£5,000-6,000 *ADT*

MAKE BMW	ENGINE cc/cyl	DATES	CONDITION		
			1	2	3
Dixi	747/4	1927-32	£5,000	£3,000	£1,500
303	1175/6	1934-36	£11,000	£8,000	£5,000
309	843/4	1933-34	£6,000	£4,000	£2,000
315	1490/6	1935-36	£9,000	£7,000	£5,000
319	1911/6	1935-37	£10,000	£9,000	£6,000
326	1971/6	1936-37	£12,000	£10,000	£8,000
320 series	1971/6	1937-38	£12,000	£10,000	£8,000
327/328	1971/6	1937-40	£20,000	£15,000	£10,000
328	1971/6	1937-40	£50,000+		

1969 BMW 2000, 1990cc, 4 cylinders.
Est. **£2,000-2,500**   *ADT*

1956 BMW Type 501 Four Door Saloon, V8 cylinder, overhead valve, water-cooled engine, bore 74mm, stroke 75mm, 2598cc, 4 speed gearbox, all-round independent suspension by adjustable torsion bars with upper and lower wishbones, and with telescopic shock absorbers front and rear, hydraulic self-adjusting brakes on all 4 wheels, live rear axle, 6.40 x 15in tyres, wheelbase 111½in.
Est. **£15,000-18,000**   *S*

By 1956 the 501 was available with a 2077cc uprated engine, and for the 1957 season could also be had with the 2½ litre V8 engine first offered in the 502.

1966/75 BMW 1602.
£1,000-2,000   *AUT*

Make: BMW	
Model: 1600/2002	
Type: Saloon/Touring Estate/Convertible	
Years Manufactured: 1966-75	
Price when new: 2002, Saloon, £1,597	
Engine Type: Overhead valve 4 cyl	
Size: 1573-1990cc	
Max Power: 96 bhp @ 5800 rpm; 100 bhp @ 5500 rpm	
Transmission: 4 speed, 5 speed or auto optional	
Performance: Max speed: 2002, 107 mph; 0-60: 10.6 secs; Mpg: 26.	

1974 BMW 2002 Cabriolet, 1990cc.
Est. **£4,000-5,000**   *HA*

1972 BMW 2002 Sports Saloon, 4 cylinder in line engine, single overhead camshaft, water-cooled monobloc, bore 89mm, stroke 80mm, 1990cc, 4 speed manual transmission, bevel rear axle, front suspension, MacPherson strutts with coil springs, rear suspension, semi-trailing arms with coil springs, wheelbase 2,500mm, 165SR x 13in tyres.   **£3,000-3,500**   *S*

1974 BMW 2002 Turbo, 1990cc,
4 cylinders, left hand drive,
mechanics good.
Est. **£8,500-9,500** *ADT*

1972 BMW 3.0 CSi, 3200cc, 6 cylinders.
Est. **£6,500-7,500** *ADT*

*The first manufacturer to offer a
turbo charged, road going
production car was BMW with their
2002 model. The car already had a
good following, especially in the Tii
format.*

1979/80 BMW M1.
£85,000-95,000 *AUT*

Make: **BMW**
Model: M1
Type: Sports Coupé
Years Manufactured: 1978-81
Quantity: 450
Engine Type: Twin cam 24
valve 6 cyl
Size: 3453cc
Max Power: 277 bhp @ 6500
rpm
Max Torque: 243 ft/lb @ 5000
rpm
Transmission: 5 speed
Wheelbase: 100.8in
Performance: Max speed: 162
mph; 0-60: 5.5 secs; Mpg: 17.

1989 BMW Z1.
£20,000-22,000 *AUT*

MAKE BMW	ENGINE cc/cyl	DATES	CONDITION 1	2	3
501	2077/6	1952-56	£7,500	£5,500	£2,000
501 V8/502	2580, 3168/8	1955-63	£8,000	£6,000	£3,000
503	3168/8	1956-59	£25,000	£20,000	£15,000
507	3168/8	1956-59	£95,000	£80,000	—
Isetta (4 wheels)	247/1	1955-62	£3,000	£2,000	£1,000
Isetta (3 wheels)	298/1	1958-64	£3,000	£2,000	£1,000
Isetta 600	585/2	1958-59	£1,000	£600	£300
1500/1800/2000	var/4	1962-68	£1,100	£700	£200
2000CS	1990/4	1966-69	£5,500	£4,000	£1,500
1500/1600/1602	1499/ 1573/4	1966-75	£2,000	£1,000	£300
1600 Cabriolet	1573/4	1967-71	£6,000	£4,500	£2,000
2800CS	2788/6	1968-71	£5,000	£4,000	£1,500
1602	1990/4	1968-74	£2,000	£1,500	£600
2002	1990/4	1968-74	£3,000	£2,000	£750
2002 Tii	1990/4	1971-75	£4,500	£2,500	£800
2002 Touring	1990/4	1971-74	£3,000	£2,000	£500
2002 Cabriolet	1990/4	1971-75	£6,000	£4,000	£2,500
2002 Turbo	1990/4	1973-74	£11,000	£7,000	£5,000
3.0 CSa/CSi	2986/6	1972-75	£9,000	£6,000	£4,000
3.0 CSL	3003/ 3153/6	1972-75	£17,000	£12,000	£9,500

1985 BMW M3.
£15,000-17,000 *S8*

BMW Isetta

1960 BMW Isetta Bubble Car.
£3,000-3,500 *S*

1961 BMW Isetta 300, 300cc.
£5,000-5,500 *LF*

1962 BMW Isetta Bubble Car,
concours in all respects, very
original, total rebuild.
£4,500-5,000 *S*

Cross Reference
Heinkel
Messerschmitt

*In post-war Germany BMW had to
adjust to changing market
conditions and, with their
motorcycle experience behind them,
BMW took a licence from the Italian
Iso company to produce the Bubble
Car in Germany. They fitted their
own 4 stroke engine and it became
one of the most successful mini cars
in post-war Germany. An English
company, Isetta of Brighton, in turn
took a licence to build the cars in the
UK in the old railway sheds at
Brighton and the cars were notable
for their publicity impact, a
forerunner to the Mini.*

1962 BMW Isetta 300 Coupé, built
by Isetta of G.B. Ltd., Brighton,
Sussex, single cylinder, 4 stroke,
overhead valve, 298cc, bore 72mm,
stroke 73mm, compression 7:1,
13bhp at 5,200rpm, single Bing
22/98 carburettor, 4 speed gearbox,
primary drive by shaft, final drive
by adjustable chain, steel tube
frame chassis with 2 seater, single
front opening door coupé bodywork,
3 wheeler, front suspension with
coil springs, swing arm,
independent, rear rigid axle,
quarter-elliptic leaf spring,
telescopic shock absorbers,
hydraulic drum brakes, 10in disc
wheels with special wire style wheel
trims, 4.50 x 10in tyres, wheelbase
1,500mm, right hand drive.
£2,500-3,000 *C*

Bristol

1950 Bristol 400, 1971cc, 6 cylinders.
£15,000-17,000   *ADT*

Bristol's diversification into motor cars began in the post-war years with the Type 400. Largely developed from earlier BMW designs, the 400 was powered by an improved version of the BMW cross pushrod 328 engine, being 6 cylinders in line with a capacity of 1971cc, performing in excess of 90mph from 80bhp. Production of the 400 ended in 1950.

1948 Bristol 400 Two Door Saloon, 6 cylinders, overhead valve, 1971cc, 4 speed manual transmission, rack and pinion, right hand drive. Engine to be rebuilt and interior re-trimmed.
Est. **£7,000-9,000**   *C*

1949/53 Bristol 401.
£18,000-20,000   *AUT*

Make: **Bristol**
Model: 401/402
Type: Sports Saloon
Years Manufactured: 1949-53
Quantity: 401, 650; 402, 24
Price when new: £2,724-£4,244
Engine Type: Overhead valve 6 cyl
Size: 1971cc
Max Power: 85 bhp @ 4500 rpm
Max Torque: 107 ft/lb @ 3500 rpm
Transmission: 4 speed
Wheelbase: 114in
Performance: Max speed: 94 mph; 0-60: 17.4 secs; Mpg: 20-25.

1951 Bristol 401, 1971cc, 6 cylinders.
Est. **£12,000-14,000**   *ADT*

1953 Bristol 403 Two Door Saloon, 6 cylinder, overhead valve, 1971cc, 4 speed manual transmission, right hand drive, complete and in running order, in need of restoration throughout.
Est. **£7,000-9,000**   *C*

1954/58 Bristol 405 Saloon.
£15,000-17,000   *AUT*

1964 Bristol 408, bodywork and interior fully restored, extensive mechanical work, right hand drive.
£12,500-14,500   *CGB*

1967 Bristol 409 Two Door Saloon, V8 Chrysler overhead valve, water-cooled engine, bore 99.31mm, stroke 84.07mm, 5211cc, push button automatic gearbox, Torqueflite transmission, independent front suspension, leaf spring rear, 6.00 x 16in tyres, wheelbase 114in.
Est. **£22,000-25,000**   *S*

MAKE Bristol	ENGINE cc/cyl	DATES	CONDITION 1	2	3
400	1971/6	1947-50	£16,000	£13,000	£9,000
401	1971/6	1949-53	£17,000	£12,000	£7,000
402	1971/6	1949-50	£28,000	£20,000	£13,000
403	1971/6	1953-55	£17,500	£12,500	£8,000
404 Coupé	1971/6	1953-57	£26,000	£18,000	£12,000
405	1971/6	1954-58	£16,000	£10,500	£8,000
405 Drophead	1971/6	1954-56	£28,000	£23,000	£15,000
406	2216/6	1958-61	£12,000	£9,000	£6,000
407	5130/8	1962-63	£11,000	£8,000	£5,500
408	5130/8	1964-65	£11,500	£8,000	£5,500
409	5211/8	1966-67	£12,500	£8,500	£6,000
410	5211/8	1969	£15,000	£10,000	£7,000
411 Mk 1-3	6277/8	1970-73	£14,000	£9,000	£7,500
411 Mk 4-5	6556/8	1974-76	£14,500	£10,000	£8,000
412	5900/ 6556/8	1975-82	£17,000	£9,500	£5,500
603	5211/ 5900/8	1976-82	£16,000	£9,000	£5,000

1964/65 Bristol 408.
£8,000-10,000   *AUT*

Make: **Bristol**
Model: 407/408/409/410/411
Type: Saloon
Years Manufactured: 1961-76
Price when new: £4,848-£6,997
Engine Type: V8
Size: 407/408, 5130cc; 409/410, 5211cc; 411, 6277cc
Max Power: 407, 250 bhp @ 4400 rpm; 411 (1973-76), 264 bhp @ 4800 rpm
Max Torque: 407, 340 ft/lb @ 2800 rpm; 411 (1973-76), 335 ft/lb @ 3600 rpm
Transmission: Auto
Wheelbase: 114in
Performance: Max speed: 407, 122 mph; 411, 138 mph; 0-60: 407, 9.9 secs; 411, 7 secs.

1971 Bristol 411 Mk II Sports Saloon.
Est. **£16,000-18,000** *S*

1979 Bristol 603.
£15,000-17,000 *S8*

1979 Bristol 412 S2, 5898cc, 8 cylinders.
Est. **£19,000-21,000** *ADT*

Make: **Bristol**
Model: 412
Type: Convertible
Years Manufactured: 1975-82
Price when new: £14,584
Engine Type: V8
Size: 5898/6556cc
Transmission: Auto
Performance: Max speed: 140 mph; 0-60: 7.4 secs; Mpg: 14.

Buick

1934 Buick Model 96S Two Door Coupé and Dickey, 3448cc, 8 cylinders.
£8,500-9,000 *ADT*

MAKE Buick	ENGINE cc/cyl	DATES	CONDITION 1	2	3
Veteran	2600/2	1903-09	£20,000	£12,000	£8,000
18/20	3881/6	1918-22	£12,000	£5,000	£2,000
Series 22	2587/4	1922-24	£9,000	£5,000	£3,000
Series 24/6	3393/6	1923-30	£9,000	£5,000	£3,000
Light 8	3616/8	1931	£18,000	£14,500	£11,000
Straight 8	4467/8	1931	£22,000	£18,000	£10,000
50 Series	3857/8	1931-39	£18,500	£15,000	£10,000
60 Series	5247/8	1936-39	£20,000	£15,000	£8,000
90 Series	5648/8	1934-35	£20,000	£15,500	£9,000
40 Series	4064/8	1936-39	£22,000	£16,000	£10,000
80/90	5247/8	1936-39	£25,000	£20,000	£15,000
McLaughlin	5247/8	1937-40	£25,000	£15,000	£10,000

Various chassis lengths and bodies will affect value. Buick chassis fitted with English bodies previous to 1916 were called Bedford-Buicks. Right hand drive can have an added premium of 25%.

BUICK

1937 Buick Straight 8, condition 1.
£9,000-10,000   *CC*

**1940 Buick Series 40 Sport
Coupé,** 4300cc, 8 cylinder.
£6,500-7,000   *ADT*

**1937 Buick Fastback.
£6,500-7,000**   *ADT*

*Manufactured by General Motors on
the Model 40 Special chassis, only
205 were produced with fastback
bodywork.*

1937 McLaughlin-Buick 38hp Series 90 Limousine, coachwork by Thrupp & Maberly, straight 8, overhead
valve, water-cooled monobloc engine, bore 3⅞in, stroke 4¼in, 5247cc, 3 speed gearbox, single plate clutch,
independent front suspension, semi-elliptic leaf springs at rear, spiral bevel rear axle, 7.50 x 16in tyres,
wheelbase 138in.   **£5,000-5,500**   *S*

MAKE Buick	ENGINE cu in	DATES	CONDITION		
			1	2	3
Special/Super 4 door	248/				
	364/8	1950-59	£6,000	£4,000	£2,000
Special/Super Riv	263/				
	332/8	1950-56	£8,000	£6,000	£3,000
Special/Super conv	263/				
	332/8	1950-56	£7,500	£5,500	£3,000
Roadmaster 4 door	320/				
	365/8	1950-58	£11,000	£8,000	£6,000
Roadmaster Riviera	320/				
	364/8	1950-58	£9,000	£7,000	£5,000
Roadmaster conv	320/				
	364/8	1950-58	£14,500	£11,000	£7,000
Special/Super Riv	364/8	1957-59	£10,750	£7,500	£5,000
Special/Super conv	364/8	1957-58	£13,500	£11,000	£6,000

Bugatti

1925 Bugatti Type 30 Sports Tourer, 8 cylinder in line as two 4 cylinder monoblocs, overhead camshaft, roller bearing crankshaft, plain big ends, 1991cc, bore 60mm, stroke 88mm, 3 valves per cylinder, 2 inlet, 1 exhaust, 2 Zenith carburettors, 75bhp at 3,800rpm, 4 speed right hand gate change gearbox, multi-plate wet clutch, back axle ratio 12/50, front suspension half-elliptic leaf springs, rear reversed quarter-elliptic leaf springs, 4 wheel cable operated drum brakes, 19in wheels, Rudge Whitworth centre lock wire spoke wheels, 5.50 x 19in tyres, right hand drive.
Est. £120,000-140,000   *C*

1927 Bugatti Type 38, English coachwork, wheelbase 122½in.
£60,000-65,000   *PMc*

Ettore Bugatti's first production cars in 1912, designated Type 13, were 4 cylinder 8 valve engined light cars, and just prior to the outbreak of WWI a 16 valve version was designed to improve the breathing and performance. These 1½ litre cars were already making a name for Bugatti in Hill Climbs and Voiturette races and the motoring press was extolling the virtues of their performance and road holding.

In 1926 Ettore Bugatti put the Type 38 into production to replace the Type 30. Its brief life (2 years) meant that only about 375 Type 38 cars were produced. Some later models were fitted with superchargers to improve the car's performance. Despite reduced performance, unsupercharged Type 38s sold well.

> **Miller's is a price GUIDE not a price LIST**

1924 Bugatti Type 23 Two Seater, 4 cylinder, monobloc, overhead valves, 4 valves per cylinder, 1496cc, bore 69mm, stroke 100mm, 40bhp at 4,000rpm, Zenith carburettor, 4 speed gearbox, right hand gear change lever, multi-plate wet clutch, 12/45 rear axle ratio, hand operated rear wheel drum brake and foot operated transmission brake, 19in wheels, Rudge Whitworth centre lock wire wheels, 4.50 x 19in tyres, front semi-elliptic leaf springs, rear reversed semi-elliptic leaf springs, right hand drive.
Est. £45,000-55,000   *C*

1929 Bugatti Type 40A Cabriolet,
4 cylinder in line engine,
water-cooled monobloc, single
overhead camshaft, bore 72mm,
stroke 100mm, 1650cc,
supercharged, 4 speed gearbox, dry
multiple plate clutch, bevel rear
axle, semi-elliptic leaf front springs,
quarter-elliptic at rear, 4.75/
5.00 x 19in tyres.
Est. **£90,000-120,000**   *S(M)*

1929 Bugatti Type 35B Racing Car, full restoration in
the 1960s, using as many original parts as possible,
non-original wheels and suspension, re-registered for
road use in 1960s.
£30,000-50,000   *C.A.R.S.*

*Introduced in 1926 as a lineal
successor to the Brescia cars, the
Type 40 was to share much of its
technical specification with the
Type 37 Grand Prix cars and is
perhaps best known in compact
4 seater Gran Sport form. The
1496cc engine was built employing a
single overhead camshaft to operate
8 inlet and 4 exhaust valves. Some
45bhp was developed at 4,500rpm
and the cars with lightweight
coachwork offered lively performance
and a 70mph top speed. The
supercharged models, the Type 40A,
had an increased engine capacity
and offered significantly enhanced
performance.*

1929 Bugatti Type 46 Saloon, coachwork unknown but of
Weymann type.   **£34,500-36,000**   *C(M)*

MAKE Bugatti	ENGINE cc/cyl	DATES	CONDITION 1	2	3
13/22/23	1496/4	1919-26	£45,000	£32,000	£25,000
30	1991/8	1922-36	£45,000	£35,000	£30,000
32	1992/8	1923	£45,000	£35,000	£30,000
35	1991/8	1924-30	£110,000	£90,000	£80,500
38 (30 update)	1991/8	1926-28	£44,500	£34,000	£28,000
39	1493/8	1926-29	£120,000	£90,000	£80,000
39A Supercharged	1496/8	1926-29	£150,000+	—	—
35T	2262/8	1926-30	£150,000+	—	—
37 GP Car	1496/4	1926-30	£110,000	£90,000	£75,000
40	1496/4	1926-30	£50,000	£42,000	£35,000
38A	1991/8	1927-28	£48,000	£40,000	£35,000
35B Supercharged	2262/8	1927-30	£17,000+	—	—
35C	1991/8	1927-30	£17,000+	—	—
37A	1496/4	1927-30	£125,000+	—	—
44	2991/8	1927-30	£50,000	£40,000	£35,000
45	3801/16	1927-30	£160,000+	—	—
43/43A Tourer	2262/8	1927-31	£180,000+	—	—
35A	1991/8	1928-30	£140,000	£110,000	£90,000
46	5359/8	1929-36	£140,000	£110,000	£90,000
40A	1627/4	1930	£55,000	£45,000	£35,500
49	3257/8	1930-34	£55,000	£45,000	£35,500
57 Closed	3257/8	1934-40	£40,000	£35,000	£30,000
57 Open	3257/8	1936-38	£80,000	£60,000	£55,000
57S	3257/8	1936-38	£250,000+	—	—
57SC Supercharged	3257/8	1936-39	£250,000+	—	—
57G	3257/8	1937-40	£250,000+	—	—
57C	3257/8	1939-40	£150,000+	—	—

Cadillac

1950 Cadillac Model 62 Convertible, V8 overhead valve, 160hp, 4 speed hydramatic transmission, wheelbase 126in.
Est. **£22,000-28,000**   *S(NY)*

1950 was the first year that Cadillac produced more than 100,000 cars, replacing Packard as the leader in the American luxury car market.

1928 Cadillac Golfer's Coupé 314.
£55,000-65,000   *BLE*

1928 Cadillac La Salle, totally original, less than 20,000 miles from new.
£20,000-30,000   *BLE*

The Cadillac Motor Company of Detroit introduced their first cars in 1903, designed by Henry M. Leland who had previously been General Engineer of Ford which these early 4 cylinder cars bore a strong resemblance. The name Cadillac derives from Antoine de la Mothe Cadillac, founder of Detroit in the 17thC, and by 1909 had become part of the General Motors group under Billy Durant.

1939 Cadillac V16 Series 90 Ceremonial Town Car, V16 cylinder 135° water-cooled side valve engine, 7200cc, 2 updraught Cadillac carburettors, compression 6:1, 185bhp at 3,800rpm, single dry plate 3 speed synchromesh gearbox, hypoid bevel final drive, pressed steel channel section frame chassis with cross members and 7 seater 4 door town car bodywork, front independent suspension, rear semi-elliptic leaf springs, hydraulic shock absorbers, pressed steel 16in wheels, 7.50 x 16in tyres, 3,630mm wheelbase, left hand drive. This second series V16 chassis with coachwork by Fleetwood, formerly a ceremonial car of The Vatican used by Pope Pius XII, was one of the last cars built in 1939.
£21,000-23,000   *C(M)*

Cadillac continued their high quality American market production for 1969 with a wide range of limousine options on the Eldorado model, and a full selection of 2 and 4 door hard-top and convertible models. The Coupé de Ville was available in fixed head or convertible styles.

1969 Cadillac Coupé de Ville Convertible, V8 cylinder, water-cooled, overhead valves, bore 4.3in, stroke 4.06in, 7800cc, 4 speed automatic gearbox, shaft drive, independent suspension, wheelbase 129.5in, 11,600 miles from new.
£11,000-12,000   *S*

73

1970 Cadillac de Ville Convertible, 7400cc, 8 cylinders, low mileage, condition 1.
£6,000-7,000   *PA*

> **Miller's is a price GUIDE not a price LIST**

1968 Cadillac Coupé de Ville Convertible, 472cu in V8 automatic.
£4,400-4,500   *SCC*

1988 Cadillac Eldorado Convertible.   **£10,000-11,000**   *S8*

MAKE Cadillac	ENGINE cc/cyl	DATES	CONDITION		
			1	2	3
4 door sedan	331/8	1949	£8,000	£4,500	£3,000
2 door fastback	331/8	1949	£10,000	£8,000	£5,000
Convertible coupé	331/8	1949	£22,000	£18,000	£7,000
Series 62 4 door	331/ 365/8	1950-55	£7,000	£5,500	£3,000
Sedan de Ville	365/8	1956-58	£8,000	£6,000	£4,000
Coupé de Ville	331/ 365/8	1950-58	£12,500	£9,500	£3,500
Convertible coupé	331/ 365/8	1950-58	£25,000	£20,000	£10,000
Eldorado	331/8	1953-55	£45,000	£35,000	£20,000
Eldorado Seville	365/8	1956/58	£11,500	£9,000	£5,500
Eldorado Biarritz	365/8	1956-58	£30,000	£20,000	£15,000
Sedan de Ville	390/8	1959	£12,000	£9,500	£5,000
Coupé de Ville	390/8	1959	£15,000	£9,000	£5,500
Convertible coupé	390/8	1959	£28,000	£20,000	£10,000
Eldorado Seville	390/8	1959	£13,000	£10,000	£6,000
Eldorado Biarritz	390/8	1959	£30,000	£20,000	£14,000
Sedan de Ville	390/8	1960	£10,000	£8,000	£4,500
Convertible coupé	390/8	1960	£27,000	£14,000	£7,500
Eldorado Biarritz	390/8	1960	£25,000	£17,000	£10,000
Sedan de Ville	390/ 429/8	1961-64	£7,000	£5,000	£3,000
Coupé de Ville	390/ 429/8	1961-64	£8,000	£6,000	£4,000
Convertible coupé	390/ 429/8	1961-64	£15,000	£9,000	£7,000
Eldorado Biarritz	390/ 429/8	1961-64	£24,000	£14,000	£9,000

Caterham

1985 Caterham 7, Ford 1600, pushrod.
£6,000-7,000   *PC*

Chenard-Walcker

1928 Chenard-Walcker Torpedo, for restoration.
Est. £6,000-8,000   *LF*

Chenard-Walcker is probably best known for being the outright winner of the first Le Mans race held in 1923. After the War the marque was absorbed by Peugeot and the last vehicles to bear the badge were some front wheel drive vans.

1928 Chenard-Walcker Type Y3, 1750cc.
£3,500-5,000   *LF*

Chevrolet

1926 Chevrolet Two Door Saloon, 2801cc, 6 cylinders.
£4,500-5,000   *ADT*

1928 Chenard-Walcker Torpedo.
Est. £5,000-7,000   *LF*

1928 Chevrolet Two Door Doctor's Coupé with Dickey Seat, coachwork by Fisher Bodyworks, 4 cylinder, overhead valve, 3 speed manual transmission, left hand drive.
£6,500-7,500   *C*

By the mid-20s Chevrolet was making inroads into the Model A Ford territory. In 1924 Ford outsold Chevrolet by more than 8:1, in 1925 4:1, in 1926 less than 3:1. In 1927 Chevrolet built 1.7 million cars. For the first time since 1906 a car other than Ford was number one in the industry.

CHEVROLET

MAKE Chevrolet	ENGINE cc/cyl	DATES	CONDITION 1	2	3
H4/H490E	2801/4	1914-29	£9,000	£5,000	£2,000
FA5	2699/4	1918	£8,000	£5,000	£2,000
D5	5792/8	1918-19	£10,000	£6,000	£3,000
FB50	3660/4	1919-21	£7,000	£4,000	£2,000
AB	2700/4	1926-32	£5,000	£3,000	£1,000
AE	3180/6	1929-36	£6,000	£4,000	£2,000
EC/EA	3358/6	1936-37	£9,000	£5,000	£2,000
9LH Series	3548/6	1938-42	£9,000	£6,000	£4,000

Value is very much dependent on being a right or left hand drive car.

1937 Chevrolet Master Series GB Six Sport Coupé, 6 cylinder in line engine, water-cooled monobloc, overhead valve, bore 3½in, stroke 3¾in, 3 speed floor shift gearbox, single plate clutch, semi-floating bevel rear axle, semi-elliptic leaf spring suspension front and rear, wheelbase 112¼in, 16in tyres.
Est. **£8,000-12,000**   *S*

1937 once again saw Chevrolet as America's best selling automobile, their Master range of 6 cylinder cars that year being offered in no less than 13 different specifications. The 1937 engines were all new with bigger bore and shorter stroke and the pressed steel coachwork with extravagant styling was by Fisher. Some 825,220 Chevrolets were built in 1937.

1928 Chevrolet, condition 2, right hand drive.
£8,500-9,000   *CC*

1936 Chevrolet Sports Roadster with Rumble Seat, coachwork by Fisher, 6 cylinder in line engine, water-cooled monobloc, bore 3⁵⁄₁₆in, stroke 4in, 3388cc, 3 speed gearbox, single dry plate clutch, bevel rear axle, wheelbase 110in, 5.50 x 17in tyres, original condition, mechanical and body restoration.
£14,250-14,750   *S*

A rebuilt car is not necessarily of more value than a car in good original condition, even if the restoration has cost thousands of pounds.

1928 Chevrolet National Model AB, 2100cc, 4 cylinders.
£4,500-5,000   *ADT*

1936 Chevrolet City Saloon,
6 cylinders.
£8,000-10,000 *ADT*

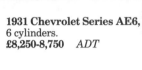

1931 Chevrolet Series AE6,
6 cylinders.
£8,250-8,750 *ADT*

1955 Chevrolet Bel Air Coupé, V8
cylinder, water-cooled, overhead
valves, bore 3.75in, stroke 3in,
162/170bhp, 4637cc, powerglide
automatic transmission, shaft drive,
semi-elliptic suspension, left hand
drive, good order throughout.
£8,900-9,200 *S*

*As part of Chevrolet's general
re-design of their 1950-52 models,
the wide range of large, comfortable
motor cars already produced was
supplemented by a series of special
option models designed to cater for a
cross section of the car-buying
community as diverse as travelling
salesmen, housewives and
sportsmen. The cars were offered as
2 and 4 doors, station wagons,
convertibles, sedans and coupés,
with the very latest in two-tone paint
and chrome trim, V8 engines and
smooth automatic gearboxes. The
Bel Air range had the V8 engine and
was considered a thoroughly modern
motor at the time, a separate series in
its own right.*

1976 Chevrolet Camero Z28
Automatic.
£2,000-2,500 *PC*

CHEVROLET

MAKE Chevrolet	ENGINE cc/cyl	DATES	CONDITION 1	2	3
Bel Air 4 door	235/6	1953-54	£6,000	£4,000	£3,000
Bel Air sports coupé	235/6	1953-54	£7,000	£4,500	£3,500
Bel Air convertible	235/6	1953-54	£12,500	£9,500	£6,000
Bel Air 4 door	283/8	1955-57	£8,000	£4,000	£3,000
Bel Air sports coupé	283/8	1955-56	£11,000	£7,000	£4,000
Bel Air convertible	283/8	1955-56	£16,000	£11,000	£7,000
Bel Air sports coupé	283/8	1957	£11,000	£7,500	£4,500
Bel Air convertible	283/8	1957	£14,500	£10,500	£8,000
Impala sports sedan	235/6, 348/8	1958	£12,500	£9,000	£5,500
Impala convertible	235/6 348/8	1958	£14,500	£11,000	£7,500
Impala sports sedan	235/6 348/8	1959	£8,000	£5,000	£4,000
Impala convertible	235/6 348/8	1959	£14,000	£10,000	£5,000
Corvette roadster	235/6	1953	£18,000	£14,000	£10,000
Corvette roadster	235/6, 283/8	1954-57	£18,000	£13,000	£9,000
Corvette roadster	283, 327/8	1958-62	£16,000	£12,000	£9,000
Corvette Stingray	327, 427/8	1963-67	£18,000	£14,000	£10,000
Corvette Stingray DHC	327, 427/8	1963-66	£20,000	£15,000	£8,000
Corvette Stingray DHC	427/8	1967	£22,000	£18,000	£13,000

1933 Chevrolet Eagle Series Roadster, completely restored, condition 1.
£17,000-18,000 *KI*

1957 Chevrolet 210 Two Door Hardtop, 30,000 miles, all original, condition 2.
£12,000-13,000 *KI*

1957 Chevrolet Bel Air Convertible, condition 2.
£24,000-26,000 *KI*

1958 Chevrolet Impala Two Door Hardtop, condition 3.
£7,500-8,000 *KI*

Miller's is a price
GUIDE not a price
LIST

1967 Chevrolet Corvette Coupé, condition 2.
£13,000-14,000 *KI*

1963 Chevrolet Corvette Stingray, 5200cc, 8 cylinders. Est. £18,000-20,000   *ADT*

The 1963 Corvette was a completely restyled car to its predecessor and took the name Stingray. The car was an immediate success with a 2 month waiting list for both the coupé and the convertible. Significant for 1963 was the split rear window which was in fact phased out from 1964 onwards. As the first of the series and with this unusual styling feature, the 1963 cars are very sought after both here and in their home country.

1959 Chevrolet Corvette Hard Top Sports, 4 speed manual gearbox with Hurst shift, chrome wire wheels, dual 4 barrel carburettors.   **£16,000-19,000**   *CGB*

Make: **Chevrolet**
Model: Corvette Sting Ray
Type: Sports/Coupé
Years Manufactured: 1963-67
Quantity: 117,964
Price when new: £3,293
Engine Type: Overhead valve V8
Size: 5359cc
Max Power: 1967, 435 bhp @ 5800 rpm
Max Torque: 1967, 460 ft/lb @ 4000 rpm
Transmission: 3/4 speed manual, 2 speed auto
Wheelbase: 98in
Performance: Max speed: 105-150 mph; 0-60: 5.4-8.0 secs.

1978 Chevrolet Corvette Stingray Targa Coupé, V8 cylinders, water-cooled, overhead valves, bore 4in, stroke 3.48in, 4 speed gearbox, shaft drive to live rear axle, carburettor fuel system, independent coil spring suspension front and rear with shock absorbers, wheelbase 98in, left hand drive. Est. £11,000-12,000   *S*

1968 Chevrolet Corvette Stingray. £10,500-11,000   *HA*

The first Corvette was unveiled by General Motors in 1953 and fitted with a V8 engine in 1956. One year later it was given a further power boost up to 283bhp by the addition of the Rochester fuel-injection system. A new Corvette range was introduced in 1961 using the 283cu in engine but this was dropped in 1962 and replaced by the 375cu in unit. The Corvette Stingray appeared in 1963 with independent suspension and disc brakes.

1989 Chevrolet Camero Z28, left hand drive. **£11,000-11,500**   *JB*

Citroën

Citroën produced cars with left hand drive in Paris, and right hand drive in Slough, Bucks, and although these shared the same basic components there were numerous detail differences, the principal ones being that the Slough cars were equipped with 12 volt Lucas electrics (the French had 6 volts), leather seats (the French were cloth), and had a wooden dashboard (painted,

metal dashboard on the French). Up until the War there were quite a few variations both in body styles and engine sizes. After the War, there was far more standardisation with only 2 and 3 litre options and fewer body sizes, not all of which were produced by the UK factory. The only other major change was a restyling of the rear body at the end of 1952; all models manufactured up to 1952 had the spare wheel mounted externally on the back, and from the end of 1952 the 'Big Boot' encased the

spare wheel, and an additional model was introduced in 1954 using hydraulic rear suspension.

All Traction Avants are front wheel drive with torsion bar suspension, hydraulic brakes, are water-cooled, engines are overhead valve, have 3 speed gearboxes with synchromesh on 2nd and 3rd, and most have rack and pinion steering which was introduced in 1936.

1922 Citroën Type C Shooting Brake, 856cc.
£5,500-6,500 *S*

André Citroën was Chief Engineer at Mors until on a visit to a water mill he saw wooden gear wheels made in a double bevel form. He subsequently founded his own firm to make a steel version. The double V of these bevel gears is commemorated to this day in the firm's double chevron emblem.

After making munitions during WWI André Citroën turned to car production in 1919. His model A was quickly superseded by the model B and this was joined in 1922 by the 856cc model C.

1931 Citroën Type AC4 12hp Paris Taxi, 12hp.
£9,000-10,000 *S*

1925 Citroën 7.5hp Cloverleaf Three Seater Tourer, 855cc.
£4,000-4,500 *S*

1953 Citroën Big 15 Saloon, Slough built.
£5,500-6,500 *CR*

MAKE Citroën	ENGINE cc/cyl	DATES	CONDITION 1	2	3
A	1300/4	1919	£4,000	£2,000	£1,000
5CV	856/4	1922-26	£7,000	£4,000	£2,000
11	1453/4	1922-28	£4,000	£2,000	£1,000
12/24	1538/4	1927-29	£5,000	£3,000	£1,000
2½ litre	2442/6	1929-31	£5,000	£3,000	£1,500
13/30	1628/4	1929-31	£5,000	£3,000	£1,000
Big 12	1767/4	1932-35	£7,000	£5,000	£2,000
Twenty	2650/6	1932-35	£10,000	£5,000	£3,000
Ten CV	1452/4	1933-34	£5,000	£3,000	£1,000
Ten CV	1495/4	1935-36	£6,000	£3,000	£1,000
11B/Light 15/ Big 15/7CV	1911/4	1934-57	£6,000	£3,000	£1,000
Twelve	1628/4	1936-39	£5,000	£3,000	£1,000
F	1766/4	1937-38	£4,000	£2,000	£1,000
15/6 and Big Six	2866/6	1938-56	£7,000	£4,000	£2,000

1940 Citroën Roadster, Slough
built, right hand drive, concours
condition.
£30,000-35,000   *CR*

1934 Citroën 7A Saloon, Paris
built, 1303cc, left hand drive,
excellent condition.
£17,000-18,000   *CR*

1938 Citroën Light 12 Saloon,
Slough built, 4 cylinder overhead
valve, bore 72mm, stroke 100mm,
1628cc.   **£9,000-10,000**   *CR*

Good originality.

1939 Citroën Roadsters, excellent
condition, good originality.
l. 11BL. **£25,000-28,000**
r. 11B. **£27,000-30,000**   *CR*

1949 Citroën Light 15 Saloon,
Slough built, 4 cylinder overhead
valve, 1911cc.
£5,500-6,000   *CR*

1936 Citroën 7C Saloon, Paris
built, 1628cc, left hand drive, low
mileage.
£5,500-6,000 *CR*

1954 Citroën Light 15 Saloon,
Slough built, fully restored.
£13,000-15,000 *CR*

1950 Citroën 11BL Saloon,
built, left hand drive,
new interior.
£5,500-6,500 *CR*

1951 Citroën 11B Saloon, Paris built, 1911cc,
left hand drive.
£5,000-6,000 *CR*

1938 Citroën Coupé, Paris built,
left hand drive.
£32,000-35,000 *CR*
Concours condition.

1955 Citroën Familiale, Paris
built, left hand drive.
£4,000-5,000 *CR*

Miller's is a price Guide not a price List

*The price ranges given
reflect the average price a
purchaser should pay for
similar vehicle. Condition,
rarity, provenance, racing
history, originality and
any restoration are factors
that must be taken into
account when assessing
values. When buying or
selling, it must always be
remembered that prices
can be greatly affected by
the condition of any
vehicle. Unless otherwise
stated, all cars shown in
Miller's are of good
merchantable quality, and
the valuations given
reflect this fact. Vehicles
offered for sale in
exceptionally fine
condition or in poor
condition may reasonably
be expected to be priced
considerably higher or
lower respectively than
the estimates given herein*

1935 Citroën Coupé,
Slough built.
£23,000-25,000   *CR*

Rare.

**1954 Citroën 11
Commerciale,**
Paris built, 1911cc,
left hand drive, hatchback,
excellent condition.
£6,000-7,500   *CR*

**1955 Citroën Light 15 11B
Normale Saloon,** 1911cc.
£5,750-6,250   *S*

1954 Citroën 11B Saloon, Paris
built, 1911cc, left hand drive,
restored.
£6,500-7,000   *CR*

1955 Citroën Light 15.
£5,500-6,000   *ADT*

MAKE Citroën	ENGINE cc/cyl	DATES	CONDITION 1	2	3
2CV	375/2	1948-54	£1,000	£500	£250
2CV/Dyane/Bijou	425/2	1954-82	£1,000	£500	£250
DS19/ID19	1911/4	1955-69	£5,000	£3,000	£250
Sahara	900/4	1958-67	£5,000	£4,000	£3,000
2CV6	602/2	1963 on	£750	£500	£250
DS Safari	1985/4	1968-75	£5,000	£3,000	£500
DS21	1985/4	1969-75	£5,000	£3,000	£500
DS23	2347/4	1972-75	£5,000	£3,000	£500
SM	2670/				
	2974/6	1970-75	£14,000	£9,000	£5,000

Clan Clover

Make: **Clan**
Model: Crusader
Type: Sports Coupé
Years Manufactured: 1972-74
Quantity: 315
Price when new: £1,118
Engine Type: 4 cyl
Size: 875cc
Max Power: 51 bhp
Transmission: 4 speed
Performance: Max speed: 100 mph; 0-60: 12.5 secs; Mpg: 40.

1988 Clan Clover, mid-engined Alfa Romeo powered coupé, one owner, 1,100 miles.   **£4,500-5,000**   *Cen*

Clement Bayard

1913 Clement Bayard Type 4M5, 4 cylinder, 10hp, swing seat tourer. **£22,000-25,000**   *SL*

Did you know

MILLER'S Collectors Cars Price Guide builds up year by year to form the most comprehensive photo-reference system available

Cord

1936 Cord 8/10 Speedster, supercharged. **£65,000-85,000**   *BLE*

1936 Cord Model 810 Supercharged Westchester Sedan, V8 cylinder engine, water-cooled, side valve, bore 88.9mm, stroke 95.2mm, 4730cc, 4 speed gearbox, single dry plate clutch, front wheel drive, independent transverse semi-elliptic leaf spring front and rear suspension, wheelbase 125in, 16in tyres, right hand drive, engine rebuilt, 4 speed synchromesh transmission overhauled, fully restored. **£14,500-15,500**   *S*

Crossley

1914 Crossley 15hp Shelsley Five Seater Tourer, 4 cylinder in line, water-cooled, monobloc engine, side valve, bore 80mm, stroke 130mm, 2614cc, 4 speed right hand gate change gearbox, cone clutch, shaft and bevel final drive, semi-elliptic leaf front springs, three-quarter elliptic rear, wheelbase 125in, 815 x 105mm tyres. Est. **£25,000-30,000**   *S*

The smaller 15hp Shelsley model, named after its successes at the famous Shelsley Hill Climb, offered the same qualities of reliability and despite the smaller horsepower offered remarkably similar performance to its larger stable mate.

Daimler

1918 Daimler, 6 cylinders, 30hp, sleeve valve, Alpine Eagles style touring body.
£45,000-50,000   *SL*

1937 Daimler 15 Cabriolet, coachwork by Martin-Walter Ltd., 2166cc, 6 cylinders.
Est. **£7,000-8,000**   *ADT*

Daimler started making the smallest model in their range, the 15, in 1933. The vehicle was substantially revised for the 1937 season, the most important innovation being independent front suspension, enlarged engine to 2166cc, and modified track. 70mph was easily obtained.

1935 Daimler 15hp, condition 1.
£8,000-10,000   *CC*

1934 Daimler Light 15, condition 1.
£8,000-10,000   *CC*

1950 Daimler DB18 Special Sports Three Seater Drophead Coupé, by Barker, 2522cc, 6 cylinders, original and unrestored.
Est. **£18,000-22,000**   *ADT*

The Special Sports was enhanced by twin carburettors and an overdrive epicyclic gearbox and produced 85bhp as against the standard 70bhp.

MAKE Daimler	ENGINE cc/cyl	DATES	CONDITION 1	2	3
Veteran (Coventry built)	var/4	1897-1904	£75,000	£60,000	£40,000
Veteran	var/4	1904-19	£35,000	£25,000	£15,000
30hp	4962/6	1919-25	£40,000	£25,000	£18,000
45hp	7413/6	1919-25	£45,000	£30,000	£20,000
Double Six 50	7136/12	1927-34	£40,000	£30,000	£22,000
20	2687/6	1934-35	£18,000	£14,000	£12,000
Straight 8	3421/8	1936-38	£20,000	£15,000	£12,000

Value is dependent on body style, coachbuilder and condition of the sleeve valve engine.

1952 Daimler 2½ Litre Special Sports Drophead Coupé. Est. **£17,000-20,000** *S*

1955 Daimler Conquest Roadster, fully restored, condition 1. **£14,000-16,000** *PA*

Daimler Conquest Century Mk II, 2433cc, 6 cylinders. **£2,750-3,250** *ADT*

Make: **Daimler**
Model: Conquest
Type: Saloon/Drop Head Coupé
Years Manufactured: 1954-57
Price when new: Saloon, £1,511
Engine Type: Overhead valve 6 cyl
Size: 2433cc
Max Power: 100 bhp @ 4400 rpm
Transmission: 4 speed; pre-selector/fluid flywheel (auto option from 1956)
Performance: Max speed: 85 mph; 0-60: 16.3 secs; Mpg: 16-20.

1957 Daimler Conquest Roadster, 6 cylinder in line engine, water-cooled monobloc, overhead valves, bore 76.2mm, stroke 88.9mm, 2433cc, 4 speed pre-select epicyclic gearbox, fluid flywheel transmission, hypoid bevel rear axle, independent wishbone and torsion bar front suspension, semi-elliptic leaf rear springs, wheelbase 104in, 15in tyres. **£11,000-12,000** *S*

1961 Daimler SP 250 Dart, V8 engine, 2500cc. **£8,750-9,500** *HA*

This Daimler Dart was one of only 55 used by the Police in the early 60s and is automatic. It was used by them from new in 1961 until disposed of in 1967. Only 2,650 were built over a period of 5 years.

1963 Daimler SP 250, low mileage, good condition. **£11,500-14,000** *GH*

MAKE Daimler	ENGINE cc/cyl	DATES	CONDITION 1	2	3
DB18	2522/6	1946-49	£7,500	£4,000	£1,000
DB18 Conv S/S	2522/6	1948-53	£11,500	£8,000	£2,000
Consort	2522/6	1949-53	£4,000	£2,000	£500
Conquest/Con. Century	2433/6	1953-58	£4,000	£2,000	£500
Conquest Roadster	2433/6	1953-56	£8,000	£4,000	£1,000
Majestic 3.8	3794/6	1958-62	£4,000	£2,000	£450
SP250	2547/8	1959-64	£15,000	£10,000	£4,500
Majestic Major	4561/8	1961-64	£5,000	£3,000	£500
2.5 V8	2547/8	1962-67	£8,000	£6,000	£2,500
V8 250	2547/8	1968-69	£7,500	£5,000	£2,000
Sovereign 420	4235/6	1966-69	£6,500	£4,500	£1,500

1962 Daimler SP 250, with hard top, good condition.
£10,000-12,000   *GH*

1964 Daimler SP 250, 2548cc, 8 cylinders.
£18,000-19,000   *ADT*

Make: **Daimler**
Model: SP250
Type: Sports
Years Manufactured: 1959-64
Quantity: 2,648
Price when new: £1,395
Engine Type: Overhead valve V8
Size: 2548cc
Max Power: 140 bhp @ 5800 rpm
Max Torque: 155 ft/lb @ 3600 rpm
Transmission: 4 speed (auto option from 1961)
Wheelbase: 92in
Performance: Max speed: 125 mph; 0-60: 8.8 secs; Mpg: 22-26.

1966 Daimler V8 250, 2548cc, 8 cylinders.
£1,800-2,200   *ADT*

1968 Daimler V8 250.
£8,000-10,000   *S8*

1968 Daimler V8 250, 2548cc, 8 cylinders.
Est. **£4,000-6,000** *ADT*

Make: **Daimler**
Model: 2½ Litre V8 250
Type: Saloon
Years Manufactured: 1962-69
Quantity: 17,620
Price when new: £1,569
Engine Type: Overhead valve V8
Size: 2548cc
Max Power: 140 bhp @ 5800 rpm
Transmission: 4 speed, optional overdrive or auto
Performance: Max speed: 112 mph; 0-60: 13 secs; Mpg: 18-22.

1968 Daimler V8 250, 2500cc, 8 cylinders.
Est. **£8,000-9,000** *ADT*

1969 Daimler Sovereign, 4235cc, 6 cylinders.
£5,500-6,500 *ADT*

Traditionally suppliers to the Carriage Trade, the Daimler Motor Co. for many years lacked a suitable chassis for such a vehicle. After the firm was taken over by Jaguar Cars in the 60s and subsequently became part of the same group as the famous coach builders Vanden Plas, the opportunity was taken to build a suitable vehicle for VIP use at State occasions.

1974 Daimler Double Six Coupé, 5343cc, 12 cylinders.
£6,600-7,500 *ADT*

1976 Daimler 4.2 litre Limousine, coachwork by Vanden Plas, 6 cylinder, water-cooled, twin overhead camshaft, bore 92.07mm, stroke 106mm, 4235cc, 3 speed Borg Warner automatic gearbox, independent front suspension, semi-elliptic rear springs, fully armoured, supplied to the Ministry of Defence.
£9,000-10,000 *S*

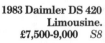

1983 Daimler DS 420 Limousine.
£7,500-9,000 *S8*

Datsun

Make: Datsun
Model: 240Z/260Z/260Z 2+2
Type: Sports Coupé
Years Manufactured: 1969-78
Quantity: 622,649
Price when new: 260Z, 2565cc
Coupé, £2,863
Engine Type: Overhead
camshaft 6 cyl
Size: 2393/2565cc
Max Power: 2393cc, 151 bhp @
5600 rpm; 2565cc, 139 bhp @
5200 rpm
Max Torque: 2393cc, 146 ft/lb @
4400 rpm; 2565cc, 137 ft/lb @
4400 rpm
Transmission: 5 speed or auto
Wheelbase: 2-seater, 90.7in;
2+2, 102.6in
Performance: Max speed: 240Z,
125 mph; 0-60: 8 secs;
Mpg: 20-30.

1971 Datsun 240Z Sports Coupé,
6 cylinder, single overhead
camshaft, 2393cc, twin SU
carburettors, bore 83mm, stroke
73mm, compression ratio 9:1,
151bhp at 5,600rpm, 5 speed
transmission, wheelbase 91in
independent all-round suspension.
£10,000-12,000   *PC*

1976 Datsun 260Z 2+2, 2565cc,
6 cylinders.
Est. **£2,000-2,500**   *ADT*

MAKE	ENGINE	DATES	CONDITION		
Datsun	cc/cyl		1	2	3
240Z	2393/6	1970-71	£8,000	£5,000	£3,500
240Z	2393/6	1971-74	£4,500	£3,250	£1,500
260Z	2565/6	1974-79	£3,000	£2,250	£1,000
260Z 2+2	2565/6	1974-79	£2,250	£1,500	£350

1978 Datsun 260Z Two Seater.
£1,000-3,000   *PC*

Darracq

1906 Darracq Four Seat Swing Seat Tonneau, 2 cylinders, 12hp.
£18,000-22,000 *SL*

c1905 Darracq 12hp Four Seat Swing Seat Tonneau, coachwork by A. Vedrine & Cie, Carrossiers, Courbevoie, Paris, vertical twin cylinder, water-cooled, side valve, bore 100mm, stroke 120mm, gearbox 3 speed and reverse, shaft drive to live axle, semi-elliptic suspension front and rear, wheelbase 85in, 760 x 90in tyres, engine complete but dismantled.
£12,750-13,500 *S*

Alexandre Darracq was one of the pioneers of motor car manufacture founding his company in 1896 and graduating from bicycle manufacture to car production at the turn of the century. Léon Bollée produced and designed the first engines, the design being conventional in most respects.

De Dion Bouton

1899 De Dion Bouton, 1 cylinder, 1¾hp, air-cooled tricycle.
£16,000-17,000 *SL*

This passenger carrying quadricycle can, in only a few minutes, be converted to a solo motor tricycle.

1900 De Dion Bouton, 1 cylinder, 2¾hp, air-cooled, quadricycle.
£12,000-13,000   *SL*

Condition Guide

1. *A vehicle in top class condition but not 'concours d'elegance' standard, either fully restored or in very good original condition*
2. *A good, clean, roadworthy vehicle, both mechanically and bodily sound*
3. *A runner, but in need of attention, probably both to bodywork and mechanics. Must have current MOT*

1912 De Dion Bouton Open Two Seater, 4 cylinder, 14hp.
£25,000-26,000   *SL*

1913 De Dion Bouton 14hp Coupé De Ville, 4 cylinder in line engine, water-cooled monobloc, side valve, bore 75mm, stroke 130mm, 2298cc, 3 speed gearbox, plate clutch, bevel rear axle, semi-elliptic leaf springs front and rear, wheelbase 121in, 815 x 105mm tyres, beaded edge.
£19,000-20,000   *S*

De Dion Bouton offered a wide range of multi-cylinder cars for the 1913 season, from the diminutive 7hp twin to the 50hp 7.8 litre 8 cylinder cars. It was the 12hp and 14hp models which contributed most to the company's success being practical mid-range models offering reliability and economic running costs.

Delage

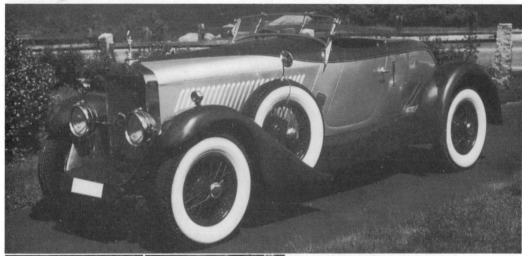

1930 Delage D8 Boat Tail, Fogoni built chassis, but with an American-looking boat tail body, by Fernandez and Darrin, wheelbase 131in.
£48,000-50,000 *PMc*

1940 Delage D6-75 Olympic Two Door Sports Saloon, coachwork by Letourner et Marchand, 6 cylinder in line, water-cooled monobloc, overhead valves, bore 81mm, stroke 90.5mm, 2800cc, Cotal 4 speed gearbox, single dry plate clutch, spiral bevel final drive, independent front suspension, semi-elliptic rear springs, wheelbase 124in, 5.50 x 17in tyres.
Est. **£25,000-28,000** *S*

1925 Delage DI, with utility body by Castraise.
£12,500-13,000 *DB*

The DI model of the 1920s was reliable as a fast sporting car, and the company turned to 6 and 8 cylinder cars in the latter part of the decade which lent themselves well to the coach builder. The final development of the company was the D6.60 engine which was to be enlarged into the D6.70 and finally the D6.75 2.8 litre model.

Delahaye

1948 Delahaye 135 M Drophead Coupé, coachwork by Chapron of Paris, 3557cc, bore 84mm, stroke 107mm, compression ratio 7.5:1, 130bhp at 4,000rpm, Rudge Whitworth centre-lock wire spoke wheels with 6.00 x 17in tyres, wheelbase 116in, right hand drive.
Est. **£41,000-47,000** *CNY*

1949 Delahaye Type 135 MS Foursome Drophead Coupé, 6 cylinder in line engine, water-cooled monobloc, pushrod operated overhead valves, bore 84mm, stroke 107mm, 3557cc, 4 speed Cotal electro-magnetic gearchange, single dry plate clutch, spiral bevel rear axle, independent transverse leaf spring suspension, semi-elliptic leaf rear springs, wheelbase 115in, 6.00 x 17in tyres. Est. £40,000-50,000   *S*

Delaunay-Belleville

1912 **Delaunay-Belleville,** bodywork by Brewster & Company, New York, 4 cylinder T-head engine, 506V, wheelbase 121in.   **£42,000-45,000**   *PMc*

De Soto

1933 De Soto Model S D Custom Sedan. Est. £8,000-12,000   *LF*

The De Soto Marque was introduced as a lower price Chrysler in 1928 and drew its name from the 16thC Explorer who discovered the Mississippi River. The S D Models had a choice of engine, and this one has the 3600cc version. The same model though with the smaller 2.7 litre engine was marketed in Britain as the Chrysler Wimbledon.

MAKE	ENGINE	DATES	CONDITION		
DeSoto	cc/cyl		1	2	3
Firedome/Fireflite	341, 383/8	1957-59	£9,000	£5,000	£3,000
Adventurer	348, 383/8	1957-59	£11,500	£8,500	£5,000

De Tomaso

1972 **De Tomaso Mangusta,** the only right hand drive Mangusta in the UK, one of only 5 built. £38,000-40,000   *PC*

1972 De Tomaso Pantera, Ford Cleveland V8 engine, 4 speed transmission, wheelbase 98.4in.
£17,500-20,000   *S(NY)*

Make: **De Tomaso**
Model: Pantera
Type: Sports Coupé
Years Manufactured: 1971-88
Quantity: est 9,500 up to 1987
Engine Type: Overhead valve V8
Size: 5763cc
Max Power: 250-350 bhp @ 5400-6000 rpm
Max Torque: 325-330 ft/lb @ 3600-3800 rpm
Transmission: 5 speed manual
Wheelbase: 99in
Performance: Max speed: 140-160 mph; 0-60: 5.2-7.5 secs.

1972 De Tomaso Pantera, left hand drive.
£13,000-15,000   *AUT*

1973 De Tomaso Pantera GTS.
£26,000-30,000   *PC*

| MAKE | ENGINE | DATES | CONDITION | | |
De Tomaso	cc/cyl		1	2	3
Mangusta	4727/8	1967-72	£24,500	£15,000	£5,500
Pantera	5763/8	1969-89	£18,500	£9,500	£6,000
Deauville	5763/8	1970-88	£8,000	£5,000	£2,000
Longchamps	5763/8	1972-	£9,000	£6,000	£2,000

1985 De Tomaso GT5S.
£25,000-30,000
S8

1990 De Tomaso Pantera GT5S.
£38,000-40,000   *PC*

Dutton Phaeton

1963 Dutton Phaeton, 1147cc, 4 cylinders, side exhaust.
£1,100-1,200 *ADT*

Duesenberg

Until the Model J, Frederick and August Duesenberg were known mainly for their achievements in motor racing.

1935 Duesenberg Model SJ Convertible Coupé, coachwork by Bohman & Schwarz, double overhead camshaft straight 8, 6885cc, bore 95.2mm, stroke 120.6mm, detachable cylinder head, 4 valves per cylinder, 320bhp at 4,750rpm, centrifugal supercharger, twin disc dry plate clutch, 3 speed manual transmission to hypoid rear axle, separate pressed steel frame with channel section side members and tubular cross members, forged front axle beam, front semi-elliptic leaf springs, hydraulic lever arm shock absorbers, rear semi-elliptic leaf springs with radius arms, lever arm shock absorbers, 4 wheel hydraulic drum brakes, 19in chromium plated centre lock wire spoke wheels, 7.00 x 19in tyres, wheelbase 142½in.
£700,000-750,000 *CNY*

Dodge

1926 Dodge 17/24hp Eleven Seater Hotel Bus, 4 cylinder in line monobloc engine, water-cooled, side valve, bore 3⅞in, stroke 4½in, 24hp, 3 speed centre change gearbox, shaft drive to bevel rear axle, semi-elliptic leaf spring suspension front and rear, disc wheels, restored.
Est. **£8,000-10,000** *S*

1946 Dodge Series D24 Kingsway Four Door Saloon, 6 cylinder in line, water-cooled L head, bore 3¼in, stroke 4⅝in, 105bhp at 3,600rpm, Stromberg carburettor, column gear change, 3 speed and reverse, single plate dry disc clutch, hypoid bevel rear axle, 6.00 x 16in tyres.
Est. **£4,000-6,000** *S*

DODGE

1953 Dodge Kingsway Coronet,
6 cylinder manual, 43,000 miles,
original leather interior,
condition 1.
£3,500-4,500   *CGB*

**1968 Dodge Charger 440
Magnum.**
£6,000-8,000   *Cen*

EMF

**1911 EMF Four Seater
Detachable Tourer,** 4 cylinders,
3.7 litre, 30hp.
£24,000-26,000   *SL*

Essex

1928 Essex Saloon, 2192cc,
owned by the same family
since new, needs restoration.
£2,800-3,000   *LAR*

**1929 Essex Super Six 4/5 Seater
Open Tourer,** coachwork by Smith
& Waddington Ltd. of Sydney,
Australia, 6 cylinder engine,
water-cooled, side valve, 2274cc,
6 volt coil ignition, 3 speed gearbox,
single dry plate clutch, hypoid rear
axle, semi-elliptic front and rear
springs, wheelbase 110in,
5.00 x 20in Dunlop tyres.
Est. £15,000-17,000   *S*

Excalibur

1973 Excalibur SS 350, 5700cc,
8 cylinders.
Est. £9,000-12,000   *ADT*

*One of the best known of replica car
builders is that of Excalibur, who
since 1964 have been building their
high performance copy of the SSK
Mercedes.*

1969 Abarth Scorpione 1300 S.S., with coachwork by Francis Lombardi, Vercelli, Italy, 4 cylinder in line engine, 1280cc, bore 75.5mm, stroke 71.5mm, pushrod overhead valve, 75bhp at 6,000rpm, compression ratio 9.5:1, 4 speed all synchromesh gearbox. **£4,000-5,000**   *C(M)*

1957 AC Ace Bristol Two Seater Sports, with coachwork by AC Cars Ltd., 6 cylinder in line engine, 1971cc, bore 66mm, stroke 96mm, inclined overhead valves by pushrod, single side camshaft, compression ratio 8.5:1, 120bhp at 5,750rpm. **£50,000-60,000**   *C(M)*

1970/77 Alfa Romeo Montreal.
£7,000-14,000   *AUT*

1931 Bentley 4½ Litre, supercharged, body by Mayfair Carriage Company, one of 50 original Blower Bentleys.
£450,000-550,000   *SL*

1937 Aston Martin 15/98 2 Litre Sports Saloon, with coachwork by Abbot, 4 cylinder in line, 1949cc, bore 78mm, stroke 102mm, overhead camshaft, compression ratio 7.75:1, 98bhp at 5,000rpm, twin SU carburettors, twin SU fuel pumps, 4 speed manual gearbox with synchromesh on 2nd, 3rd and 4th, spiral bevel rear axle, steel box section chassis with braced crossover bars. Est. **£25,000-28,000**   *C*

Further detail of the dashboard and steering wheel of the **1927 Bentley 3 Litre 'Speed Model'**.

1927 Bentley 3 Litre 'Speed Model' Four Seater Tourer, by Vanden Plas, with long-stroke overhead camshaft 2996cc engine, over 80bhp, Smith's carburettors, Hartford shock absorbers, rear mounted spare wheel, running board tool boxes.
Est. **£60,000-80,000**   *ADT*

1913 Brasier Two Seater 'Type de Course' Raceabout, 4 cylinder, 1500cc, 10/14hp engine.
£18,000-20,000 *SL*

1937 Bentley 4¼ Litre Saloon, with coachwork by Park Ward, in good original condition.
£20,000-25,000 *RCC*

1988 Bentley Turbo R.
£40,000-48,000 *PJF*

1950 Bentley MkVI 4¼ Litre Standard Steel Saloon, with coachwork by Rolls-Royce Motors, Crewe, 6 cylinder in line, cast iron monobloc engine, with alloy cylinder head, wheelbase 3,050mm. Est. **£12,000-15,000** *C*

1909 Buick Model 10 Tourer, with 4 cylinder overhead valves, water-cooled cast iron block engine, 2702cc, bore and stroke 95.2mm, compression ratio 5:1, 23bhp at 2,400rpm, Schebler mechanical carburettor, Stewart speedometer. Est. **£20,000-25,000** *C*

1917 Crane Simplex Model 5, Seven Passenger Victoria Phaeton, 6 cylinder, 9.2 litre, 46hp.
£70,000-80,000 *SL*

1913 De Dion Bouton, Coupé de Ville, 4 cylinder, 14hp monobloc engine.
£30,000-40,000 *SL*

1913 De Dion Bouton, Open Drive ¾ Landaulette, 4 cylinder, 20hp, by Botwoods Limited of Ipswich.
£45,000-55,000 *SL*

1901 Delin, with 1 cylinder, 4hp engine, 2 seater and spyder seat.
£20,000-30,000 *SL*

1975 Dodge Demon, with V8 Standard engine, super-tuned semi-race, 340bhp, 4 speed gearbox.
£8,000-9,000 *AC*

l. **1982 De Tomaso Pantera GTS CS,** with unique custom body styling, steel arches, side slats and skirts, front spoiler, recessed lights, nitrous injection. **£30,000-40,000** *PC*

1956 Ferrari 250GT Coupé, with coachwork by Carrozzeria Boano, Turin, Italy, V12 cylinder engine, single overhead camshaft per bank, 2953cc, bore 73mm, stroke 58.8mm, compression ratio 8.5:1, triple Weber carburettors, single distributor, twin disc dry plate clutch, 4 speed all synchromesh gearbox plus reverse, rigid rear axle, welded tubular steel ladder frame type chassis, wheels and tyres 16in, wheelbase 2,600mm. **£120,000-150,000**   *C(M)*

1953 Ferrari 250 'Millemiglia', with an aluminium bodyshell by Pinin Farina, Colombo V12 3 litre engine, chain driven camshafts, three 36mm 4-barrel Weber carburettors, 240bhp, an overall weight of about 850kg, a genuine 22,665km recorded, unique Hermes upholstery in original condition, restored.   **£700,000-750,000**   *O*

1959 Ferrari 250GT California Spyder, with coachwork by Scaglietti, designed by Pinin Farina, V12 cylinder engine, single overhead camshaft per bank, 2953cc, bore 73mm, stroke 58.8mm, compression ratio 9.1:1, 250bhp at 7,000rpm, triple Weber 36 DCL-3 carburettors, Abarth exhaust system, single dry plate clutch with 4-speed all synchromesh gearbox, live rear axle, welded tubular steel ladder style chassis frame with steel and alloy 2-door Spyder bodywork, wheels and tyres 16in. Est. **£550,000-650,000**   *C(M)*

1957 Ferrari 625/250 TRC Testarossa Sports Racing Car, with coachwork by Scaglietti, 250 T.R. 128 DF type, V12 cylinder, single overhead camshaft per bank, 2953cc, bore 73mm, stroke 58.8mm, compression ratio 9.8:1, 300bhp at 7,200rpm, 6 Weber 38 DCN carburettors, twin distributors, 2 valves per cylinder, outside cylinder plug location. Est. **£700,000-750,000**   *C(M)*

r. **1959 Ferrari 250 GT,** with coachwork by Pinin Farina, V12 cylinder, single camshaft per bank, 2953cc, bore 73mm, stroke 58.8mm, compression ratio 8.5:1, 220bhp at 7,000rpm, triple Weber DCF carburettors, single plate clutch, 4-speed all synchromesh gearbox, rigid rear axle, welded tubular steel ladder frame chassis, independent front suspension with Helicoidal springs, semi-elliptic leaf springs rear, Houdaille shock absorbers, disc brakes on all 4 wheels, wheels and tyres 15in, Borrani wire spoke centre lock wheels, wheelbase 2,600mm, left hand drive. **£47,000-57,000**   *C(M)*

Make the Most of Miller's

Price ranges in this book reflect what one should expect to pay for a similar example. When selling, however, one should expect to receive a lower figure. This will fluctuate according to a dealer's stock, saleability at a particular time, etc. It is always advisable, when selling, to approach a reputable specialist dealer or an auction house which has specialist sales

At the end of 1957 Pinin Farina developed several alternative designs for the 250 GT and this one first appeared at the 1958 Paris Salon, was delivered to France in mid-1959 and recently has been totally restored, rear bumper missing.

1966 Ferrari 500 Superfast, with coachwork by Pinin Farina, V12 cylinder single overhead camshaft per bank, 4963cc, bore 88mm, stroke 68mm, compression ratio 9:1, 400bhp at 6,500rpm, triple Weber 40 DCZ/6 carburettors, single dry plate clutch, 5-speed all synchromesh gearbox, hypoid bevel, rigid rear axle. Est. **£160,000-180,000**   *C(M)*

1968 Ferrari 330 GTC, one of 600 built, this model was unveiled at the Geneva Motorshow in March 1966, with V12 engine, 3967cc, compression ratio 8.8:1, 6 Weber DCZ carburettors, 300bhp, independent suspension on all 4 wheels, in good overall working order and resprayed a few years ago. **£60,000-65,000**   *O*

1971 Ferrari 365 GTS/4 'Daytona', with bodywork by Scaglietti, designed by Pininfarina, V12, 4.4 litre engine, 4 overhead camshafts, 6 twin choke Weber carburettors, 4 wheel independent suspension, renewed leather upholstery, resprayed and completely restored. **£365,000-400,000**   *O*

1972 Dino 246 GT, with all the mechanical components in good general working order, having been recently overhauled.
£40,000-45,000 *O*

Further detail of the **1972 Ferrari 365 GTB/4.**

1972 Ferrari 365 GTB/4 'Daytona', with coachwork by Pininfarina, V12 cylinder, 4.4 litre engine, compression ratio 8.8:1, 6 Weber 40 DCN 20 carburettor 352bhp DIN at 7,500rpm, fully independent suspension with double wishbones and coil springs, mechanics overhauled. **£120,000-130,000** *O*

1914 Fiat Salamanca Landaulette, Type 52B, by Brewster of New York, 4 cylinder, 20hp.
£35,000-40,000 *SL*

1971 Ferrari 365 GTB/4 'Daytona Competition', with coachwork by Scaglietti, designed by Pininfarina, V12 cylinder, 2 camshafts per bank, 2 valves per cylinder, light alloy block and cylinder heads, 4390cc, bore 81mm, stroke 71mm, compression ratio 9.3:1, 425bhp at 7,600rpm, 6 Weber 40 DCN-20 twin choke carburettors, 2 fuel pumps, single dry plate clutch.
Est. **£450,000-500,000** *C(M)*

1978 Ferrari 512 BB-LM, with coachwork by Pininfarina, flat 12 cylinder horizontally opposed, twin overhead camshafts per bank, alloy crankcase and cylinder heads, bore 82mm, stroke 78mm, compression ratio 9.2:1, 460bhp at 7,250rpm, 4 Weber 401F3C carburettors, dry sump lubrication, single dry plate clutch, rear mounted 5-speed all synchromesh gearbox. Est. **£250,000-275,000** *C(M)*

1907 Itala, Open Driver Landaulette, by Locati Viarengo-Toreno, 4 cylinder, 14hp.
£35,000-40,000   *SL*

1937 Ford 8 Y Type, this car was one of the last 'Y' models produced, was purchased in 1989 as a non-runner but has since been restored.
£2,500-3,500   *PC*

1913 Ford Model T, with 4 cylinder, 2900cc engine, a later overhead valve 'Roof Sixteen' head, a 'fast-cool' V radiator, acetylene gas headlights, correct type sidelights, monocle screen.
Est. **£9,000-11,000**   *ADT*

1955 Ford Thunderbird, with 8 cylinder, 292cu in engine, in good mechanical condition and is to original specification following restoration.
£11,000-12,000   *ADT*

Detail of the dashboard and left hand drive steering column of the **1955 Ford Thunderbird.**

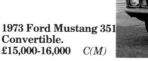

1973 Ford Mustang 351 Convertible.
£15,000-16,000   *C(M)*

1938 Jaguar SS 2½ Litre, with standard Swallow styled body, 6 cylinder, 2663cc engine, it is believed this car was rebodied with a SS100 type body and rebuilt 4 years ago. **£50,000-55,000** *ADT*

1972 Jensen Interceptor Series III. £4,000-6,000 *AUT*

Jaguar XK150 'S' FHC, believed to be one of only 39 built specifically for racing and supplied without bumpers, gold seal 3.8 E-type engine, restored. Est. **£30,000-32,000** *ADT*

1955 Jaguar XK140 Roadster, with 6 cylinder in line engine, twin overhead camshaft, 3442cc, bore 83mm, stroke 106mm, compression ratio 8.0:1, 190bhp at 5,500rpm, twin SU H6 carburettors, single dry plate clutch. Est. **£30,000-40,000** *C(M)*

1961 Jaguar 3.8 Litre MkII Saloon, with 6 cylinder in line, cast iron block engine, light alloy cylinder heads, overhead valves, twin overhead camshafts, 3781cc, bore 87mm, stroke 106mm, compression ratio 8:1, 220bhp at 5,500rpm, twin SU HD6 carburettors, single dry plate clutch, 4-speed manual and overdrive gearbox. **£8,000-10,000** *C*

1971 Jaguar V12 Series III E-Type 2+2 Coupé, V12 cylinder, 2 overhead in line valves per cylinder, single overhead camshaft per bank, 5343cc, bore 90mm, stroke 70mm, compression ratio 9:1, 272bhp at 5,850rpm, 4 Zenith Stromberg 175 CDSE carburettors. **£21,000-25,000** *C*

1984 Lamborghini Countach, with V12 cylinder 5 litre engine, 4795cc, 5-speed manual gearbox, all round disc brakes, mechanically superb, bodywork above average for the year, leather upholstery, full service history from new.
Est. **£55,000-60,000**   *ADT*

1962 Mercedes Benz 300 SL Roadster, with coachwork by Daimler Benz AG, Stuttgart, 6 cylinder in line engine, 2996cc, bore 85mm, stroke 88mm. Est. **£170,000-190,000**   *C(M)*

1970 Maserati 115 Ghibli Coupé, with coachwork by Giugiaro Ghia, V8 cylinder engine, twin overhead camshafts per bank, 2 valves per cylinder, 4719cc. **£35,000-40,000**   *C(M)*

1962 Mercedes 190SL Roadster.
£12,000-18,000   *AUT*

1976 Maserati-Type 117 Bora, with coachwork by Ital Design, 90° V8 cylinder, 4719cc engine, bore 93.9mm, stroke 85mm, twin valves per cylinder, 4 overhead camshafts, compression ratio 8.1:1, 310bhp at 6,000rpm, 4 Weber 42 DCNF carburettors. Est. **£45,000-50,000**   *C(M)*

1971 Jaguar Series III V12 E-Type Coupé, with 2 overhead in line valves per cylinder operated by single overhead camshaft per bank, 5343cc, bore 90mm, stroke 70mm, compression ratio 9:1, 272bhp at 5,850rpm, 4 Zenith Stromberg 175 CDSE carburettors, single dry plate clutch, 3-speed BW12 automatic gearbox. **£11,000-13,000**   *C*

1974 Porsche 911 2.7 Carrera, right hand drive.
£15,000-17,000   AUT

1964 Porsche 356SC Coupé LHD, engine stripped and refinished, black interior original and perfect, all original body and underbody panels, except longitudinals.
£18,500-20,000   HCI

1915 Morgan-Adler Six Seater Station Wagon, 4 cylinder Lycoming engine, 30hp.
£15,000-20,000   SL

1956 Riley Pathfinder.
£3,000-4,000   WCC

1910 Rolls-Royce 40/50hp Silver Ghost, with double Pullman coachwork by S. A. Fuller of Bath.
£500,000-600,000   SL

l. 1904 Rambler Rear Entrance Tonneau, 1 cylinder, 8hp. £18,000-20,000 *SL*

r. 1903 Panhard Levassor Rear Entrance Tonneau, twin cylinder, 7hp chain drive, 4 forward speeds. £70,000-75,000 *SL*

1928 Rolls-Royce 20hp Sedanca De Ville. £30,000-35,000 *S*

1925 Rolls-Royce 20hp 'Howdah' Saloon, ordered by Maharajah of Bharatpur, to go tiger shooting, it has a sliding roof and special tip-up seats to enable the Maharajah to shoot from safety of the cockpit. £50,000-60,000 *C*

1933 Rolls-Royce Phantom II Continental Touring Limousine, with coachwork by Park Ward, 6 cylinder, in 2 blocks of 3 with one-piece detachable aluminium cylinder head, 2 overhead valves per cylinder operated by pushrods, 7688cc, with built in retracting vanity sets. Est. £50,000-55,000 *C*

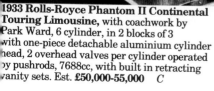

1922 Rolls-Royce 40/50hp Silver Ghost Hooper Open Drive Limousine, in good condition. £65,000-75,000 *RCC*

l. **1935 Rolls-Royce Phantom II Kellner Limousine De Ville,** all original. **£30,000-40,000** *RCC*

r. **1936 Rolls-Royce Phantom III,** with coachwork by H. J. Mulliner. **£65,000-95,000** *PJF*

1911 Sizaire Naudin 12/16hp Two Seater with Dickey Seat, coachwork by Jarrot, Ballot engine, 4 cylinder monobloc water-cooled, 1800cc, right hand drive.   Est. **£18,000-22,000** *C*

1954 Rolls-Royce Silver Wraith Saloon, by Freestone & Webb, in very good condition throughout. **£15,000-20,000** *RCC*

1937 Rolls-Royce Phantom III Limousine, with coachwork by Barker & Co., 12 cylinder, 7340cc engine, sliding roof. Est. **£50,000-55,000** *ADT*

l. **1964 Rolls-Royce Silver Cloud III Continental,** by James Young. **£75,000-115,000** *PJF*

l. 1959 Austin Healey Sprite Race Car. £5,000-7,000 *CA*

r. 1924 Vauxhall 14/40 Type LM Five Seater Open Tourer, 2297cc. £24,000-34,000 *SL*

1921 Sunbeam 24hp Semi-Sporting Tourer, with 6 cylinder engine. £60,000-75,000 *SL*

1961 Cooper Type 56 MkII Formula Junior, with BMC 1100cc engine, Citroën Ersa gearbox. £22,000-26,000 *SL*

1925 Vauxhall 30/98 'OE' 4 Seater Velox Tourer. £140,000-180,000 *SL*

1988 Caterham Seven, built from a kit for hill climbing and sports also road legal. £7,000-8,000 *CA*

1959 Gemini MkII Formula Junior.
£16,000-20,000 *CA*

1962 Lotus 22 Formula Junior.
£23,000-27,000 *CA*

1961 Lotus 20 Formula Junior, totally
restored in 1989. **£20,000-30,000** *CA*

1963 Marcos Gullwing, this car has
recently finished 2nd in an historic
endurance race. **£14,000-18,000** *CA*

1967 Ford GT40 MkII, came 2nd at Le Mans driven
by Gurney and McLaren. **£350,000-450,000** *SL*

1971 Merlyn MK20 Formula Ford, in immaculate, fully restored, condition. **£5,000-6,000** *CA*

986 Metro 6R4, Group B Rally car, V6, litre engine, 440bhp, 4-wheel drive, rst 6R4 to win International rally ircuit of Ireland. **£45,000-55,000** *SL*

1976 McClaren M23. £150,000-180,000 *DHA*

068 McLaren M6B Can/Am, with 5.9 Chevrolet V8, 600hp engine, Hewland LG 0 gearbox, 5-speed, 0-60 in 2½secs, raced by Soames Langton for 4 years, inning its class in 1988 and 1990. **£130,000-150,000** *SL*

1960 O.S.C.A. Tipo S.F. 392 1600 Two Seater Sports Race Car, with coachwork by Morelli, Ferrara, 4 cylinder in line engine, with overhead camshaft, 1568cc, bore 80mm, stroke 78mm, compression ratio 9.5:1, 140bhp at 6,700rpm, twin Weber 42 DCOE6 carburettors, twin plugs per cylinder, 2 distributors, single dry plate clutch, 4 speed gearbox, 4 wheel Girling disc brakes. Est. **£150,000-160,000**   *C(M)*

Did you know

MILLER'S Collectors Cars Price Guide builds up year by year to form the most comprehensive photo-reference system available

1929 Scott Squirrel Motorcycle and Sidecar. **£6,750-7,250**   *DB*

l. **Caterham Super Seven,** with 1700cc Ford-based power unit. **£12,000-16,000**   *KSC*

1913 Royal Enfield 6hp 770cc Motorcycle with Wicker Chair, V twin cylinder engine, air-cooled, side valve 4 stroke, bore 76mm, stroke 85mm, 770cc, 2 speed hand change gearbox, chain final drive, girder forks and coil spring front suspension, rigid rear with C spring leaf suspension to chair, tyres 650 x 65mm and 26 x 3in. **£12,000-14,000**   *S*

Miller's is a price GUIDE not a price LIST

1929 Sunbeam, 350cc motorcycle. **£3,250-3,500**   *DB*

Ferrari

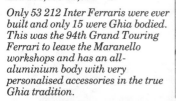

1951 Ferrari 212 Inter.
Est. £65,000-70,000   *O*

Only 53 212 Inter Ferraris were ever built and only 15 were Ghia bodied. This was the 94th Grand Touring Ferrari to leave the Maranello workshops and has an all-aluminium body with very personalised accessories in the true Ghia tradition.

1955 Ferrari 250 GT Europa.
Est. £120,000-150,000   *O*

1957 Ferrari 250 GT Tour de France.
Est. **£420,000-460,000**   *O*

Make: **Ferrari**
Model: 250GT long wheelbase
Type: Sports Coupé
Years Manufactured: 1954-62
Quantity: All types, 905
Engine Type: Single overhead
camshaft V12
Size: 2953cc
Max Power: 220-260 bhp @
7000 rpm
Transmission: 4 speed manual,
with overdrive from 1960
Wheelbase: 102.3in
Performance: Max speed:
124-155 mph; 0-60: 7.0-8.0 secs.

**1958 Ferrari 250 GT
California.**
£380,000-420,000   *O*

1958 Ferrari 250 GT Cabriolet Série 1.
£200,000-250,000   *O*

1959 Ferrari 250 GT Pinin Farina.
Est. £40,000-50,000   *O*

1960 Ferrari 250 GT Cabriolet Pinin Farina.
Est. £100,000-130,000   *O*

1963 Ferrari 400 Super America.
£140,000-160,000   *PiK*

1964 Ferrari 250 GT/L Lusso.
Est. £120,000-140,000   *O*

> *Make:* **Ferrari**
> *Model:* 250GT short wheelbase
> *Type:* Sports Coupé
> *Years Manufactured:* 1959-64
> *Quantity:* Berlinetta, 175;
> Spyder California, 57;
> Berlinetta Lusso, 350
> *Engine Type:* Single overhead
> camshaft V12
> *Size:* 2953cc
> *Max Power:* 280 bhp @ 7000
> rpm
> *Transmission:* 4 speed manual
> *Wheelbase:* 94.5in
> *Performance:* Max speed:
> 140-150 mph; 0-60: est. 6.5-7.0
> secs.

1965 Ferrari 275 GTS Spyder.
£100,000-140,000   *O*

1966 Ferrari 275 GTB Series II, coachwork by Pinin Farina, built by Scaglietti in alloy, V12 cylinder, single overhead camshaft per bank, 3286cc, bore 77mm, stroke 58.8mm, compression ratio 9.2:1, 280bhp at 7,600rpm, triple Weber 40 DCN carburettors, single dry plate clutch, 5 speed all synchromesh gearbox rear mounted in transaxle, welded tubular steel ladder frame chassis with all alloy, 2 door, 2 seater coupé bodywork, independent all round suspension of unequal A arms combined with a coaxial unit of adjustable tubular shock absorbers and helicoidal springs, disc brakes on all 4 wheels, 14in Borrani wire spoke centre lock wheels with 205 x 14in tyres, wheelbase 94½in. Est. **£180,000-220,000**   *CNY*

1966 Ferrari 275 GTB Aluminium. Est. **£200,000-240,000**   *O*

FERRARI

1967 Ferrari 330 GTS Spyder.
Est. £140,000-160,000   *O*

1965 Ferrari 330 GT 2+2 MkI,
3300cc, 12 cylinders.
Est. £45,000-48,000   *ADT*

1968 Ferrari 365 GTC.
£70,000-100,000   *PiK*

MAKE Ferrari	ENGINE cc/cyl	DATES	CONDITION 1	2	3
166 Inter	1995/12	1948-53	£120,000	£90,000	—
212 Inter	2563/12	1951-53	£135,000	£95,000	—
250 GT	2953/12	1959-63	£65,000	£60,000	£50,000
250 GT SWB (steel)	2953/12	1959-62	£235,000	£185,000	—
250 GT Lusso	2953/12	1962-64	£135,000	£115,000	£95,000
250 GT 2+2	2953/12	1961-64	£65,000	£45,000	£30,000
275 GTB	3286/12	1964-66	£140,000	£115,000	£105,000
275 GTS	3286/12	1965-67	£150,000	£145,000	£140,000
275 GTB 4-cam	3286/12	1966-68	£185,000	£160,000	—
330 GT 2+2	3967/12	1964-67	£35,000	£26,000	£18,000
330 GTC	3967/12	1966-68	£85,000	£65,000	£55,000
330 GTS	3967/12	1966-68	£110,000	£95,000	£80,000
365 GT 2+2	4390/12	1967-71	£30,000	£26,000	£21,500
365 GTC	4390/12	1967-70	£80,000	£65,000	£45,000
365 GTS	4390/12	1968-69	£135,000	£100,000	£90,000
365 GTB (Daytona)	4390/12	1968-74	£125,000	£95,000	£80,000
365 GTC4	4390/12	1971-74	£85,000	—	—
365 GT4 2+2/400GT	4390/ 4823/12	1972-79	£28,000	£21,500	£19,500
365 BB	4390/12	1974-76	£115,000	£85,000	£70,000
512 BB/BBi	4942/12	1976-81	£80,000	£65,000	£60,000
246 GT Dino	2418/6	1969-74	£38,000	£25,000	£18,000
246 GTS Dino	2418/6	1972-74	£42,000	£34,000	£25,000
308 GT4 2+2	2926/8	1973-80	£15,500	£12,500	£7,500
308 GTB (fibreglass)	2926/8	1975-76	£32,000	£26,000	£22,000
308 GTB	2926/8	1977-81	£30,000	£24,000	£22,000
308 GTS	2926/8	1978-81	£35,000	£28,000	£24,000
308 GTBi/GTSi	2926/8	1981-82	£29,000	£23,000	£21,000
308 GTB/GTS QV	2926/8	1983-85	£28,500	£24,500	£22,500
400i manual	4823/12	1981-85	£16,000	£13,500	£11,000
400i auto	4823/12	1981-85	£14,500	£12,000	£9,500

1969 Ferrari 365 GTC, coachwork by Pininfarina, V12 60° engine, 4390cc, single overhead camshaft per bank, bore 81mm, stroke 71mm, 320bhp at 6,600rpm, 3 double choke Weber carburettors, front and rear double wishbone coil spring suspension, 5 speed synchromesh gearbox integral with final drive, servo-assisted disc brakes all round.
£140,000-150,000   *PC*

1970 Ferrari 365 GTS Spyder, 33,000 miles, original.
£260,000-280,000   *HWA*

Make: **Ferrari**
Model: Daytona 365GTB/4
Type: Sports Coupé/Convertible
Years Manufactured: 1968-74
Quantity: 1,412
Price when new: Coupé, £9,167; Sports, £8,749
Engine Type: V12 cyl
Size: 4390cc
Max Power: 352 bhp @ 7500 rpm
Max Torque: 365 ft/lb @ 5500 rpm
Transmission: 5 speed
Wheelbase: 94.5in
Performance: Max speed: 174 mph; 0-60: 5.4 secs; Mpg: 14.

1972 Ferrari Daytona right hand drive.
£90,000-110,000   *AUT*

1972 Ferrari 365 GTC/4, Borrani wire wheels, 14,000 miles.
£86,000-92,000
HWA

1972 Ferrari 365 GTC/4.
£50,000-70,000   *O*

1973 Ferrari Dino 246 GTS.
£65,000-70,000 *O*

Make: **Ferrari**
Model: Dino 206/246GT/GTS
Type: Sports Coupé/Convertible
Years Manufactured: 1967-73
Quantity: 4,033
Price when new: 206GT, £6,243;
246GT, £5,288
Engine Type: Transverse V6 cyl
Size: 1987cc/2418cc
Max Power: Dino 206GT, 180
bhp @ 8000 rpm; Dino
246GT/GTS, 175 bhp @ 7000
rpm
Max Torque: 246GT/GTS, 160
ft/lb @ 5500 rpm
Transmission: 5 speed
Wheelbase: Dino 206GT, 90in;
Dino 246GT/GTS, 92.1in
Performance: Max speed:
206GT, 148 mph; 246GT/GTS,
140 mph; 0-60: 206GT, 7.1 secs;
246GT/GTS, 8.0 secs;
Mpg: 206GT, 23.

1973 Ferrari 246 GT Dino, 2418cc,
6 cylinders, extensively restored.
Est. **£42,000-45,000** *ADT*

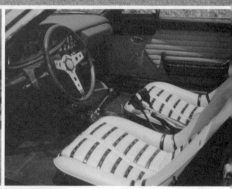

1975 Ferrari 308 Dino GT4.
Est. **£18,000-24,000** *LF*

**1977 Ferrari Type 512 Berlinetta
Boxer,** 62,000 miles from new, full
engine and gearbox rebuilt 2,000
miles ago.
Est. **£65,000-75,000** *HA*

1978 Ferrari Boxer, right hand drive.
£85,000-100,000   *AUT*

1975 Ferrari Dino 308 GT4, 2926cc, 8 cylinders.
Est. **£15,000-16,000**   *ADT*

1980 Ferrari 400i, 4823cc,
12 cylinders, right hand drive,
automatic with fuel injection,
recorded mileage of 58,500.
Est. **£21,000-23,000**   *ADT*

1981 Ferrari 308 GTSi, 2926cc,
original car, only 44,000 miles from
new.
£28,000-30,000   *HA*

*The Ferrari 308 GTS was
introduced in 1978 having been
offered for preview at the 1977
Frankfurt Motor Show. The GTS
was based on the 308 GTB which
was introduced into the Ferrari
range in 1975.*

1986 Ferrari Mondial
Drophead Coupé.
£35,000-40,000   *S8*

1987 Ferrari Testarossa.
£60,000-80,000   *S8*

Fiat

1914 Fiat 15/20hp Tipo 52B Salamanca, coachwork by Brewster, 4 cylinder in line engine, water-cooled monobloc, side valve, bore 80mm, stroke 140mm, 2816cc, 4 speed gearbox, shaft final drive to bevel rear axle, semi-elliptic leaf spring suspension front and rear, wheelbase 111in, 33 x 4in tyres. Est. **£27,000-32,000**   *S*

During 1914 five different models were offered by Fiat in Italy and America, ranging from the 1847cc Tipo 1 and Zero to the giant 9 litre Tipo 5. American equivalents were prefixed by 50 differentiating them from the Italian cars. The 52B had a top speed in excess of 50mph and would cruise at 35-40mph.

1928 Fiat 505 Tourer, 4 cylinders, 2.2 litres, needs total restoration. **£4,350-4,750**   *DB*

MAKE Fiat	ENGINE cc/cyl	DATES	CONDITION 1	2	3
501	1460/4	1920-26	£6,000	£3,500	£1,500
519	4767/6	1923-29	£9,000	£7,000	£3,000
503	1473/4	1927-29	£8,000	£4,000	£2,000
507	2297/4	1927-28	£9,000	£5,500	£3,500
522/4	2516/6	1932-34	£10,000	£8,000	£3,500
508	994/4	1934-37	£5,000	£2,500	£1,500
527 Sports	2516/6	1935-36	£14,000	£8,000	£3,500
1.5 litre Balilla	1498/6	1936-39	£10,000	£7,000	£3,000
500	570/4	1937-55	£6,000	£2,500	£1,000
1100 Balilla	1089/4	1938-40	£4,500	£2,000	£1,000

1964 Fiat 1500 Cabriolet 118K, coachwork by Pinin Farina, 4 cylinder in line alloy cylinder heads with overhead valves, twin overhead camshafts, 1995cc, bore 84mm, stroke 90mm, compression ratio 8.2:1, 120bhp at 5,500rpm, twin Weber carburettors, single dry plate clutch with 5 speed manual synchromesh gearbox, hypoid bevel rear axle, integral box frame, front independent coil springs, wishbones, anti-roll bar, rear half-elliptic leaf springs, hydraulic telescopic shock absorbers all round, hydraulic servo-assisted disc brakes on front, drum brakes on rear, 14in steel disc type wheels, 175 x 14in tyres, wheelbase 2,340mm, left hand drive. Est. **£10,000-15,000**   *C*

> **Did you know**
> *MILLER'S Collectors Cars Price Guide builds up year by year to form the most comprehensive photo-reference system available*

1968 Fiat Dino Coupé, V6 cylinder engine, water-cooled, twin overhead camshaft per bank, bore 86mm, stroke 57mm, 1987cc, 5 speed ZF gearbox, single dry plate clutch, hypoid bevel final drive, independent front suspension, semi-elliptic rear, wheelbase 90in, 14in tyres, good condition, right hand drive.
Est. **£8,000-10,000** *S*

1969 Fiat Dino Coupé. £5,000-8,000 *AUT*

MAKE Fiat	ENGINE cc/cyl	DATES	CONDITION 1	2	3
500B Topolino	569/4	1945-55	£3,000	£1,500	£750
500C	569/4	1948-54	£4,000	£1,700	£1,000
500 Nuova	479, 499/2	1957-75	£3,000	£1,500	£750
600/600D	633, 767/4	1955-70	£4,000	£2,000	£1,000
500F Giardiniera	479, 499/2	1957-75	£3,000	£1,500	£1,000
2300S	2280/6	1961-68	£3,000	£1,700	£1,000
850	843/4	1964-71	£1,000	£750	—
850 Coupé	843, 903/4	1965-73	£1,500	£1,000	—
850 Spyder	843, 903/4	1965-73	£5,000	£3,000	£1,500
128 Sport Coupé 3P	1116/ 1290/4	1971-78	£4,000	£2,500	£1,500
130 Coupé	3235/6	1971-77	£8,000	£6,500	£3,000
131 Mirafiori Sport	1995/4	1974-84	£2,000	£1,000	£750
124 Sport Coupé	1438/ 1608/4	1966-72	£3,500	£2,000	£1,000
124 Sport Spyder	1438/ 1608/4	1966-72	£4,500	£2,500	£1,500
Dino Coupé	1987/ 2418/6	1967-73	£8,500	£6,000	£3,500
Dino Spyder	1987/ 2418/6	1967-73	£12,000	£8,500	£5,000
X1/9	1290/ 1498/4	1972-89	£3,000	£1,500	£750

1972 Fiat 500. £750-2,000 *AUT*

Make: **Fiat**
Model: 500/600
Type: Saloon/Convertible/ Station Wagon
Years Manufactured: 1960-73
Price when new: 500D/500F, £556
Engine Type: Overhead valve twin
Size: 499cc
Max Power: 18 bhp @ 4600 rpm
Transmission: 4 speed
Performance: Max speed: 60 mph; 0-50: 33 secs; Mpg: 45-60.

1973 Fiat 130 Pinin Farina Coupé.
Est. £2,000-2,500   *Cen*

Pinin Farina designed the body for the 130 Coupé. Fiat added the 3235cc, V6, double overhead camshaft engine provided by Ferrari which produced 165bhp. This gave the vehicle a maximum speed of 116mph with a 0-60 time of 10.6 seconds.

1985 Fiat X19, low mileage.   £5,000-6,000   *PC*

1975 Fiat 124 Sport, 1756cc, 4 cylinders.
Est. £3,000-4,000   *ADT*

Make: **Fiat**
Model: 124 Coupé/Spyder
Type: Coupé/Sports Car
Years Manufactured: 1969-73
Price when new: 124 Sport Coupé, £1,429
Engine Type: Twin overhead camshaft 4 cyl
Size: 1438cc/1995cc
Max Power: 1438cc, 96 bhp @ 6500 rpm; 1995cc, 80 bhp @ 5500 rpm
Max Torque: 1438cc, 83 ft/lb @ 4000 rpm; 1995cc, 100 ft/lb @ 3000 rpm
Transmission: 4 speed, 5 speed or auto
Wheelbase: Coupé, 95.3in; Spyder, 89.8in
Performance: Max speed: 95-104 mph; 0-60: 9.4-14.5 secs; Mpg 24.

1978 Fiat 124 Spyder, 1800cc, 4 cylinders.   £5,000-6,000   *ADT*

Fisson

1897 Fisson 6hp Rallycart, twin cylinder vertical in line side valve, water-cooled engine, bore 130mm, stroke 120mm, 2920cc, 3 speed gearbox, chain final drive, bent layshaft in the gearbox, otherwise mechanically sound and good overall condition, original accumulator, trembler coil and spark plugs appear unmodified, surface Benz-type carburettor, VCC Dating certificate.
Est. £42,000-45,000   *S*

Possibly one of the last types of Fisson built, it is quite a handful to drive. A separate lever operates each gear, 2 spoon type brakes operate directly on the solid rubber tyres, and these are augmented by foot pedal-operated strangling rope strangling brake on the transmission, and contracting brakes on the rear wheels. There are no front wheel brakes. The near 3 litre engine is controlled by a hand lever on the steering column, there being no accelerator pedal, and the car is built with left hand drive.

Ford

1911 Ford Model T Roadster, 2895cc, 4 cylinders, acetylene gas projector headlamps, acetylene gas generator, bolster tank, raked windscreen, original trembler coils and canopy hood. **£9,000-10,000** *ADT*

1914 Ford Model T Four Seater Tourer, 4 cylinders, sound condition, engine rebuilt in 1986. Est. **£8,500-11,500** *ADT*

1918 Ford Model T Shooting Brake. Est. **£6,000-7,000** *S*

1919 Ford Model T Speedster, 4 cylinder water-cooled monobloc, side valve, bore 95mm, stroke 102mm, 2896cc, 22.4hp, 2 speed planetary transmission, shaft drive to bevel rear axle, transverse single semi-elliptic spring suspension at front and rear with multiple leaves, mechanical rear wheel brakes and transmission, 30 x 3½in beaded edge tyres. **£5,000-5,500** *S*

Henry Ford's inimitable Model T was designed in 1907, introduced in late 1908 and produced until late 1928 with only minor mechanical revisions and modest streamlining to the coachwork. The car's unique features were its extremely simple, flexible and robust construction, using fine quality vanadium steel almost entirely, straight forward controls with an ingenious 2 speed planetary transmission, able to be adjusted by the completely uninitiated with a spanner and an informative instruction manual, and an unprecedented low retail price. Ford's marketing for the Model T was no less than brilliant and the price was constantly lowered over nearly 20 years, resulting at one point in sales of over one million cars in a year. More than 15 million were produced in total and the company prospered to become the world's leading motor vehicle manufacturer for a considerable period of time.

1914 Ford Model T 20hp Four Seater Tourer, 4 cylinders, side valve, water-cooled monobloc engine, bore 95mm, stroke 102mm, 2900cc, 2 speed epicyclic gearbox with reverse, pedal control, hand throttle, transverse leaf springs front and rear, spiral bevel rear axle, wheelbase 100in, 30 x 3in tyres. Est. **£10,500-11,000** *S*

1915 Ford Model T 20hp Two Seater Roadster. Est. **£8,000-10,000** *S*

FORD

MAKE	ENGINE	DATES	CONDITION		
Ford	cc/cyl		1	2	3
Model T	2892/4	1908-27	£10,000	£7,500	£4,000
Model A	3285/4	1928-32	£8,500	£6,000	£3,500
Models Y and 8	933/4	1933-40	£4,500	£3,000	£1,500
Model C	1172/4	1933-40	£4,000	£2,000	£1,000
Model AB	3285/4	1933-34	£11,000	£8,000	£4,500
Model ABF	2043/4	1933-34	£9,000	£6,000	£4,000
Model V8	3622/8	1932-40	£9,500	£6,000	£4,500
Model V8-60	2227/8	1936-40	£7,000	£5,000	£2,000
Model AF (UK only)	2033/4	1928-32	£9,000	£6,000	£3,500

A right hand drive vehicle will always command more interest than left hand drive. Coachbuilt vehicles and in particular drophead coupés achieve a premium at auction.

1926 Ford Model T, 2700cc, Canadian model discovered on a farm and fully renovated by a Canadian enthusiast before being imported to UK in 1990. **£6,750-7,500** *LF*

1926 Ford Model T Four/Five Seater Open Tourer, 20hp, 4 cylinder, water-cooled, monobloc engine, 2890cc, 2 speed epicyclic gear with pedal control and hand throttle, transverse leaf spring suspension front and rear, spiral bevel rear axle, wheelbase 100in, 30 x 3in front, 30 x 3½in rear tyres. Est. **£11,000-12,000** *S*

1926 Ford Model T Four Door Saloon, 2300cc, 4 cylinders, restored to a very high standard, in need of some cosmetic work. Est. **£8,000-9,000** *ADT*

1925 Ford Model T De Luxe Four Seater Tourer, concours d'élégance winner in Denmark, unusual chrome plated radiator surround, original condition. **£8,500-9,000** *S*

> **Miller's is a price GUIDE not a price LIST**

1920 Ford T Saloon, centre door. **£6,750-7,250** *DB*

1928 Ford Model A Two Door Coupé and Rumble, 2300cc, 4 cylinders.
Est. **£9,000-13,000** *ADT*

A far more complex vehicle than its predecessor, the Model T, there were nevertheless several similarities which included an L shaped cylinder head, semi-elliptical transverse springing and 4 cylinder engines. Ancillary parts were very different with coil ignition replacing the magneto system, a 3 speed, sliding gear unit, Hordaille hydraulic shock absorbers and 4 wheel braking controlled by handbrake, which after a short time was outlawed.

c1930 Ford Model A Two Door Coupé, with dickey, 3250cc, 4 cylinders. **£7,500-8,000** *ADT*

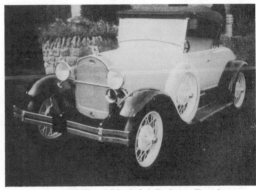

1930 Ford Model A Two Door Coupé, restored in the USA.
£7,500-8,000 *C*

1930 Ford Model A, 24hp, right hand drive, condition 2.
£9,000-9,500 *CC*

1929 Ford Model A Deluxe Roadster, 4 cylinder side valve, water-cooled monobloc, bore 3⅞in, stroke 4½in, 3 speed manual gearbox with centre change, multi-plate clutch, shaft drive to live rear axle, semi-elliptic leaf spring suspension front and rear, wheelbase 103½in, wire wheels with 21in tyres, left hand drive, first class order throughout, engine recently overhauled. **£15,500-16,000** *S*

More than 200 different body prototypes were built in the search for the new shape, and the powerful L head engine had been completely redesigned from the robust but less efficient Model T's 2400cc unit. Every component of the Model A was new or redesigned, and there were 6,800 components, 1,800 more than the Model T; the car had 4 wheel brakes, a great deal more style and comfort, and a modern 3 speed and reverse gearbox. The first cars were released in 1928, after extensive testing with experimental models thinly disguised as Model T Fords.

1930 Ford Model A Saloon, 1939cc, 4 cylinders.
Est. **£7,000-8,000** *ADT*

1931 Ford Model A Roadster,
4 cylinder in line, water-cooled, cast iron block, detachable cylinder head, side valves, 3300cc, bore 98mm, stroke 107mm, compression ratio 4.2:1, 40bhp at 2,300rpm, Ford positive feed carburettor, electric start, single dry plate clutch, 3 speed synchromesh type gearbox, spiral bevel rear axle, rigid frame steel chassis with cross members, 2 seater Roadster bodywork with Dickey seat and side-mounted spare wheel, front beam axle, reverse Elliott type, transverse semi-elliptic springs, three-quarter floating Ford rear axle with semi-elliptic springs, Houdaille lever arm shock absorbers, 4 wheel drum brakes, 19in Ford wire spoke, well based rimmed wheels, 5.25 x 19in tyres, wheelbase 2,700mm, left hand drive.
£14,750-15,250 *C*

1934 Ford V8 Roadster, 3285cc, 8 cylinders. Est. **£8,000-9,000** *ADT*

Locate the source
The source of each illustration in Miller's can be found by checking the code letters below each caption with the list of contributors

1931 Ford Model A, 2300cc, 4 cylinders, some work required.
£7,000-7,500 *ADT*

1934 Ford Model BF Fordor Sedan, 4 cylinder in line engine, water-cooled monobloc, side valve, bore 77.6mm, stroke 108mm, 2043cc, 3 speed gearbox, multiple plate clutch, spiral bevel rear axle, transverse semi-elliptic leaf spring suspension, wheelbase 105½in, 5.25 x 18in tyres, original right hand drive car, photographically documented restoration.
£7,750-8,250 *S*

MAKE Ford (British built)	ENGINE cc/cyl	DATES	CONDITION 1	2	3
Anglia E494A	993/4	1948-53	£2,000	£850	£250
Prefect E93A	1172/4	1940-49	£3,500	£1,250	£900
Prefect E493A	1172/4	1948-53	£2,500	£1,000	£300
Popular 103E	1172/4	1953-59	£1,875	£825	£300
Anglia/Prefect 100E	1172/4	1953-59	£1,350	£625	£250
Prefect 107E	997/4	1959-62	£1,150	£600	£200
Escort/Squire 100E	1172/4	1955-61	£1,000	£850	£275
Popular 100E	1172/4	1959-62	£1,250	£600	£180
Anglia 105E	997/4	1959-67	£1,400	£500	£75
Anglia 123E	1198/4	1962-67	£1,550	£575	£150
V8 Pilot	3622/8	1947-51	£7,500	£4,000	£1,500
Consul Mk I	1508/4	1951-56	£2,250	£950	£400
Consul Mk I DHC	1508/4	1953-56	£4,750	£3,000	£1,250
Zephyr Mk I	2262/6	1951-56	£3,000	£1,250	£600
Zephyr Mk I DHC	2262/6	1953-56	£6,800	£3,250	£1,500
Zodiac Mk I	2262/6	1953-56	£3,300	£1,500	£700
Consul Mk II/Deluxe	1703/4	1956-62	£2,900	£1,500	£650
Consul Mk II DHC	1703/4	1956-62	£5,000	£3,300	£1,250
Zephyr Mk II	2553/6	1956-62	£3,800	£1,800	£750
Zephyr Mk II DHC	2553/6	1956-62	£8,000	£4,000	£1,500
Zodiac Mk II	2553/6	1956-62	£4,000	£2,250	£750
Zodiac Mk II DHC	2553/6	1956-62	£8,500	£4,250	£1,800
Zephyr 4 Mk III	1703/4	1962-66	£2,100	£1,200	£400
Zephyr 6 Mk III	2552/6	1962-66	£2,300	£1,300	£450
Zodiac Mk III	2553/6	1962-66	£3,000	£1,500	£500
Zephyr 4 Mk IV	1994/4	1966-72	£1,750	£600	£150
Zephyr 6 Mk IV	2553/6	1966-72	£1,800	£700	£150
Zodiac Mk IV	2994/6	1966-72	£2,000	£800	£150
Zodiac Mk IV Est.	2994/6	1966-72	£2,200	£950	£150
Zodiac Mk IV Exec	2994/6	1966-72	£2,300	£950	£150
Classic 315	1340/ 1498/4	1961-63	£1,400	£800	£500
Consul Capri	1340/ 1498/4	1961-64	£2,100	£1,350	£400
Consul Capri GT	1498/4	1961-64	£2,600	£1,600	£800

1937 Ford V8 Fordor Deluxe Saloon, V8 cylinder engine, water-cooled, bore 3¹⁄₁₆in, stroke 3¾in, 3 speed floor shift gearbox, single dry plate clutch, three-quarter floating bevel rear axle, wheelbase 112in, 16in tyres, original specification, museum stored for past 5 years, right hand drive.
£6,250-6,750 *S*

1937 Y Type Ford, 933cc, 4 cylinders.
£2,500-2,800 *ADT*

c1948 Ford Mercury 8 Town Sedan, V8 engine, 3622cc, recently rebuilt, currently painted in yellow to create a New York taxi cab of the early 50s.
Est. **£2,000-3,000** *ADT*

1953 Ford Anglia E93A.
£2,800-3,000   *WCC*

1953 Ford Popular Saloon,
4 cylinder, side valve, water-cooled,
monobloc engine, bore 63.5mm,
stroke 92.5mm, 1172cc, 3 speed
gearbox, transverse elliptic springs,
live rear axle, wheelbase 90in,
4.50 x 17in tyres.
Est. £2,000-2,500   *S*

*The last of the 'sit-up-and-beg'
Fords, the Popular inherited the
bodyshell of the 8hp Anglia and the
mechanics of the Prefect, and was
first seen in 1953, costing £390 when
new.*

1953 Ford Anglia, excellent
condition.
£2,000-2,250   *CC*

1955 Ford Popular, condition 1.
£2,000-2,500   *CC*

1959 Ford Prefect, in need of
restoration.
£200-800   *PC*

1959 Ford Prefect, 1172cc,
4 cylinders, original example,
warranted mileage of 18,000 mile
from new, excellent condition.
£2,250-2,500   *WH*

1955 Ford Consul Saloon, 1508cc
4 cylinders.
£1,300-1,500   *ADT*

MAKE Ford (British built)	ENGINE cc/cyl	DATES	CONDITION 1	2	3
Cortina Mk I	1198/4	1963/66	£1,550	£600	£150
Cortina Crayford Mk I	1198/4	1963-66	£3,500	£1,800	£950
Cortina GT	1498/4	1963-66	£1,800	£1,000	£650
Lotus Cortina Mk I	1558/4	1963-66	£10,000	£7,500	£4,500
Cortina Mk II	1599/4	1966-70	£1,000	£500	£100
Cortina GT Mk II	1599/4	1966-70	£1,200	£650	£150
Cortina Crayford Mk II DHC	1599/4	1966-70	£4,000	£2,000	£1,500
Lotus Cortina Mk II	1558/4	1966-70	£5,500	£3,000	£1,800
Cortina 1600E	1599/4	1967-70	£2,800	£1,000	£450
Consul Corsair	1500/4	1963-65	£1,100	£500	£250
Consul Corsair GT	1500/4	1963-65	£1,200	£600	£250
Corsair V4	1664/4	1965-70	£1,150	£600	£250
Corsair V4 Est.	1664/4	1965-70	£1,400	£600	£250
Corsair V4GT	1994/4	1965-67	£1,300	£700	£250
Corsair V4GT Est.	1994/4	1965-67	£1,400	£700	£350
Corsair Convertible	1664/ 1994/4	1965-70	£4,300	£2,500	£1,000
Corsair 2000	1994/4	1967-70	£1,350	£500	£250
Corsair 2000E	1994/4	1967-70	£1,500	£800	£350
Escort 1300E	1298/4	1973-74	£1,900	£1,000	£250
Escort Twin Cam	1558/4	1968-71	£8,000	£5,000	£2,000
Escort GT	1298/4	1968-73	£3,000	£1,500	£350
Escort Sport	1298/4	1971-75	£1,750	£925	£250
Escort Mexico	1601/4	1970-74	£4,000	£2,000	£750
RS1600	1601/4	1970-74	£5,000	£2,500	£1,500
RS2000	1998/4	1973-74	£4,500	£2,200	£1,000
Escort RS Mexico	1593/4	1976-78	£3,500	£2,000	£850
Escort RS2000 Mk II	1993/4	1976-80	£6,000	£3,500	£2,000
Capri Mk I 1300/ 1600	1298/ 1599/4	1969-72	£1,500	£1,000	£550
Capri 2000/ 3000GT	1996/4 2994/6	1969-72	£2,000	£1,000	£500
Capri 3000E	2994/6	1970-72	£4,000	£2,000	£1,000
Capri RS3100	3093/6	1973-74	£6,500	£3,500	£2,000
Cortina 2000E	1993/4	1973-76	£2,500	£550	£225
Granada Ghia	1993/4 2994/6	1974-77	£4,000	£900	£350

Make: **Ford**
Model: Classic/Capri
Type: Classic, Saloon; Capri, Fixed Head Coupé
Years Manufactured: 1961-63
Price when new: £745; Capri £863
Engine Type: 4 cyl
Size: 1340cc/1498cc
Max Power: 54 bhp @ 4900 rpm; 60 bhp @ 4600 rpm
Transmission: 4 speed
Performance: Max speed: 79/81 mph; 0-60: 22/20 secs; Mpg: 25-30.

1964 Ford Classic Capri Coupé.
£4,000-4,500   *WCC*

1959 Ford Zephyr Mk II.
£500-1,500   *PC*

The Zodiac was more popular than the Zephyr.

1965 Ford Zephyr Six Mk III Saloon, 30,000 miles.
£4,500-5,000
WCC

1965 Ford Lotus Cortina Mk I, 1580cc, 4 cylinders.
Est. **£20,000-22,000**   *ADT*

This was one of the left hand drive Boreham works team cars that in 1966, at the hands of Bengt Soderstrom and Gunnar Palm, won the 1966 RAC Rally. It was reshelled and, in its restored condition, was also used by Roger Clarke and Tony Mason on the 1989 Pirelli Classic Marathon.

1970 Ford Cortina 1300 Deluxe Mk II.
£800-1,800   *PC*

1966 Ford Lotus Cortina Mk I, 1558cc, rebuilt in 1981, excellent condition, completely standard.
Est. **£8,000-10,000**   *LF*

1967 Ford Lotus Cortina Mk II, resprayed, original Dunlop alloy wheels, condition 1.
Est. **£3,000-4,000**   *Cen*

1968 Ford Anglia Saloon, 997cc, very good condition. **£1,400-1,600** *LF*

The Anglia was produced from late 1959 until early 1968.

Make: **Ford**
Model: Anglia 105E
Type: Saloon/Estate
Years Manufactured: 1959-67
Price when new: £589
Engine Type: Overhead valve 4 cyl
Size: 997cc
Max Power: 39 bhp @ 5000 rpm
Transmission: 4 speed
Performance: Max speed: 75 mph; 0-60: 27 secs; Mpg: 35-45.

Make: **Ford**
Model: Capri I/II/III
Type: Coupé
Years Manufactured: 1969-88
Quantity: 1,709,765
Engine Type: 4 cyl or V6 cyl
Size: 1298-3093cc
Max Power: 52-160 bhp
Transmission: 4 speed, 5 speed or auto
Performance: Max speed: 2.8 injection, 127 mph; 0-60: 2.8 injection, 7.9 secs; Mpg: 2.8 injection, 21.

1974 Ford Capri RS 3100, 6 cylinders, excellent condition. **£4,750-5,250** *ADT*

Approximately 250 of these cars were built by Ford although not many have survived.

1968 Ford Cortina 1600GT. **£1,500-4,000** *PC*

1974 Ford Escort RS 2000 Mk I. Est. **£2,500-3,000** *Cen*

The Mk I RS 2000 was only produced between 1973 and 1974 and was fitted with the 2 litre, overhead cam Pinto engine and German transmission. Built by Ockenden, it was a smoother and better road car than the RS 1600. With 100hp it had a near 110mph maximum speed.

1978 Ford Escort RS 2000 Mk II,
original example.
Est. **£2,500-3,000**   *Cen*

*When the Mk II Escort arrived in
1976, Ford continued the RS 2000
and gave it a special identity with a
polyurethane droopsnoot and quad
headlamps. The output from the
Pinto engine was raised to 100bhp.*

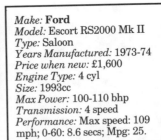

Make: **Ford**
Model: Escort RS2000 Mk II
Type: Saloon
Years Manufactured: 1973-74
Price when new: £1,600
Engine Type: 4 cyl
Size: 1993cc
Max Power: 100-110 bhp
Transmission: 4 speed
Performance: Max speed: 109
mph; 0-60: 8.6 secs; Mpg: 25.

1980 Ford Escort RS 2000, good
condition.
£2,000-4,000   *PC*

1974 Ford Capri 2000 GT, 1998cc,
4 cylinders.
£2,500-2,750   *ADT*

Condition Guide

1. *A vehicle in top class
   condition but not
   'concours d'elegance'
   standard, either fully
   restored or in very good
   original condition*
2. *A good, clean,
   roadworthy vehicle,
   both mechanically and
   bodily sound*
3. *A runner, but in need of
   attention, probably
   both to bodywork and
   mechanics. Must have
   current MOT*

1978 Ford Capri Mk II Ghia,
2996cc, 6 cylinders, recorded
mileage of 70,000, automatic
transmission, good condition.
Est. **£1,500-2,000**   *ADT*

**1969 Ford Mustang 302
Convertible,** V8 engine,
power hood, automatic transmission.
£9,000-10,000   *AC*

1969 Ford Mustang 289 Hard Top, engine rebuilt, condition 1 after restoration.
Est. **£4,000-5,000**   *Cen*

Make: **Ford**
Model: Mustang
Type: Hardtop, Convertible, Fastback
Years Manufactured: 1964-67
Price when new: £2,044
Engine Type: Overhead valve V8
Size: 289cu in
Max Power: 232 bhp @ 6000 rpm
Transmission: 4 speed (manual)
Performance: Max speed: 115+ mph; 0-60: 8.2 secs; Mpg: 10-15.

Introduced in 1964 the 289 Mustang was powered by a V8, 289cu in engine that produced 232bhp with a maximum speed of 115mph plus with a 0-60mph time of 8.2 seconds.

1973 Ford Mustang Mach 1, 351 Cleveland engine, good condition.   **£4,500-5,000**   *JB*

1966 Ford Mustang 289 Automatic, air conditioning, rally pack wheels, hypo engine, left hand drive, one owner from new, good condition.
£5,500-6,000   *CCTC*

1959 Ford Galaxy 500 Skyliner Retractable, restored to fair condition.
£9,500-10,000   *JB*

MAKE	ENGINE	DATES	CONDITION		
Ford (American built)	cc/cyl		1	2	3
Thunderbird	292/				
	312/8	1955-57	£22,000	£13,500	£9,000
Edsel Citation	410/8	1958	£9,000	£4,500	£2,500
Edsel Ranger	223/6-				
	361/8	1959	£6,000	£3,500	£2,000
Edsel Citation conv	410/8	1958	£12,000	£6,000	£4,000
Edsel Corsair conv	332/				
	361/8	1959	£10,500	£7,000	£4,500
Fairlane 2 door	223/6-				
	352/8	1957-59	£8,000	£4,500	£3,000
Fairlane 500 Sunliner	223/6-				
	352/8	1957-59	£12,000	£8,000	£6,500
Fairlane 500 Skyliner	223/6-				
	352/8	1957-59	£16,000	£10,000	£8,000
Mustang hardtop	170/6-				
	289/8	1965-66	£8,000	£5,000	£4,000
Mustang fastback	170/6-				
	289/8	1965-66	£9,000	£6,000	£5,000
Mustang conv	170/6-				
	289/8	1965-66	£12,500	£8,500	£6,000
Mustang hardtop	260/6-				
	428/8	1967-68	£6,000	£4,000	£3,000
Mustang fastback	260/6-				
	428/8	1967-68	£6,000	£4,000	£3,000
Mustang convertible	260/6-				
	428/8	1967-68	£12,000	£6,000	£4,000

FORD

The Cobra Mustang project was initially intended to promote the image of stock production Mustangs with the success of the racing GT350s. The 1966 GT350 had a few features that would set it apart from the 1965 GT350 as well as the stock 1966 Mustangs. Clear plexiglass rear quarter windows and functional side scoops to cool the rear brakes were the most visible differences.

1966 Shelby GT350, V8 engine, 4 speed gearbox, wheelbase 108in, recent restoration. Est. **£20,000-25,000** *S(NY)*

1971 Mustang Mach I 351 Cobrajet. £8,000-12,000 *AUT*

1955 Ford Thunderbird Convertible. £20,000-30,000 *BLE*

1960 Ford Thunderbird Tudor Coupé, 5700cc, 8 cylinders, recorded mileage 85,000. Est. **£7,000-8,000** *ADT*

Over 90% of the V8 cars were automatic.

Frazer Nash

1934 Frazer Nash, chain driven, body style TT replica, ex Le Mans car. **£75,000+** *SL*

Gardner

The Gardner Brothers transferred their business from horse-drawn vehicles to motor cars in 1915, when a deal was negotiated to produce Chevrolet cars in their Saint Louis factory. Russell Gardner was to become President and produce 60,000 cars there prior to the General Motors takeover in 1919. The first Gardner was built in a matter of weeks and 12,000 were produced in the first year.

1925 Gardner Town Coupé, 4500cc, 8 cylinders. Est. **£9,000-11,000**   *ADT*

Georges Richard

1900 Georges Richard Four Seater Swing-Seat Tonneau, 2 cylinder, 10hp. **£30,000-33,000**   *SL*

Glas

1967 Glas GT Coupé, 1700cc single overhead camshaft, limited production model of German design. **£3,000-4,000**   *PMc*

Gordon Keeble

1964 Gordon Keeble. Est. **£10,000-13,000**   *LF*

The Turtle symbol adopted as the trademark for John Gordon and J. D. S. Keeble's brainchild seems inappropriate for this exhilarating grand touring sports car as, with a top speed of 136mph and 0-60mph time of 7.5 seconds. The Bertone styled coachwork was fibreglass on a multi-tube construction chassis and was propelled by a 5.3 litre Chevrolet engine.

Only 99 Gordon Keebles were produced.

1965 Gordon Keeble GKI/GT Sports Saloon, rebuilt engine, condition 1. **£18,000-20,000**   *Cen*

MAKE	ENGINE	DATES	CONDITION		
Gordon Keeble	cc/cyl		1	2	3
GKI/GKIT	5395/8	1964-67	£10,000	£6,000	£4,000

Hanomag

In common with many motor car manufacturers, Hanomag traced its roots back through heavy engineering, in this case the manufacture of steam locomotives and lorries, and it was not until 1924 that Hannoversche Maschinenbau AG, abbreviated to Hanomag, commenced motor car production.

1939 Hanomag Type 13 1.3 litre Two Door Aerodynamic Coupé, 4 cylinder, water-cooled petrol engine, bore 71mm, stroke 82mm, 1300cc, 4 speed gearbox, independent front and rear suspension, 16in tyres, sympathetically restored.
£7,000-8,000 *S*

Haynes

The Haynes Automobile Company of Kokomo, Indiana, USA, imported cars into the UK from 1918 until 1925, in which year production ceased; Elwood Haynes was a pioneer US manufacturer who built his original buggy-type car in 1894, forming Haynes-Apperson with the Apperson brothers in 1898, but separating from them again in 1902. Thereafter the 2 makes pursued independent existences in Kokomo.

1923 Haynes Model 55 Sports Tourer, 6 cylinder, side valve, water-cooled monobloc engine, bore 88.8mm, stroke 126.9mm, 29.4hp, 3 speed gearbox, semi-elliptic springs, dry plate clutch, shaft and bevel final drive, wheelbase 121in, 32 x 4½in tyres.
£10,250-12,000 *S*

> **Miller's is a price GUIDE not a price LIST**

H.E.

1927 H.E. 16/55 Four Seater Tourer, coachwork by Corsica of London, 6 cylinder in line monobloc, with detachable aluminium cylinder head and pistons, side valves, 2290cc, bore 65mm, stroke 115mm, 55bhp at 3,800rpm, coil ignition, triple 1¼in SU carburettors, H.E. 4 speed manual gearbox with multi-plate dry clutch enclosed propeller shaft, spiral bevel final drive with 4.7:1 ratio, 4 wheel drum brakes with driver controlled adjustment mechanism, long flat semi-elliptic leaf springs underslung on front and rear, shock absorbers, H section front axle, 19in Rudge Whitworth centre lock wire wheels with Olympic Balloon 5.50 x 19in tyres, pressed steel ladder frame chassis with cross members, right hand drive.
£24,250-26,000 *C*

Healey

1952 Healey Drophead Coupé, coachwork by Abbott of Farnham, 2443cc, 4 cylinders, excellent condition.
£16,000-17,000 *ADT*

Heinkel

1958 Heinkel Three Wheeler Cabin Cruiser, air cooled single cylinder, overhead valve, 175cc, 4 speed manual gearbox, left hand drive, engine complete and in good running order, original condition.
£1,250-1,350 *C*

1959 Heinkel Bubble Car Tri-Car, single cylinder, air-cooled, 2 stroke, 200cc, 3 speed gearbox, leaf spring suspension.
£1,600-2,000 *S*

> **Cross Reference**
> Isetta
> BMW Isetta
> Messerschmit

The Heinkel was a post-war product of a German company far better known for its aeroplanes, but like fellow aircraft builders Messerschmit and Dornier, Heinkel turned to cars as an alternative product. In 1955 the company launched its bubble car, known as the Cabin Cruiser. It was a short, high, egg-shaped device which closely resembled the Isetta, introduced in 1953. The first model was a three-wheeler, with two front wheels and a single rear wheel driven by an air-cooled overhead valve single cylinder 175cc engine of Heinkel's own design and manufacture.

Hillman

1929 Hillman 14hp Six Light Saloon, 4 cylinder in line engine, water-cooled monobloc, side valve, bore 72mm, stroke 120mm, 1954cc, 4 speed gate change gearbox, single dry plate clutch, spiral bevel final drive, semi-elliptic leaf springs front and rear, wheelbase 114in, original example.
£6,000-7,000 *S*

1937 Hillman 16 Four Door Saloon, 6 cylinders, 2192cc, 4 speed manual gearbox, wheelbase 108½in, extensive restoration, excellent condition.
£8,000-9,000 *DDM*

> *A rebuilt car is not necessarily of more value than a car in good original condition, even if the restoration has cost thousands of pounds.*

1952 Hillman Minx Convertible.
£2,500-2,750 *DB*

1956 Hillman Minx Drophead Coupé, condition 1.
£3,200-3,500 *CC*

1958 Hillman Minx SII Deluxe, 1390cc, good condition, 26,000 miles since new.
£1,850-2,250 *LF*

The Series II Hillman Minx, the mainstay of the Rootes Group for many years, always offered total reliability as a family car.

1963 Hillman Minx Convertible Series IIIA, 6,000 miles from new, excellent condition.
£9,500-10,000 *WCC*

MAKE	ENGINE	DATES	CONDITION		
Hillman	cc/cyl		1	2	3
Minx Mk I-II	1184/4	1946-48	£1,750	£800	£250
Minx Mk I-II DHC	1184/4	1946-48	£3,500	£1,500	£250
Minx Mk III-VIIIA	1184/4	1948-56	£1,750	£700	£350
Minx Mk III-VIIIA DHC	1184/4	1948-56	£3,750	£1,500	£350
Californian	1390/4	1953-56	£1,500	£750	£200
Minx SI/II	1390/4	1956-58	£1,250	£450	£200
Minx SI/II DHC	1390/4	1956-58	£3,500	£1,500	£500
Minx Ser III	1494/4	1958-59	£1,000	£500	£200
Minx Ser III DHC	1494/4	1958-59	£3,750	£1,500	£400
Minx Ser IIIA/B	1494/4	1959-61	£1,250	£500	£200
Minx Ser IIIA/B DHC	1494/4	1959-61	£3,750	£1,250	£500
Minx Ser IIIC	1592/4	1961-62	£900	£500	£200
Minx Ser IIIC DHC	1592/4	1961-62	£3,000	£1,500	£500
Minx Ser V	1592/4	1962-63	£1,250	£350	£150
Minx Ser VI	1725/4	1964-67	£1,500	£375	£100
Husky Mk I	1265/4	1954-57	£1,000	£600	£200
Husky SI/II/III	1390/4	1958-65	£1,000	£550	£150
Super Minx	1592/4	1961-66	£1,500	£500	£100
Super Minx DHC	1592/4	1962-64	£3,500	£1,250	£450
Imp	875/4	1963-73	£800	£300	£70
Husky	875/4	1966-71	£800	£450	£100
Avenger	var/4	1970-76	£550	£250	£60
Avenger GT	1500/4	1971-76	£950	£500	£100
Tiger	1600/4	1972-73	£1,250	£650	£200

Make: **Hillman**
Model: Imp
Type: Saloon/Estate/Coupé
Years Manufactured: 1963-76
Quantity: 440,032 all types
Price when new: £532
Engine Type: Rear engine 4 cyl
Size: 875cc
Max Power: 39 bhp @ 5000 rpm
Transmission: 4 speed
Performance: Max speed: Imp,
80+; Imp Sport, 90 mph;
0-60: Imp, 23.5 secs; Imp Sport,
16.3 secs; Mpg: Imp, 35-45;
Imp Sport, 33.

1966 Hillman Imp, 1725cc,
4 cylinders, 23,882 miles from new,
good all round condition.
£1,500-1,750   *ADT*

**1975 Hillman Avenger Ex Works
1600 GT,** completely rebuilt in
1987.
Est. **£7,000-9,000**   *ADT*

*Driven in the 1975 Avon Tour of
Britain and was in fact a class
winner at the hands of Bernard
Unett.*

Hispano Suiza

1914 Hispano Suiza Boat-Tail,
coachbuilder presumed Spanish,
engine bears 'La Hispano Suiza' in
casting of crankcase, wheelbase
113in.
£17,000-20,000   *PMc*

*This 1914 is an extremely early
model, built before the flying stork
emblem was adopted for a bonnet
ornament.*

1928 Hispano Suiza H6.B Sedanca De Ville,
coachwork by Janssen.
£35,000-45,000   *C(M)*

141

1929 Hispano Suiza H6.B Limousine, coachwork by Devillars of Paris.
£45,000-55,000   *C(M)*

The Town Car coachwork was always in demand and no better example is there than this 1928 H6.B Limousine built by Devillars of Paris, who were renowned for their Hispano Suiza bodywork. The car is finished in royal maroon and black livery and the chauffeur's compartment is upholstered in black leather. The rear compartment, separated by a wind-up division, is extravagantly appointed in red cloth with matching carpets. The instrumentation is original and the car is well appointed throughout.

1928 Hispano Suiza H6.B Full Convertible Landaulet, coachwork considered to be by Kellner of Paris, 6 cylinder in line, water-cooled, monobloc, non-detachable cylinder head, overhead camshaft, 2 overhead valves per cylinder, 6597cc, bore 100mm, stroke 140mm, single up-draught Hispano Suiza carburettor, 135bhp at 3,000rpm, single dry plate clutch and 3 speed gearbox, remote control right hand gear change, 2 piece prop shaft connected to spiral bevel live rear axle, separate pressed steel chassis frame with channel section side members and pressed and tubular cross members, forged front axle beam, semi-elliptic leaf springs front and rear, friction type dampers, 4 wheel mechanically operated drum brakes with Hispano Suiza mechanical servo assistance driven off the gearbox, Rudge Whitworth centre lock wire spoke 21in wheels, 6.00 x 21in tyres, wheelbase 3,680mm, right hand drive.
£60,000-80,000   *C(M)*

Approximately 204 examples of the K6 were produced.

1937 Hispano Suiza K6 Sedanca de Ville, right hand drive, totally original condition.
Est. £50,000-75,000   *C(M)*

1936 Hispano Suiza K6 30/120 Four Door Convertible Cabriolet, 6 cylinder in line, single overhead camshaft, water-cooled monobloc, bore 100mm, stroke 110mm, 5184cc, 3 speed and reverse gearbox, centre change, large single disc clutch, 4 wheel brakes, spiral bevel rear axle, semi-elliptic leaf springs front and rear, 16 x 45in tyres.
£52,000-55,000   *S*

Honda

1969 Honda S800 Coupé.
£2,000-2,200   *WCC*

1966-69 Honda S800 Mk I, double overhead camshaft,
4 carburettors, 791cc, 70bhp, top speed 97mph.
£2,500-10,000   *JC*

Make: **Honda**
Model: S800
Type: Sports Car/Fixed Head Coupé
Years Manufactured: 1966-71
Price when new: Both types, £779
Engine Type: Twin overhead camshaft 4 cyl
Size: 791cc
Max Power: 70 bhp @ 8000 rpm
Transmission: 4 speed
Performance: Max speed: 94 mph; 0-60: 13.4 secs; Mpg: 27.

1968-69 Honda S800 Mk II.
£3,000-12,000   *JC*

1967 Honda S800 Mk I Coupé,
original condition.
£4,000-5,000   *OBA*

1966-69 Honda S800 Mk I Coupé.
£1,000-6,000   *JC*

There is very little price difference between the Mk I and the Mk II Coupé as condition is more important.

1967 Honda Mk I Convertible,
restored, excellent condition.
£8,000-9,000   *OBA*

MAKE Honda	ENGINE cc/cyl	DATES	CONDITION 1	2	3
S800 Mk I Convertible	791/4	1966-69	£10,000	£6,000	£2,500
S800 Mk I Coupé	791/4	1966-69	£6,000	£3,500	£1,000
S800 Mk II Convertible	791/4	1968-69	£12,000	£7,000	£3,000
S800 Mk II Coupé	791/4	1968-69	£6,500	£4,000	£1,200

143

1968 Honda Mk II Convertible, 791cc, all alloy twin cam engine, recently restored, rare model. **£10,000+** *OBA*

Hotchkiss

1928 Hotchkiss AM 12CV, 2.4 litres, original bodywork, good mechanics, poor interior, needs restoration.
£2,000-2,200 *LF*

The Hotchkiss Company was set up in France in the 1870s by a French armaments manufacturer, Benjamin Berkeley Hotchkiss, hence the mascot. Their first car was built in 1903 and in 1924 they introduced the 2.4 litre 12CV AM model. The car was designed by Maurice Sinturat who joined Delage in 1924. The AM model was given overhead valve in 1926 and became designated the AM 2.

HRG

1937 HRG 1½ litre Two Seater, 4 cylinder in line engine, water-cooled monobloc, overhead valve, bore 69mm, stroke 100mm, 1496cc, 4 speed Moss gearbox, remote control, single dry plate, open shaft, spiral bevel rear axle, quarter-elliptic leaf front springs, semi-elliptic at rear, wheelbase 103in, 4.75 x 17in tyres.
Est. £42,000-48,000 *S*

H. R. Godfrey of G.N. fame, E. A. Halford, a motor sport enthusiast of long standing, and G. Robins, formerly of Trojan,

joined forces to build and unveil the first HRG in 1935. Flying somewhat in the face of contemporary trends the new car was traditional in most respects, almost spartan, and featured radiator and engine set well behind the front axle with quarter-elliptic front springs.

1939/1946 HRG 1500 Aerodynamic (prototype), 4 cylinder, single overhead camshaft, 1496cc, bore 68mm, stroke 103mm, 61bhp at 4,800rpm, compression ratio 7:1, twin 1¼in SU carburettors, 4 branch manifold, deep sectioned ladder frame chassis with tubular front axle, 4 speed synchromesh close ratio gearbox, 4.0-1 ENV rear axle, 11in hydraulic operated drum brakes, fly-off handbrake on rear wheels, front quarter-elliptic leaf springs with friction type shock absorbers, rear half-elliptic leaf springs with hydraulic type shock absorbers, Rudge Whitworth centre lock wire spoke wheels, 4.75 x 17in tyres, wheelbase 103½in, maximum speed 90mph, 0-60mph in 17 seconds, right hand drive.
£22,000-25,000 *C*

1954 HRG Sports Special, Emperor, 4 cylinder in line engine, water-cooled monobloc, overhead valve, bore 73mm, stroke 89mm, 1489cc, 6 speed gearbox, Volkswagen independent front suspension, De Dion type rear axle, 5.60 x 15in tyres.
£12,000-13,000   *S*

Anthony Fidlater, with David Blakely, built a new car for the 1955 season, known as the Emperor. He installed an HRG engine with a twin overhead camshaft engine in this car, from one of the ex Le Mans cars. Its debut was to be the Boxing Day meeting at Brands Hatch in 1954 and Blakely drove the car into 2nd place in the Kent Cup 1500cc class. Blakely had great plans for the car for the 1955 season and indeed he had been nominated also to drive for Bristol at Le Mans that year.

Hudson

1938 Hudson 28.8hp Straight Eight Drophead Coupé, coachwork by Salmons of Newport Pagnell, straight 8 cylinder, side valve, water-cooled monobloc, 4168cc, 3 speed manual gearbox, right hand drive, fair condition, engine runs well.
£10,500-11,000   *C*

Humber

For the 1925 season Humber of Coventry were to increase the capacity of their 11.4hp model to 1795cc and listed the car as the 12/25hp model. It was produced alongside the 9/20hp and 15/40hp models and the 4/5 seat touring car sold for £440 with a £25 surcharge if front wheel brakes were required. This was approximately £200 more expensive than the Morris Oxford and £100 dearer than the Austin 12 Clifton Tourer, however, the Humber was arguably better appointed and certainly attracted a more well-to-do customer.

1913 Humberette Two Seater Roadster, 2 cylinders, 8hp, air-cooled engine.   **£9,000-10,000**   *SL*

1925 Humber 12/25hp Tourer, 4 cylinder in line, water-cooled monobloc engine, pushrod operated overhead valves, bore 69mm, stroke 120mm, 1795cc, 4 speed gearbox, cone clutch, spiral bevel final drive, semi-elliptic leaf spring suspension front and rear, wheelbase 109in, 4.50 x 20in tyres, engine re-assembled, needs attention to restore it to the open road after museum storage.
£12,000-13,000   *S*

1926 Humber 12/25hp Saloon, 4 cylinder in line, water-cooled monobloc engine, pushrod operated overhead valves, bore 69mm, stroke 120mm, 1795cc, 4 speed gearbox, cone clutch, spiral bevel final drive, semi-elliptic leaf spring suspension front and rear, wheelbase 109in, 20in tyres.
£13,000-13,500   *S*

1905 Humber 8/10hp Four Seater Swing Seat Tonneau, 4 cylinder side valve, water-cooled engine, bore 3⅛in, stroke 3¾in, 8/10hp, 3 speed gearbox with Quadrant type change, semi-elliptic springs front and rear, shaft drive to live rear axle with direct drive on top gear, wheelbase 80in, 750 x 75 tyres, condition 1.
Est. **£20,000-22,000**   *S*

MAKE Humber	ENGINE cc/cyl	DATES	CONDITION 1	2	3
Hawk Mk I-IV	1944/4	1945-52	£2,750	£1,500	£600
Hawk Mk V-VII	2267/4	1952-57	£2,500	£1,500	£400
Hawk Ser I-IVA	2267/4	1957-67	£2,500	£850	£325
Snipe	2731/6	1945/48	£5,000	£2,600	£850
Super Snipe Mk I-III	4086/6	1948-52	£4,700	£2,400	£600
Super Snipe Mk IV-IVA	4138/6	1952-56	£5,500	£2,300	£550
Super Snipe Ser I-II	2651/6	1958/60	£3,800	£1,800	£475
Super Snipe Ser I-II	2651/6	1958-60	£4,000	£1,850	£575
Super Snipe SIII-VA	2965/6	1961-67	£3,500	£1,800	£400
Super Snipe S.III-VA Est.	2965/6	1961-67	£3,950	£1,850	£525
Pullman	4086/6	1946-51	£4,500	£2,350	£800
Pullman Mk IV	4086/6	1952-54	£6,000	£2,850	£1,200
Imperial	2965/6	1965-67	£3,900	£1,600	£450
Sceptre Mk I-II	1592/4	1963-67	£2,050	£900	£300
Sceptre Mk III	1725/4	1967-76	£1,600	£600	£200

1928 Humber 9/20 Two Seater Tourer with Dickey, 4 cylinder, overhead inlet valves, bore 58mm, stroke 100mm, 1057cc, 3 speed forward gearbox with reverse, 4 wheel mechanical brakes, leaf spring suspension, wheelbase 102in, right hand drive, original specification, very good condition throughout.
£9,000-9,500   *C*

1946 Humber Super Snipe MkI Saloon, 6 cylinder in line side valve engine, 4086cc, 100bhp, 4 speed manual gearbox, wheelbase 114in, restored.
£4,000-5,000   *PC*

1949/50 Humber Super Snipe MkII Tickford Drophead Coupé, 6 cylinder in line side valve engine, 4086cc, 100bhp, 4 speed gearbox, wheelbase 117in, fully restored. **£20,000-30,000** *PC*

934 Humber Snipe 80, 6 cylinder line side valve engine, 3498cc, speed manual gearbox, 77bhp, heelbase 132in, original condition. **4,000-5,000** *PC*

1950 Humber Imperial Limousine, 4086cc, totally rebuilt body, replaced interior, mechanics overhauled, coachwork by Thrupp and Maberley. Est. **£5,000-7,000** *LF*

955 Humber Hawk Mk6A Saloon, 4 cylinder verhead valve in line engine, 267cc, 75bhp, 4 speed earbox, wheelbase 105in, riginal condition. **2,500-3,500** *C*

> *Make:* **Humber**
> *Model:* Super Snipe/Imperial
> *Type:* Saloon/Estate
> *Years Manufactured:* 1958-67
> *Quantity:* approx. 32,000; Imperial approx. 3,032
> *Price when new:* Super Snipe Series I-III, £1,110
> *Engine Type:* Overhead valve 6 cyl
> *Size:* 2651cc/2965cc
> *Max Power:* 105-129 bhp
> *Transmission:* 4 speed
> *Performance:* Max speed: 100 mph; 0-60: 14.3 secs; Mpg: 20.

950 Humber Pullman MkII Limousine, 6 cylinder in line side valve ngine, 4086cc, 100bhp, 4 speed manual gearbox, wheelbase 31in, original condition. **£5,000-6,000** *PC*

1961 Humber Super Snipe Series 3, 6 cylinder in line overhead valve engine, 2965cc, 129.5bhp, 3 speed gearbox, wheelbase 110in, some restoration. **£3,500-5,500** *PC*

The earlier the cars the more difficult spares are to come by, especially body panels. There are specialist suppliers who can provide the majority of mechanical parts. Repair panel sections are soon to be made available through the post-Vintage Humber Car Club probably for the 'Series' type Hawk/Super Snipe.

964 Humber Super Snipe. **£3,000-3,300** *WCC*

HUMBER

MAKE Humber	ENGINE cc/cyl	DATES	CONDITION 1	2	3
Veteran	var	1898-1918	£26,000	£20,000	£14,000
10	1592/4	1919	£7,000	£5,000	£3,000
14	2474/4	1919	£8,000	£6,000	£4,000
15.9-5/40	2815/4	1920-27	£10,000	£7,000	£4,000
8	985/4	1923-25	£7,000	£5,000	£2,500
9/20-9/28	1057/4	1926	£7,000	£5,000	£4,000
14/40	2050/4	1927-28	£14,000	£8,000	£5,000
Snipe	3498/6	1930-35	£8,000	£6,000	£4,000
Pullman	3498/6	1930-35	£8,000	£6,000	£4,000
16/50	2110/6	1930-32	£9,000	£7,000	£5,000
12	1669/4	1933-37	£7,000	£5,000	£3,000
Snipe/Pullman	4086/6	1936-40	£7,000	£5,000	£3,000
16	2576/6	1938-40	£7,000	£5,000	£3,000

Pre-1905 or Brighton Run cars are very popular.

1965 Humber Hawk Series 4, 4 cylinder in line overhead valve engine, 2267cc, 78bhp, 4 speed gearbox, wheelbase 110in, restored **£3,000-4,000**   *PC*

Make: **Humber**
Model: **Hawk**
Type: Saloon
Years Manufactured: 1957-67
Quantity: approx. 43,000
Price when new: £1,261
Engine Type: Overhead valve 4 cyl
Size: 2267cc
Max Power: 73 bhp @ 4400 rpm
Transmission: 4 speed, optional overdrive or auto
Performance: Max speed: 83 mph; 0-60: 20.6 secs; Mpg: 25.

1966 Humber Super Snipe, 20,000 miles. **£6,000-6,500**   *WCC*

International Harvester

c1909 International Harvester Model A Runabout, 2 cylinders. Est. **£14,000-18,000**   *ADT*

Produced between 1907 and 1911 the International was a 2 cylinder, friction transmission, solid-tyred vehicle which became available as either a passenger carrying car or light delivery pick-up. It was probably the most rugged high wheeler built in America at the time and perhaps this is a reason why the survival rate of these vehicles is fairly high.

Invicta

1934 Invicta 4½ litre Type S Low Chassis Tourer, coachwork by Carbodies Ltd., Coventry, 6 cylinder in line engine, water-cooled monobloc, pushrod operated overhead valves, bore 85.5mm, stroke 120.64mm, 4476cc, twin SU carburettors, 4 speed and reverse gearbox right hand gate, single plate dry clutch, hypoid bevel rear axle, semi-elliptic leaf springs front and rear, 19in tyres, wheelbase 118in. **£155,000-165,000**   *S*

148

1932 Invicta 1500, 6 cylinder Blackburn engine.
£13,500-14,000   *DB*

Isetta

Cross Reference
BMW Isetta

1932 Invicta 1½ litres, 1600cc overhead cam Blackburn engine, original condition.
£30,000-35,000   *DG*

961 Isetta Bubble Car.
2,800-3,000   *WCC*

Iso Grifo

969 Iso Grifo 5.7 V8 Series 1, left hand drive.   **£19,500-20,000**   *AUT*

Iso Lele

Make: **Iso**
Model: Lele
Type: Saloon
Years Manufactured: 1967-74
Quantity: 192
Price when new: 5359cc, £7,450
Engine Type: V8 cyl
Size: 5359-5769cc
Max Power: 300-355 bhp
Transmission: 4 speed, 5 speed, auto
Performance: Max speed: 133 mph; 0-60: 8.1 secs; Mpg: 12.

1974 Iso Lele, 5762cc, 8 cylinder rebuilt engine, condition of bodywork well above average.   Est. **£12,000-14,000**   *ADT*

Jaguar

1937 Jaguar SS100, 2½ litre.
£95,000-100,000 *PiK*

1935 Jaguar SS1 Special,
6 cylinder in line, cast iron cylinder block, 2 overhead valves per cylinder operated by single block mounted camshaft, pushrods and rockers, 3485cc, bore 82mm, stroke 110mm, twin SU carburettors, compression ratio 7:1, 130+bhp at 4,500rpm, 4 speed manual gearbox, single dry plate clutch, hypoid spiral bevel final drive with 3.78:1 ratio, 4 wheel rod operated drum brakes, front semi-elliptic leaf springs in trunnion bearings, adjustable

hydraulic and friction dampers, rear live axle with semi-elliptic springs with hydraulic adjustable dampers, pressed steel underslung chassis with box section main members fore and aft of cruciform centre section, 2 door, 2 seater sports one-off special racing type body, right hand drive. **£17,000-18,000** *C*

The Swallow Sidecar and Coachbuilding Co. of Blackpool started by William Lyons and

William Walmsley, originally built attractive motorcycle sidecars and in 1927 introduced their first special bodywork on an Austin 7 chassis. This was followed by offering attractive alternative bodyworks on a number of small cars and in particular on a range of Standard motor cars. New manufacturing premises were opened in Coventry, and the SS1 Sports Coupé was launched at the 1931 London Motor Show.

1947 Jaguar 2½ litre Sports Saloon, 6 cylinder in line, water-cooled monobloc, pushrod operated overhead valves, bore 73mm, stroke 106mm, 2663cc, 4 speed manual gearbox, single dry plate clutch, hypoid bevel rear axle, semi-elliptic suspension front and rear, wheelbase 120in. This model has been in dry storage for several years.
£8,500-9,500 *S*

By 1947 the SS badge had disappeared from the radiator and hubcaps. However, there was no mistaking the ancestry of the new

Jaguar cars. The new 6 cylinder engines fitted to the 2½ litre and 3½ litre cars were now built in-house at the top of Swallow Road and the

2½ litre engine developed 120bhp at 4,600rpm, giving a top speed approaching 90mph.

MAKE	ENGINE	DATES	CONDITION		
Jaguar	cc/cyl		1	2	3
SSI	2054/6	1932-33	£22,000	£18,000	£14,000
SSI	2252/6	1932-33	£25,000	£18,000	£14,000
SSII	1052/4	1932-33	£18,000	£15,000	£11,000
SSI	2663/6	1934	£30,000	£25,000	£15,000
SSII	1608/4	1934	£18,000	£15,000	£12,000
SS90	2663/6	1935	£60,000+		
SS3 (100)	3485/6	1938-39	£70,000+		
SS2 (100)	2663/6	1936-39	£60,000+		
SS2 Saloon	2663/6	1938-49	£14,000	£10,000	£8,000

Very dependent on body styles, completeness and originality, particularly original chassis to body.

1948 Jaguar 1½ litre Four Door Sports Saloon, 4 cylinder, monobloc, overhead valves by pushrods, single camshaft, 1767cc, bore 73mm, stroke 106mm, compression ratio 7.5:1, 65bhp at 4,500rpm, single SU carburettor, coil ignition, manual controlled, single dry plate clutch, 4 speed synchromesh gearbox, hypoid bevel rear axle, welded steel frame chassis with box section cross bracing, 4 door, 4 seater all steel Sports Saloon bodywork, front and rear rigid axles, semi-elliptic leaf springs, hydraulic shock absorbers, 4 wheel, 2 leading shoe drum brakes, 18in centre lock wire spoke wheels, 5.28 x 18in tyres, wheelbase 2,860mm, right hand drive.
Est. **£6,000-8,000**   *C*

1947 Jaguar 3½ litre Saloon.
£15,000-16,000   *ADT*

1948 Jaguar 1.5 Saloon, 1775cc.
Est. **£8,000-12,000**   *LF*

1961 Jaguar Mk9 Automatic, original UK car with service history and low mileage.
£10,000-11,000   *CCTC*

1951 Jaguar Mk V Cabriolet, 6 cylinder, condition 3.
£26,000-27,500   *KI*

1950 Jaguar XK120 Roadster.   **£28,000-30,000**   *AUT*

1953 Jaguar XK120 Drophead Coupé, 6 cylinder in line engine, water-cooled monobloc, twin overhead camshaft, overhead valves, bore 83mm, stroke 106mm, 3442cc, 4 speed synchromesh gearbox, Borg and Beck single dry plate clutch, hypoid bevel rear axle, independent front suspension, semi-elliptic leaf springs at rear, wheelbase 102in, 6.00 x 16in tyres.
£17,000-18,000   *S*

1955 Jaguar XK140 Roadster, restored, excellent condition, left hand drive.
Est. **£28,000-32,000**   *HA*

1954 Jaguar XK120 Drophead Coupé, one owner, totally original, 19,000 miles from new.   **£25,000-30,000**   *DG*

MAKE Jaguar	ENGINE cc/cyl	DATES	CONDITION 1	2	3
Jaguar 1½ Litre	1775/4	1945-49	£8,500	£5,500	£2,000
Jaguar 2½ Litre	2663/6	1946-49	£10,000	£7,500	£2,000
Jaguar 2½ Litre DHC	2663/6	1947-48	£18,000	£10,000	£8,000
Jaguar 3½ Litre	3485/6	1947-49	£12,000	£6,000	£4,000
Jaguar 3½ Litre DHC	3485/6	1947-49	£19,000	£13,500	£5,500
Jaguar Mk V 2½ Litre	2663/6	1949-51	£8,000	£5,000	£1,500
Jaguar Mk V 3½ Litre	3485/6	1949-51	£13,000	£7,000	£1,800
Jaguar Mk V 3½ Litre DHC	3485/6	1949-51	£20,000	£17,000	£8,500
Jaguar Mk VII	3442/6	1951-57	£10,500	£7,500	£2,500
Jaguar Mk VIIM	3442/6	1951-57	£12,000	£8,500	£2,500
Jaguar Mk VIII	3442/6	1956-59	£8,500	£5,500	£2,000
Jaguar Mk IX	3781/6	1958-61	£11,000	£9,000	£2,500
Jaguar Mk X 3.8/4.2	3781/6	1961-64	£8,500	£3,500	£1,500
Jaguar Mx X 420G	4235/6	1964-70	£6,000	£3,000	£1,200
Jaguar Mk I 2.4	2438/6	1955-59	£7,000	£5,500	£2,000
Jaguar Mk I 3.4	3442/6	1957-59	£9,000	£8,000	£2,500
Jaguar Mk II 2.4	2483/6	1959-67	£6,000	£5,000	£2,000
Jaguar Mk II 3.4	3442/6	1959-67	£9,000	£6,500	£3,000
Jaguar Mk II 3.8	3781/6	1959-67	£9,850	£9,000	£4,000
Jaguar S-Type 3.4	3442/6	1963-68	£10,000	£6,500	£2,000
Jaguar S-Type 3.8	3781/6	1963-68	£12,500	£6,500	£2,000
Jaguar 240	2438/6	1967-68	£8,000	£5,000	£2,500
Jaguar 340	3442/6	1967-68	£9,000	£7,000	£3,000
Jaguar 420	4235/6	1966-68	£6,000	£3,000	£2,000

Manual gearboxes with overdrive are at a premium.

Make: **Jaguar**
Model: XK120, 140, 150
Type: Drop Head Coupé, Fixed Head Coupé, Roadster
Years Manufactured: 1953-61
Price when new: XK150, £2,007
Engine Type: Twin overhead camshaft 6 cyl
Size: 3442cc
Max Power: XK120, 160/180 bhp @ 5000 rpm; XK150, 252 bhp @ 5500 rpm
Max Torque: XK120, 195/203 ft/lb @ 2500/4000 rpm
Transmission: 4 speed, optional overdrive
Wheelbase: 102in
Performance: Max speed: XK150, 130+ mph; 0-60: XK150, 7.5 secs; Mpg: XK150, 18-22.

1955 Jaguar XK140, American restoration.
£20,000-25,000   *DG*

1957 Jaguar XK140 Roadster, USA import, needs restoration, runs and drives, left hand drive.
£14,000-14,500   *CCTC*

Wire wheels increase the value.

1960 Jaguar XK150 Drophead Coupé, right hand drive.
£25,000-35,000   *AUT*

The final version of the XK family was the 150 model which became available in early 1957, almost 10 years after the original XK120. The car was similar in size to the XK140, but there were now a number of changes for the better, including the Jaguar mascot and the single wrap around windscreen.

1960 Jaguar XK150 Drophead Coupé, 3781cc, 6 cylinders, chrome wire wheels.
Est. **£32,000-35,000**   *ADT*

1959 Jaguar MkI, 3400cc, 6 cylinders, imported from South Africa, original right hand drive.
£4,500-5,000   *ADT*

1959 Jaguar MkI 3.4, 3442c, 6 cylinders, manual gearbox with overdrive, professionally restored in 1989/90. Est. **£12,500-14,500** *ADT*

1962 Jaguar MkII Saloon, 3442cc. **£7,400-7,600** *LAI*

Make: **Jaguar**
Model: Mk II
Type: Saloon
Years Manufactured: 1959-69
Quantity: 90,640
Price when new: £1,611
Engine Type: 6 cyl
Size: 2483cc/3781cc
Max Power: 120-220 bhp
Transmission: 4 speed, optional overdrive, auto
Performance: Max speed: 3.8 Mk II, 125 mph; 0-60: 3.8 Mk II, 8.5 secs; Mpg: 3.8 Mk II, 16.

1961 Jaguar MkII 3.8, 3800cc, 4 cylinders, restored 2 years ago, manual gearbox with overdrive, 48,400 recorded miles. Est. **£9,000-12,000** *ADT*

1961 Jaguar MkII 3.8 litre Sports Saloon, 6 cylinder, in line, water-cooled, twin overhead camshafts, bore 87mm, stroke 106mm, 3781cc, 3 speed automatic gearbox, hypoid bevel rear axle, independent front suspension by double wishbones, rear suspension by cantilevered semi-elliptic springs, wheelbase 108in, left hand drive. **£9,500-10,000** *S*

The MkII Jaguar was introduced at the 1959 Earls Court Motor Show. Initially it only came with the 2.4 litre or 3.4 litre versions of the twin overhead camshaft Jaguar XK engine. The 3.8 litre version was offered in 1960.

Make the Most of Miller's

CONDITION is absolutely vital when assessing the value of a vehicle. Top class vehicles on the whole appreciate much more than less perfect examples. However a rare, desirable car may command a high price even when in need of restoration

1964 Jaguar 3.8S, 3798cc, 6 cylinders.   Est. **£5,000-6,000**   *ADT*

MAKE	ENGINE	DATES	CONDITION		
Jaguar	cc/cyl		1	2	3
Jaguar XJ6 2.8 Ser I	2793/6	1968-73	£2,600	£1,500	£1,000
Jaguar XJ6 4.2 Ser I	4235/6	1968-73	£3,000	£2,000	£1,000
Jaguar XJ6 Coupé	4235/6	1974-78	£7,000	£3,000	£2,000
Jaguar XJ6 Ser II	4235/6	1973-79	£3,500	£2,000	£750
Jaguar XJ12 Ser I	5343/12	1972-73	£4,500	£2,250	£1,500
Jaguar XJ12 Coupé	5343/12	1973-77	£8,000	£4,000	£2,000
Jaguar XJ12 Ser II	5343/12	1973-79	£2,000	£1,500	—
Jaguar XK120 DHC	3442/6	1953	£28,000	£18,000	£12,000
Jaguar XK120 DHC	3442/6	1949-54	£30,000	£20,000	£13,000
Jaguar XK120 FHC	3442/6	1951-54	£25,000	£17,000	£10,000
Jaguar XK140 DHC	3442/6	1954-57	£30,000	£20,00	£12,000
Jaguar XK140 roadster	3442/6	1954-57	£33,000	£24,000	£14,000
Jaguar XK140 FHC	3442/6	1954-57	£20,000	£15,000	£10,000
Jaguar XK140MC			£35,000	£27,500	£18,00
Jaguar XK150 DHC	3442/6	1957-60	£30,000	£20,000	£15,000
Jaguar XK150 roadster	3442/6	1958-60	£32,000	£22,000	£15,000
Jaguar XK150S			£38,000	£28,000	£18,000
Jaguar XK150 FHC	3442/6	1957-61	£20,000	£15,000	£10,000

1966 Jaguar MkII 3.8, total restoration, 80,000 miles. **£12,000-14,000** *DG*

1962 Jaguar E-Type Series 1, American full restoration, left hand drive. **£25,000-30,000** *DG*

1961 Jaguar E-Type 3.8 Roadster (flat floor), 3781cc, 6 cylinders. **£47,000-48,000** *ADT*

1965 Jaguar E-Type Roadster 4.2 litre Series 1, front 6 cylinder in line 7-bearing cast iron block and aluminium alloy cylinder heads, twin overhead camshafts, 2 inclined overhead valves per cylinder, 4235cc, bore 92.07mm, stroke 106mm, compression ratio 9:1, 265bhp at 5,400rpm, triple SU HD8 carburettors, coil and distributor ignition, single dry plate clutch with 4 speed manual gearbox, hypoid bevel final drive with limited slip differential, steel monocoque centre section with square tube front subframe and pressed steel rear frame with 2 seater roadster bodywork, 4 wheel Dunlop disc brakes inboard at rear, hydraulic servo assistance, 5½in J x 15in wire spoke centre lock wheels with 6.40 x 15in tyres, wheelbase 96in, fully restored.
£15,000-20,000   *CNY*

MAKE Jaguar	ENGINE cc/cyl	DATES	CONDITION 1	2	3
E-type 3.8 flat 'floor roadster'		1961	£40,000	£30,000	£21,500
E-type S1 3.8 roadster	3781/6	1961-64	£28,000	£18,000	£13,000
E-type 3.8 FHC	3781/6	1961-64	£18,000	£13,000	£9,000
E-type S1 4.2 roadster	4235/6	1964-67	£22,000	£18,000	£12,000
E-type 2+2 manual FHC	4235/6	1966-67	£15,000	£10,000	£8,000
E-type S.1 2+2 auto FHC	4235/6	1966-68	£13,000	£9,000	£7,000
E-type S.II roadster	4235/6	1968-70	£22,000	£18,000	£12,000
E-type S.II FHC	4235/6	1968-70	£18,000	£12,000	£8,000
E-type S.II 2+2 manual FHC	4235/6	1968-70	£15,000	£10,000	£8,000
E-type S.III roadster	5343/12	1971-75	£32,000	£22,000	£15,000
E-type S.III 2+2 manual FHC	5343/12	1971-75	£19,000	£14,000	£10,000
E-type S.III 2+2 auto FHC	5343/12	1971-75	£17,000	£12,000	£9,000
Jaguar XJS manual	5343/12	1975-78	£6,000	£4,500	£2,500
Jaguar XJS auto	5343/12	1975-81	£4,000	£2,200	£1,500

1965 Jaguar E-Type 4.2 Roadster.
Est. **£25,000-30,000**   *S(M)*

The XK engine was further developed and this vehicle is fitted with the 4.2 litre engine which developed 265hp at 54rpm.

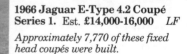

1966 Jaguar E-Type 4.2 Coupé Series 1. Est. **£14,000-16,000**   *LF*
Approximately 7,770 of these fixed head coupés were built.

Locate the source
The source of each illustration in Miller's can be found by checking the code letters below each caption with the list of contributors

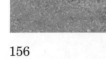

1962 Jaguar E-Type 3.8 Roadster. Est. £28,000-34,000 *LF*

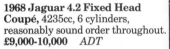

1968 Jaguar 4.2 Fixed Head Coupé, 4235cc, 6 cylinders, reasonably sound order throughout. **£9,000-10,000** *ADT*

1970 Jaguar E-Type Series 2 2+2, manual gearbox, Concours condition. **£18,000-19,000** *SC*

1972 Jaguar E-Type V12 Fixed Head Coupé, imported from USA, right hand drive. **£11,000-11,500** *Cen*

1971 Jaguar E-Type V12 2+2 Fixed Head Coupé, V12 overhead camshaft, water-cooled bi-bloc engine, 5343cc, automatic gearbox, independent front suspension, live rear axle, wheelbase 105in. Est. **£15,000-17,000** *S*

Introduced in 1971 the Jaguar V12 engine was in fact a modified version of the unit designed by Walter Hassan and W. M. Heynes for the XJ 13, a mid-engined monocoque racer which was completed in 1966, but which did not progress beyond the prototype stage. The production version was enlarged from 4994cc to 5343cc and fitted with 4 dual choke downdraught Zenith carburettors. The first recipient of the new unit was the E-Type, and this example is an early one from the production run.

1971 Jaguar XKE 4.2 Convertible Roadster, 41,000 miles. **£20,000-25,000** *HWA*

Make: **Jaguar**
Model: E-Type, Series III
Type: Sports Car/Coupé
Years Manufactured: 1971-74
Quantity: 15,287
Price when new: Fixed Head Coupé, £3,369
Engine Type: V12 cyl
Size: 5343cc
Max Power: 272 bhp @ 5850 rpm
Max Torque: 304 ft/lb @ 3600 rpm
Transmission: 4 speed or auto
Wheelbase: 104.7in
Performance: Max speed: 142 mph; 0-60: 6.8 secs; Mpg: 16.

1973 Jaguar V12 E-Type Roadster, complete bare chassis restoration, full mechanical rebuild, chrome wire wheels. **Est. £40,000-50,000** *LF*

1973 Jaguar E-Type V12 2+2, 5343cc, 12 cylinders. **Est. £17,000-19,000** *ADT*

Jaguar E-Type V12 Coupé Automatic. £14,000-16,000 *AUT*

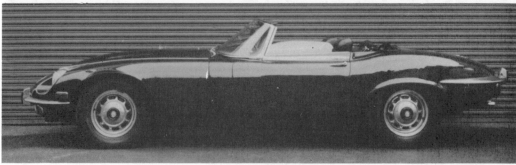

1974 Jaguar E-Type V12 Roadster. £30,000-32,000 *AUT*

1974 Jaguar E-Type Series III, as new, with full restoration history, 2 owners. £30,000-35,000 *DG*

**1976 Jaguar E-Type V12
Roadster,** chrome wire wheels,
sympathetic restoration over recent
years, original right hand drive, UK
supplied car.
£28,000-29,000 *HA*

*The Series III E-Types were in
production from 1971 until 1975. In
total, 7,990 Roadsters were made
and 7,297 2+2 FHC.*

1968 Jaguar 420 G, 4235cc,
6 cylinders.
£2,800-3,200 *ADT*

**1982 Jaguar
XJS.**
£6,000-6,500
S8

1936 Jaguar SS100, rebodied from 2.5 litre saloon.
£45,000-55,000   BLE

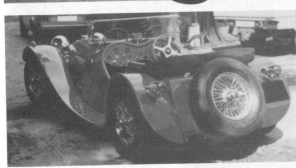

1977 Jaguar XJ6 Two Door Coupé Convertible.
Est. £8,000-12,000   LF

1988 Heritage Jaguar SS100 3.8 litre Roadster, 6 cylinder in line water-cooled monobloc, twin overhead camshafts, bore 87mm, stroke 106mm, 3781cc, twin SU carburettors, 4 speed manual all synchromesh gearbox, hypoid bevel rear axle, fully independent suspension front and rear, servo assisted dual circuit disc brakes, 15 x 6in wheels, chassis 3mm steel box section to Heritage Engineering design.   Est. £22,000-26,000   S

Heritage Engineering (Herts) Ltd. successfully produced both Jaguar C-Type and SS100 replicas and fielded their cars competitively in the Paladin racing series with success. The cars were built to a high specification utilising a chassis of their own design in 3mm steel with a GRP body incorporating an aluminium bonnet. E-Type disc brakes and XJ6 running gear are used and Connolly hide trim and mohair hood and cover with Jaguar/Smiths instruments complete the interior.

1991 Jaguar D-Type Replica, 4200cc, 6 cylinders.   £9,000-10,000   ADT

1989 Jaguar D-Type Replica, by Proteus, hand built all aluminium body.   £80,000-90,000   S8

Jensen

1952 Jensen Interceptor Drophead Coupé, 6 cylinder in line, water-cooled, monobloc engine, pushrod operated overhead valve, bore 87.3mm, stroke 111.1mm, 3993cc, 4 speed manual gearbox, hypoid bevel final drive, independent front suspension by coil spring and wishbone, rear suspension by half-elliptic leaf spring front and rear drum brakes, wheelbase 112in, 6.00 x 16in tyres, a rare post-war classic car, in overall good condition.
Est. **£12,000-14,000**   *S*

1963 Jensen CV8.
£8,000-9,000   *PC*

The name Interceptor was coined by Lord Strathcarron, a close friend of Richard Jensen, and production was at the rate of approximately 2/3 per week. Performance was good and it

could manage 100mph. Later models were fitted with overdrive. Production of the new 541 model in 1953 caused the Interceptor to be phased out.

1958 Jensen 541R Four Litre Four Seater Grand Tourer, Austin 135, 6 cylinder, overhead valve, 4 litre, 150bhp, 4 speed synchromesh gearbox with overdrive, independent front suspension, live rear axle, power disc brakes, wire spoke centre lock wheels, rack and pinion steering, right hand drive, in need of total restoration.
£2,500-3,000   *C*

1965 Jensen CV8 MkIII. £12,500-13,000   *WCC*

1963 Jensen 541S Sports Coupé, straight 6 cylinder, water-cooled monobloc, overhead valve, bore 87mm, stroke 111mm, 3993cc, automatic transmission, shaft drive to live rear axle, coil spring and wishbone front suspension, semi-elliptic leaf springs rear with Panhard rods, wheelbase 105in, 6.40 x 15in tyres, very good overall condition.
Est. **£12,000-14,000**   *S*

JENSEN

MAKE Jensen	ENGINE cc/cyl	DATES	CONDITION		
			1	2	3
541/541R/541S	3993/6	1954-63	£8,000	£5,000	£3,500
CV8 Mk I-III	5916/ 6276/8	1962-66	£10,000	£6,000	£4,000
Interceptor SI-SIII	6276/8	1967-76	£10,000	£7,000	£4,500
Interceptor SP	7212/8	1971-76	£14,000	£11,000	£8,500
FF	6766/8	1967-71	£18,000	£12,000	£9,000
Healey	1973/4	1972-76	£5,000	£3,000	£1,500
Healey GT	1973/4	1975-76	£6,000	£3,000	£2,000

1965 Jensen CV8.
Est. £14,000-16,000   *HA*

Make: **Jensen**
Model: Interceptor/FF
Type: Coupé/Convertible
Years Manufactured: 1966-76
Quantity: 5,577/320
Price when new: 6276cc, £3,743
Engine Type: V8 cyl
Size: 6276cc/7210cc
Max Power: 325-385 bhp
Transmission: 4 speed or auto
Performance: Max speed: Mk I,
133 mph; 0-60: Mk I, 7.3 secs;
Mpg: Mk I, 14.

1968 Jensen FF, 6276cc,
8 cylinders, excellent condition.
Est. £10,000-14,000   *ADT*

1969 Jensen Interceptor Saloon,
rebuilt and all mechanics
overhauled.
Est. **£6,000-8,000**   *LF*

*The body of this car was executed by
Vignale with a 6.2 litre Chrysler
engine with automatic box.*

*Introduced in 1967, the Touring of
Milan styled Interceptor used a
6276cc V8 Chrysler engine
producing 330bhp. A powerful
4 seater, it was comprehensively
equipped and luxuriously furnished.
Between 1971 and 1973 a limited
production of only 105 SPs were
built. These had a triple carburettor,
7212cc engine and is easily
identifiable by its louvred bonnet
panel.*

1969 Jensen Interceptor MkI,
6276cc, 8 cylinders.
Est. **£7,000-10,000**   *ADT*

1972 Jensen Interceptor MkIII,
30,000 miles.
£16,000-17,000   *WCC*

Make the Most of Miller's

Price ranges in this book reflect what one should expect to pay for a similar example. When selling, however, one should expect to receive a lower figure. This will fluctuate according to a dealer's stock, saleability at a particular time, etc. It is always advisable, when selling, to approach a reputable specialist dealer or an auction house which has specialist sales

1972 Jensen Interceptor SP Automatic.
Est. **£10,000-12,000**   *Cen*

1972 Jensen Interceptor MkIII,
6276cc, 8 cylinders, good condition.
£7,000-7,500   *ADT*

1972 Jensen Interceptor MkIII,
V8 cylinder, overhead valve,
6276cc, automatic transmission,
right hand drive.
Est. **£8,000-12,000**   *C*

Jensen Interceptor MkI.
£5,000-6,000   *CB*

163

1975 Jensen Interceptor Convertible.
£20,000-30,000 *S8*

Jensen Interceptor Convertible.
£15,000-35,000 *CB*

Considered to be THE best luxury 4 seater convertible built in modern times. It does NOT suffer from scuttle shake! Based on the Interceptor, it has a stylish and well-fitting power hood that sits proud of the rear when down giving a useful protection against draughts round the back of the neck for rear seat passengers. The very last handful built has a full length walnut dash fitted, as did the Interceptor Saloon. Many were supplied to North America.

Jensen Interceptor MkII.
£8,000-9,000 *CB*

Jensen FF MkI.
£8,000-9,000 *CB*

Derived from the Interceptor shape this was the highly advanced 4 wheel drive anti-lock braking car that set new standards in road safety 20 years before Audi Quattro developed the idea.

Jensen Healey

Make: **Jensen**	
Model: **Jensen-Healey**	
Type: Sports Car	
Years Manufactured: 1972-76	
Quantity: 10,926	
Price when new: £1,810	
Engine Type: twin overhead camshaft 4 cyl	
Size: 1973cc	
Max Power: 144 bhp @ 6500 rpm	
Max Torque: 130 ft/lb @ 5000 rpm	
Transmission: 4 speed or 5 speed from November 1974	
Performance: Max speed: 120 mph; 0-60: 8.5 secs; Mpg: 21-25.	

Jensen Healey MkII, 4 speed gearbox.
£4,500-5,000   *CB*

A small 2 seater sports car making a radical move away from the luxury market Jensen had always pursued. Aimed at the export market, it used a Lotus 2 litre twin cam mated to Rootes/Chrysler 4 speed gearbox, later Getrag 5 speed box.
The early cars are less desirable.

1974 Jensen Healey MkII, restored 5 years ago, excellent condition.
£8,500-9,000   *APP*

1976 Jensen Healey MkII, 5 speed gearbox, restored 3 years ago, excellent condition.
£9,500-10,000   *APP*

1972 Jensen Healey, 2 litre Lotus, twin cam, 4 cylinders, 4 speed gearbox, unrestored, low mileage, well maintained.   **£4,500-5,000**   *Ree*

1973 Jensen Healey, 1973cc, 4 cylinders. Est. **£4,500-5,500**   *ADT*

Jowett

1924 Jowett 7hp Two Seater with Dickey, twin cylinder, horizontally opposed, water-cooled engine, side valves, non-detachable cylinder heads, bore 75.4mm, stroke 101.5mm, 907cc, 3 speed gearbox, cone clutch spiral bevel rear axle, semi-elliptic leaf springs front and rear, 26 x 3in tyres.
£6,500-7,000 *S*

Built in Idle, Yorkshire, the twin cylinder Jowett was the brainchild of William and Benjam Jowett and earned an enviable reputation for reliability, hill-climbing ability and economy, justifying its advertising slogan 'The little engine with the big pull'. The Edwardian-designed engine, in only marginally developed form, was to power Jowett products right through to the Jowett Bradford vans of the early 1950s with their distinctive exhaust beat.

MAKE Jowett	ENGINE cc/cyl	DATES	CONDITION 1	2	3
7hp	907/2	1910-36	£10,000	£8,000	£6,000
8hp	946/2	1936-39	£9,000	£6,000	£4,000
J Series 10hp	1166/4	1936-39	£7,000	£5,000	£2,500
A fun car that is somewhat undervalued and underrated.					

Kennedy

1986 Kennedy Squire, Ford 2.0 engine, low mileage, condition 1.
£8,000-10,000 *PA*

Lagonda

1928 Lagonda 2 litre, original, maintained to an excellent standard.
£50,000-60,000 *DG*

MAKE Lagonda	ENGINE cc/cyl	DATES	CONDITION 1	2	3
12/24	1421/4	1923-26	£14,000	£10,000	£8,000
2 litre	1954/4	1928-32	£28,000	£25,000	£19,000
3 litre	2931/6	1928-34	£30,000	£30,000	£22,000
M45	4429/6	1934-36	£35,000	£26,000	£18,000
LG45	4429/6	1936-37	£40,000	£30,000	£20,000
LG6	4453/6	1937-39	£35,000	£28,000	£20,000
V12	4480/V12	1937-39	£65,000	£50,000	£40,000
Prices very dependent on body type, originality and competition history.					

1932 Lagonda 3 litre Tourer, full restoration, excellent condition.
£60,000-65,000   *DG*

1933 Lagonda 2 litre Low Chassis Tourer, 4 cylinder in line engine, water-cooled monobloc, overhead valve, bore 72mm, stroke 120mm, 1954cc, 4 speed gearbox, single plate clutch, spiral bevel rear axle, semi-elliptic leaf springs front and rear, wheelbase 120in, 21in tyres, extensively restored, retrimmed.
Est. £35,000-40,000   *S*

1933 Lagonda 16/80 Four Seater Tourer, 1991cc, 6 cylinders.
Est. £42,000-45,000   *ADT*

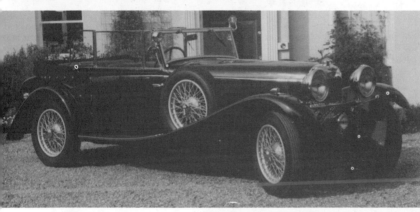

1934 Lagonda M45, Vanden Plas body, unique body style to order of Oxborrow and Fuller, history known from new.
£90,000-100,000
DG

1934 Lagonda M45 Saloon, original condition.
£30,000-35,000   *DG*

1932 Lagonda 3 litre Saloon, engine rebuilt, original car in very good order.
£35,000-37,000   *OC*

1935 Lagonda 16/80 Special Six Tourer, 6 cylinder, 1991cc, 4 speed manual gearbox with Wilson preselector, right hand drive.
£31,000-34,000   *C*

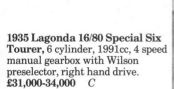

LAGONDA

1935 Lagonda 3½ litre Tourer,
6 cylinder in line, overhead valve,
3619cc, 4 speed manual
transmission, right hand drive,
coachwork and interior in very good
condition.
£30,000-32,000   *C*

*Wilbur Gunn who founded Lagonda
emigrated to England from a suburb
of Springfield, Ohio, called
Lagonda. The name derived from a
local tribe of Indians.*

1935 Lagonda 4½ litre, exact
replica of 1935 Le Mans winning
car, total restoration.
£60,000-65,000   *DG*

> *A rebuilt car is not
> necessarily of more value
> than a car in good original
> condition, even if the
> restoration has cost
> thousands of pounds.*

1936 Lagonda LG45 Rapide Replica, total restoration and rebody, one
of 6 exact replicas made c1986.   **£90,000-100,000**   *DG*

1937 Lagonda LG45, American Concours winner, full American restoration.   **£85,000-90,000**   *DG*

1938 Lagonda V12 Short Chassis Saloon, by Freestone & Webb. £25,000-26,000 *PiK*

1938 Lagonda V12 Sport Saloon. £28,000-30,000 *PMc*

1938 Lagonda V12 Rapide Drophead Coupé. £85,000-95,000 *PMc*

1939 Lagonda V12 Short Chassis, with sporting saloon body by Freestone & Webb. £35,000-55,000 *SL*

1939 Lagonda V12 Medium Chassis Four Door Saloon. £24,000-25,000 *SL*

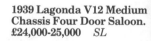

1953 Lagonda 3 Litre Drophead Coupé, coachwork by Tickford, 6 cylinder in line, water-cooled monobloc, twin overhead camshaft, bore 83mm, stroke 90mm, 2992cc, 4 speed manual gearbox, single dry plate clutch, hypoid bevel rear axle, independent front and rear suspension, wheelbase 113½in, 16in tyres. £19,000-20,000 *S*

169

LAGONDA

Make: **Lagonda**
Model: Rapide
Type: Saloon
Years Manufactured: 1961-64
Quantity: 55
Price when new: £4,951
Engine Type: 6 cyl
Size: 3995cc
Max Power: 236 bhp
Transmission: 4 speed or auto
Performance: Max speed: 125 mph; 0-60: 10.0 secs; Mpg: 15.

1963 Lagonda Rapide, 3995cc.
Est. **£18,000-20,000** *HA*

The Lagonda Rapide was the last of only 54 to be built before a long gap in operations occurred, resuming with the Aston Martin Lagonda in the 70s. The Rapide featured the same 3995cc engine as the Aston Martin DB6, powering a large saloon styled by Touring of Milan.

1939 Lagonda V12 De Ville Saloon.
£26,500-27,000 *DB*

Before and after WWI Lagonda concentrated on light car production, however the introduction of the 2 litre from 1925 changed their image. The fine 4 cylinder twin high camshaft engine designed by Arthur Davidson moved Lagonda into the sports car league and examples competed in many of the famous events of the time. This engine continued through to 1932 with various modifications and was then replaced by a 6 cylinder 2 litre Crossley unit and was named the 16/80. Like most pre-war Lagondas, coachwork was built in-house and in this case consists of the 3 door T7 Tourer body style

MAKE	ENGINE	DATES	CONDITION		
Lagonda	cc/cyl		1	2	3
3 Litre	2922/6	1953-58	£12,000	£7,000	£4,500
3 Litre DHC	2922/6	1953-56	£14,000	£12,000	£8,500
Rapide	3995/6	1961/64	£11,000	£7,000	£4,500

Lamborghini

1986 Lamborghini.   **£20,000-25,000**   *S8*

1972 Lamborghini Espada Series II 400GT 2+2 Coupé, 60° V12 cylinder engine, water-cooled, twin overhead camshaft, bore 82mm, stroke 62mm, 3929cc, 5 speed synchromesh gearbox, single dry plate clutch, independent coil spring front and rear suspension, 4 wheel disc brakes, wheelbase 104.3in, 15in tyres, good overall condition.
£22,000-25,000 *S*

It was his astralogical sign of Taurus that made Ferrucio Lamborghini adopt the Bull as the emblem for his supercars. The millionaire industrialist introduced the most advanced Gran Turismo cars of their time, and there has been great speculation as to why he turned to the automobile world as his third career. Folklore has it that having owned several exotic high performance cars he decided he could make a better car himself.

1973 Lamborghini Espada.
£25,000-30,000 *S8*

Lanchester

1928 Lanchester 21hp Limousine, 3327cc, 6 cylinders.
£16,000-17,500 *ADT*

George, Fred and Frank Lanchester were pioneers in the development of the motorcar from 1895 in England. What so many people do not realise is that prior to 1930 the quality of construction and their innovative ability created a car that would equal Rolls-Royce in its ability to please.

The 21hp was introduced in 1923 and was in fact a scaled-down simplified and modernised model 40. Its 6 cylinder engine comprised a 3327cc capacity and was created from 2 monoblocs holding 3 cylinders each. Drive to the rear wheels is via a 4 speed gearbox and shaft and Lanchester worm drive.

MAKE Lanchester	ENGINE cc/cyl	DATES	CONDITION		
			1	2	3
LD10	1287/4	1946-49	£3,500	£1,500	£750
LD10 (Barker bodies)	1287/4	1950-51	£3,800	£1,500	£700

1933 Lanchester 10 Martin Walter Romney Coupé. £5,500-6,000   *DB*

Condition Guide

1. A vehicle in top class condition but not 'concours d'elegance' standard, either fully restored or in very good original condition
2. A good, clean, roadworthy vehicle, both mechanically and bodily sound
3. A runner, but in need of attention, probably both to bodywork and mechanics. Must have current MOT

Lancia

1928 Lancia Lambda 8th Series Two Seat Drophead Coupé and Dickey, coachwork by The Albany Carriage Co. of London W7, V4 cylinder engine, water-cooled overhead valve, overhead camshaft, bore 79.4mm, stroke 120mm, 2400cc, 4 speed gearbox, multi-plate clutch, independent telescopic front suspension, semi-elliptic leaf spring rear, wheelbase 122in, 15/16 x 50 tyres.
£14,600-15,600   *S*

1930 Lancia Dilambda Fabric Saloon, coachwork by Mulliner, 24° V8 monobloc, water-cooled engine, overhead camshaft, bore $3\frac{1}{8}$in, stroke $3\frac{15}{16}$in, 3959cc, 100bhp at 4,000rpm, single plate Borg & Beck clutch, 4 speed and reverse gearbox, hypoid bevel final drive, deep box-section chassis with tubular and boxed cruciform bracing, mechanical 4 wheel brakes, front independent suspension, Lancia sliding pillar, underslung semi-elliptic leaf springs rear, centralised Bijur chassis lubrication, wheelbase 137in, 16 x 5.00 tyres, right hand drive.
Est. £30,000-35,000   *C*

1963 Lancia Flavia Vignale Spider, right hand drive.
£13,000-14,000   *AUT*

1963 Lancia Flavia Coupé.
£2,100-2,500   *Cen*

Styled by Pinin Farina, the Lancia Flavia Coupé was introduced in 1962 with a 1488cc engine later uprated to 1800cc as employed by today's example. Production of this 4 seater coupé continued until 1968.

1971 Lancia Fulvia Zagato 1600, Series II.
Est. **£7,000-8,000**   *Cen*

1974 Lancia Fulvia Coupé, V4 cylinder, water-cooled monobloc, overhead valves, bore 77mm, stroke 69.7mm, 1298cc, 5 speed gearbox, single dry plate, independent coil spring front and rear suspension, front wheel drive, wheelbase 90in, 205/70/14in tyres.
£3,500-4,000   *S*

1969 Lancia 1.3 Fulvia Sport Zagato, Series 1, condition 1.
£8,000-10,000   *PA*

LANCIA

1975 Lancia Fulvia 1.3 S3, 1298cc, V4, overhead camshaft, 108bhp,
5 speed gearbox, mechanically sound.
£2,000-2,500   *SCC*

1974 Lancia Stratos, solid condition.
Est. **£80,000-90,000**   *S(NY)*

1975 Lancia Fulvia 1.3, condition 1.
£4,500-5,500   *PA*

| MAKE | ENGINE | DATES | CONDITION | | |
Lancia	cc/cyl		1	2	3
Theta	4940/4	1913-19	£24,000	£16,500	£8,000
Kappa	4940/4	1919-22	£24,000	£16,000	£8,000
Dikappa	4940/4	1921-22	£24,000	£16,000	£8,000
Trikappa	4590/4	1922-26	£25,000	£18,000	£10,000
Lambda	2120/4	1923-28	£28,000	£20,000	£10,000
Dilambda	3960/8	1928-32	£24,000	£16,000	£8,000
Astura	2604/8	1931-39	£25,000	£18,000	£9,000
Artena	1925/4	1931-36	£9,000	£5,000	£2,000
Augusta	1196/4	1933-36	£9,000	£4,000	£2,000
Aprila 238	1352/4	1937-39	£10,000	£5,000	£3,000

Land Rover

**1949/51 Land Rover Station
Wagon,** based on 80in chassis with
coachbuilt aluminium clad body,
very rare.
£18,000-20,000   *DL*

**1954 Land Rover SWB Canvas
Top,** wheelbase 86in, excellent
condition.
£1,700-2,000   *LF*

Make: **Land Rover**
Model: Series I
Type: Utility
Years Manufactured: 1948-58
Price when new: 1948-51, £450;
1952-58, £598
Engine Type: Inlet-over-exhaust
4 cyl
Size: 1595cc (1997cc from 1952)
Max Power: 1955cc, 50 bhp @
4000 rpm; 1997cc, 52 bhp @
4000 rpm
Transmission: 4 speed plus
transfer gearbox
Performance: Max speed: 65
mph; 0-60: 25+ secs; Mpg: 15-25.

957 Land Rover Station Wagon,
wheelbase 107in.
5,000-8,000 *DL*

Lea Francis

1957 Land Rover Series One
Hard Top, wheelbase 88in.
£3,500-4,000 *DL*

Manufactured between 1946 and
1952 these models were similar in
principle to the pre-war cars but
considerably modified in detail.

951 Lea Francis 14 Saloon,
767cc, 4 cylinders.
2,750-3,250 *ADT*

1950 Lea Francis,
condition 2.
£3,250-3,750 *CC*

Lea Francis started
making cars in 1904.
One of their best
post-war models was
the 18hp 2½ litre
Sportscar introduced
in 1950. The engine
developed 100bhp and
the newly introduced
torsion bar
independent front
suspension greatly
improved handling.

950 Lea Francis 2½ litre 2+2 Open Sports Touring Special, 4 cylinder, overhead
alve, water-cooled monobloc engine, 2496cc, 4 speed gearbox, independent front
uspension by torsion bar, leaf spring at rear, spiral bevel rear axle, wheelbase
11in, 6.00 x 16in tyres. **£40,000-50,000** *S*

LEA FRANCIS

1951 Lea Francis, 14hp, needs
restoration.
£750-1,000   *Cen*

MAKE Lea-Francis	ENGINE cc/cyl	DATES	CONDITION		
			1	2	3
12/14HP	1496/ 1767/4	1946-54	£8,000	£5,000	£1,500
14HP Sports	1767/4	1947-49	£14,000	£8,000	£3,000
14/7018HP	1767/ 2496/4	1949-53	£9,000	£4,000	£2,000
2½ Litre Sports	2496/4	1950-53	£18,000	£15,000	£7,000

Lincoln

1928 Lincoln Limousine 6.3 litre,
V8 cylinder, side valve, cast iron
block and cylinder heads, 6300cc,
bore 88.9mm, stroke 127mm, 90bhp
at 2,800rpm, Stromberg 03
updraught carburettor, multi-disc
plate clutch, 3 speed manual
gearbox, spiral bevel live rear axle,
rigid pressed steel chassis frame
with cross members, 4 door, 7 seater
limousine coachwork, forged front
axle beam suspension, semi-elliptic
transverse leaf springs, lever arm,
hydraulic shock absorbers,
transverse rear semi-elliptic leaf
springs, radius arms, live rear axle,
4 wheel drum brakes, 20in five-stud
wire spoke wheels, 20 x 7.00in
tyres, wheelbase 3,654mm.
Est. **£20,000-25,000**   *C*

Liver Benz

1897 Liver Benz, 1050cc,
1 cylinder, 3½hp, only one known to
exist.
£50,000+   *SL*

*Liver Benz was a British-built Benz
made in Liverpool by the William
Lea Motor Company Ltd. Using a
genuine Benz engine they had a
British-built chassis and body
closely following the Benz design.*

Locomobile

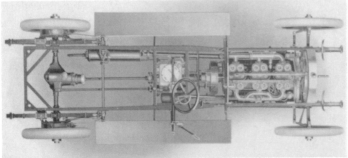

**1912 Locomobile Model 38
Chassis,** 6 cylinder, 60hp, bronze
crank case, 7 main bearings,
4 speed selective transmission,
bronze gear case, multiple 43 disc
clutch, drive shaft through bevel
gears and live axles, half-elliptic
front springs, three-quarter
elliptical rear, full floating rear
axle, 36in artillery wheels,
wheelbase 128in, 36 x 4.5in tyres.
Est. **£22,000-25,000**   *S(NY)*

Detail of the striped bonnet of the **1966 AC Cobra 427.**

1966 AC Cobra 427 Two Seater Sportscar, with Ford V8 overhead valve water-cooled engine, bore 107.7mm, stroke 90.62mm, 6997cc, 4 speed manual gearbox, live rear axle, wheelbase 96in, tyres 8.15 x 14in. Est. **£150,000-160,000** *S(M)*

1902 Arrol-Johnston 12hp Six Seat Dog Cart, with rear mounted flat twin, opposed piston, water-cooled engine, bore 108mm, stroke 165mm, 12hp, 4 speed gearbox, inverted tooth chain final drive, transmission braking and spoon brakes to solid tyred rear wheels, full-elliptic leaf front springs, semi-elliptic leaf rear springs, 32in front and 38in rear wheels. **£32,000-35,000** *S*

Detail of the left side and back of **1902 Arrol-Johnston 12hp Six Seat Dog Cart.**

1962 Alfa Romeo Giulietta Sprint Zagato Coupé, with coachwork by Zagato, 4 cylinder in line engine, water-cooled, twin overhead camshaft, bore 74mm, stroke 75mm, 1290cc, 5 speed gearbox, single dry plate clutch, hypoid bevel rear axle, independent coil spring front and rear suspension, wheelbase 94in. Est. **£90-100,000** *S(M)*

1930 Aston Martin 1½ Litre International Two Seater Sports, with coachwork by E. Bertelli Ltd., Feltham, 4 cylinder in line, water-cooled monobloc, overhead camshaft, bore 69.3mm, stroke 99mm, 11.9hp, 1495cc, 4 speed and reverse gearbox, final drive by shaft and worm drive, dry sump lubrication, wheelbase 102in. Est. **£60,000-65,000** *S*

Detail of the driving column and dashboard of **1924 Bentley 3 Litre.**

1962 Aston Martin DB4 Series 4 Sports Saloon, with 6 cylinder in line engine, water-cooled monobloc, twin overhead camshafts, bore/stroke 92mm, 3670cc, 4 speed gearbox, hypoid bevel final drive.
Est. **£30,000-35,000** *S*

1924 Bentley 3 Litre Tourer, with coachwork by Pearce, after Vanden Plas, 4 cylinder, water-cooled monobloc engine, single overhead camshaft, 4 valves per cylinder, bore 80mm, stroke 149mm, 2996cc, 4 speed gearbox, right hand change, inverted cone clutch.
Est. **£80,000-120,000** *S*

1931 Bentley 4 Litre Sports Saloon, with coachwork by H. J. Mulliner, 6 cylinder in line, water-cooled monobloc engine, inlet over side exhaust valve, bore 85mm, stroke 115mm, 26.8hp, 3915cc, 4 speed 'F' type gearbox, single dry plate clutch, spiral bevel final drive, 4 wheel brakes.
Est. **£80,000-90,000** *S*

1924 Bentley 3 Litre Tourer, with 4 cylinder in line engine, water-cooled monobloc, single overhead camshaft, 4 valves and twin plugs per cylinder, bore 80mm, stroke 149mm, 2996cc, 4 speed gearbox with right hand change, inverted cone clutch, underslung semi-floating rear axle, wheelbase 117½in. Est. **£70,000-80,000** *S*

1923 Bentley 3 Litre Speed Model Vanden Plas Tourer, with 4 cylinder in line, water cooled monobloc engine, overhead camshaft, bore 80mm, stroke 149mm, 2996cc. **£85,000-100,000** *S*

1925 Bentley 3 Litre Tourer, with 4 cylinder in line engine, water-cooled monobloc, single overhead camshaft, 4 valves and twin plugs per cylinder. Est. **£75,000-90,000** *S*

1956 Bentley SI Continental Two Door Coupé, with coachwork by Park Ward, 6 cylinder, water-cooled monobloc engine, with pushrod operated overhead inlet and side exhaust valves actuated by camshaft, bore 3¾in, stroke 4½in, 4887cc, 4 speed automatic gearbox. **£34,000-36,000** *S*

1927 Bentley 6½ Litre Fixed Head Sportsman's Coupé, with coachwork by Park Ward, 6 cylinder in line, water-cooled monobloc engine, overhead valves, bore 100mm, stroke 140mm, 6597cc, 4 valves per cylinder, single plate clutch, 4 speed manual gearbox, right hand gate change, shaft drive to live rear axle, semi-elliptic leaf spring suspension front and rear, wheelbase 152½in. Est. **£220,000-250,000** *S*

1952 Bentley Mark VI Four Door Sports Saloon, with coachwork by H. J. Mulliner Ltd., F-head engine, bore 3⅝in, stroke 4½in, 4566cc, 4 speed gearbox with synchromesh on 2nd, 3rd and top, single dry plate clutch, wheelbase 120in, 16in tyres. Est. **£13,000-16,000** *S*

1928 Bentley 6½ Litre Weymann Sports Saloon, with coachwork by Freestone and Webb, 6 cylinder, water-cooled monobloc engine, non-detachable head, single overhead camshaft, 4 valves per cylinder, bore 100mm, stroke 140mm, 6597cc, single plate clutch, 4 speed gearbox with right hand change. Est. **£185,000-200,000** *S*

1931 Bentley 8 Litre Sports Saloon, with coachwork by Thrupp & Maberly, 6 cylinder, overhead camshaft, water-cooled monobloc engine, bore 110mm, stroke 140mm, 7983cc, 2 sparking plugs per cylinder, 3 carburettors, 4 speed and reverse 'F' type gearbox, single plate clutch, hypoid bevel rear axle, cooling by pump and fan, wheelbase 157in, tyres 7.0 x 21in. Est. **£100,000-150,000** *S*

179

1931 Bentley 8 Litre Two Seater 'Boat Tail' Sports, with coachwork by Smith & Cave, Blandford Forum, Dorset, 6 cylinder in line, water-cooled engine, single overhead camshaft, bore 110mm, stroke 140mm, 7983cc, 4 valves per cylinder, twin SU carburettors, F type 4 speed and reverse gearbox, right hand change, single plate clutch, semi-elliptic leaf spring suspension with hydraulic shock absorbers to rear, wheelbase 156in. Est. **£220,000-250,000** *S*

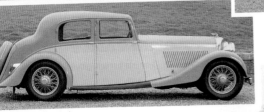

1937 Bentley 4¼ Litre Sports Saloon, with coachwork by Park Ward, 6 cylinder in line, water-cooled monobloc engine, bore 89mm, stroke 114mm, 4257cc. **£25,000-30,000** *S*

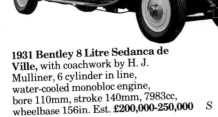

1931 Bentley 8 Litre Sedanca de Ville, with coachwork by H. J. Mulliner, 6 cylinder in line, water-cooled monobloc engine, bore 110mm, stroke 140mm, 7983cc, wheelbase 156in. Est. **£200,000-250,000** *S*

1934 Bentley 3½ Litre Two Seater Drop-head Coupé, with coachwork by Hooper, 6 cylinder in line, water-cooled monobloc engine, pushrod operated overhead valves, bore 3¼in, stroke 4½in, 3669cc, 4 speed gearbox with right hand change, single dry plate clutch, hypoid bevel rear axle, semi-elliptic leaf spring suspension, wheelbase 126in, 5.50 x 18in tyres. Est. **£65,000-85,000** *S*

Further detail of the **1934 Bentley 3½ Litre,** showing its fully overhauled engine.

1928 Bugatti Type 37A Grand Prix Two Seater, with 4 cylinder in line, water-cooled monobloc engine, single overhead camshaft, supercharged bore 69mm, stroke 100mm, 1496cc, 4 speed gearbox, multi-plate clutch, bevel rear axle, semi-elliptic leaf front springs, quarter-elliptic rear, tyres 19in.
£195,000-215,000   *S*

1937 Bugatti Type 57 Three Position Sports Cabriolet, with coachwork by Mylord, 8 cylinder in line, water-cooled engine, cast in 2 blocks of 4, overhead valve, bore 72mm, stroke 100mm, 3257cc, 4 speed manual gearbox, shaft drive to live rear axle, wheelbase 330mm, tyres 550 x 18in.
£180,000-200,000   *S(M)*

1956 Ferrari Boano 250 GT Coupé, with coachwork designed by Pinin Farina, built by Carrozzeria Boano, V12 60° Colombo, overhead camshaft, water-cooled engine, bore 73mm, stroke 58.8mm, 2953cc, triple Weber carburettors, 4 speed gearbox, single dry plate clutch, 6.50 x 16in tyres.
Est. **£160,000-180,000**   *S(M)*

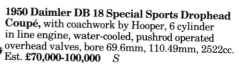

1950 Daimler DB 18 Special Sports Drophead Coupé, with coachwork by Hooper, 6 cylinder in line engine, water-cooled, pushrod operated overhead valves, bore 69.6mm, 110.49mm, 2522cc.
Est. **£70,000-100,000**   *S*

The first registered owner was H.M. King George VI.

1952 Bentley Mk VI Series N Two Door Drophead Coupé, with coachwork by Park Ward, 6 cylinder in line, water-cooled monobloc engine, pushrod operated inlet valves, side exhaust valves, bore 92.1mm, stroke 114.3mm, 4566cc, 4 speed manual and reverse gearbox, wheelbase 120in, 16in tyres. Est. **£55,000-60,000**   *S*

1965 Ferrari 500 Superfast Coupé, with coachwork by Pinin Farina, V12 cylinder, water-cooled monobloc engine, single overhead camshaft per bank, bore 88mm, stroke 68mm, 4963cc, single dry plate clutch, 4 speed manual gearbox with overdrive, spiral bevel gear live axle, wheelbase 2,650mm.
Est. **£200,000-240,000**   *S(M)*

Detail of the steering wheel and dashboard of the **1925 Frazer Nash Super Sports Two Seater.**

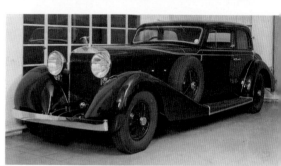

1934 Hispano-Suiza Type 56 8 Litre Pillarless Four Door Sports Saloon, with 6 cylinder in line, water-cooled monobloc engine, overhead camshaft, non-detachable cylinder head, 2 valves per cylinder, bore 100mm, stroke 140mm, 7983cc, single updraught carburettor, single dry plate clutch, 3 speed gearbox, spiral bevel live rear axle, semi-elliptic leaf springs front and rear, wheelbase 3,690mm, 7.00 x 17in tyres.
£63,000-70,000   *S*

1925 Frazer Nash Super Sports Two Seater, with 4 cylinder in line, water-cooled monobloc engine, overhead valve, bore 69mm, stroke 100mm, 1496cc, 3 speed gearbox, plate clutch, chain final drive, leaf spring suspension front and rear. **£30,000-40,000**   *S(M)*

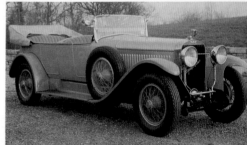

1925 Hispano-Suiza H6 32CV Dual Cowl Seven Seat Tourer, with coachwork by Million Guiet, Paris, 6 cylinder in line, water-cooled monobloc engine, bore 100mm, stroke 140mm, 6597cc, dual coil ignition. **£120,000-130,000**   *S*

1972 Ferrari Dino 246 GT Berlinetta, with V6 cylinder, water-cooled engine, double overhead camshaft, bore 92.5mm, stroke 60mm, 2418cc, 5 speed gearbox, independent coil spring front and rear suspension. **£38,000-45,000**   *S(M)*

1932 Hispano-Suiza Type 64 Close-Coupled Fixed Head Coupé, with coachwork attributed to Balthasar Fiol, Spain, 6 cylinder in line, overhead camshaft, water-cooled monobloc engine, bore 90mm, stroke 120mm, 4581cc, 3 speed and reverse gearbox, centre change, multiple clutch, spiral bevel rear axle, semi-elliptic leaf springs front and rear.
£65,000-75,000   *S*

1955 Jaguar XK 140 Roadster, with 6 cylinder, water-cooled monobloc engine, twin overhead camshafts, bore 83mm, stroke 106mm, 3442cc, 4 speed manual gearbox plus overdrive, independent front suspension by torsion bars, semi-elliptic leaf spring rear with telescopic shock absorbers, live rear axle, wheelbase 102in, 16in tyres.
Est. **£60,000-75,000**   *S(M)*

1953 Jaguar XK 120 Roadster, with 6 cylinder in line, water-cooled monobloc engine, twin overhead camshaft, bore 83mm, stroke 106mm, 3442cc, 160bhp at 5,000rpm, dry plate clutch, 4 speed manual synchromesh gearbox, wheelbase 102in, 6.00 x 16in tyres.
Est. **£40,000-50,000**   *S(M)*

'L'Aventure', A Unique and Historically Important Prototype French Road Vehicle, c1882, with a metal and wooden chassis, canvas body panels, metal 'coal scuttle' nose, rear wheel block brake, sliding 'piston' treadles connected to rear cam axle, foot rests and rear wooden box, together with some original body panels and spare parts.
Est. **£8,000-12,000**   *S*

1921 Lanchester 40hp Four Door Seven Seat Tourer, 6 cylinder engine, set in threes, vertical overhead valve, overhead camshaft, bore 4in, stroke 5in, 6.2 litre, 3 speed epicyclic and reverse gearbox, single plate clutch shaft and worm final drive, wheelbase 150in, 895 x 135mm tyres.
Est. **£28,000-30,000** *S*

1961 Jaguar E-Type 3.8 Roadster, with 6 cylinder in line, water-cooled monobloc engine, twin overhead camshafts, bore 87mm, stroke 106mm, 3781cc, 4 speed gearbox, single dry plate clutch, hypoid bevel rear axle, independent front and rear suspension, wheelbase 96in, 15in tyres.
Est. **£30,000-40,000** *S(M)*

1934 Lagonda M 45 T7 Tourer, with 6 cylinder in line, water-cooled monobloc engine, overhead valve, bore 88.5mm, stroke 120mm, 4467cc, 4 speed gate change gearbox, single dry plate clutch, spiral bevel rear axle, semi-elliptic leaf spring suspension front and rear, 129in wheelbase, 5.25/5.50 x 19in tyres.
£52,000-55,000 *S*

1955 Maserati A6GCS Sports Racing Two Seater, with 6 cylinder in line, water-cooled engine, twin overhead camshaft, bore 76.5mm, stroke 72mm, 1986cc, 4 speed gearbox with synchromesh on 3rd and top, remote control gearshift, independent coil spring and wishbone front suspension with Houdaile hydraulic shock absorbers and anti-roll bar, quarter-elliptic leaf rear springs.   Est. **£150,000-160,000** *S*

1955 Maserati 300S Sports Racing Car, with 6 cylinder in line, water-cooled monobloc engine, twin overhead camshaft, overhead valve, bore 84mm, stroke 90mm, 2992.5cc, 4 speed rear mounted transaxle, dry multi-plate clutch, bevel drive rear axle, independent front suspension by unequal length double wishbones and coil springs with hydraulic shock absorbers, wheelbase 2,310mm. Est. **£500,000-650,000**   *S(M)*

The first of only 29 **Maserati 300S Sports Cars,** this car won more championship points than any other 300S and was driven by Moss, Fangio, Musso, Villoresi, Perdisa and Valenzano.

Detail of the **1966 Maserati Mistral Four Litre Spyder,** showing dashboard, steering wheel and bonnet.

1966 Maserati Mistral Four Litre Spyder, 6 cylinder twin overhead camshaft, water-cooled monobloc engine, bore 86mm, stroke 106mm, 4000cc, 5 speed manual gearbox, live rear axle, independent coil spring front, semi-elliptic leaf spring rear, with telescopic shock absorbers front and rear. Est. **£55,000-65,000**   *S(M)*

1955 Maserati 300S Sports Racing Car, one of a team of 3 cars campaigned by the Cunningham team and the first official Works Team Car achieving an illustrious history and enjoying a reputation for endurance, quality of engineering and excellent handling characteristics.

Detail showing the boot of the **1954 Mercedes-Benz 220 A,** containing a matching set of luggage.

1954 Mercedes-Benz 220 A Cabriolet, with 6 cylinder in line, water-cooled monobloc engine, single overhead camshaft, overhead valve, bore 80mm, stroke 72.8mm, 2195cc, single dry plate clutch, 4 speed gearbox, hypoid bevel final drive, independent front and rear suspension, wheelbase 2,845mm, 15in tyres. Est. **£38,000-42,000**   *S(M)*

1977 Mercedes-Benz 450 SLC Factory Race Team Car, with V8 cylinder, water-cooled engine, overhead camshaft, 3 speed automatic gearbox, bevel rear axle, independent front and rear suspension, 210/595 x 15in tyres. Est. **£40,000-50,000** *S(M)*

1914 Peugeot Bébé 6hp Cyclecar, with 4 cylinder in line, water-cooled monobloc, side valve, bore 55mm, stroke 90mm, 856cc, 2 speed gearbox, shaft drive to live rear axle, semi-elliptic front spring suspension, quarter-elliptic spring rear suspension, wheelbase 60in, 550 x 65mm tyres. **£13,000-15,000** *S(M)*

1958 Mercedes-Benz 300 SL Sports Roadster, with 6 cylinder in line, water-cooled monobloc engine, overhead camshaft, bore 85mm, stroke 88mm, 2996cc, 4 speed manual gearbox, single dry plate clutch, bevel rear axle, independent coil spring front and rear suspension. Est. **£140,000-160,000** *S(M)*

1957 Mercedes-Benz 300 SL Sports Roadster, with 6 cylinder in line, water-cooled monobloc engine, overhead camshaft, bore 85mm, stroke 88mm, 2996cc, bevel rear axle, independent coil spring front and rear suspension, wheelbase 94.6in, 15in tyres. Est. **£155,000-165,000** *S(M)*

1923 Rolls-Royce 40/50hp R Series Silver Ghost Limousine, with coachwork by Maythorn & Son Ltd. Biggleswade, Beds, 6 cylinder, in 2 groups of 3, engine, side valves operated by single camshaft, through rocking levers, non-detachable cylinder heads, bore/stroke 4½in. Est. £45,000-50,000 *S*

1923 Rolls-Royce 20hp Barrel Sided Tourer, with coachwork in the style of Barker, 6 cylinder in line, water-cooled monobloc engine, pushrod operated overhead valves, bore 3in, stroke 4½in, 3127cc, 3 speed centre change gearbox, single dry plate clutch, wheelbase 129in. £51,000-60,000 *S*

1910 Rolls-Royce Silver Ghost 40/50hp Double Pullman Limousine, with coachwork by S & A Fuller Ltd., of Bath, 6 cylinder, in blocks of 3, side valve, water-cooled, bore 4½in, stroke 4¾in, 7428cc, 3 speed gearbox, cone clutch, open propeller shaft, spiral bevel rear axle, semi-elliptic front, three-quarter elliptic rear springs. Est. £400,000-500,000 *S*

1920 Rolls-Royce 40/50hp Silver Ghost Drophead Coupé, with coachwork by Dansk Karossarywagan, 6 cylinder in line, cast in threes, water-cooled, side valve engine, bore 4½in, stroke 4¾in, 7428cc, 4 speed, right hand change gearbox, cone clutch, enclosed shaft spiral bevel rear axle, semi-elliptic leaf spring front suspension, cantilever rear springs. £45,000-50,000 *S*

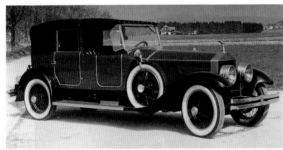

1926 Rolls-Royce 40/50hp Silver Ghost Town Car, with coachwork by Belvallette, 6 cylinder in line, 2 blocks of 3, side valve, water-cooled engine, bore 4½in, stroke 4¾in, 7428cc, 3 speed centre change gearbox, cone clutch, wheelbase 144in, 7.00 x 21in tyres. Est. **£88,000-94,000** *S(M)*

Detail of the engine of **1926 Rolls-Royce 40/50hp Silver Ghost Town Car.**

1932 Rolls-Royce Phantom II 40/50hp Series N2 Continental Sports Saloon, with coachwork by Park Ward, 6 cylinder in line, 2 groups of 3, overhead valve, water-cooled, bore 108mm, stroke 139.7mm, 7668cc, magneto and coil ignition, 4 speed and reverse, right hand change gearbox, single plate clutch, hypoid final drive, semi-elliptic springs front and rear suspension, with hydraulic dampers, wheelbase 144in. Est. **£50,000-55,000** *S*

1927 Rolls-Royce 20hp Landaulette, with coachwork by Park Ward, 6 cylinder in line, water-cooled monobloc engine, overhead valve, bore 82mm, stroke 114.3mm, 3669cc, 4 speed right hand change gearbox, single dry plate clutch, spiral bevel rear axle, semi-elliptic leaf springs front and rear. **£40,000-45,000** *S*

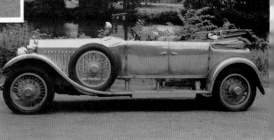

1926 Rolls-Royce Phantom I Series V 40/50hp All Weather Cabriolet, with coachwork by H. J. Mulliner, 6 cylinder, in 2 groups of 3, with one-piece detachable cylinder head, water-cooled, pushrod operated overhead valves, bore 5½in, stroke 4¼in, 7668cc, 4 speed and reverse gearbox, single dry plate clutch, enclosed propeller shaft to live rear axle, spiral bevel final drive, semi-elliptic front springs, cantilever rear suspension, 7.00 x 21in tyres. **£75,000-85,000** *S*

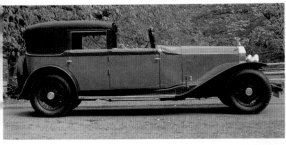

1929 Rolls-Royce Phantom II Series J2 40/50hp Sedanca de Ville, with coachwork by Hibbard & Darrin, Paris, 6 cylinder, in 2 blocks of 3, overhead valve, water-cooled engine, bore 108mm, stroke 139.7mm, 7688cc, 4 speed and reverse right hand change gearbox, hypoid bevel final drive, semi-elliptic front and rear springs, wheelbase 150in, 7.00 x 21in tyres. Est. **£45,000-50,000**   *S*

1935 Rolls-Royce 40/50hp Phantom II Series S2 Continental Saloon, with coachwork by Park Ward, 6 cylinder in line, 2 groups of 3, water-cooled, pushrod operated overhead valves, bore 4¼in, stroke 5½in, 7668cc, 4 speed and reverse gearbox, single dry plate clutch, 19in wheels. Est. **£48,000-50,000**   *S*

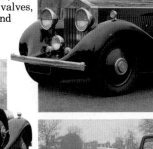

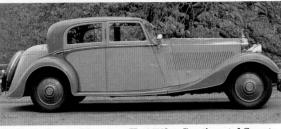

1933 Rolls-Royce Phantom II 40/50hp Continental Sports Saloon, with coachwork by Thrupp & Maberly, 6 cylinder in line, water-cooled engine, with pushrod operated overhead valves, bore 4¼in, stroke 5½in, 7668cc, 4 speed gearbox, single dry plate clutch, hypoid bevel fully floating rear axle, wheelbase 144in, 21in tyres. Est. **£70,000-75,000**   *S*

1936 Rolls-Royce 20/25hp Series K2 Two Door Drophead Coupé, with coachwork by Windovers, 6 cylinder in line, water-cooled monobloc engine, pushrod operated overhead valves, bore 3¼in, stroke 4½in, 3669cc, 4 speed and reverse right hand change gearbox, single dry plate clutch, spiral bevel final drive, semi-elliptic leaf spring front and rear suspension, wheelbase 121in, 6.00 x 19in tyres, electrically operated hood, in good overall condition. Est. **£30,000-40,000**   *S*

1958 Rolls-Royce Silver Cloud I Series B Saloon, with coachwork by Freestone and Webb Ltd., 6 cylinder in line, water-cooled monobloc engine, pushrod operated inlet valves, side exhaust valves, bore 3¾in, stroke 4½in, 4887cc, automatic transmission shaft drive to hypoid bevel differential and semi-floating half shafts, independent front suspension by wishbone, coil spring and hydraulic damper, semi-elliptic rear with electrically controlled damper and anti-roll bar. Est. £30,000-32,000 *S*

1932 Rolls-Royce Phantom II 40/50hp Series 02 Continental Touring Sports Saloon, with coachwork by Barker & Co., London, 6 cylinder in line, 2 blocks of 3, water-cooled engine, pushrod operated overhead valves, bore 4¼in, stroke 5½in, 7668cc, 4 speed and reverse gearbox, single dry plate clutch, hypoid bevel fully floating rear axle, semi-elliptic leaf spring suspension front and rear, wheelbase 144in, 21in tyres. Est. £38,000-42,000 *S*

1968 Shelby Mustang GT-500 KR Cabriolet, with V8 cylinder, water-cooled engine, overhead valve, bore 4.13in, stroke 3in, 6774cc, 3 speed automatic transmission, bevel rear axle, independent coil spring front, semi-elliptic leaf rear spring suspension, wheelbase 108in. This 2 door cabriolet is one of 318 built in 1968, the modified 428cu in engine developed to 400bhp, it underwent an 8 year restoration programme during the 1980s and since has taken part successfully in European rallies, including the Austrian Alpine Event, its total mileage from new is only 31,000, 1,000 or so since restoration, in excellent running order, and offered with Austrian papers. Est. £20,000-24,000 *S(M)*

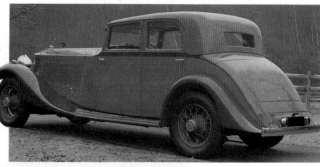

1912 Unic Model J2 10/12hp Torpedo Spyder, with coachwork by Carrosserie Automobile A.Minot, Paris, 4 cylinder, side valve, water-cooled monobloc engine, bore 65mm, stroke 110mm, 1300cc, 3 speed sliding pinion gearbox, semi-elliptic front springs, three-quarter elliptic rear, live axle, wheelbase 103in, 710 x 90 tyres. The Unic Model J2 was built at the Puteaux factory of Georges Richard, and has been fully restored in the USA by John W. Ironside of Massachusetts to a very high standard but retaining the original coachwork, this open 2 seater with dickey seat has been fully authenticated and dated by the Veteran Car Club of GB's Dating Committee.
£20,000-22,000   S

SOTHEBY'S
FOUNDED 1744

34-35 New Bond Street, London W1A 2AA
Telephone: 071-493 8080   Telex: 24454 (SPBLON·G)   Telefax: 071-409 3100

IMPORTANT, EARLY, HISTORIC AND CLASSIC MOTOR VEHICLES, AUTOMOBILIA AND AUTOMOBILE ART

FORTHCOMING SPECIALIST SALES 1992

March 30th 1992	Important, Early, Historic and Classic Motor Vehicles and Automobilia to be held at The Royal Air Force Museum, Hendon
April 26th 1992	Early and Classic Motorcycles at the International Classic Bike Show, Stafford
May 9th 1992	Veteran, Vintage and Classic Motor Vehicles and Automobilia to be held at The Royal Air Force Museum, Hendon
June 13th 1992	Rolls-Royce and Bentley Motor Cars and related Material at the Rolls-Royce Enthusiasts Club Annual Rally
June 29th 1992	Important, Early, Historic and Classic Motor Vehicles and Automobilia to be held at The Royal Air Force Museum, Hendon
October 24th 1992	Veteran, Vintage and Classic Motor Vehicles and Automobilia to be held at The Royal Air Force Museum, Hendon
November 28th 1992	Early and Classic Motorcycles to be held at The Royal Air Force Museum, Hendon
November 30th 1992	Important, Early, Historic and Classic Motor Vehicles and Automobilia to be held at The Royal Air Force Museum, Hendon

1929 Stutz Model M 36.4hp Four Door Sports Saloon, with coachwork by Lancefield, straight 8 cylinder, water-cooled monobloc engine, overhead camshaft, bore 85.7mm, stroke 114.3mm, 5274cc, Detroit 4 speed gearbox, Delco duplicated coil ignition, single dry plate clutch, semi-elliptic springs front and rear, wheelbase 145in. This car was found derelict in the early 60s, restoration begun but not completed, was stored away until 1986 when the present owner commenced restoration, now complete, and recently has covered 4,000 miles in rallies. The car comes with old style log book.
Est. **£38,000-45,000**   S

1915 Vauxhall D Type 25hp Army Staff Car
with 4 cylinder in line, water-cooled
monobloc engine, side valve, bore
95mm, stroke 140mm, 3964cc, 4 speed gearbox,
disc clutch, bevel rear axle, semi-elliptic
leaf springs front and rear, wheelbase 132in,
880 x 120mm tyres. This car has been used
for transporting many members of the Royal
family and is fitted with a black duck
hood, full side screens and an Auster rear
screen. It has been dated by The Veteran Car
Club of GB.
£40,000-50,000 *S*

A further view of the **1915 D Type
25hp Army Staff Car,** this model
was produced at the rate of
8 per week to the order of the
War Office during World War I.

**1909 Vulcan Model 35hp Open Drive Single
Landaulette,** with 6 cylinder in line, in
pairs, water-cooled engine, side valve,
T-head, bore 102mm, stroke 120mm, 5883cc,
3 speed gate change gearbox, cone clutch,
shaft drive to live rear axle, 815 x 135mm
beaded edge tyres. This vehicle has been
restored by H. F. Welham of Surbiton,
retaining originality in all major respects,
rear compartment is furnished with occasional
seats and original deep buttoned leather
upholstery, a speaking tube communicates
with the driver who is separated by a
curved glass division from the rear
passengers. Est. **£35,000-45,000** *S*

A rear and side view of the **1911 White Model
GA 30hp Torpedo Tourer,** showing its superb
brass fittings, included are a full lighting
set, oil and acetylene, and a folding brass
frame windscreen.

**1911 White Model GA 30hp Torpedo
Tourer,** with 4 cylinder in line,
water-cooled monobloc engine,
side valve, bore 3¾in, stroke 5⅛in,
30hp, 4 speed gearbox, cone clutch,
shaft drive to bevel rear axle,
semi-elliptic leaf spring front
suspension, three-quarter elliptic
rear, wheelbase 110in, 32 x 4in
tyres, right hand drive, in good
mechanical condition.
Est. **£26,000-30,000** *S*

Lombard

1927 Lombard/Salmson Grand Prix, Salmson 1100cc engine, unknown French coachbuilder, wheelbase 95in.
£23,000-25,000   *PMc*

Lotus

1962 Lotus Elite Climax, restored,
original Coventry Climax engine,
twin Weber carburettors fitted.
£25,000-27,000   *KSC*

1959 Lotus Elite Series 1, Coventry Climax engine, 1.2 litre, overhead valve, 4 cylinders, 4 speed gearbox. **£22,000-25,000**   *S(NY)*

1968 Lotus 7 Series 3, unrestored. **£9,000-11,000**   *CA*

1963 Lotus 7 SII Cosworth, original engine tuned by Jack Brabham Engineering in the 1960s, one owner from new, very rare original example. **£17,500-18,500**   *KSC*

1963 Lotus Elan.
£9,500-10,000 *CA*

1964 Lotus Elan S1, total restoration.
£16,000-18,000 *KSC*

1966 Lotus Elan S3/SE, fixed head coupé, with replacement chassis, resprayed, original fittings.
£14,000-15,000 *KSC*

1969 Lotus Elan Series 4/SE, restored, only 17,000 miles.
£16,000-17,000 *KSC*

1969 Lotus Elan S4, 1558cc, 4 cylinders.
Est. **£10,000-11,000**   *ADT*

1972 Lotus Elan Sprint Drophead,
replacement galvanised chassis, rebuilt engine, original condition.
£16,000-17,000   *KSC*

1972 Lotus Elan Sprint Drophead,
new galvanised chassis,
rebuilt engine,
Lenham hardtop,
original interior.
£16,000-17,000
KSC

1972 Lotus Elan 130/5,
excellent condition,
33,000 miles.
£10,000-11,000
AUT

1971 Lotus Elan 130.
£6,000-7,000   *AUT*

1968 Lotus Cortina, by Crayford, 1558cc, 4 cylinders.
£1,750-2,000 *ADT*

Cross Reference
Ford Lotus Cortina

Miller's is a price GUIDE not a price LIST

1972 Lotus Europa Twin Cam, original alloy wheels.
£9,000-10,000 *KSC*

1972 Lotus Europa Twin Cam, rebuilt on a Spyder space frame chassis.
£9,000-10,000 *KSC*

1973 Lotus Europa Twin Cam Special,
5 speed gearbox, new suspension, original alloy wheels.
£12,000-13,000 *KSC*

1973 Lotus Europa Twin Cam Special, 5 speed gearbox, new chassis, original factory alloy wheels.
£12,000-13,000 *KSC*

1973 Lotus Europa Twin Cam Special, 5 speed gearbox.
£12,000-13,000 *KSC*

LOTUS

1980 Lotus Esprit S2.2, leather interior, good condition.
£9,000-10,000 *KSC*

Less than 50 of this model were produced.

1982 Lotus Esprit Turbo, leather interior, air conditioning.
£12,000-13,000 *KSC*

1985 Lotus Esprit S3, leather interior, glass targa sunroof.
£11,000-12,000 *KSC*

1985 Lotus Esprit Turbo, leather interior, air conditioning, glass targa sunroof.
£16,000-17,000 *KSC*

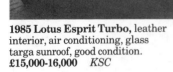

1985 Lotus Esprit Turbo, leather interior, air conditioning, glass targa sunroof, good condition.
£15,000-16,000 *KSC*

1985 Lotus Esprit S3, leather interior, glass targa sunroof, 'turbo' side sills.
£12,000-13,000 *KSC*

1985 Lotus Esprit Turbo, leather interior, air conditioning, glass Targa sunroof.
£15,000-16,000 *KSC*

1987 Lotus Esprit Turbo HC, leather interior, air conditioning, glass sunroof.
£18,000-19,000 *KSC*

Now becoming collectable.

1986 Lotus Esprit Turbo, leather interior, air conditioning, glass Targa sunroof.
£16,000-17,000 *KSC*

1985 Lotus Excel SIII, leather interior, power assisted steering, air conditioning. **£7,500-8,500** *KSC*

1988 Lotus Esprit Turbo, leather interior, air conditioning and full width glass sunroof, 26,000 miles.
£18,000-19,000 *KSC*

Maserati

1959 Maserati 3500 GT, restoration project.   £15,000-15,500   *CA*

Make: **Maserati**
Model: 3500GT/GTI
Type: Coupé/Convertible
Years Manufactured: 1957-64
Quantity: 2,223
Engine Type: Double overhead camshaft 6 cyl
Size: 3485cc
Max Power: GT/GTI, 220/235 bhp @ 5500/5800 rpm
Max Torque: GT/GTI, 253/261 ft/lb @ 3500/4000 rpm
Transmission: 4 speed manual; 5 speed manual optional 1960; standard from 1961
Wheelbase: Coupé, 102in; Spyder, 100in
Performance: Max speed: 140 mph; 0-60: 8.1 secs.

1961 Maserati 3500 GT Coupé, 3485cc.   Est. £20,000-22,000   *HA*

1963 Maserati 3500 GT, fuel injection, left hand drive. **£22,000-23,000**   *AUT*

1968 Maserati Ghibli Coupé, 90° V8 cylinder engine, water-cooled, twin overhead camshafts per bank, bore 93.9m, stroke 85mm, 4719cc, 5 speed manual ZF gearbox, single dry plate clutch, hypoid bevel rear axle, independent coil spring front suspension, leaf springs and hydraulic shock absorbers at rear, wheelbase 2,550mm, 215/70 x 15in tyres, original factory specification, one owner.
Est. **£30,000-35,000**   *S(M)*

1969 Maserati Mexico Sports Coupé, V8 engine, 4 overhead camshafts, water-cooled, bore 93.9mm, stroke 85mm, 4719cc, 5 speed ZF gearbox, single dry plate clutch, front suspension coil spring and hydraulic shock absorbers, rear suspension semi-elliptic leaf spring with hydraulic shock absorbers, wheelbase 2,640mm, 215 x 70 VR15 tyres.
£9,000-11,000   *S*

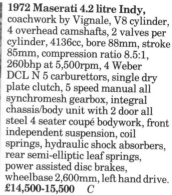

1972 Maserati 4.2 litre Indy, coachwork by Vignale, V8 cylinder, 4 overhead camshafts, 2 valves per cylinder, 4136cc, bore 88mm, stroke 85mm, compression ratio 8.5:1, 260bhp at 5,500rpm, 4 Weber DCL N 5 carburettors, single dry plate clutch, 5 speed manual all synchromesh gearbox, integral chassis/body unit with 2 door all steel 4 seater coupé bodywork, front independent suspension, coil springs, hydraulic shock absorbers, rear semi-elliptic leaf springs, power assisted disc brakes, wheelbase 2,600mm, left hand drive.
£14,500-15,500   *C*

Maserati Ghibli.
£60,000-65,000   *S8*

1975 Maserati Merak 3 litre, V6 cylinder, 2965cc, bore 91.6mm, stroke 75mm, 4 overhead camshafts, compression ratio 8.75:1, 190bhp at 6,000rpm, 5 speed manual gearbox, single dry plate clutch, 4.357:1 final drive ratio with LSD, independent wishbones and coil spring suspension front and rear, telescopic shock absorbers, anti-roll bar, 4 wheel disc brakes, hydraulic power assisted with dual master cylinder, 15in Compagnolo cast light alloy wheels with 205 VR x 15in tyres on rear and 185 VR x 15in on front, right hand drive.
Est. **£20,000-25,000**   *C*

1975 Maserati Merak Sports Coupé.
Est. **£18,000-22,000**   *S*

The engine was similar to that which had been used in the Citroën SM, itself the result of the Citroën take-over of Maserati in 1968. Of medium capacity, the Merak engine was classic Italian high performance automotive engineering at its best and 190 (DIN) horse power was produced from the 4 cam engine.

1975 Maserati Khamsin.   **£30,000-32,000**   *S8*

1974 Maserati Bora, manual gearbox, left hand drive, good condition.
£10,000-11,000   *PC*

1978 Maserati Khamsin V8, totally original condition.
£20,000-22,000   *Cen*

Make: **Maserati**
Model: Khamsin
Type: Coupé
Years Manufactured: 1973-82
Quantity: 421
Price when new: £12,929
Engine Type: V8 cyl
Size: 4930cc
Max Power: 320 bhp @ 5500 rpm
Max Torque: 354 ft/lb @ 4000 rpm
Transmission: 5 speed or auto
Wheelbase: 100.3in
Performance: Max speed: 160 mph; 0-60: 8.1 secs; Mpg: 14.

1977 Maserati Khamsin 4.9 litre, original right hand drive.
£30,000-32,000   *FOR*

One of only 400 cars ever built.

1979 Maserati Merak SS, 2965cc, superb condition.
£19,000-20,000   *HA*

Maserati Karif.
£25,000-26,000   *FOR*

Maserati's fastest road car since the Bora.

Maserati Biturbo, 27,000 miles.
£13,000-13,500   *FOR*

Maserati Merak SS, rebuilt.
£35,000-36,000   *FOR*

Only 243 of these cars were built.

Mercedes-Benz

1908 35hp Mercedes-Benz Shaft-Drive Tourer.
£50,000-55,000   *PMc*

This is a low production edition, shaft-driven car, as opposed to the more common chain and gear operated vehicles, like the French Grand Prix winner.

Shaft drives were manufactured en masse at a much later time, but in 1908 this touring car was one of a mere handful of experimental models.

1952 Mercedes W194 SLR, wheelbase 94½in.
£420,000-450,000   *PMc*

Of the 11 Works race cars scheduled to be built during 1952, only ten were actually constructed, and this model is chassis number 6. 194/6 has a clearly documented racing history: Le Mans, Nurburgring, Carrera Pan Americana and the Mille Miglia. According to factory records it finished 4th at the Nurburgring sporting an alloy roadster body and was a test car, or DNF, at other races.

1956 Mercedes-Benz 300SL Gullwing Coupé, 6 cylinder in line, 2966cc, bore 85mm, stroke 88mm, single overhead camshaft, 2 valves per cylinder operated by rocker arms, compression ratio 8.55:1, 240bhp at 6,100rpm, Bosch direct fuel injection, dry sump lubrication, cast-iron block, detachable light alloy cylinder head, 4 speed all synchromesh manual gearbox in unit with engine, single dry plate clutch, direct acting central gearchange, open propeller shaft to chassis-mounted hypoid bevel final drive with limited slip differential, separate multi-tube spaceframe with coupé bodywork and 2 gullwing doors, steering wheel hinged for access to driving seat, front independent coil spring suspension and swing axles, telescopic shock absorbers, 4 wheel hydraulically operated drum brakes, vacuum servo-assisted Alfin drums, 15in pressed steel wheels, 6.70 x 15in tyres, wheelbase 94½in, left hand drive.
£149,000-151,000   *CNY*

1955 Mercedes-Benz 300SL Gullwing.
£170,000-190,000   *PiK*

1956 Mercedes-Benz 300SL Gullwing, coachwork by Daimler Benz Ag, Stuttgart, totally original. £167,000-170,000   *C(M)*

1956 Mercedes-Benz 300SL Gullwing Coupé. Est. £160,000-120,000   *S(NY)*

The roadster engine developed some 250hp from its Bosch fuel injected engine and offered smooth top gear acceleration from 15mph to its maximum top speed. All roadsters enjoyed the benefit of the sports camshaft.

1960 Mercedes-Benz 300SL Roadster, 6 cylinder in line, water-cooled, overhead camshaft, overhead valve, bore 85mm, stroke 88mm, 2996cc, 4 speed gearbox, single dry plate clutch, hypoid bevel rear axle, independent front suspension with coil springs and parallel wishbone arms, single joint swing axle, coil springs, shock absorbers with compensating springs at rear, wheelbase 94½in, 15in tyres. £110,000-112,000   *S(M)*

Make: **Mercedes-Benz**
Model: 190SL
Type: Sports
Years Manufactured: 1954-63
Quantity: 25,881
Engine Type: Overhead camshaft 4 cyl
Size: 1897cc
Max Power: 105 bhp @ 5700 rpm
Max Torque: 105 ft/lb @ 3200 rpm
Transmission: 4 speed
Wheelbase: 94.5in
Performance: Max speed: 105+ mph; 0-60: 13.3-14.5 secs.

1960 Mercedes-Benz 190SL, 1897cc, 4 cylinders. £11,500-12,500   *ADT*

1964 Mercedes 230 SL Sports. £12,500-13,500 *HA*

The Pagoda-top 230SL heralded a new age in luxury sports cars. Its ability to become either a hard-topped coupé or an exciting open-topped roadster gave the car great appeal because of its flexibility. Produced from 1963 to 1967 nearly 20,000 left the Stuttgart factory. The 2.3 litre engine was fuel-injected and gave the car 120mph performance.

1964 Mercedes-Benz 230SL Coupé, overall good example. Est. **£14,000-15,000** *S*

Make: **Mercedes-Benz**
Model: 230SL/250SL/280SL
Type: Coupé/Convertible
Years Manufactured: 1963-71
Quantity: 19,831
Price when new: 250SL, £3,414
Engine Type: 6 cyl
Size: 2306cc/2496cc/2778cc
Max Power: 150-170 bhp
Transmission: 4 speed, 5 speed or auto
Wheelbase: 94.5in
Performance: Max speed: 280SL, 121 mph; 0-60: 280SL, 9.3 secs; Mpg: 280SL, 19.

Introduced in 1963 the 230SL typified the thoroughness of Mercedes-Benz research and development under Rudolph Ullenhaut.

1966 Mercedes-Benz 230SL, 6 cylinder in line water-cooled, overhead camshaft, bore 82mm, stroke 72.8mm, 2306cc, automatic 4 speed gearbox, independent suspension front and rear by coil springs, wheelbase 94½in, 185HR14 tyres. **£11,500-12,500** *S*

1969 Mercedes 280SL Sports. £14,000-18,000 *BLE*

Mercedes-Benz 280SL, rebuilt, right hand drive. **£25,000-26,000** *FOR*

1968 Mercedes-Benz 280SL Coupé Convertible.
£11,500-12,500   *S*

1967 Mercedes-Benz 250SL Coupé, 6 cylinder in line water-cooled monobloc, single overhead camshaft, bore 82mm, stroke 72.8mm, 2496cc, 4 speed automatic gearbox, hypoid bevel final drive, independent front and rear suspension, wheelbase 94½in, 16in tyres.
£16,750-17,500   *S*

1959 Mercedes 220S Station Wagon, Belgian coachbuilder, unrestored condition, running.
£1,000-1,200   *PMc*

This example is built on the 6 cylinder, 2 carburettor sport chassis, all other examples are on the 4 cylinder 219 chassis.

1960 Mercedes-Benz 300D Four Door Convertible, 6 cylinder in line, cast iron block, single overhead camshaft, overhead valves, 2996cc, bore 85mm, stroke 88mm, compression ratio 8.5:1, 160bhp at 5,700rpm, Bosch fuel injection, torque converter 3 speed automatic gearbox, open propeller shaft, hypoid bevel rear axle, tubular steel cruciform structure chassis with 4 door drophead convertible bodywork, independent front and rear suspension, with coil springs, wishbones, anti-roll bar and telescopic shock absorbers, divided rear axle, 4 wheel servo-assisted hydraulic drum brakes, 15in steel disc type wheels with 7.60 x 15in tyres, wheelbase 124in.
£81,000-83,000   *CNY*

MAKE Mercedes	ENGINE cc/cyl	DATES	CONDITION 1	2	3
300AD	2996/6	1951-62	£12,000	£10,000	£8,000
220A/S/SE Ponton	2195/6	1952-60	£7,500	£3,500	£1,800
220S/SEB Coupé	2915/6	1956-59	£9,000	£5,000	£3,500
220S/SEB Cabriolet	2195/6	1958-59	£22,000	£18,000	£7,000
190SL	1897/4	1955-63	£15,000	£12,000	£9,000
300SL 'Gullwing'	2996/6	1954-57	£140,000	£100,000	£70,000
300SL Roadster	2996/6	1957-63	£130,000	£90,000	£70,000
230/250SL	2306/				
	2496/6	1963-68	£13,000	£9,000	£7,000
280SL	2778/6	1967-71	£14,000	£10,000	£8,000
220/250SE	2195/				
	2496/6	1960-68	£8,000	£6,000	£3,000
300SE	2996/6	1961-65	£10,000	£8,000	£5,000
280SE Conv	2778/6	1965-69	£20,000	£16,000	£12,000
280SE V8 Conv	3499/8	1969-71	£25,000	£18,000	£15,000
280SE Coupé	2496/6	1965-72	£7,000	£4,000	£3,000
300SEL 6.3	6330/8	1968-72	£12,000	£7,000	£3,500
600 & 600 Pullman	6332/8	1964-81	£15,000	£10,000	£8,000

1959 Mercedes-Benz 300D Four Door Saloon, 6 cylinder overhead camshaft, water-cooled monobloc engine, bore 85mm, stroke 88mm, 2996cc, 4 speed automatic transmission, tubular cruciform frame, independent suspension, live rear axle, 7.60 x 15in tyres, wheelbase 124in, generally sound condition, original upholstery, chromium plating requires attention.
Est. **£10,000-12,000**   S

1965 Mercedes-Benz 220SE Convertible, 2200cc, 6 cylinders.
Est. **£15,000-20,000**   ADT

The 220 range of medium-sized cars was superseded in 1959 by the uprated and mechanically improved B models. Distinguished from their forebears by a wider radiator, and being 5in longer and lacking overriders, they now employed a safety cage and were introduced to the British market in right hand drive form in 1962.

1964 Mercedes-Benz 220SEB Cabriolet.
Est. **£22,000-26,000**   LF

1969 Mercedes-Benz 280SE Convertible, 2778cc, 6 cylinders, new automatic gearbox, new steering box, new suspension, new rear discs and callipers.
Est. **£20,000-23,000**   ADT

1971 Mercedes-Benz 280SE, 2778cc, 6 cylinders.
£975-1,250   ADT

1971 Mercedes-Benz 300SEL, 6329cc, 8 cylinders.
£4,700-5,200   ADT

1971 Mercedes-Benz 280SE 3.5 Convertible, front V8 cylinder, light alloy cylinder heads, cast iron block, single overhead camshaft, 3499cc, bore 92mm, stroke 65.8mm, compression ratio 9:1, 230bhp at 6,000rpm, Bosch fuel injection, automatic 4 speed gearbox, unitary construction pressed steel body/chassis with 2 door, 4 seater convertible bodywork, front and rear independent suspension with coil springs, wishbones and anti-roll bar, low pivot swing rear axle, telescopic hydraulic shock absorbers, 4 wheel servo assisted disc brakes, pressed steel disc wheels with 185 x 14in tyres, wheelbase 106in, extensively restored.
£60,000-65,000   *CNY*

1978 Mercedes-Benz 450SEL, 6.9 litres, hydropneumatic suspension, air-conditioning and steel sliding sun roof, generally good condition.
Est. £5,500-6,500   *HA*

Mercer

1921 Mercer, 6 cylinder, 5½ litre, staggered 2 seater raceabout.
£75,000-85,000   *SL*

Make the Most of Miller's

Veteran Cars are those manufactured up to 31 December 1918 although only vehicles built before 31 December 1904 are eligible for the London/Brighton Commemorative Run. Vintage Cars are vehicles that were manufactured between 1 January 1919 and 31 December 1930

Mercury

950 Mercury V8 4½ Litre Monterey Sedan, excellent original condition. **£8,000-10,000** *BC*

1940 Mercury DeLuxe Convertible, in very good condition. **£13,000-15,000** *KI*

Messerschmitt

958 Messerschmitt KR200 Cabriolet, with single cylinder ngine, 2 stroke, bore 65mm, stroke 8mm, 191cc, 4 speed gearbox with everse, multiple wet plate clutch, hain final drive to rear wheel, Neimann bonded rubber uspension, wheelbase 82in, 00 x 8in tyres. **£4,600-5,500** *S*

The 200cc engine gave the KR200 a top speed of around 60mph and despite appearances it was remarkably stable.

1959 FMR Messerschmitt Tiger 500 Roadster, with vertical twin cylinder Sachs engine, 2 stroke, rear mounted, air-cooled, 500cc, 4 speed gearbox, multiple plate clutch, chain drive to rear wheels, wheelbase 82in, 10in tyres. **£15,000-17,000** *S*

Messerschmitt took over the Fend-designed 'Bubble Car' in 1953 and production took place in a converted aircraft factory in Regensburg between 1953 and 1962. The first model was the KR 175, being replaced by the 200cc version in 1955 which was built until the company closed in 1962. The scooters were all equipped with Sachs engines, but the rarest of all models and the most interesting was the Tiger 500, a four-wheeled version built between 1958 and 1960.

1959 Messerschmitt KR200 Three Wheel Cabin Scooter, restored to highest concours standards. **£13,500-14,500** *S*

1960 Messerschmitt KR200 Cabin Scooter. **£7,800-8,400** *LF*

The designation KR is an abbreviation of 'Kabinenrollor' which translates as 'scooter with cabin'·

MG

1930 MG M-Type Midget Two Seater Sports, with 4 cylinder in line engine, water-cooled monobloc, overhead valves, overhead camshaft, bore 57mm, stroke 83mm, 847cc, 3 speed gearbox, multi-plate clutch, open shaft, spiral bevel drive, semi-elliptic leaf spring suspension front and rear, wheelbase 78in, 4.00 x 19in tyres, fully restored.
£11,500-13,500 S

Developed from the Morris Minor of 1928 the M-Type Midget was the first of a long line of Midgets to leave the Oxfordshire factory. The model distinguished itself on the race track in blown and unblown guise, however in standard production form was an agile sports car capable of 60mph. Its lightweight pointed tail coachwork was to be copied by other manufacturers and the M-Type was to continue in production until 1932.

1936 MG PB Midget Sports Two Seater.
Est. **£12,000-14,000** C

1937 MG TA, fully restored in 1985, condition 1.
£14,000-15,000 CC

1938 MG TA, mechanically very good, bodywork and interior in good condition.
£10,000-12,000 DG

MG

MAKE MG	ENGINE cc/cyl	DATES	CONDITION 1	2	3
14/28	1802/4	1924-26	£30,000	£25,000	£20,000
18/80 Mk I/Mk II	2468/4	1927-33	£45,000	£28,000	£20,000
M-Type Midget	847/4	1928-32	£12,000	£10,000	£8,000
J-Type Midget	847/4	1932-34	£15,000	£13,000	£10,000
J3 Midget	847/4	1932-33	£18,000	£14,000	£12,000
PA Midget	847/4	1934-46	£13,000	£10,000	£8,000
PB Midget	936/4	1935-36	£14,000	£10,000	£8,000
F Type Magna	1271/6	1931-33	£22,000	£18,000	£12,000
L Type Magna	1087/6	1933-34	£22,000	£16,000	£12,000
K1/K2 Magnette	1087/6	1932-33	£45,000	£40,000	£35,000
N Series Magnette	1271/6	1934-36	£40,000	£30,000	£20,000
TA Midget	1292/4	1936-39	£15,000	£12,000	£9,000
SA 2 litre	2288/6	1936-39	£22,000	£18,000	£15,000
VA	1548/4	1936-39	£12,000	£8,000	£5,000
TB	1250/4	1939-40	£15,000	£11,000	£9,000

Value will depend on body style, history, completeness, racing history, the addition of a supercharger and originality.

1946 MG TC, in condition 1 in all respects. **£13,500-14,500** *Mot*

1946 MG TC, with 4 cylinder, overhead valve, 1250cc engine, original bodywork and chassis, restored to a very good condition. **£19,000-20,000** *Ree*

1948 MG TC Midget, with 4 cylinder, 1250cc engine. Est. **£14,000-18,000** *ADT*

A rebuilt car is not necessarily of more value than a car in good original condition, even if the restoration has cost thousands of pounds.

1948 MG TC, good condition. **£14,000-15,000** *LF*

1950 MG TD Two Seater Sports, with 4 cylinder overhead valve, water-cooled monobloc engine, 1250cc, bore 66.5mm, stroke 90mm, 4 speed gearbox, independent front suspension, semi-elliptic leaf springs at rear, live rear axle, wheelbase 94in, 5.50 x 15in tyres. **£14,750-15,250** *S*

211

c1950 MG TD Two Seater Sports,
with 4 cylinder overhead valve,
water-cooled monobloc engine,
1250cc, bore 66.5mm, stroke 90mm,
4 speed gearbox, independent front
suspension, semi-elliptic leaf
springs at rear, live rear axle,
wheelbase 94in, 5.50 x 15in tyres,
left hand drive.
Est. **£9,000-10,000**   *S*

*The MG T Series was the lineal
successor to the M type Midget
introduced in 1929 and the
archetypal British sportscar.*

**1951 MG TD Midget Two Seater
Sports.**
£9,000-10,000   *S*

*When post-war car production was
resumed at Abingdon in 1946 the
popular Midget series was
represented by the TC, essentially a
derivative of the pre-war TB. Then in
1949 came the TD, an almost entirely
revised car designed largely by
Gerald Palmer who had also been
responsible for the MG Y type.*

1952 MG TD Two Seater Sports,
left hand drive.
£9,750-10,250   *DB*

1954 MG TF, unrestored.
£8,000-12,000   *PC*

*Beware of left hand drive
conversions.*

1952 MG TD, condition 2.
£10,000-11,000   *PA*

Condition Guide

1. *A vehicle in top class
   condition but not
   'concours d'elegance'
   standard, either fully
   restored or in very good
   original condition*
2. *A good, clean,
   roadworthy vehicle,
   both mechanically and
   bodily sound*
3. *A runner, but in need of
   attention, probably
   both to bodywork and
   mechanics. Must have
   current MOT*

1954 MG TF 1500.
£20,000-22,000   *LF*

1955 MG TF, 4 cylinder, 1250cc engine, originally exported in 1955, previously left hand drive, now thoroughly restored.
£12,000-13,000 *ADT*

1955 MG TF 1500 Two Seater Sports, 4 cylinder in line, 2 overhead valves per cylinder operated by pushrods from single block mounted camshaft, 1466cc, bore 72mm, stroke 90mm, compression ratio 8.3:1, 63bhp at 5,250rpm, twin SU downdraught carburettors, SU electric fuel pump, single dry plate clutch, 4 speed manual gearbox, hypoid bevel final drive, ladder type box section steel chassis, independent front suspension with wishbones, coil springs and telescopic shock absorbers, live rear axle with semi-elliptic leaf springs, telescopic shock absorbers, Lockheed drum brakes with twin leading shoes, 15in bolt-on steel disc wheels with 5.50 x 15in tyres, wheelbase 2,388mm, right hand drive.
£13,000-14,000 *C*

1956 MGA 1500 Roadster.
£7,500-8,000 *Cen*

1956 MGA 1500 Roadster, left hand drive USA import, cosmetically restored, rust-free, UK registered.
£5,250-5,750 *CCTC*

1956 MGA Roadster, left hand drive.
£8,000-8,500 *AUT*

1957 MGA 1500 Roadster, in excellent condition. £14,500-15,000 *WCC*

1958 MGA Roadster, with 4 cylinder, 1489cc engine, in excellent original condition, recently returned from South Africa.
Est. **£9,000-11,000** *ADT*

1958 MGA.
£6,000-7,000 *LF*

Make: **MG**
Model: A
Type: Sports, later also Coupé
Years Manufactured: 1489cc, 1955-59; 1588cc, 1959-61; 1622cc, 1961-62; twin cam, 1958-60
Price when new: 1489cc Sports, £844; twin cam Coupé, £1,357
Engine Type: Overhead valve 4 cyl, or twin cam 4 cyl
Size: 1489cc, 1588cc, 1622cc and 1588cc twin cam
Max Power: 1489cc, 72 bhp @ 5500 rpm; 1588cc, 80 bhp @ 5500 rpm; 1622cc, 86 bhp @ 5500 rpm; twin cam, 108 bhp @ 6700 rpm
Max Torque: 1489cc, 77 ft/lb @ 3500 rpm; 1588cc, 87 ft/lb @ 3800 rpm; 1622cc, 97 ft/lb @ 4000; twin cam, 104 ft/lb @ 4500 rpm
Transmission: 4 speed
Wheelbase: 94in
Performance: Max speed: 1489cc, 98 mph; 1588cc, 101 mph; 1622cc, 105 mph; twin cam, 114 mph; 0-60: 1489cc, 15.5 secs; 1588cc, 14.0 secs; 1622cc, 13.5 secs; twin cam, 13.0 secs; Mpg: 20-30.

1959 MGA Twin Cam, with 4 cylinder in line, twin overhead camshaft, 1588cc engine, bore 75.39mm, stroke 88.9mm, compression ratio 9.8:1, 108bhp at 6,700rpm, twin SU carburettors, 4 speed synchromesh manual gearbox, no synchromesh on 1st, live rear axle, separate steel chassis frame with 2 door steel roadster bodyshell and aluminium bonnet, doors and boot, rack and pinion steering, independent front suspension by coil springs and wishbones, half-elliptic leaf springs rear, 4 wheel Dunlop disc brakes, Dunlop centre lock wheels with 165 x 15in tyres, wheelbase 94in, left hand drive.
£10,500-12,500 *CNY*

1959 MGA 1600 Roadster, with 4 cylinder, overhead valve, 1588cc, 4 speed manual gearbox, left hand drive, in excellent condition throughout.
Est. **£9,000-12,000**   *C*

1965 MG Midget MkII, in average condition.
£1,500-2,500   *PC*

1961 MGA 1600 Roadster, with 4 cylinder, overhead valve, 1588cc, 4 speed manual gearbox, left hand drive.
£4,620-5,000   *C*

Miller's is a price GUIDE not a price LIST

1969 MG Midget.
£3,700-4,200   *LF*

1978 MG Midget, late rubber bumper model and Rostyle wheels, poor restoration and respray in 1980s.
£1,500-2,000   *C.A.R.S.*

1980 MG Midget Sports Roadster.
£3,500-3,750   *HA*

1964 MGB Roadster, with 4 cylinder, 1798cc engine.
£4,750-5,250   *ADT*

1965 MGB Sports Roadster, with 4 cylinder in line, water-cooled monobloc, 1798cc engine, pushrod operated overhead valve, bore 80.26mm, stroke 88.9mm, 4 speed and reverse gearbox, hypoid bevel final drive, front wheel disc brakes, drum rear, independent front suspension by coil springs and wishbones, half-elliptic rear, 15.5 x 14in tyres, completely restored and rebuilt.
£8,000-8,500 *S*

1966 MGB Roadster, after receiving a full mechanical and body restoration in 1990, most body panels replaced, now in condition 1.
£6,500-7,000 *Cen*

1967 MGB Roadster.
£8,500-9,000 *Cen*

> ### Did you know
> *MILLER'S Collectors Cars Price Guide builds up year by year to form the most comprehensive photo-reference system available*

1968 MGB MkII Roadster, overdrive and wire wheels.
£4,000-5,000 *PC*

1971 MGB, 4 cylinder, 1800cc engine, restored.
£5,600-6,000 *ADT*

Make: **MG**
Model: B
Type: Sports
Years Manufactured: 1962-80
Price when new: 1962-64, £950;
1964-67, £870
Engine Type: Overhead valve
4 cyl
Size: 1798cc
Max Power: 62-95 bhp @ 5400
rpm
Max Torque: 87-110 ft/lb @
3000 rpm
Transmission: 4 speed (auto
option 1967-73, overdrive
option 1963 on, standard 1975
on)
Wheelbase: 91in
Performance: Max speed: 105
mph; 0-60: 13.0 secs; Mpg: 26-30.

1971 MGB Roadster MkII, totally renovated.
£5,600-6,000 *LF*

1972 MGB V8 Roadster, 3.5 litre
V8 engine.
£6,750-7,500 *ADT*

1971 MGB, in very good condition, 50,000 miles recorded.
£8,000-8,500 *FOR*

1974 MGB Tourer, 1798cc engine,
built on B.M.H. body shell, all new
or reconditioned parts, chrome
wheels, black leather seats, as
original specification.
£8,100-8,600 *Hus*

217

1979 MGB Roadster, 4 cylinder, 1798cc engine.
£5,000-6,000   *ADT*

1967 MGC GT Lightweight Race Car.
Est. **£15,000-20,000**   *S(NY)*

Encouraged by the success of the B, MG's design office at Abingdon decided to pursue the idea of a 'new generation' Healey 3000. Displayed at the 1967 Motor Show, the new MGC featured a 3 litre, 145hp BMC engine which produced tremendous low-end torque. In spite of this power, however, the MGC was not a sales success and production was discontinued in 1969.

1968 MGC GT, in concours condition.
£9,000-10,000   *SC*

1968 MGB GT, in unrestored original condition.
£2,000-2,500   *PC*

Make: **MG**
Model: C
Type: Sports
Years Manufactured: 1967-69
Quantity: 8,999
Price when new: £1,257
Engine Type: Overhead valve 6 cyl
Size: 2912cc
Max Power: 145 bhp @ 5250 rpm
Max Torque: 170 ft/lb @ 3400 rpm
Transmission: 4 speed or auto, overdrive optional from 1968
Wheelbase: 91in
Performance: Max speed: 120+ mph; 0-60: 10.0 secs; Mpg: 20-27.

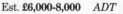

1968 MGC GT, 6 cylinder, 2912cc engine.   Est. **£6,000-8,000**   *ADT*

1969 MGC GT, 6 cylinder, 2912cc engine, totally rebuilt to original specification.
Est. **£7,000-8,000**   *ADT*

1968 MGC GT, 6 cylinder, 2912cc engine, totally rebuilt. £7,500-8,000 *ADT*

1973 MGB GT, 4 cylinder, 1798cc engine.
£3,000-3,500 *ADT*

1973 MGB GT.
£6,000-6,500 *SC*

MAKE MG	ENGINE cc/cyl	DATES	CONDITION 1	2	3
TC	1250/4	1946-49	£15,000	£11,000	£7,000
TD	1250/4	1950-52	£13,000	£9,000	£5,000
TF	1250/4	1953-55	£17,000	£13,000	£8,000
TF 1500	1466/4	1954-55	£18,000	£14,000	£9,000
Ser. YA/YB	1250/4	1947-53	£5,500	£2,750	£1,500
Magnette ZA/ZB	1489/4	1953-58	£3,000	£2,000	£500
Magnette Mk III/IV	1489/4	1958-68	£2,500	£850	£350
MGA 1500	1489/4	1955-59	£9,000	£6,500	£3,500
MGA 1500 FHC	1489/4	1956-59	£7,000	£5,000	£3,000
MGA 1600	1588/4	1959-61	£11,000	£9,000	£4,500
MGA 1600 FHC	1588/4	1959-61	£7,000	£5,000	£3,000
MGA Twin Cam	1588/4	1958-60	£17,000	£12,000	£9,000
MGA Twin Cam FHC	1588/4	1958-60	£14,000	£9,000	£7,000
MGA 1600 Mk II	1622/4	1961-62	£12,000	£10,000	£4,000
MGA 1600 Mk II FHC	1622/4	1961-62	£9,000	£7,000	£3,000
MGB Mk I	1798/4	1962-67	£7,000	£4,000	£1,200
MGB GT Mk I	1798/4	1965-67	£5,000	£3,500	£1,000
MGB Mk II	1798/4	1967-69	£7,500	£4,000	£1,500
MGB GT Mk II	1798/4	1969	£4,500	£2,500	£850
MGB Mk III	1798/4	1969-74	£7,500	£4,000	£1,100
MGB GT Mk III	1798/4	1969-74	£4,500	£2,500	£1,000
MGB Roadster (rubber)	1798/4	1975-80	£6,000	£4,500	£1,200
MGB GT	1798/4	1975-80	£4,000	£3,000	£1,000
MGB Jubilee	1798/4	1975	£6,000	£3,000	£1,200
MGB LE	1798/4	1980	£8,500	£4,750	£2,250
MGB GT LE	1798/4	1980	£6,000	£3,750	£2,000
MGC	2912/6	1967-69	£8,000	£6,500	£4,000
MGC GT	2912/6	1967-69	£6,000	£4,500	£2,000
MGB GT V8	3528/8	1973-76	£8,250	£6,000	£3,000
Midget Mk I	948/4	1961-62	£4,000	£2,000	£850
Midget Mk II	1098/4	1962-66	£3,000	£2,000	£850
Midget Mk III	1275/4	1966-74	£3,200	£2,000	£850
Midget 1500	1491/4	1975-79	£3,000	£2,000	£850

All these prices are for British right hand drive cars. Deduct 10-15% for left hand drive varieties even if converted to right hand drive.

1976 MGB GT, Webasto
sunroof.
£1,500-2,000   *SCC*

1975 MGB GT, new leather interior.
£4,000-4,500   *FOR*

1973 MGB GT V8.
£5,500-6,500   *PC*

1975 MGB GT V8, 8 cylinder,
3520cc engine.
£2,000-2,500   *ADT*

1976 MGB GT V8, 4 cylinder, 3250cc engine.
£5,100-5,500   *ADT*

Miller's is a price Guide not a price List

*The price ranges given
reflect the average price a
purchaser should pay for
similar vehicle. Condition,
rarity, provenance, racing
history, originality and
any restoration are factors
that must be taken into
account when assessing
values. When buying or
selling, it must always be
remembered that prices
can be greatly affected by
the condition of any
vehicle. Unless otherwise
stated, all cars shown in
Miller's are of good
merchantable quality, and
the valuations given
reflect this fact. Vehicles
offered for sale in
exceptionally fine
condition or in poor
condition may reasonably
be expected to be priced
considerably higher or
lower respectively than
the estimates given herein*

Make: **MG**
Model: B GT V8
Type: Fixed Head Coupé
Years Manufactured: 1973-76
Quantity: 2,591
Price when new: 1973-74, £2,294
Engine Type: Overhead valve V8
Size: 3528cc
Max Power: 137 bhp @ 5000 rpm
Transmission: 4 speed plus overdrive
Performance: Max speed: 125 mph; 0-60: 8.6 secs; Mpg: 20-27.

1976 MGB GT V8, 8 cylinder, 3520cc engine.
Est. **£7,000-8,000**   *ADT*

1978 MGB GT V8,
4500cc engine, Super B bodykit, 365bhp, top speed 170mph.
£20,000-21,000   *SC*

Built as a design and PR exercise.

1937 MGA SA Two Litre Sports Saloon, with 6 cylinder in line, water-cooled monobloc engine, 2288cc, pushrod operated overhead valves, bore 69.5mm, stroke 102mm, twin SU carburettors, 4 speed gearbox, synchromesh and reverse, single plate clutch, open shaft spiral bevel rear axle, semi-elliptic leaf spring suspension, wheelbase 123in, 18in tyres, requires minor cosmetic attention.
£8,750-9,250   *S*

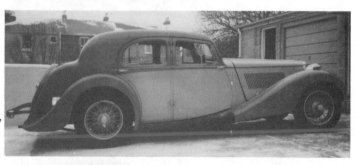

1951 MG YA, in all round excellent condition.
£6,000-6,500   *CC*

1950 MG YA Saloon.
£4,500-5,000   *WCC*

1956 MG Magnette Varitone,
4 cylinder, 1489cc engine.
£3,550-4,000   *ADT*

1957 MG Magnette ZB Varitone.
£5,500-6,000   *WCC*

Make: **MG**
Model: Magnette ZA/ZB
Type: Saloon
Years Manufactured: ZA,
1953-56; ZB, 1956-58
Price when new: £914
Engine Type: Overhead valve
4 cyl
Size: 1489cc
Max Power: ZA, 60 bhp @ 4600
rpm; ZB, 68 bhp @ 5250 rpm
Transmission: 4 speed
Performance: Max speed: ZA, 85
mph; ZB, 90 mph; 0-60: ZA, 22.5
secs; ZB, 18.5 secs; Mpg: 28-32.

1969 MG 1300, 4 cylinder, 1275cc
engine.
£1,200-1,500   *ADT*

Moon

1920 Moon 20HP Six Touring, 6 cylinder in line, cast iron monobloc
detachable head, overhead valves by pushrod, 3208cc, bore 79mm,
stroke 108mm, compression ratio 5:1, 60bhp at 4,000rpm, single
carburettor, magneto ignition, single dry plate clutch, 3 speed manual
gearbox with central gear lever, spiral bevel live rear axle, steel frame
channel section side members with pressed and tubular cross bracing,
4 door, 4 seater open touring coachwork, front beam axle suspension,
semi-elliptic leaf springs, rear semi-elliptic leaf springs underset the
chassis frame, live axle, cantilever shock absorbers, rear wheel only
mechanical drum brakes, 32in centre lock wire spoke wheels with
detachable flange rims, 32 x 4in tyres, plus 2 spare wheels,
wheelbase 122in.
£10,000-12,000   *CNY*

Joseph W. Moon was one of five Ohio
farming brothers who, at the age of
21, were given a horse, a saddle and
a bridle to make their own way in the
world. Joseph Moon made his way to
St. Louis, Missouri, where he set
himself up in the buggy business and
in 1905 introduced his first car, a
Model A 4 cylinder 30/35hp model
promoted as 'The Ideal American
Car'. Four cylinder engines were
replaced by 6 cylinder in 1913 as a
38hp Tourer and remained that
configuration thereafter. The Moon
was, in fact, an assembled car using
Rutenber, Falls and Continental
engines and other proprietary
components. The total assembly
produced a high quality, refined
motor car boasting such refinements
by the early 20s as demountable rims
on detachable wheels, balloon tyres
and Lockheed hydraulic brakes. The
various body styles ranging from
Sport Runabout, Torpedo Tourers to
De-luxe Sedans were well recognised
by their distinctive square
Rolls-Royce look-alike radiator with
crescent moon designed mascot.

Morgan

1925 Morgan 8hp Two Seat Grand Prix Tourer, Anzani V-twin overhead valve, water-cooled engine, 8hp, 2 speed gearbox, chain final drive, sliding pillar front suspension.
£10,000-11,000   *S*

The first Morgan Runabout was produced in prototype form in 1909 by H. F. S. Morgan and was exhibited initially at The Olympia Motorcycle Show in November 1910 as a single seater. The public responded with a demand for a 2 seater as well as for a proven competition record. Morgan provided both and by 1912 had captured the Cyclecar Trophy. During WWI Morgan produced munitions and with these successful government contracts Morgan was able to provide new machinery to develop cars with the onset of peacetime. The Grand Prix, Aero and Family models followed together with greater competition successes.

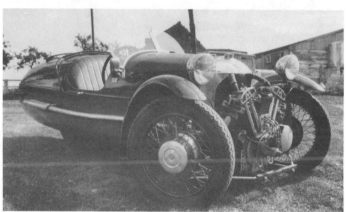

1935 Morgan 1000cc Super Sports Two Seater, V-twin 50° Matchless overhead valve engine, water-cooled, 998cc, 4 stroke, single plate clutch, chain final drive, vertical coil spring, 18in Dunlop Magna wheels.   **£12,500-13,500**   *S*

1930 Morgan Super Aero 1000cc Sports Three Wheeler, excellent condition.
£10,500-11,000   *S*

1928 Morgan Super Sports Aero Two Speed Three Wheeler, JAP 10/40hp, racing body, fully restored.
£12,000-15,000   *C.A.R.S.*

Make: **Morgan**
Model: 4/4
Type: Drop head Coupé, Sports
Years Manufactured: 1946-63
Price when new: Drop head
Coupé (1956), £684
Engine Type: Overhead valve
4 cyl
Size: 1267cc, 1340cc and other
engines used
Max Power: 1267cc, 39 bhp @
4300 rpm
Transmission: 3 speed manual
to 1960, then 4 speed
Wheelbase: 96in
Performance: Max speed:
1267cc, 75 mph; 1340cc, 80+
mph; 0-60: 1267cc, 25.0 secs;
1340cc, 18.5 secs; Mpg: 25-32.

1948 Morgan SI 4/4, 1267cc, 4 cylinder, manual transmission.
£11,500-12,500   *WH*

1938 Morgan Series I 4/4, T.T.
racing replica with Coventry
Climax engine, fully restored.
£15,000-18,000   *C.A.R.S.*

1951 Morgan 4/4 Two Seater,
Standard Vanguard engine, sports
wheels with twin spars, flat radiator
model, fully restored.
£15,000-18,000   *C.A.R.S.*

*A rebuilt car is not
necessarily of more value
than a car in good original
condition, even if the
restoration has cost
thousands of pounds.*

1969 Morgan 4/4, 1599cc, 4 cylinders.   **£6,750-7,000**   *ADT*

1961 Morgan 4/4 Series II Drophead Coupé, Ford 100E engine, 4 cylinders, cowelled
radiator, wire wheels, fully restored in 1980s.   **£16,000-18,000**   *C.A.R.S.*

MAKE Morgan	ENGINE cc/cyl	DATES	CONDITION		
			1	2	3
4/4 Series I	1098/4	1936-50	£11,000	£9,000	£6,000
Plus 4	2088/4	1950-53	£12,000	£9,000	£7,000
Plus 4	1991/4	1954-68	£12,000	£10,000	£8,000
4/4 Series II/III/IV	997/4	1954-68	£8,000	£6,000	£3,000
4/4 1600	1599/4	1960 on	£11,000	£9,000	£6,000
Plus 8	3528/8	1969 on	£18,000	£13,500	£10,000

1990 Morgan 4/4 Two Seater, Ford CVH 1600cc engine, with 5 speed gearbox, 95bhp at 5,750rpm. **£16,000-18,000** *BHM*

1959 Morgan +4 Two Seater, Triumph TR3 engine, 1991cc, 100bhp at 5,000rpm. **£15,000-50,000** *BHM*

1984 Morgan 4/4 Two Seater, aluminium body, wire wheels, leather upholstery. **£10,000-12,000** *C.A.R.S.*

1952 Morgan Series I +4 Drophead Coupé, Standard Vanguard 2088cc engine, flat radiator, restored with new leather upholstery, chromework, paintwork and double duck hood. **£18,000-20,000** *C.A.R.S.*

1962 Morgan +4 Two Seater Drophead Coupé, TR4 engine, 2138cc, 100bhp at 4,600rpm.
£35,000-40,000   *BHM*

Make: **Morgan**
Model: Plus 8
Type: Sports
Years Manufactured: 1968 to date
Quantity: Still in production
Price when new: £1,510
Engine Type: Overhead valve V8
Size: 3528cc
Max Power: 143 bhp @ 5000 rpm to 190 bhp @ 5200 rpm; injection, Sept 1984 on, 190 bhp @ 5280 rpm
Max Torque: 202 ft/lb @ 4700 rpm to 220 ft/lb @ 4000 rpm
Transmission: 4 speed, 5 speed from Oct 1976
Wheelbase: 98in
Performance: Max speed: 124 mph; Injection, 126 mph; 0-60: 6.7 secs; Injection, 6.0 secs; Mpg: 19-25.

1991 Morgan +8, Rover V8 3.9 litre engine, fuel injection system, 190bhp at 4,750rpm.   **£28,000-30,000**   *BHM*

1986 Morgan +4, Fiat 2 litre engine, standard steel body, wire wheels, leather upholstery,excellent condition
£16,000-18,000   *C.A.R.S.*

1990 Morgan +4 Four Seater, Rover 2 litre engine, chrome wire wheels, aluminium body and wings, leather upholstery, double duck hood, excellent condition.
£20,000-21,000   *C.A.R.S.*

1986 Morgan 4/4, 1600cc, aluminium body and wings.
£9,000-10,000   *C.A.R.S.*

Morris

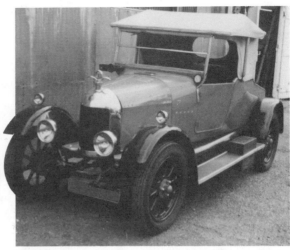

1927 Morris Cowley Four Seater Tourer, running and partly restored, needs painting, trim and nickel, hood.
£6,500-7,000 *Mot*

1924 Morris Cowley Two Seater with Dickey.
£12,000-13,000 *DB*

| MAKE | ENGINE | DATES | CONDITION | | |
Morris	cc/cyl		1	2	3
Prices given are for saloons					
Cowley	1550/4	1913-26	£9,000	£8,000	£6,000
Cowley	1550/4	1927-39	£8,000	£6,000	£4,000
14/28 Oxford	1803/4	1924-33	£10,000	£8,000	£6,000
16/40	2513/4	1928-33	£8,000	£7,000	£6,000
18	2468/6	1928-35	£9,000	£7,000	£5,000
8 Minor	847/4	1929-34	£5,500	£4,000	£2,000
10/4	1292/4	1933-35	£5,000	£3,000	£1,500
25	3485/6	1933-39	£10,000	£8,000	£5,000
Eight	918/4	1935-39	£4,000	£3,000	£1,500
10hp	1140/4	1939-47	£4,500	£3,000	£1,500
16hp	2062/6	1936-38	£5,000	£3,500	£2,000
18hp	2288/6	1935-37	£5,000	£3,500	£2,500
21hp	2916/6	1935-36	£6,000	£4,000	£2,500

A touring version of the above is worth approximately 20% more and price is very dependent on body type and has an increased value if coachbuilt.

The early Bullnose Morris cars, first equipped with White and Poppe engines, later with Continental and finally with the Hotchkiss engine, had earned a justifiable reputation for durability and economy during the 1913 to 1926 period and it was with some reluctance that the company abandoned the bullnose radiator for the 1927 season in favour of the more fashionable flatnose radiator design. The new car retained most of the characteristics of its predecessors, front wheel braking was now standard and Morris shock absorbers assisted a smooth ride.

1928 Morris Cowley 11.9hp Two Seater with Dickey, 4 cylinder in line, water-cooled monobloc engine, 1550cc, side valve, bore 69.5mm, stroke 102mm, 3 speed gearbox, cork inset multi-plate clutch, spiral bevel final drive, semi-elliptic leaf spring suspension front and rear, wheelbase 105in, 19in tyres, requires recommissioning following a period of museum display.
£9,000-10,000 *S*

1926 Bullnose Morris Cowley Two Seater with Dickey, calorimeter, spare wheel, petrol can, battery box, hood and side screens. **£10,000-11,000** *RBB*

1929 Morris Cowley Four Seater Tourer, 4 cylinder, 1548cc engine.
£9,000-9,500 *ADT*

1929 Morris Cowley, condition 1.
£10,500-11,000 *CC*

1929 Morris Oxford Sportsman's Coupé, 6 cylinder, 1928cc engine. Est. **£9,000-11,000** *ADT*

The only known survivor of this particular body style.

1929 Morris Cowley Domed Coupé, all original New Zealand car. Est. **£7,000-9,000** *LF*

1929 Morris Cowley Tw Seater with Dickey, condition 2.
£8,000-8,500 *Mot*

1930 Morris Cowley, condition 1.
£8,900-9,200 *CC*

1931 Morris Cowley 11.9hp Folding Head Saloon, with 4 cylinder in line, water-cooled engine, 1550cc, side valve, bore 69.5mm, stroke 102mm, 3 speed gearbox, cork inset plate clutch, spiral bevel final drive, semi-elliptic leaf spring suspension front and rear, wheelbase 105in, 29 x 5in tyres, extensively restored.
£9,500-10,000   S

The range of 1931 Morris cars displayed at the Olympia Motor Exhibition in 1930 included the Minor, the Cowley, the Major, the Oxford Six and the Isis Six, a wide range indeed from a manufacturer battling with Austin for the lucrative share of the first time car buyer market. The 11.9hp Cowley had earned its colours first in famous Bullnose guise and the new Flatnose design appeared for the 1927 season cars. Nickel fittings had given way to chrome plating by 1931 and the front and rear bumpers reflected contemporary fashion and some American influence. The patent folding head operated on a neat scissor action and gave the Cowley a dual role as saloon or semi-open car, an interesting transition to the sliding sunshine roofs later adopted.

1930 Morris Minor, with overhead camshaft engine, condition 1.
£5,500-6,500   PA

1933 Morris Minor Saloon, 4 cylinder, 847cc engine, manual gearbox, in good running order.
£3,500-3,750   WH

1934 Morris Minor, 4 cylinder, 804cc engine, manual gearbox, restored to showroom condition, opening windscreen, luggage rack and the traditional Morris winged calorimeter.
£6,250-6,750   WH

Introduced by Morris Motors in 1928 the Minor, in its original overhead valve form, was aimed at the lucrative small car market in which Herbert Austin had already achieved some considerable success. The later side valve version in saloon form was competitively priced at £122.10s.0d in 1932 and offered lively performance living up to its advertising slogan 'Built like a big car'.

1934 Morris 10/4 Special Coupé, condition 1.
£7,500-8,000   C

1936 Morris 8, condition 1.
£3,600-4,000   *CC*

Introduced in September 1934 to replace the Minor, the new Morris 8 had a slightly longer stroke engine with a capacity of 918cc. It competed with the Austin 7hp and 10hp cars and was offered in 2 and 4 door saloon versions and also in Open Tourer form as a 2 or 4 seater.

1938 Morris 8 Four Door Saloon, condition 1.
£3,800-4,200   *PA*

1937 Morris 10, condition 2.
£2,700-3,000   *CC*

1938 Morris 8 Four Door Saloon, in need of restoration.
£1,500-1,750   *DB*

1939 Morris 8 Series E Saloon.
£3,000-4,000   *WCC*

Make: **Morris**
Model: Oxford
Type: Saloon
Years Manufactured: 1954-58 (Series II, III, IV)
Price when new: £745
Engine Type: Overhead valve 4 cyl
Size: 1489cc
Max Power: 50 bhp @ 4200 rpm; Series III (from 1956), 53 bhp @ 4350 rpm
Transmission: 4 speed
Performance: Max speed: 75 mph; Series III, 80 mph; 0-60: 25.0+ secs; Mpg: 28-32.

1954 Morris Oxford, condition 3, needing further restoration.
£450-550   *Mot*

MAKE Morris	ENGINE cc/cyl	DATES	CONDITION 1	2	3
Minor Series MM	918/4	1948-52	£1,800	£1,000	£300
Minor Series MM Conv	918/4	1948-52	£3,250	£1,500	£650
Minor Series II	803/4	1953-56	£1,500	£850	£300
Minor Series II Conv	803/4	1953-56	£3,000	£2,000	£650
Minor Series II Est	803/4	1953-56	£2,500	£1,000	£350
Minor 1000	948/4	1956-63	£1,750	£925	£250
Minor 1000 Conv	948/4	1956-63	£3,000	£2,000	£750
Minor 1000 Est	948/4	1956-63	£2,000	£1,200	£350
Minor 1000	1098/4	1963-71	£2,000	£950	£250
Minor 1000 Conv	1098/4	1963-71	£3,500	£2,250	£750
Minor 1000 Est	1098/4	1963-71	£3,000	£1,200	£400
Cowley 1200	1200/4	1954-56	£1,675	£1,000	£300
Cowley 1500	1489/4	1956-59	£1,750	£950	£350
Oxford MO	1476/4	1948-54	£2,000	£850	£250
Oxford MO Est	1476/4	1952-54	£3,000	£1,500	£350
Series II/III	1489/4	1954-59	£2,000	£1,200	£300
Series II/III/IV Est	1489/4	1954-60	£2,250	£1,350	£250
Oxford Series V Farina	1489/4	1959-61	£1,800	£800	£250
Oxford Series VI Farina	1622/4	1961-71	£1,750	£750	£200
Six Series MS	2215/6	1948-54	£2,500	£1,500	£500
Isis Series I/II	2639/6	1955-58	£2,500	£1,300	£450
Isis Series I/II Est	2639/6	1956-57	£2,600	£1,350	£500

The Sir Alec Issigonis inspired 2 door, 4 seater Morris Minor MM saloon was introduced in October 1948. The car was powered by the 28bhp, 918cc side valve engine with a 4 speed gearbox. From late 1952, following the merger with Austin, the Minor was fitted with the overhead valve 803cc engine from the Austin A30. From October 1956 the Minor was revised in Minor 1000 form receiving BMC's more robust and powerful 37bhp, 948cc A-series engine and at the same time replacing the split windscreen.

1956 Morris Minor, 4 cylinder, 948cc, manual gearbox, right hand drive, in good original condition. £2,000-2,500   *C*

> **Cross Reference**
> Commercial Vehicles

1968 Morris Minor Pick-Up, 4 cylinder, 1298cc, overhead valve engine, manual gearbox, right hand drive, in first-class condition. Est. £4,500-5,500   *C*

Make: **Morris**
Model: Minor 1000
Type: Saloon
Years Manufactured: 1948-71
Price when new: 1956, 948cc, £628
Engine Type: Side valve 4 cyl, overhead valve 4 cyl
Size: 918cc/803cc/948cc/1098cc
Max Power: 918cc, 28 bhp @ 4400 rpm; 803cc, 30 bhp @ 4800 rpm; 948cc, 37 bhp @ 4750 rpm; 1098cc, 48 @ 5100 rpm
Transmission: 4 speed
Performance: Max speed: 918cc, 60 mph; 803cc, 62mph; 948cc, 75 mph; 1098cc, 80 mph; 0-60: 803cc, 50.0+ secs; 948cc, 26.0+ secs; 1098cc, 24.0 secs;
Mpg: 38-43

1949 Morris Minor, 4 cylinder, 918cc engine. £3,300-3,500   *ADT*

1956 Morris Minor 1000, 805cc engine.
£3,000-3,250   *CA*

1968 Morris Minor 1000 Saloon, 1098cc engine, some work required
£500-700   *LAR*

1961 Morris Minor Convertible, 4 cylinder, 948cc engine, manual gearbox, in good running order throughout.
£2,400-2,600   *WH*

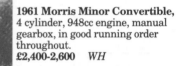

1968 Morris Minor, 4 cylinder, 1098cc engine, in original condition.
Est. £1,000-2,000   *ADT*

1970 Morris Minor 1100cc, 2 owners from new.
£3,500-4,000   *FOR*

This vehicle is one of the last produced.

1956 Morris Minor Series 2, 12,000 miles recorded.
£4,500-5,000   *WCC*

1966 Morris Minor 1000 Convertible, 1098cc engine, independent front suspension using torsion bars, semi-elliptic leaf springs rear, rack and pinion steering, 12 volt electrics, fully restored to highest standard.
£7,500-8,500   *ESM*

1,619,958 Morris Minors were produced between 1948 and 1971.

1959 Morris Minor 1000 Convertible, 948cc engine, leather interior.
£5,000-5,500 *ESM*

Use the Index!

Because certain items might fit easily into any of a number of categories, the quickest and surest method of locating any entry is by reference to the index at the back of the book.

1956 Morris Minor Series II Convertible, 803cc engine, leather interior. **£5,000-6,000** *ESM*

1952 Morris Minor Series MM Convertible, fully restored and fitted with later type 1098cc engine, gearbox and brakes. **£6,500-7,000** *ESM*

The Minor is one of the only cars where modifications/standard upgrading can increase the value. Price when new £358. Manufactured from 1949-53.

1949 Morris Minor Series MM Two Door Saloon.
£10,000-10,500 *ESM*

Fully restored and now fitted with 1300cc Morris Ital type engine, servo assisted disc brakes, early type 'lowlight' headlights fitted in front grille and not on wings as on later cars. Bumpers made up in 2 halves due to last minute widening of the car when the bumpers had already been made. A 4in fillet was inserted in the middle.

1954 Morris Minor Series II Saloon, 803cc overhead valve engine, bore 57.9mm, stroke 76.2mm, 4 speed gearbox, 0-50mph in 25secs, some restoration required.
£900-1,000   *ESM*

1971 Morris Minor 1000 Traveller, 1098cc, original 30,000 miles recorded.
£4,500-5,500   *ESM*

1970 Morris Minor 1000 Two Door Saloon, 66,000 miles recorded, in average condition.
£2,500-3,000   *ESM*

1971 Morris Minor Two Door Saloon, 1098cc reconditioned engine, excellent bodywork, 62,000 miles recorded.
£3,600-4,000   *ESM*

1970 Morris Minor 1000 Four Door Saloon, 1098cc, 15,000 miles recorded, all original.
£4,500-5,000 *ESM*

Condition Guide

1. *A vehicle in top class condition but not 'concours d'elegance' standard, either fully restored or in very good original condition*
2. *A good, clean, roadworthy vehicle, both mechanically and bodily sound*
3. *A runner, but in need of attention, probably both to bodywork and mechanics. Must have current MOT*

1968 Morris Mini Cooper MkII, genuine Mini Cooper with 998cc engine. **£2,000-2,500** *LF*

1967 Morris Minor 1000 Traveller, 1098cc, bore 64.5mm, stroke 83.7mm, 4 speed gearbox, 0-50mph in 16.1secs, 70,000 miles recorded, replaced rear wood made in original ash.
£4,000-5,000 *ESM*

Miller's is a price Guide not a price List

The price ranges given reflect the average price a purchaser should pay for similar vehicle. Condition, rarity, provenance, racing history, originality and any restoration are factors that must be taken into account when assessing values. When buying or selling, it must always be remembered that prices can be greatly affected by the condition of any vehicle. Unless otherwise stated, all cars shown in Miller's are of good merchantable quality, and the valuations given reflect this fact. Vehicles offered for sale in exceptionally fine condition or in poor condition may reasonably be expected to be priced considerably higher or lower respectively than the estimates given herein

Mini Cooper, 998cc. **£5,000-5,500** *AUT*

Cross Reference
Austin

1975 Morris Marina Two Door Coupé, 4 cylinder, 1300cc engine, manual gearbox, 21,000 miles, in excellent order throughout.
£800-9 00 *WH*

| MAKE | ENGINE | DATES | CONDITION | | |
Mini	cc/cyl		1	2	3
Mini	848/4	1959-67	£2,000	£900	—
Mini Countryman	848/4	1961-67	£1,800	£900	—
Cooper Mk I	997/4	1961-67	£5,000	£3,000	£1,500
Cooper Mk II	998/4	1967-69	£3,500	£3,000	£1,500
Cooper S Mk I	var/4	1963-67	£6,000	£4,000	£2,000
Cooper S Mk II	1275/4	1967-71	£5,000	£4,000	£2,000
Innocenti					
Mini Cooper	998/4	1966-75	£3,000	£1,500	—

Nash

1928 Nash Standard Six Tourer, with 6 cylinder, 3000cc engine, restored some time ago, right hand drive.
£7,750-8,250 *ADT*

The model 321 was introduced in June 1927 and was the smaller of the series 360 and 330 cars. The engine is an overhead valve, 6 cylinder unit of 3000cc, the price when new $365.00. Power to the rear wheels was through a disc clutch and 3 speed gearbox with 108in wheelbase.

Nash-Healey

1954 Nash-Healey Coupé, with coachwork by Pinin Farina, Nash Ambassador 6 cylinder in line, overhead valves operated by pushrods and rockers, 3820cc engine, bore 85mm, stroke 112mm, compression ratio 8.2:1, 140bhp at 4,200rpm, twin SU H6 carburettors, coil ignition, single dry plate clutch, 3 speed manual with Borg Warner overdrive gearbox, Nash torque tube hypoid bevel rear axle, steel box section chassis frame, boxed pressed and tubular cross members with 2 door, 2 seater steel and alloy coachwork, independent front suspension with coil springs, trailing arms, hydraulic shock absorbers, coil springs, panhard rod, hydraulic shock absorbers rear, 4 wheel dual servo drum brakes, 15in wheels and tyres, steel disc type with embellishers and 6.40 x 15in tyres, wheelbase 102in, left hand drive, excellent overall condition.
Est. £18,000-23,000 *CNY*

One of the very rare fixed head Coupés of which 90 were thought to have been built and today only 3 or 4 are known to exist.

Neustadt & Perry

1902 Neustadt & Perry, 1 cylinder, 5hp, 2 seater, 'Genevieve' runabout.
£18,000-19,000 *SL*

Noble

1991 Noble Motorsport Mk 4, manufactured by Phoenix Sports Cars as a replica of the Ferrari P4.
Est. £24,000-25,000 *ADT*

NSU

1971 NSU Ro80 Rotary Saloon, with twin chamber rotary engine, water-cooled, 1990cc, 3 speed semi-automatic gearbox, shaft drive, all coil independent suspension, disc brakes front and rear, power assisted steering, left hand drive, in good order throughout but in need of some cosmetic restoration.
Est. **£3,500-4,500**   *S*

The NSU Works in Neckarsulm, West Germany, became established through bicycle and motorcycle manufacturing before embarking on motor cars in 1905.

MAKE NSU	ENGINE cc/cyl	DATES	CONDITION		
			1	2	3
Prinz 1-4	583/598/2	1958-73	£1,000	£750	—
Sport Prinz	583/598/2	1959-67	£2,000	£1,000	£500
Wankel Spyder	497/rotary	1964-67	£3,200	£2,000	£1,000
1200TT	1177/4	1965-72	£1,500	£1,000	—
Ro80	994/rotary	1967-76	£3,000	£1,500	£500

Oakland

1924 Oakland Model 6-54 Touring, left hand drive, 'Californian top', fully restored.
£9,500-11,500   *CGB*

Did you know
MILLER'S Collectors Cars Price Guide builds up year by year to form the most comprehensive photo-reference system available

Ogle

1961 Ogle, 4 cylinder, 998cc Cooper engine, interior in first class condition, trimmed in leather.
Est. **£8,000-9,000**   *ADT*

Only 15 or so of these cars are still in existence.
Ogle are well known for their unusual styling exercises and in the early 1960s produced a handful of Mini based cars. In fact the company designs and moulds were subsequently bought by Norman Fletcher of the boat building company bearing his name.

Oldsmobile

1902 Oldsmobile Curved Dash.
Est. **£16,000-20,000**   *C*

The curved dash runabout, so named after the profile of the bodywork in front of the passenger legs, is claimed to be the world's first true mass production car with 2,100 cars being sold in 1902 and 5,000 in 1904.

1903 Oldsmobile 5hp Curved Dash Runabout, with single cylinder, T-head, side valve, horizontally mounted, RAC rating 8.1hp, 2 speed and reverse epicyclic gearbox, low speed and reverse clutch by contracting brakes on epicyclic drums, metal cone clutch for top gear, chain drive to live rear axle, longitudinal semi-elliptic springs/chassis side members, 700 x 80mm tyres.
£13,750-14,500   *S*

MAKE Oldsmobile	ENGINE cc/cyl	DATES	CONDITION 1	2	3
Curved Dash	1600/1	1901-04	£18,000	£15,000	£11,000
30	2771/6	1925-26	£9,000	£7,000	£4,000
Straight Eight	4213/8	1937-38	£12,000	£8,000	£6,000

1936 Oldsmobile Straight 8, original right hand drive. Est. **£6,000-8,000**   *LF*

A US car which has been in this country from outset.

1966 Oldsmobile 442 Two Door Hardtop, excellent condition. **£5,000-6,000**   *KI*

Opel

1972 Opel GT Sports Coupé, 1897cc, one owner, 45,000 miles recorded, left hand drive. **£3,200-3,500**   *DDM*

Make: **Opel**
Model: GT
Type: Coupé
Years Manufactured: 1968-73
Quantity: 103,373
Price when new: 1897cc, £2,057
Engine Type: 4 cyl
Size: 1078cc/1897cc
Max Power: 1078cc, 60 bhp @ 5200 rpm; 1897cc, 90 bhp @ 5100 rpm
Max Torque: 1078cc, 61 ft/lb @ 3800 rpm; 1897cc, 108 ft/lb @ 2500 rpm
Transmission: 4 speed or auto
Wheelbase: 95.7in
Performance: Max speed: 1900cc, 115 mph; 0-60: 1900cc, 12.0 secs; Mpg: 1900cc, 30.

Packard

1931 Packard 833 5 Passenger Coupé, condition 3. **£24,000-26,000**   *KI*

1932 Packard De Luxe Eight Sedanca De Ville, 6300cc, 8 cylinders.
£19,000-20,000 *ADT*

1937 Packard Super Eight Town Car, coachwork by Brewster & Company, New York, 8 cylinder in line, L-head, 2 side valves per cylinder, cast-iron block, detachable alloy cylinder heads, 5240cc, bore 80mm, stroke 127mm, compression ratio 6.5:1, 135bhp at 3,200rpm, single coil ignition, Detroit Lubricator carburettor, single dry plate clutch with 3 speed synchromesh manual gearbox, pressed steel chassis frame with channel side sections and cross bracings, 4 door Sedanca de Ville style Town Car with glass division, 2 occasional folding seats, rear mounted leather covered boot, front independent Safe T. Flex suspension with lever type hydraulic shock absorbers, rear, semi-elliptic leaf springs with lever type hydraulic shock absorbers, 4 wheel hydraulic drum brakes, 16in steel disc wheels with chrome hub caps and wheel trims, 7.15 x 16in whitewall tyres, wheelbase 3,700mm, left hand drive, leather interior.
£42,000-43,000 *C*

James Ward Packard, an electric lamp manufacturer of Warren, Ohio, and his brother William Doud bought their first car, a Winton, in 1898. Dissatisfied with it they decided to design and build their own car and in 1903 opened their new factory in Detroit, becoming within a few years one of America's leading car manufacturers.

1937 Packard 1501 Roadster, rare rear mounted spare wheel, complete restoration.
£68,000-70,000 *KI*

MAKE Packard	ENGINE cc/cyl	DATES	CONDITION		
			1	2	3
Twin Six	6946/12	1916-23	£30,000	£25,000	£18,000
6	3973/6	1921-24	£20,000	£15,000	£12,000
6, 7, 8 Series	5231/8	1929-39	£40,000	£30,000	£22,000
12	7300/12	1936-39	£40,000	£30,000	£18,000

1939 Packard Six (1700) Station Wagon (Woody), coachwork by J. T. Cantrell, 6 cylinder in line cast iron monobloc, side valve, L-head, 245cu in, bore 3½in, stroke 4¼in, compression ratio 6.52:1, 100bhp at 3,200rpm, single downdraught Chandler carburettor, Delco distribution ignition, single dry plate clutch with 3 speed Packard selective silent synchronised gearbox, Packard hypoid angleset differential, pressed steel channel section parallel beams with tubular cross-members, rigid front axle, semi-floating rear, front independent coil springs, Safe T. Flex, rear semi-elliptic leaf springs, hydraulic shock absorbers, 4 wheel hydraulic drum brakes, 16in steel disc wheels with hub caps and embellishers, 6.00 x 16in tyres, wheelbase 122in, left hand drive.
£21,000-25,000   *CNY*

Make the Most of Miller's

CONDITION is absolutely vital when assessing the value of a vehicle. Top class vehicles on the whole appreciate much more than less perfect examples. However a rare, desirable car may command a high price even when in need of restoration

1948 Packard Super 8 Convertible, condition 2.
£10,000-12,000   *KI*

Panhard & Levassor

1910 Panhard & Levassor Seven Seater Tourer, by Henri La Bourdette, 6 cylinder, 5 litre, 30hp, T-head engine.
£100,000-110,000   *SL*

Panther

Make:	**Panther**
Model:	Lima
Type:	Sports
Years Manufactured:	1976-82
Quantity:	897
Engine Type:	4 cyl
Size:	2279cc
Max Power:	108 bhp
Transmission:	4 speed or auto
Performance:	Max speed: 98 mph; 0-60: 9.9 secs; Mpg: 25.

1979 Panther Lima Mk II, 2.3 Vauxhall Magnum engine and floor pan, with fibreglass bodyshell, leather interior, mohair weather equipment, restored.
£8,000-10,000   *C.A.R.S.*

1978 Panther Lima Mk I, 2.3 Vauxhall Magnum engine and floor pan, egg box alloy grille, fibreglass bodyshell, hardtop, good original condition.
£5,000-6,000 *C.A.R.S.*

Panther, based at Byfleet in Surrey, produced only 100 of these hand built cars over some ten years. The styling was heavily based on the Bugatti Royale and was a luxury, 4 seat exponent of the replica vintage car era. At over 4,360lb it weighs substantially more than the Jaguar XJ6/12 cars from which it derives most of its mechanical components. It has a rectangular section steel ladder chassis with all aluminium hand beaten coachwork. The doors are pressed steel and are Austin Maxi units.

1977 Panther De Ville Coupé, Jaguar V12 engine, 5300cc.
£47,000-49,000 *S*

This was built for Elton John and his name is on the engine plate. It made an appearance in the video for his single 'I'm Still Standing' in 1983.

1977 Panther Lima Mk I, special limited edition for the Silver Jubilee, official ER II Silver Jubilee door plaques, original condition.
£10,000-12,000 *C.A.R.S.*

1984 Panther Kallista, 2.8i fuel injection Ford engine, all aluminium bodywork.
£15,000-16,000 *C.A.R.S.*

1989 Panther Kallista, 2.8 litre Ford engine, all aluminium body and wings, chrome fittings, wire wheels and mesh grille with spot and driving lamps, excellent condition.   **£15,000-16,000** *C.A.R.S.*

| MAKE | ENGINE | DATES | CONDITION | | |
Panther	cc/cyl		1	2	3
J72	various	1972-81	£12,000	£10,000	—
Lima	2279/4	1976-82	£5,500	£4,400	—

Peugeot

1926 Peugeot 172R Tourer, 720cc, 4 cylinders.
£2,500-3,000 *ADT*

**1931 Peugeot 201C Four Door
Saloon,** 2 cylinder, 1300cc, manual
gearbox, left hand drive.
£1,000-1,250 *C*

*Peugeot is the second oldest
surviving car company in the world
after Daimler-Benz and the oldest
still in the same family.*

1933 Peugeot Type 201B Saloon,
1100cc, 4 cylinders.
Est. **£6,500-7,500** *ADT*

MAKE	ENGINE	DATES	CONDITION		
Peugeot	cc/cyl		1	2	3
153	2951/4	1913-26	£5,000	£4,000	£2,000
163	1490/4	1920-24	£5,000	£4,000	£2,000
Bebe	676/4	1920-25	£7,000	£6,000	£3,000
156	5700/6	1922-24	£7,000	£5,000	£3,000
174	3828/4	1922-28	£6,000	£4,000	£2,000
172	714/4	1926-28	£4,000	£3,000	£1,500
183	1990/6	1929-30	£4,000	£3,000	£1,500
201	996/4	1930-36	£4,000	£3,000	£1,500
402	2140/4	1938-40	£4,000	£3,000	£1,000

Right hand drive cars will always achieve more interest than left hand drive. Good solid cars.

1972 Peugeot 504 Convertible, condition 1, right hand drive.
£8,000-10,000 *PA*

1972 Peugeot 504 Cabriolet,
right hand drive.
£6,000-9,000 *AUT*

Make: **Peugeot**
Model: 404
Type: Coupé/Convertible
Years Manufactured: 1962-69
Quantity: 6,837/10,387
Price when new: £2,291
Engine Type: 4 cyl
Size: 1618cc
Max Power: 88 bhp
Transmission: 4 speed or auto
Performance: Max speed:
Coupé, 105 mph; 0-60: Coupé,
14.0 secs; Mpg: Coupé, 26.

Phoenix

1903 Phoenix Fourcar, 1 cylinder, 3½hp.
€12,000-12,500 *SL*

Plymouth

c1913 Phoenix Two Seater,
4 cylinder, in line, water-cooled side
valve, bore 69mm, stroke 110mm,
11.9hp, 3 speed gearbox, metal to
metal clutch, shaft drive to worm
rear axle, semi-elliptic leaf spring
suspension front and rear,
760 x 90mm tyres, beaded edge.
£6,500-7,000 *S*

**1970 Plymouth Road Runner
Superbird 440,** automatic gearbox,
230 recorded mileage, condition 1.
£37,000-39,000 *KI*

Pontiac

Condition Guide

1. *A vehicle in top class
condition but not
'concours d'elegance'
standard, either fully
restored or in very good
original condition*
2. *A good, clean,
roadworthy vehicle,
both mechanically and
bodily sound*
3. *A runner, but in need of
attention, probably
both to bodywork and
mechanics. Must have
current MOT*

1929 Pontiac Big 6 Roadster.
£9,000-9,500 *DB*

1959 Pontiac Bonneville, V8, 300bhp, sport coupé, 2 door, 4 barrel, hard top, power steering, disc brakes, totally original, very rare.
£11,500-12,500 *AC*
This car was the USA Car of the Year for 1959.

1958 Pontiac Bonneville Convertible, fuel injected, factory bucket seats front and rear, frame-off restoration, original condition.
£42,000-45,000 *KI*

1974 Pontiac Firebird, 4100cc, 6 cylinders, manual gearbox, restored, left hand drive.
£1,100-1,200 *ADT*

Make: **Pontiac**
Model: Firebird
Type: Coupé/Convertible
Years Manufactured: 1966-81
Engine Type: various 6 cyl, V6 cyl, V8 cyl
Size: 3.8-7.5 litre
Max Power: 165-375 bhp
Transmission: 4 speed or auto

1978 Pontiac Trans Am 400, T Tops, 6 cylinders, imported from USA in 1990.
£3,000-3,500 *JB*

1986 Pontiac Firebird, 2.8 injection, left hand drive.
£5,000-5,500 *JB*

Pope

1904 Pope Tribune Two Seat Runabout,
forward mounted, vertical single cylinder,
water-cooled, atmospheric side inlet valve,
6hp, bore 4½in, stroke 4in, 2 speed sliding gear
transmission and reverse, three-quarter
elliptic front and rear suspension, shaft final
drive to live axle, wheelbase 65in, 2½ x 28in
tyres, original body and wings, repainted and
restored.   Est. **£16,000-18,000**   *S*

*The smallest and the least expensive in the Pope
domain, the Tribune was built in Hagerstown,
Maryland, USA, in the factory which had
previously been used for the Crawford bicycle.
The car was shaft driven and introduced in
1904 as a single cylinder runabout, later to
increase to 2 and 4 cylinders.*

Porsche

**1955 Porsche 356 Speedster
1600/90,** coachwork by Reutter,
Zuffenhausen, Stuttgart,
4 cylinders horizontally opposed,
3 bearing crankshaft, light alloy
block/crankcase, air-cooled, 1583cc,
bore 82.5mm, stroke 74mm, 2 alloy
cylinder heads, 2 overhead valves
per cylinder operated by pushrods
and rockers from single camshaft
mounted in crankcase, 9:1
compression ratio, 90bhp at
5,500rpm, twin downdraught
Zenith carburettors, single dry plate
clutch, 4 speed all synchromesh
gearbox, both in unit with rear
mounted engine, remote control
central gear change, spiral bevel
final drive and exposed universally
jointed drive shafts to rear wheels,
pressed steel punt type chassis
frame with pressed steel and light
alloy speedster 2 door bodywork,
factory Glasspar hard top, front
independent VW type
suspension by trailing arms,
transverse torsion bars and
anti-roll bar, telescopic
shock absorbers, rear swing
half transverse axles radius
arms and bars, 4 wheel
hydraulic operated drum
brakes, 15in Rudge
Whitworth knock-on wheels,
5.60 x 15in tyres, wheelbase
2,100mm, left hand drive,
exported to USA in 1955.
£40,000-50,000   *C(M)*

1952 Porsche 356 V-Screen Cabriolet.   **£25,000-26,000**   *DF*

1958 Porsche Speedster.
£32,000-33,000   *AUT*

MAKE Porsche	ENGINE cc/cyl	DATES	CONDITION 1	2	3
356	var/4	1949-53	£20,000	£15,000	£10,000
356 Cabriolet	var/4	1951-53	£25,000	£17,000	£12,000
356A	1582/4	1955-59	£12,000	£7,000	£3,000
356A Cabriolet	1582/4	1956-59	£18,000	£11,000	£8,000
356A Speedster	1582/4	1955-58	£28,000	£20,000	£15,000
356 Carrera	1582/ 1966/4	1960-65	£30,000	£25,000	£18,000
356C	1582/4	1963-65	£12,000	£9,000	£4,000
356C Cabriolet	1582/4	1963-64	£18,000	£14,000	£8,000
911/911L/T/E	1991/6	1964-68	£10,500	£6,500	£4,500
912	1582/4	1965-68	£8,000	£6,000	£2,500
911S	1991/6	1966-69	£12,000	£9,000	£6,000
911S	2195/6	1969-71	£14,000	£10,500	£6,500
911T	2341/6	1971-73	£13,000	£9,000	£6,500
911E	2341/6	1971-73	£15,000	£11,500	£7,000
914/4	1679/4	1969-75	£4,000	£3,000	£1,000
914/6	1991/6	1969-71	£5,000	£3,500	£1,500
911S	2341/6	1971-73	£17,000	£14,000	£9,500
Carrera RS lightweight	2687/6	1973	£50,000	£40,000	£25,000
Carrera RS Touring	2687/6	1973	£45,000	£30,000	£20,000
Carrera 3	2994/6	1976-77	£15,000	£10,000	£7,000
924 Turbo	1984/4	1978-83	£7,000	£5,500	£4,500

Sportmatic cars are less desirable.

1958 Porsche 356 A Coupé, rally prepared.
£22,000-23,000   *DF*

1960 Porsche 356 B Sunroof Coupé.   £15,000-16,000   *DF*

1960 Porsche 356 B Roadster.   **£30,000-32,000**   *DF*

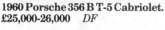

1960 Porsche 356 B T-5 Cabriolet.
£25,000-26,000   *DF*

1963 Porsche 356 B T-6 Cabriolet.
£27,000-30,000   *DF*

Make: **Porsche**
Model: 356B/356C
Type: Coupé/Convertible/Hard Top
Years Manufactured: 1960-65
Quantity: 47,866 all models
Price when new: 356C Convertible (1582cc), £2,313
Engine Type: Overhead valve flat 4 cyl; double overhead camshaft flat 4 cyl
Size: 1582cc; Carrera 2 (1961-65), 1966cc
Max Power: 1582cc 60 bhp @ 4500 rpm; 1966cc, Carrera 2, 130 bhp @ 6200 rpm
Max Torque: 1582cc, 78 ft/lb @ 2800 rpm; 1966cc, Carrera 2, 116 ft/lb @ 4600 rpm
Transmission: 4 speed manual
Wheelbase: 82.7in
Performance: Max speed: 110-130 mph; 0-60: 9.2-14.5 secs.

1965 Porsche 356C Coupé, one owner, show quality engine detail, original upper and underbody panels except battery box floor which has been correctly replaced, fully restored, left hand drive.
£17,000-18,500   *HCI*

1962 Porsche 356 B Roadster, original engine in good running order, Nardi steering wheel, new hood and carpets.   **£24,000-26,000**   *HCI*

Make the Most of Miller's

Veteran Cars are those manufactured up to 31 December 1918 although only vehicles built before 31 December 1904 are eligible for the London/Brighton Commemorative Run. Vintage Cars are vehicles that were manufactured between 1 January 1919 and 31 December 1930

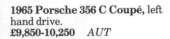

1965 Porsche 356 C Coupé, left hand drive.
£9,850-10,250   *AUT*

1967 Porsche 911 2 litre Coupé, 1991cc, right hand drive, good condition throughout.
Est. **£6,000-8,000**   *LF*

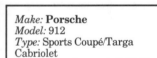

1967 Porsche 911S, right hand drive.   **£11,000-12,000**   *AUT*

Make: **Porsche**
Model: 912
Type: Sports Coupé/Targa Cabriolet
Years Manufactured: 1965-69
Quantity: 30,745
Price when new: £2,467
Engine Type: Flat 4 cyl
Size: 1582cc
Max Power: 90 bhp @ 5800 rpm
Max Torque: 87 ft/lb @ 3500 rpm
Transmission: 4 speed or 5 speed
Wheelbase: 1965-68, 87.1in; 1969, 89.3in
Performance: Max speed: 119 mph; 0-60: 11.9 secs; Mpg: 25.

1969 Porsche 912, 1600cc, 5 speed gearbox.
£2,000-3,000   *LF*

The 912 is basically a 911 with the 356 flat four engine rather than the 6 cylinder. Some 30,700 912s were produced, but of those only 290 were imported to the UK in right hand drive form.

1970 Porsche 911T, excellent condition, USA import.
£11,950-13,950   *HCI*

1971 Porsche 911 Carrera 2.7. £30,000-40,000 *S8*

1987 Porsche 911 Flat Front Cabriolet Turbo.
Est. £45,000-55,000 *LF* *Only 100 were made.*

1973 Porsche 911T, period wheels and trim improvements. £8,000-9,000 *PC*

1972 Porsche 911E Coupé, right hand drive. £9,000-9,500 *AUT*

1986 Porsche 911 Turbo Cabriolet, special Ruff conversion, 385bhp. £40,000-42,000 *SC*

1989 Porsche 911 Speedster Turbo. £38,000-39,000 *AUT*

Powerdrive

1957 Powerdrive, 322cc.
£1,500-2,200   *LF*

Railton

1935 Railton 4.2 Litre Fairmile MkI Three Position Drophead Coupé, with coachwork by Coachcraft Ltd., Hanwell, London, 8 cylinder in line, water-cooled monobloc, side valve, 4168cc, bore 76mm, stroke 114mm, 3 speed and reverse gearbox, single plate clutch, shaft and spiral bevel final drive, wheelbase 116in, 16 x 6.25in tyres. Est. **£20,000-23,000**   *S*

1938 Railton Eight Two Seater Sports Special. This car possibly started life as something more formal but later built in the style of a 1930s sports 2 seater. Est. **£10,000-12,000**   *S*

Range Rover

Railton cars of Cobham, Surrey, were the result of the work of Reid Railton, well known for his work on land speed record cars at the time. The cars were Anglo-American in their construction with a 4.2 litre Hudson engine coupled with a lowered 4 litre Terraplane chassis with stiffened suspension.

1969 Pre-Production Prototype Range Rover, originally a Company Management Assessment vehicle, completely restored, right hand drive.
£12,000-14,000   *PC*

Design of the Range Rover started in 1966 and, following the building of 7 engineering prototypes, 27 pre-production prototypes were built in 1969 on the new production line, and then 20 press cars used at the launch in May/June 1970.

1969 Pre-Production Prototype Range Rover, one of the earliest left hand drive vehicles surviving, in original condition.
£7,000-10,000   *PC*

Make: **Range Rover**
Type: Estate car
Years Manufactured: 1970 onwards
Quantity: Still in production
Engine Type: Overhead valve V8 or 4 cyl diesel
Size: 3528cc or 2393cc diesel
Max Power: 132 bhp @ 5000 rpm
Transmission: 4 speed, 5 speed from July 1983, plus transfer gearbox. Overdrive optional from Feb 1978, auto optional from Aug 1982
Performance: Max speed: 96 mph; 0-60: 14.5 secs; Mpg: 15-22.

1969 Pre-Production Prototype Range Rover, originally an Engineering Test Vehicle, right hand drive.   **£55,000+**   *PC*

1971 Range Rover, 3.5 litre V8 2 door, in totally original condition with guaranteed 22,000 miles, right hand drive.
£6,000-8,000   *PC*

1987 Range Rover Vogue EFi, automatic.
£10,000-12,000   *WCC*

1969 Pre-Production Prototype Range Rover, originally a Quality Control vehicle, totally restored, right hand drive.
£10,000-12,000   *PC*

Reliable Dayton

Most of the pre-production prototypes survive, all registered in the series YVB 151H to YVB 177H, all 3.5 litre V8 2 door vehicles, and these are held in high esteem by collectors. Some have been fully restored, some are currently being restored, some are still original.

c1907 Reliable Dayton, 2 cylinder 3000cc engine.
£9,500-10,000   *ADT*

The Reliable Dayton Motor Company of Chicago manufactured cars from 1906 to 1909.

Reliant

1971 Reliant Regal 21E, 30,000 miles recorded from new.
£1,500-1,750
WCC

This vehicle is the actual Robin featured in the current Hamlet Cigars commercial and still bears the battle scars of the dodgem scene.

1974 Reliant Robin Three Wheeler, 4 cylinder, in line, water-cooled monobloc, 850cc engine, overhead valve, 4 speed gearbox, bevel rear axle, wheelbase 84in, 5.20 x 10in tyres, to original specification.
£1,300-1,500   *S*

1968 Reliant Rebel Saloon, restored to mint condition, new chassis.
£2,500-3,000   *PC*

1971 Reliant Scimitar GTE, 6 cylinder, 2994cc engine.
Est. **£4,500-6,500**   *ADT*

Make: **Reliant**
Model: Scimitar GTE
Type: Sports hatchback
Years Manufactured: 1968-82
Quantity: 9,705
Price when new: £1,863
Engine Type: V6 cyl
Size: 2994cc
Max Power: 138 bhp
Transmission: 4 speed, optional overdrive, optional auto
Performance: Max speed: 121 mph; 0-60: 8.9 secs; Mpg: 24.

1974 Reliant Scimitar SE5, Ford engine, fibreglass body.
£2,000-3,000   *PC*

MAKE	ENGINE	DATES	CONDITION		
Reliant	cc/cyl		1	2	3
Sabre	1703/4	1961-63	£4,000	£2,000	£1,000
Sabre Six	2553/8	1962-64	£4,500	£2,000	£1,000
Scimitar GT	2553/8	1964-70	£2,500	£1,000	—
Scimitar GTE	2994/8	1969-86	£4,000	£1,500	£1,000
Scimitar GTC	2792/8	1980-86	£5,000	£3,500	£2,000

1981 Reliant Scimitar, 6 cylinder, 2792cc engine, in good overall condition.
£6,500-7,000   *ADT*

Following the success of the Ogle-designed Scimitar GTE in 1980 Reliant introduced a drophead Scimitar, namely the GTC.

Renault

Make the Most of Miller's

Veteran Cars are those manufactured up to 31 December 1918 although only vehicles built before 31 December 1904 are eligible for the London/Brighton Commemorative Run. Vintage Cars are vehicles that were manufactured between 1 January 1919 and 31 December 1930

1901 Renault Type D, 1 cylinder, 6½hp De Dion Bouton engine.
£28,000-30,000   *SL*

1907 Renault Type V 20/30hp Roi-des-Belges Tourer, with 4 cylinder, water-cooled engine, 4398cc, side valve, cast in pairs, bore 100mm, stroke 140mm, 4 speed gearbox with right hand quadrant change, shaft and bevel final drive, semi-elliptic leaf spring front suspension, three-quarter elliptic leaf springs rear, 880 x 120mm tyres.
Est. **£18,000-22,000**   *S*

1906 Renault AH Landaulet, 4 cylinder, 2120cc engine, 3 speed manual gearbox, right hand drive.
£17,500-18,000   *C*

Louis Renault built his first car in 1898 in the grounds of his family home. In 1902 the Renault factory started to make its own 4 cylinder engines, and later singles and twins, but De Dion units were still used in 1903. The radiator moved to the dashboard in 1904, a trend followed by many imitators for a while, although none kept it up until 1928 as Renault did.

RENAULT

1928 Renault NN Tourer,
4 cylinder, 951cc engine, restored in
the early 1980s.
Est. **£9,000-14,000**   *ADT*

1932 Renault Saloon, 1700cc engine, condition 2.
£7,000-9,000   *PA*

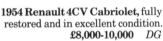

1954 Renault 4CV Cabriolet, fully
restored and in excellent condition.
£8,000-10,000   *DG*

Make: **Renault**
Model: 5 Turbo
Type: Saloon
Years Manufactured: 1981-85
Engine Type: Turbocharged
overhead valve 4 cyl
Max Power: 160 bhp @ 6000
rpm
Transmission: 5 speed
Performance: Max speed: 112
mph; 0-60: 9.8 secs; Mpg: 28-34.

1984 Renault 5 Turbo 2, mid-engine.   **£9,000-9,500**   *AUT*

MAKE Renault	ENGINE cc/cyl	DATES	CONDITION		
			1	2	3
40hp	7540/6	1919-21	£30,000	£20,000	£10,000
SR	4537/4	1919-22	£10,000	£7,000	£5,000
EU–15.8HP	2815/4	1919-23	£5,000	£3,000	£2,000
GS–IG	2121/4	1920-23	£5,000	£3,000	£2,000
JP	9123/6	1922-29	£30,000	£20,000	£15,000
KJ	951/4	1923-29	£6,000	£4,000	£2,000
Mona Six	1474/6	1928-31	£7,000	£5,000	£3,000
Reinastella	7128/8	1929-32	£30,000	£20,000	£15,000
Viva Six	3181/6	1929-34	£10,000	£7,000	£3,000
14/45	2120/4	1929-35	£7,000	£5,000	£2,000
Nervahuit	4240/8	1931	£15,000	£10,000	£7,000
UY	1300/4	1932-34	£7,000	£5,000	£2,000
ZC/ZD2	4825/8	1934-35	£15,000	£10,000	£7,000
YN2	1463/4	1934-39	£7,000	£5,000	£2,000
Airline Super and Big 6	3620/6	1935	£10,000	£8,000	£5,000
18	2383/4	1936-39	£9,000	£5,000	£3,000
26	4085/6	1936-39	£12,000	£8,000	£5,000

Veteran pre-war models like the two cylinder AX, AG and BB are very popular with values ranging
between £6,000 and £15,000. The larger four cylinder cars like the AM, AZ, XB and VB are very reliable
and coachbuilt examples command £25,000+.

Reo

1925 Reo T6 Five Passenger Sedan, with 6 cylinder engine, complete body-off restoration a few years ago.
£9,500-11,500   *CGB*

Riley

1924 Riley 11.9hp Four Seat Tourer, 4 cylinder, in line, water-cooled monobloc engine, 1645cc, side valve, bore 69mm, stroke 110mm, cone clutch, 4 speed gearbox and reverse, shaft and spiral bevel final drive, wheelbase 90in, 4.95 x 29in tyres.
Est. **£16,000-17,000**   *S*

1933 Riley 9hp Lynx, manual gearbox, in excellent condition.
£21,000-22,000   *DB*

1932 Riley Monaco, with manual gearbox, all original.
£10,750-11,250   *OC*

1937 Riley 9 Merlin Special, condition 1.
£10,000-12,000   *PA*

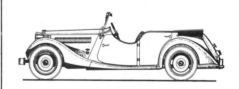

MAKE Riley	ENGINE cc/cyl	DATES	CONDITION 1	2	3
9hp	1034/2	1906-07	£9,000	£6,000	£3,000
Speed 10	1390/2	1909-10	£10,000	£6,000	£3,000
11	1498/4	1922-27	£7,000	£4,000	£2,000
9	1075/4	1927-32	£10,000	£7,000	£4,000
9 Gamecock	1098/4	1932-33	£15,000	£10,000	£6,000
Lincock 12hp	1458/6	1933-36	£9,000	£7,000	£5,000
Imp 9hp	1089/4	1934-35	£32,000	£28,000	£20,000
Kestral 12hp	1496/4	1936-38	£8,000	£5,000	£2,000
Sprite 12hp	1496/4	1936-38	£40,000	£35,000	£20,000

1934 Riley 9hp Brooklands Replica, 4 cylinder in line, water-cooled monobloc, 1089cc engine, pushrod operated overhead valves, bore 60.3mm, stroke 95.22mm, 4 speed crash gearbox, single plate clutch, spiral bevel rear axle, semi-elliptic leaf springs front and rear, wheelbase 95in, 4.50 x 19in tyres, stripped and rebuilt by Gillams of Wincanton.
£18,000-20,000   *S*

1950 Riley RMA, condition 2.
£3,000-3,500   *CC*

Introduced in 1946 the RMA is considered a 'real' Riley from Nuffield with a classic twin camshaft, 1496cc, high pushrod engine that gave the car a top speed of 75mph. Production continued until 1952 by which time just over 10,500 had been built.

1950 Riley 1.5 Litre RMA Saloon, all original, condition 2.
£4,000-4,500   *Cen*

1953 Riley 1.5 Litre RME, in condition 2
£3,500-4,000   *PA*

Rochet

1963 Riley 1.5 Litre, in excellent condition.
£4,000-4,500   *WCC*

1899/1900 Rochet Quadricycle, 1 cylinder, 2¾bhp, 2 speed Bozier gearbox.
Est. £13,000-16,000   *C*

931 Bentley 4.5 Litre Sports Tourer,
riginal Thrupp & Maberly coachwork
nd 4398cc engine.
st. **£155,000-160,000**   *S(NY)*

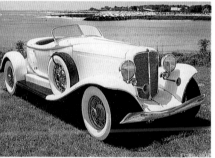

**1929 Bentley 6½ Litre Speed
Six,** with coachwork by Hunt
of Horley, 6 cylinder in line
engine, single overhead
camshaft, 4 valves per cylinder,
6597cc, bore 100mm, stroke
140mm, 160bhp at 3,500rpm.
Est. **£270,000-300,000**   *CNY*

**1932 Auburn V12 Boat-Tail
Speedster,** with 'Salon
Speedster' body, Lycoming V12
160hp engine, fitted with
2 speed rear axle, 134in
wheelbase, engine and
drivetrain are in excellent
condition, the body was
stripped and repainted in hand
rubbed lacquer 20 years ago.
£43,500-45,000   *PMc*

Detail of the boat-tail
eature **1932 Auburn
12 Speedster.**

1935 Aston Martin Mk II Ulster Replica,
4 cylinder E5/575/S engine, 103in wheelbase,
the creation of this car was supervised by
A. C. Bertelli, and is one of only 5 short
chassis models built.
£52,000-55,000   *PMc*

948 Alfa Romeo 6C 2500 Super Cabriolet,
cylinder in line, cast iron monobloc twin
verhead camshafts, 2443cc, bore 72mm, stroke
00mm, 105bhp at 4,800rpm, triple Weber
arburettors. **£63,000-65,000**   *CNY*

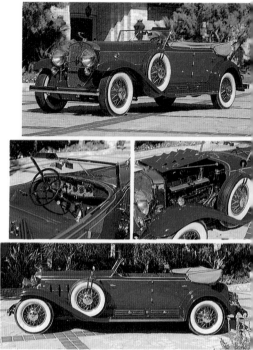

1956 Bentley S.I. Continental Drophead Coupé, with coachwork by Park Ward, London, 6 cylinder in line, cast iron monobloc engine, aluminium pistons, overhead inlet valves, side exhaust valves, 4887cc, bore 92.25mm, stroke 114.3mm, compression ratio 8.0:1 178bhp at 4,000rpm, twin SU HD6 carburettors, coil and distributor ignition. Est. **£153,000-155,000**   *CNY*

1930 Cadillac V16 Convertible Sedan, coachwork by Murphy, 45° V16 engine, bore 3in, stroke 4in, 452cu in, 7412cc, compression ratio 5.5:1, 2 in line valves per cylinder, single block mounted camshaft, updraft Cadillac carburettor to each bank, with vacuum fuel pump, dual 6 volt ignition, 165bhp at 3,400rpm, 148in wheelbase. Est. **£210,000-250,000**   *CNY*

1959 BMW 507 Roadster, with 3.2 litre, overhead valve V8 engine, capable of 150hp, body designed by Prince Albert Goertz, double radiator for more efficient cooling. The 507 experienced some success in competition, driven by Hans Stuck it outpaced racing Ferraris by winning a German mountain title, and less than 250 model 507s were built.   Est. **£145,000-150,000**   *S(NY)*

1936 Bentley 4¼ Litre Airline Saloon, with coachwork by Gurney Nutting, 6 cylinder in line, cast iron cylinder block and detachable cast iron cylinder head, 2 overhead valves per cylinder operated by pushrods and rockers from side mounted camshaft, 4257cc, bore 89mm, stroke 114mm, compression ratio 6.8:1 125bhp at 4,500rpm. **£70,000-75,000**   *CNY*

1927 Bugatti Tipo 35C 2 Litre 8 Cylinder Supercharged, 94.5in wheelbase, the type 35C was a successful model in its own right, winning the 1927 Targa Florio, the San Sebastian G.P. and the 1928 French Grand Prix. **£195,000-200,000**   *PMc*

1950 Jaguar XK120 Roadster, with alloy body, all major drive line components have been replaced with components from an XK140, c1956, an original type engine is included, a 'quick fill' has been fitted along with other modifications.
Est. **£30,000-35,000**   *S(NY)*

1957 Ferrari 500 TRC Sports Racing Car, with coachwork by Scaglietti, type 158C 4 cylinder in line twin overhead camshaft, inclined overhead valves, 1984cc. Est. **£535,000-550,000**   *CNY*

1955 Jaguar XK140 Roadster, 6 cylinder, double overhead camshaft, 3442cc, 4 speed manual with overdrive, rebuilt engine with a 'C' cylinder head.
£20,000-30,000   *S(NY)*

1929 Duesenberg Model J Sport Sedan, with coachwork by Murphy, double overhead camshaft straight 8, 420cu in, 6885cc, bore 95.2mm, stroke 120.6mm, detachable cylinder head, 4 valves per cylinder, 265bhp at 4,250rpm, 142½in wheelbase. Est. **£295,000-300,000**   *CNY*

1949 Delahaye 135M Cabriolet, with coachwork by Marcel Pourtout, France, 6 cylinder in line engine with cast iron cylinder block and head with 2 pushrod operated valves per cylinder, single side mounted camshaft, 3557cc. Est. **£240,000-260,000**   *CNY*

1950 Jaguar XK120 Roadster, 6 cylinder in line engine, twin overhead camshaft, 3442cc, bore 83mm, stroke 106mm, compression ratio 8.0:1 160bhp at 5,200rpm, twin horizontal SU carburettors, single dry plate clutch and 4 speed synchromesh manual gearbox, 102in wheelbase. **£26,000-28,000**   *CNY*

Detail of the mascot
**1926 Isotta
Fraschini Tipo 8A.**

1926 Isotta Fraschini Tipo 8A Phaeton, with wheelbase 147in and coachwork by Castagna of Milan. Isotta's customers ranged from the Pope to film stars like Rudolf Valentino.
£65,000-70,000   *PMc*

1885 Benz Replica, built by J Bentley and Sons, with gear ratio engine/countershaft 1 to 1, front wheel 730, rear 1125mm diam, wheelbase 1450mm. **£21,000-23,000**   *S(NY)*

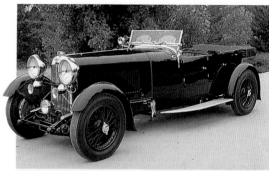

1933 Lagonda 3 Litre Open Tourer, with 6 cylinder in line, overhead valve, 3181cc, bore 75mm, stroke 120mm, twin SU carburettors, 4 speed gearbox, single plate clutch, enclosed shaft, spiral bevel rear axle, 4 wheel drum brakes, right hand drive. **£47,000-50,000**   *CNY*

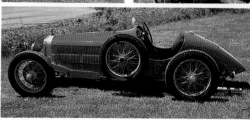

1927 Lombard Grand Prix 1100cc Supercharged, with Priou and Gausse Levallois-Perret body, 'Legere' racing coachwork and 95in wheelbase, all original. **£65,000-70,000**   *PMc*

1962 Jaguar E-Type Roadster 3.8 Litre, 6 cylinder in line engine, 7 bearing cast iron block and aluminium alloy cylinder head, twin overhead camshafts, 2 inclined overhead valves per cylinder, 3781cc, bore 87mm, stroke 106mm. Est. **£23,750-26,750**   *CNY*

1926 Lincoln Sport Roadster Model L-151, with coachwork by Locke & Co, V8 side valve engine, cast iron block and cylinder heads, 357.8cu in, 5865cc, bore 85.7mm, stroke 127mm, 90bhp at 2,800rpm, multiple disc clutch, 3 speed manual transmission, bevel rear live axle, semi-elliptic leaf front and rear suspension, 2 wheel mechanical brakes, wheelbase 144in, left hand drive.
£45,500-47,500   *CNY*

Left. The engine of the Maserati 300 S, which came from the second of Briggs Cunningham's race cars, and also the dashboard.

The 1957 Maserati 300 S Sports Racing Car.

1957 Maserati 300S Sports Racing Car, with coachwork by Fantuzzi, 6 cylinder in line engine, alloy block and cylinder heads, twin overhead camshaft, 2 overhead valves, 2993cc, bore 84mm, stroke 90mm, compression ratio 9:1, 250bhp at 6,800rpm, triple Weber 45 DCO3 carburettors, twin plugs per cylinder, twin Marelli magnetos, multi-dry plate clutch with 4 speed rear mounted transaxle, bevel drive rear axle, 6.00 x 16in and 6.50 x 16in Dunlop racing tyres, right hand drive. Est. **£600,000-650,000**   *CNY*

Above and above right detail of the headlight radiator, wing, spare wheel, and bonnet mascot of the 1927 Mercedes K Supercharged Victoria Cabriolet.

1927 Mercedes K Supercharged Victoria Cabriolet, with coachwork by Erdmann & Rossi of Berlin, wheelbase 133.9. **£85,000-90,000**   *PMc*

Detail of front and engine, 1923 Mercedes 28/95 Tourer.

1923 Mercedes 28/95 Tourer, with coachwork by Fleetwood, 6 cylinder, 3 blocks of 2 cylinders, overhead valves, overhead camshaft, 7250cc, bore 105mm, stroke 140mm, 95bhp at 1,800rpm, twin Miller carburettors, twin ignition, electric starter, dynamo electric lighting, double cone clutch with 4 speed manual gearbox, torque tube 'live' rear axle bevel drive, steel ladder frame chassis with tubular and box section cross members, 4 wheel mechanical drum brakes, handbrake on rear wheels only, 21in wheels and tyres, right hand drive. Est. **£165,000-200,000**   *CNY*

1927 Mercedes K Supercharged Skiff Body, Boudeman restored mahogany plank on frame, brass trimmed, 133.9in wheelbase. This car is the only one of its kind.
£100,000-150,000
PMc

Detail of the dashboard and steering wheel of **1927 Mercedes K Supercharged Skiff Body.**

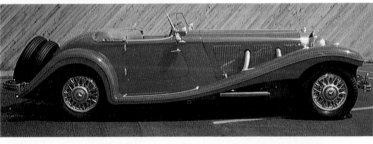

1935 Mercedes 500K 'Sport Two-Seater' Roadster, with coachwork by Daimler Benz, Sindelfingen, 8 cylinder in line engine, 9 main bearings, cast iron block and crankcase, detachable cast iron cylinder head, 2 overhead valves per cylinder by pushrods and rockers from single camshaft, 5018cc.
Est. **£1,300,000-1,500,000**
CNY

1929 Mercedes SSK Supercharged 'Zatuszec', with replacement 'S' block engine with SS accessories, 129½in wheelbase. Carlos Zatuszec purchased this SSK in 1929 and campaigned it successfully in South America between 1929 and 1938.
£228,000-235,000 *PMc*

Detail of left hand drive and dashboard of **1957 Mercedes Benz 300 SC Roadster.**

1957 Mercedes Benz 300 SC Roadster, with coachwork by Daimler Benz, Sindelfingen, 6 cylinder in line engine, 2996cc, bore 85mm, stroke 88mm, 175bhp at 5,400rpm, 4 speed all synchromesh gearbox. **£330,000-400,000** *CNY*

Further detail of the **1913 Minerva Knight,** showing bonnet and mascot.

1913 Minerva Knight, with coachwork by Carrosserie-Minerva, Anvers, with Knight sleeve valve 4 cylinder engine, 129in wheelbase. **£33,000-35,000** *PMc*

Further detail of **1933 Packard 12-1006 Convertible Sedan.**

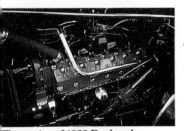

The engine of **1933 Packard 12-1006 Convertible Sedan.**

1957 Mercedes Benz 300 SL Roadster with Gullwing Top, 6 cyliner in line engine, 2996cc, bore 85mm, stroke 88mm, single overhead camshaft, 2 valves per cylinder operated by rocker arms, compression ratio 8.55:1 240bhp at 6,100rpm, 4 speed all synchromesh manual gearbox in unit with engine, Est. **£133,000-135,000** *CNY*

1933 Packard 12-1006 Convertible Sedan, with coachwork by Dietrich, V12 cylinder engine, cast iron monobloc, aluminium detachable cylinder heads, 2 valves per cylinder, L-head and hydraulic valve lifters, 7297cc, bore 87.3mm, stroke 101.5mm, compression ratio 6.0:1 160bhp at 3,200rpm, 3 speed manual gearbox. Est. **£265-270,000** *CNY*

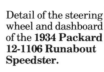

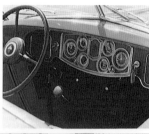

Detail of the steering wheel and dashboard of the **1934 Packard 12-1106 Runabout Speedster.**

1934 Packard Model 1107 Coupé Roadster, V12, 160hp engine, bore 3.4375in, stroke 4in, 3 speed transmission, semi-elliptic spring suspension, 142in wheelbase. This vehicle has been owned by one family for the past 25 years, and restored in the mid-60s. Est. **£85,000-90,000** *S(NY)*

1934 Packard 12-1106 Runabout Speedster, with coachwork by Le Baron, V12 cylinder engine, cast iron monobloc, 7297cc, bore 87.3mm, stroke 101.5mm, compression ratio 6.0:1 160bhp at 3,200rpm. Est. **£600,000-650,000** *CNY*

1963 Porsche 356B Super 90 Cabriolet, was conceived and built as a sports car. This vehicle is one of the last models and is fitted with a later engine. **£17,000-20,000** *S(NY)*

1912 Rolls-Royce Silver Ghost, with hood raised.

1912 Rolls-Royce Silver Ghost 40/50 Tourer, with coachwork by Barker & Co, London, 6 cylinder in line engine, 7428cc, bore 114mm, stroke 121mm, compression ratio 3.2:1 65bhp at 1,500rpm. Est. **£240-245,000** *CNY*

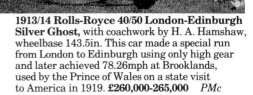

Detail of the serpent shaped horn, **1913/14 Rolls-Royce 40/50 Silver Ghost.**

Detail of wing, bonnet and boot of **1930 Rolls-Royce 40/50 Phantom II Charleston Tourer.**

1913/14 Rolls-Royce 40/50 London-Edinburgh Silver Ghost, with coachwork by H. A. Hamshaw, wheelbase 143.5in. This car made a special run from London to Edinburgh using only high gear and later achieved 78.26mph at Brooklands, used by the Prince of Wales on a state visit to America in 1919. **£260,000-265,000** *PMc*

1930 Rolls-Royce 40/50 Phantom II Charleston Tourer, with coachwork by Woodall Nicholson Ltd., wheelbase 150½in. Only 2 of this model known to exist, the other in the Stratford-on-Avon Museum. **£48,000-55,000** *PMc*

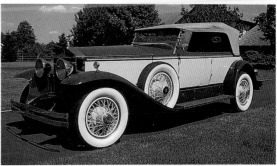

1931 Rolls-Royce Phantom I Ascot Tourer, with coachwork by Brewster of New York, 6 cylinder in 2 blocks of 3 engine, overhead valves, pushrod operated, 7668cc, bore 108mm, stroke 140mm, 4 speed manual gearbox, semi-elliptic leaf springs front, hydraulic shock absorbers cantilever leaf springs, adjustable friction type shock absorbers rear. Est. **£150-175,000** *CNY*

1931 Rolls-Royce Phantom I Regent Convertible, with coachwork by Brewster of New York, 6 cylinder engine in 2 blocks of 3, overhead valves, pushrod operated, 7668cc, bore 108mm, stroke 140mm, single dry plate clutch with 4 speed manual gearbox, semi-elliptic leaf springs, hydraulic shock absorbers front, cantilever leaf springs rear. **£170,000-175,000** *CNY*

1965 Shelby GT350, 289cu in overhead valve V8 engine, 306hp, 4 speed gearbox, wheelbase 108in, 16in steering wheel, all fibreglass bonnet, side-exit exhaust, completely restored. This car is one of the earliest of the 515 GT350s produced, and less than half are currently accounted for. Est. **£60,000-65,000**   *S(NY)*

Detail of steering wheel and dashboard of **1963 FIA Cobra.**

1963 FIA Cobra, 260cu in overhead valve V8 260hp engine, 4 speed gearbox, 90in wheelbase, built in America by Carroll Shelby from an AC chassis, recently restored and fitted with period Weber carburettors. Est. **£110,000-115,000**   *S(NY)*

1911 Simplex Speed Car, No. 649, built by Hermann Broesel, Simplex Co., New York, 4 cylinder T-head, cast in pairs, dual camshaft engine, bore 5.75in, stroke 5.75in, 597cu in, 53hp, 4 forward, 1 reverse double chain drive transmission, 124in wheelbase.
Est. **£120,000-150,000**   *S(NY)*

1951 Tuffanelli-Derrico, with Deidt chassis, the Offenhauser 270cu in engine has been removed from the car which competed in the 1951 Indianapolis 500 race, driven by Mack Hellings, but lost a piston on the 18th lap and has never been driven again. Est. **£60,000-65,000**   *S(NY)*

1914 Kline-Duesenberg, with Duesenberg 4 cylinder 'walking beam' design engine, 300cu in displacement, 4918cc, 16 valve. This car won 19 races between 1914 and 1919, was restored by Stu Laidlaw and Phil Reilly, a second unrestored body is included with the car.
Est. **£180,000-185,000**   *CNY*

Belanger Special No. 97, with 262cu in Offenhauser engine, Lesovsky chassis. This car was entered in the 1952 Indianapolis race carrying No. 1 and driven by Duane Carter finished fourth, the car was also entered for the 1953 and 54 Indianapolis but in 1953 was forced to retire with ignition problems and in 1954, carrying No. 97 and driven by Walt Faulkner, failed to qualify. Est. **£86,000-96,000** *S(NY)*

1952 Bandini Open Sports Racer, with 750cc Crosley engine and Weber carburettor. This car was produced using components from the Fiat Topalino and competed successfully in the under 2 litre racing class in Europe and later in America, restored to its now excellent condition 20 years ago. Est. **£24,000-30,000** *S(NY)*

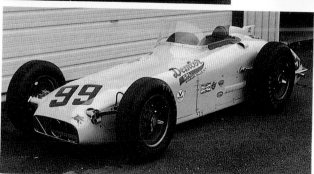

Demler Special No. 99, with 255cu in double overhead valve, 4 cylinder, Offenhauser engine, Epperly chassis, now meticulously restored to the state in which George Amick drove it to second place in the Indianapolis 500. Est. **£95,000-110,000** *S(NY)*

A further view of the **Alfa Romeo TZ1,** showing its aerodynamic design.

1964 Alfa Romeo Giulia TZ1, with coachwork by Zagato, 4 cylinder in line aluminium block and cylinder head, twin overhead camshaft, twin overhead valves, 1570cc, bore 78mm, stroke 82mm, compression ratio 9.7:1, 125bhp at 7,000rpm. **£156,000-170,000** *CNY*

1964 Alfa Romeo Giulia TZ1.

A further view of the **North American Van Lines Special, No. 3.**

North American Van Lines Special, No. 3, with 161cu in, Cosworth turbocharged engine, and Penske PC-6 chassis. This car was one of the Penske team cars which raced in the 1979 Indianapolis 500, driven by Gordon Johncock finishing sixth, and now believed in excellent conditon. Est. **£27,000-37,000** *S(NY)*

Detail of the engine of **1939 Clyde Adams Race Car.**

1946 Kurtis Offenhauser-Drake Midget Race Car, designed and built by Kurtis Kraft Race Cars, Los Angeles, Offenhauser-Drake water-cooled, in line 4 cylinder, 1680cc engine, 2 valves per cylinder operated by gear driven twin overhead camshafts, 2 side draught Riley carburettors. Est. **£30,000-35,000** *CNY*

1939 Clyde Adams Offenhauser Midget Race Car, built and designed by Clyde Adams, with Offenhauser, water-cooled, in line 4 cylinder engine, 1680cc, 2 valves per cylinder operated by gear driven twin overhead camshafts, 2 side draught Riley carburettors, single transverse leaf spring assembly at each end, beam axles front and rear, and brakes on the rear wheels only, wheelbase 70½in.
Est. **£30,000-35,000** *CNY*

1959 O.S.C.A. TIPO J Formula Junior, with 1.1 litre overhead valve Fiat engine, 85bhp at 6,800rpm, 4 speed gearbox, the front suspension was constructed using unequal length wishbones and coil spring damper units, rear live axle sprung by vertical coil springs, one of only 14 ever built, capable of 120mph, the engine and gearbox completely rebuilt but paint and upholstery in original condition. Est. **£55,000-65,000** *S(NY)*

Detail of the engine
15 Harley Conversion Midget.

15 Harley Conversion Midget, a Drake water-cooled conversion, previously owned by Ray Janell, who helped to restore it.
£8,500-9,500 *PMc*

Detail of the engine **99 Offenhauser Midget.**

44 Ardun Mercury Sprint Car, with overhead valve conversion of a Mercury flathead.
£14,000-15,000 *PMc*

99 Offenhauser Midget, Bardahl Special.
£14,000-15,000 *PMc*

Detail of 44 **Ardun Mercury Sprint Car.**

Detail of the radiator of the **6 Ford 60 Midget.**

6 Ford 60 Midget, completely restored, by Sam Packard of Daytona, Florida.
£10,000-11,000 *PMc*

1957 Kurtis Midget Roadster, with 105cu in double overhead camshaft, 4 cylinder Offenhauser engine, Kurtis chassis, and cross frame torsion bars, 4 wheel brakes, magnesium wheels and rear end spindles made by Halibrand, total car length 123in, total width 28in, one of only 6 produced, fully restored.
Est. **£35,000-45,000** *S(NY)*

l. **83 Ford 60 Midget.**
This car succcessfully
campaigned in the
A.R.D.C. circuit
in the U.S.A.
£9,500-10,500 *PMc*

r. **93 Crosley 3/4
Midget,**
powered by a Crosley
motor. This car is in
'as raced' condition.
£2,500-3,000 *PMc*

l. **8 Promo Midget,**
built by Sam Packard
for advertising
and has no engine.
£3,750-4,000 *PMc*

r. **17 Offenhauser Midget.**
This car was owned by Ted
Koopman and driven to
several New England
championships, fully
restored.
£14,000-15,000 *PMc*

**66 Offset Ford 60 Indy
Midget,** fully
restored.
£7,000-8,000 *PMc*

**11 Ford Ferguson
Midget,** powered
by the Ferguson
tractor engine modified
for racing.
£5,500-6,500 *PMc*

l. **52 GM Mid-
Engine Midget,**
fully restored in
the 1980s.
£3,500-4,500 *PMc*

Detail of the
nose of **11 Ford
Ferguson Midget**.

1 Ford Smith Jiggler Midget, with Smith Jiggler overhead valve conversion of a Ford 60 engine, fully restored. £12,500-13,500 *PMc*

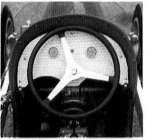

24 Elto Midget, converted Elto outboard motor, completely restored car. £8,500-9,500 *PMc*

2 Ford 60 Midget, with early Ford 60 engine, totally restored, with a quick change rear end. £10,500-11,500 *PMc*

Rear side view of **Elto Midget.**

73 Offenhauser Midget, used in the movie 'Big Wheel', featuring Mickey Rooney. £15,500-16,500 *PMc*

61 Ford Tractor Powered Midget, 4 cylinder engine, formerly owned by Mike Budniewski. £9,000-10,000 *PMc*

Detail of **Offenhauser Midget.**

9 Ford B Sprint Car, 'B' engine, fully restored, raced in New England 1930s-40s. £12,000-13,000 *PMc*

Ford B Sprint Car.

Midget, 4 cylinder in line Ace engine as used for Indian motorcycles of the early 1930s, former National 1st prize winner.
£10,000-11,000 *PMc*

38 JAP Dreyer Midget, an early 'flat tail'. This James A. Prescott conversion of a Harley Davidson.
£9,000-10,000 *PMc*

14 Ford 60 Midget, completely resto...
£12,000-13,000 *PMc*

22 Ford 60 Midget, owned by Nemo Russo of Watertown, driven by Bob Blair in several New England championships.
£5,000-6,000 *PMc*

c1900 Crouch Motorcycle, the first motorised bicycle to be built in the United States from the Stoneham, Massachusetts Crouch factory, with company name on crank, fully restored.
£7,000-8,000 *PMc*

1978 NCR Ducati Motorcycle, 1000cc Desmo 2 cylinder engine, completely rebuilt.
£16,000-17,000 *PMc*

Rolls-Royce

1920 Rolls-Royce 40/50hp Silver Ghost Tourer, 6 cylinder in line engine, cast in blocks of 3, water-cooled, side valve, bore 4½in, stroke 4¾in, 7428cc, 4 speed right hand change gearbox, cone clutch, enclosed shaft bevel rear axle, semi-elliptic leaf front springs, cantilever rear, wheelbase 147½in.   Est. **£60,000-70,000**   *S*

1920 Rolls-Royce 40/50 London to Edinburgh Style Tourer, rebodied by Wilkinson in 1950s. **£100,000-150,000** *BLE*

A rebuilt car is not necessarily of more value than a car in good original condition, even if the restoration has cost thousands of pounds.

1922 Rolls-Royce Silver Ghost, 7668cc. **£51,000-55,000** *LF*

1924 Rolls-Royce 20hp Doctor's Coupé with Dickey Seat, 6 cylinder in line, water-cooled monobloc, overhead valves, bore 3in, stroke 4½in, 3127cc, 3 speed centre change gearbox, single dry plate clutch, open shaft, spiral bevel rear axle, semi-elliptic leaf springs front and rear, wheelbase 129in, Barker coachwork, rear part of the body and dickey rebuilt in period style. **£32,000-35,000**   *S*

1924 Rolls-Royce Silver Ghost Piccadilly Speedster, 4 speed gearbox, right hand drive.
£250,000-300,000   *BLE*

1922 Rolls-Royce Silver Ghost, body by Mulliner, wheelbase 145in.
£34,000-38,000   *PMc*

1926 Rolls-Royce 20hp Sports Saloon, by Southern Motor Bodies, good condition.
£17,000-17,500   *BA*

1924 Rolls-Royce 20hp Tourer, originally supplied with a Park Ward saloon body.   Est. **£27,500-32,500**   *S*

Introduced in 1922 as a companion model to the Silver Ghost, the Twenty was intended to appeal more to the owner-driver rather than the traditional chauffeur driven customer. It was an instant success and in the following 7 years a total of just over 2,900 were supplied, the earlier examples being fitted with 2 wheel brakes. From 1926 4 wheel brakes became standard and very many of the earlier cars were subsequently modified to the later specification.

MAKE Rolls-Royce	ENGINE cc/cyl	DATES	CONDITION		
			1	2	3
40/50	7035/6	pre-WWI	£350,000	→	£50,000
40/50	7428/6	post-WWI	£90,000	£68,000	£35,000
20hp	3127/6	1922-25	£38,000	£30,000	£22,000
20hp	3127/6	1925-29	£40,000	£32,000	£24,000
Phantom I	7668/6	1925-29	£38,000	£28,000	£22,000
20/25	3669/6	1925-26	£25,000	£18,000	£15,000
Phantom II	7668/6	1929-35	£42,000	£30,000	£22,000
Phantom II Continental	7668/6	1930-35	£59,000	£40,000	£28,000
25/30	4257/6	1936-38	£24,000	£18,000	£12,000
Phantom III	7340/12	1936-39	£44,000	£28,000	£16,000
Wraith	4257/6	1938-39	£42,000	£32,000	£25,000

Prices will vary considerably depending on heritage, originality, coachbuilder, completeness and body style. A poor reproduction body can often mean the value is dependent only upon a rolling chassis and engine.

1926 Rolls-Royce 20hp Sedanca de Ville, coachwork by Brewster. £38,000-42,000   *BA*

1927 Rolls-Royce 20hp Saloon, by Cockshoot, opening 'V' windscreen and peaked roof, Barker dipping headlights.
£25,000-30,000   *OC*

1926 Rolls-Royce Phantom I Hooper, restored, engine overhauled.
£20,000-25,000   *BA*

1928 Rolls-Royce Phantom I 40/50hp Open Tourer, coachwork by Pioneer and Chapman, originally a limousine, rebodied in early 1970s in the style of a Park Ward open tourer.   Est. £40,000-45,000   *C*

1928 Rolls-Royce Phantom I Boat Tail Speedster.   £65,000-75,000   *BLE*

1928 Rolls-Royce 20hp Three Position Drophead Coupé, 6 cylinder in line, water-cooled monobloc, pushrod operated overhead valves, bore 3in, stroke 4½in, 3127cc, 4 speed right hand change gearbox, single dry plate clutch, open shaft, spiral bevel, fully floating rear axle, semi-elliptic leaf spring suspension front and rear, wheelbase 129in, 6.00 x 19in tyres.
£35,000-40,000 *S*

1929 Rolls-Royce Phantom II Sedanca de Ville, coachwork by Hibbard & Darrin, Paris.
Est. **£55,000-65,000** *C*

1929 Rolls-Royce 20hp Sedanca de Ville.
Est. **£35,000-40,000** *LF*

1928 Rolls-Royce 20hp Town Car, coachwork by Windovers.
Est. **£18,000-24,000** *S*

1930 Rolls-Royce Series L2 Phantom II Limousine, 6 cylinder pushrod operated, overhead valve, water-cooled engine, bore 4¼in, stroke 5½in, 7668cc, unit construction 4 speed gearbox, single dry plate clutch, open type propeller shaft with hypoid rear axle, semi-elliptic springs front and rear, wheelbase 150in, 7.00 x 21in tyres.
Est. **£23,000-25,000** *S*

1929 Rolls-Royce Phantom I Open Tourer.
£55,000-65,000   *BLE*

1929 Rolls-Royce Phantom I Sedanca de Ville, by Brewster.
£60,000-70,000   *BLE*

1930 Rolls-Royce Phantom II Limousine, by Croall.
£35,000-37,000   *DB*

1930 Rolls-Royce 20/25hp Four Light Saloon, with division by H. J. Mulliner, needs restoration.
£12,500-13,500   *RCC*

1932 Rolls-Royce Phantom II Croydon Convertible Coupé, coachwork by Brewster of New York, original interior.
Est. £70,000-80,000   *CNY*

In 1931 the American Springfield Phantom I production came to a close and Rolls-Royce Derby had already begun to build their AJS and AMS Series with left hand drive only for the American market. These cars, in completed or chassis-only form, were shipped to Rolls-Royce America for final preparation prior to delivery, and many of them had coachbuilt bodies by The Brewster Co. of New York which in 1926 became an integral part of Rolls-Royce Motors.

1930 Rolls-Royce Phantom I Golfer's Coupé, by Judkins, left hand drive.   £60,000-70,000   *BLE*

1931 Rolls-Royce Phantom II Roadster. £20,000-22,000 *F*

1932 Rolls-Royce Phantom II Continental Saloon, 6 cylinder in line engine, water-cooled, pushrod operated overhead valves, bore 4¼in, stroke 5½in, 7668cc, 4 speed gearbox with right hand change, hypoid bevel final drive, semi-elliptic front and rear suspension, wheelbase 144in, 6.50 x 20in tyres, interior trim poor. Est. £35,000-40,000 *S*

This was Hooper's 1932 show car and is mechanically in excellent condition.

1932 Rolls-Royce Phantom II Continental Sedanca de Ville, Barker. £175,000-185,000 *F*

Rolls-Royce Phantom II Touring Limousine, coachwork by Park Ward, modern fuel system, original equipment retained, excellent condition. Est. £35,000-40,000 *C*

1932 Rolls-Royce Phantom II Continental Sports Saloon, coachwork by Park Ward, interior woodwork needs attention, good condition. Est. £60,000-70,000 *C*

1932 Rolls-Royce 20/25hp Sports
Saloon, coachwork by Freestone
and Webb, 6 cylinder in line engine,
water-cooled monobloc, pushrod
operated overhead valves, bore
3¼in, stroke 4½in, 3669cc, 4 speed
right hand change gearbox with
synchromesh on 3rd and top, single
dry plate clutch, spiral bevel fully
floating rear axle, semi-elliptic leaf
springs front and rear, wheelbase
132in, 19in tyres, interior restored,
woodwork replaced.
£50,000-55,000   S

1934 Rolls-Royce 20/25hp Tickford
Cabriolet.   £25,000-30,000   BA

Condition Guide

1. *A vehicle in top class*
   condition but not
   'concours d'elegance'
   standard, either fully
   restored or in very good
   original condition
2. *A good, clean,*
   roadworthy vehicle,
   both mechanically and
   bodily sound
3. *A runner, but in need of*
   attention, probably
   both to bodywork and
   mechanics. Must have
   current MOT

1933 Rolls-Royce, coachwork by Gurney
Nutting.   Est. £40,000-50,000   LF

In all 3,827 20/25s were built with various
bodies and the 6 cylinder engine continued
in the best of Rolls-Royce traditions. By
1933 synchromesh had been introduced
on 3rd and top gears.

1933 Rolls-Royce 20/25hp Series
X Sports Saloon, coachwork by
Freestone and Webb, 6 cylinder in
line engine, water-cooled monobloc,
pushrod operated overhead valves,
bore 3¼in, stroke 4½in, 3669cc,
4 speed right hand change gearbox
with synchromesh on 3rd and top,
single dry plate clutch, spiral bevel
fully floating rear axle, semi-elliptic
leaf springs front and rear,
wheelbase 132in, 19in tyres, engine
rebuilt and requires running in.
Est. £30,000-34,000   S

1932 Rolls-Royce 20/25hp
Sedanca de Ville, coachwork by
Kellner of Paris, very original.
£25,000-30,000   C(M)

1932 Rolls-Royce 20/25hp, sports
saloon body by Freestone and Webb,
engine rebuilt.
£26,000-28,000   LF

1934 Rolls-Royce 20/25hp, good original condition.
£16,000-21,000 *BA*

Gurney Nutting established themselves as coachbuilders for Rolls-Royce in 1925 and subsequently were granted a Royal Warrant by the Prince of Wales for the years 1933-35.

1934 Rolls-Royce 20/25hp Owen Sedanca Drophead Coupé, coachwork by J. Gurney Nutting & Co. good condition.
£58,000-60,000 *S*

The Rolls-Royce 25/30hp was developed from the highly successful 20/25hp model and had the engine bored out to 3½in, giving a capacity of 4257cc.

1936 Rolls-Royce 25/30hp Sedanca De Ville, with coachwork by Gurney Nutting, 6 cylinder in line, water-cooled monobloc, 4257cc engine, pushrod operated overhead valves, bore 3½in, stroke 4½in, 4 speed gearbox with synchromesh on 3rd and top gears, single dry plate clutch, fully floating hypoid rear axle, semi-elliptic leaf springs front and rear, automatically controlled hydraulic dampers with manual override, wheelbase 132in, 19in tyres.
£39,000-42,000 *S*

1935 Rolls-Royce 20/25hp Limousine, with coachwork by Thrupp & Maberly.
Est. **£25,000-30,000** *S*

1937 Rolls-Royce 25/30hp Touring Limousine, with coachwork by Thrupp & Maberly, in original and sound condition throughout.
£18,000-21,000 *RCC*

1936 Rolls-Royce 25/30hp Series N2 Owner/Driver Saloon, with coachwork by Mann Egerton.
Est. **£26,000-28,000** *S*

1937 Rolls-Royce 25/30hp Hooper Limousine, in generally good order, excellent interior.
£25,000-27,000   *BA*

1950 Rolls-Royce Silver Wraith Saloon, coachwork by Park Ward.
£16,500-18,500   *DB*

1950 Rolls-Royce Silver Wraith, coachwork by Freestone & Webb.
£30,000-32,000   *DB*

ROLLS-ROYCE

1937 Rolls-Royce Phantom III Sports Saloon, coachwork by Barker, V12 cylinder, water-cooled 7338cc engine, overhead valve, bore 3½in, stroke 4½in, 4 speed manual gearbox, shaft drive to live rear axle, independent front suspension, semi-elliptic leaf spring rear, wheelbase 142in, 7.00 x 18in tyres, good overall condition, original interior trim.
Est. **£42,000-46,000**   *S*

1937 Rolls-Royce Phantom III Coupé, by Inskip.
£200,000-220,000   *PiK*

Deliveries of the Phantom III started in 1936 and 710 were made before WWII.

1952 Rolls-Royce Silver Wraith, coachwork by Park Ward.
£25,000-29,000   *BA*

MAKE Rolls-Royce	ENGINE cc/cyl	DATES	CONDITION 1	2	3
Silver Wraith LWB	4566/ 4887/6	1951-59	£22,000	£15,000	£9,000
Silver Wraith SWB	4257/ 4566/6	1947-59	£20,000	£12,000	£9,000
Mark VI	4257/6	1946-54	£20,000	£12,000	£7,000
Mark VI Coachbuilt	4257/6	1946-54	£22,000	£13,000	£6,000
Silver Wraith Drophead	4257/ 4566/6	1947-59	£60,000	£35,000	£25,000
Silver Dawn St'd Steel	4257/ 4566/6	1949-52	£30,000	£15,000	£10,000
Silver Dawn St'd Steel	4257/ 4566/6	1952-55	£30,000	£20,000	£15,000
Silver Dawn Coachbuilt	4257/ 4566/6	1949-55	£35,000	£25,000	£18,000
Silver Dawn Drophead	4257/ 4566/6	1949-55	£70,000	£50,000	£35,000
Silver Cloud I	4887/6	1955-59	£20,000	£10,000	£8,000
SCI Coupé Coachbuilt	4887/6	1955-59	£30,000	£20,000	£15,000
SCI Conv (HJM)	4887/6	1955-59	£80,000	£60,000	£40,000
Silver Cloud II	6230/8	1959-62	£19,000	£10,000	£8,000
SCII Conv (HJM)	6230/8	1959-62	£80,000	£75,000	£40,000
SCII Conv (MPW)	6230/8	1959-62	£60,000	£40,000	£32,000
Silver Cloud III	6230/8	1962-65	£25,000	£12,000	£10,000
SCIII Conv (MPW)	6230/8	1962-65	£75,000	£45,000	£35,000
Silver Shadow	6230/ 6750/8	1965-76	£11,000	£8,000	£6,000
S Shadow I Coupé (MPW)	6230/ 6750/8	1965-70	£15,000	£10,000	£8,000
SSI Drophead (MPW)	6230/ 6750/8	1965-70	£33,000	£25,000	£18,000

Coachbuilt cars can often command less than standard steel bodied cars due to general ugliness.
Continental specification cars are still the most popular models.

1954 Rolls-Royce Silver Dawn.
£25,000-40,000   *PJF*

1955 Rolls-Royce Silver Dawn Standard Steel Saloon, with coachwork by Rolls-Royce Ltd., Crewe.
£15,000-17,000   *C*

1955 Rolls-Royce Silver Wraith Touring Limousine, coachwork by Park Ward, 6 cylinder in line, water-cooled monobloc, 4887cc engine, pushrod operated overhead inlet valves and side exhaust valves, bore 3⅝in, stroke 4½in, 4 speed automatic gearbox with hypoid bevel rear axle, independent front suspension, semi-elliptic leaf springs rear, wheelbase 133in, 7.50 x 16in tyres.
Est. **£16,000-18,000**   *S*

1957 Rolls-Royce Silver Cloud I Four Door Saloon, coachwork by H. J. Mulliner & Co., Ltd., 6 cylinder in line, water-cooled monobloc, 4887cc engine, pushrod operated overhead inlet valves, side exhaust valves, bore 3¾in, stroke 4½in, 4 speed automatic gearbox, hypoid bevel rear axle with semi-floating half shafts, independent wishbone and coil spring front suspension, semi-elliptic leaf springs rear with piston dampers and anti-roll bar, wheelbase 123in, 8.20 x 15in tyres.
Est. **£28,000-32,000**   *S*

1956 Rolls-Royce Silver Cloud I, 6 cylinder, 4887cc engine.
Est. **£13,000-16,000**   *ADT*

The first standard steel Silver Cloud saloon left Crewe on 25th April 1955 at a cost of £4,797 including taxes.

1956 Rolls-Royce Silver Cloud I, right hand drive.
£41,500-45,000
HWA

1959 Rolls-Royce Silver Cloud I, with coachwork by H. J. Mulliner.
£100,000-110,000   S8

Special rear fin design.

1959 Rolls-Royce Silver Cloud I Standard Steel Saloon, 2 owners from new, has undergone a major mechanical overhaul.
£10,000-11,000   S

1961 Rolls-Royce Silver Cloud II, requires some attention.
£12,500-13,000   BA

1961 Silver Cloud II Convertible, with coachwork by H. J. Mulliner.
£150,000-250,000   PJF

1961 Rolls-Royce Silver Cloud II Standard Steel Sports Saloon.
£15,000-20,000   C.A.R.S.

Similar to Silver Cloud Series I but with revised dashboard and interior fittings.

1962 Silver Cloud II Standard Steel Saloon.
£25,000-50,000   PJF

1964 Rolls-Royce Phantom V James Young Touring Limousine.
£75,000-85,000   BLE

**1963 Rolls-Royce Silver Cloud
III Standard Steel Saloon,** V8
cylinder, water-cooled, 6230cc
engine, pushrod operated overhead
valves, with hydraulic tappets, bore
4.1in, stroke 3.6in, 4 speed gearbox,
hypoid bevel drive, independent coil
spring front suspension, semi-
elliptic leaf spring rear, wheelbase
123in, 15in tyres, in original state,
meticulously maintained.
Est. **£30,000-35,000**   *S*

**1964 Rolls-Royce
Silver Cloud III
Convertible
Continental,**
by Graber.
£55,000-65,000
BLE

**1964 Rolls-Royce Phantom V
James Young Touring
Limousine.
£75,000-125,000**   *PJF*

Use the Index!

*Because certain items
might fit easily into any of
a number of categories,
the quickest and surest
method of locating any
entry is by reference to
the index at the back of the
book.*

*This has been fully cross-
referenced for absolute
simplicity*

1964 Rolls-Royce Phantom V,
with coachwork by Park Ward.
£45,000-95,000   *PJF*

**1964 Rolls-Royce Silver Cloud
III Standard Steel Saloon,**
believed to be to original
specification.
£20,000-22,000   *S*

**1964 Rolls-Royce Silver Cloud
III Continental,** with coachwork by
H. J. Mulliner.
£75,000-115,000 *PJF*

**1964 Rolls-Royce Silver Cloud
III Standard Steel Saloon.
£25,000-40,000** *PJF*

**1965 Rolls-Royce Silver Cloud
III Drophead Coupé,** coachwork
by Mulliner Park Ward of Chiswick,
London, fully restored.
£65,000-70,000 *C.A.R.S.*

**1965 Rolls-Royce Silver Cloud
III,** in need of some attention.
£10,000-11,000 *LF*

*Distinguishable from the Silver
Cloud II by virtue of quadruple
headlamps, the Silver Cloud III was
introduced in 1962 and was in
production until 1965. It had the
6230cc V8 engine inherited from the
Series II, 200bhp at 4,500rpm.*

**1965 Rolls-Royce Silver Cloud
III Standard Steel Saloon.
£25,000-40,000** *PJF*

**1967 Rolls-Royce Drophead
Coupé,** by Mulliner Park Ward.
£22,000-23,000 *HA*

*Originally available with the 6230cc
engine, the cars were upgraded to
6.7 litres from 1970. The Drophead
was in production from 1965 to 1970
of which only 505 were built before
giving way to the Corniche.*

**1967 Rolls-Royce Phantom V
Limousine,** 90° V8 cylinder,
water-cooled, pushrod operated
overhead valves, bore 4.1in, stroke
3.6in, 6230cc, 4 speed automatic
gearbox, hypoid spiral bevel rear
axle, independent coil spring front
suspension, semi-elliptic leaf rear
springs, wheelbase 145in,
8.90 x 15in.
Est. **£35,000-45,000** *S*

*The Rolls-Royce Phantom IV had
been produced in limited numbers
exclusively for Royalty and Heads of
State. Over 500 Phantom Vs were
produced between 1959 and 1968.*

**1965/1970 Rolls-Royce
Convertible,** with coachwork by
Mulliner Park Ward.
£24,000-25,000 *AUT*

**1967 Rolls-Royce
Drophead
Coupé,** by
Mulliner.
£20,000-25,000
S8

**1968 Rolls-Royce Silver Shadow
Two Door Saloon,** coachwork by
H. J. Mulliner, Park Ward Ltd., 90°
V8 cylinder, water-cooled, pushrod
operated overhead valve engine,
bore 4.1in, stroke 3.6in, 6230cc,
3 speed automatic gearbox, hypoid
bevel final drive, independent front
and rear suspension, wheelbase
119½in, 15in tyres.
Est. **£18,000-20,000** *S*

Make: **Rolls-Royce**
Model: Silver Shadow
Type: Saloon
Years Manufactured: 1965-80
Quantity: 32,339 inc. Bentley-
badged cars
Price when new: Mk 1, £6,557
Engine Type: V8 cyl
Size: 6230cc/6750cc
Transmission: Auto
Performance: Max speed: 117
mph; 0-60: 10.2 secs; Mpg: 25.

1970 Rolls-Royce Silver Shadow,
76,000 miles.
£13,000-15,000 *HWA*

1971 Rolls-Royce Phantom VI Limousine, coachwork by Mulliner, Park Ward Ltd., 90° V8 cylinder engine, water-cooled, pushrod operated overhead valves, bore 4.1in, stroke 3.9in, 6750cc, 4 speed automatic gearbox, hypoid bevel final drive, independent coil spring and wishbone front suspension, semi-elliptic leaf rear springs with piston type dampers, wheelbase 145in, 8.90 x 15in tyres. Est. **£45,000-55,000** *S*

1971 Rolls-Royce Silver Shadow I Long Wheelbase Saloon, V8 cylinder engine, water-cooled, pushrod operated overhead valves, bore 4.1in, stroke 3.9in, 6750cc, 4 speed automatic gearbox, hypoid bevel final drive, independent front and rear coil spring suspension with hydraulic dampers, wheelbase 123½in, 205 x 15in tyres. Est. **£24,000-26,000** *S*

The introduction of the Silver Shadow to replace the Silver Cloud in 1965 marked the end of the traditional car with its separate chassis.

1972 Rolls-Royce Corniche Convertible, V8 cylinder, water-cooled, pushrod operated overhead valve with hydraulic tappets, bore 4.1in, stroke 3.9in, 6750cc, 3 speed automatic transmission, hypoid bevel rear axle, independent front and rear suspension with coil springs and hydraulic dampers, single trailing arms to the rear, wheelbase 119½in, 235/70 HR 15in tyres. **£36,000-38,000** *S*

1972 Rolls-Royce Corniche Convertible. **£35,000-48,000** *PJF*

Service history adds value.

1973 Rolls-Royce Corniche Fixed Head Coupé. **£17,000-18,000** *S*

1977 Rolls-Royce Silver Shadow II Saloon. **£17,000-18,000** *S*

1973 Rolls-Royce Corniche Fixed Head Coupé.
£14,000-18,000   *BLE*

> *Make:* **Rolls-Royce**
> *Model:* Corniche
> *Type:* Coupé/Convertible
> *Years Manufactured:* 1971-84
> *Quantity:* 4,061 inc. Bentley-badged cars
> *Price when new:* Coupé, £12,829; Convertible, £13,410
> *Engine Type:* V8 cyl
> *Size:* 6750cc
> *Transmission:* Auto
> *Performance:* Max speed: 120 mph; 0-60: 9.6 secs; Mpg: 12.

1973 Rolls-Royce Corniche Convertible.
£35,000-38,000   *HWA*

1980 Rolls-Royce Silver Shadow II.
£15,000-16,000   *WCC*

1978 Rolls-Royce Corniche Series II Fixed Head Coupé, bodywork by Mulliner Park Ward, US specification.   £25,000-30,000   *C.A.R.S.*

1979 Rolls-Royce Corniche Convertible.
£40,000-55,000   *PJF*

1971 Rolls-Royce Silver Shadow.
£8,000-12,000   *PC*

1984 Rolls-Royce Silver Spirit.   £23,000-25,000   *WCC*

1980 Rolls-Royce Corniche Convertible, excellent condition throughout.
£38,000-40,000   *HWA*

1982 Rolls-Royce Corniche Drophead Coupé.
£45,000-50,000   *S8*

1982 Rolls-Royce Camargue.
£50,000-55,000   *S8*

Make: **Rolls-Royce**
Model: Camargue
Type: Coupé
Years Manufactured: 1975-86
Quantity: 526
Engine Type: V8 cyl
Size: 6750cc
Transmission: Auto
Performance: Max speed: 120 mph; 0-60: 10.0 secs; Mpg: 13.

1986 Rolls-Royce Camargue, new condition.
£88,000-100,000   *HWA*

1986 Rolls-Royce Camargue.
£88,000-100,000   *HWA*

1990 Rolls-Royce Corniche Series III Drophead Coupé, 6750cc, excellent original condition.
£80,000-90,000   *C.A.R.S.*

Revised rear light cluster and up-graded dashboard and interior in the last of the line of these coachbuilt cars by Mulliner Park Ward.

Rover

1932 Rover 10, one owner from new, original logbook, excellent condition.
£9,500-10,500 *LF*

The Rover family 10 of 1932 was the successor to the earlier 10/25.

1946 Rover P216, condition 2.
£3,000-3,500 *CC*

1938 Rover 14 Saloon, 4 cylinder, 1577cc engine.
£5,750-6,250 *ADT*

1961 Rover 100.
£1,250-1,350 *LF*

1962 Rover 110.
£4,000-4,500 *WCC*

1961 Rover 100 Saloon,
6 cylinder,
2635cc engine.
£750-850 *ADT*

ROVER

MAKE Rover	ENGINE cc/cyl	DATES	CONDITION 1	2	3
P2 10	1389/4	1946-47	£2,900	£2,000	£500
P2 12	1496/4	1946-47	£3,200	£2,300	£600
P2 12 Tour	1496/4	1947	£6,500	£3,000	£1,000
P2 14/16	1901/6	1946-47	£4,000	£2,800	£700
P2 14/16 Sal	1901/6	1946-47	£3,700	£2,500	£700
P3 60	1595/4	1948-49	£2,900	£2,000	£500
P3 75	2103/6	1948-49	£3,800	£2,700	£600
P4 75	2103/6	1950-51	£2,800	£1,000	—
P4 75	2103/6	1952-64	£2,500	£900	—
P4 60	1997/4	1954-59	£2,300	£750	—
P4 90	2638/6	1954-59	£2,900	£1,100	—
P4 75	2230/6	1955-59	£2,500	£900	—
P4 105R	2638/6	1957-58	£3,000	£1,600	—
P4 105S	2638/6	1957-59	£3,000	£1,600	£250
P4 80	2286/4	1960-62	£2,500	£900	—
P4 95	2625/6	1963-64	£2,800	£1,600	—
P4 100	2625/6	1960-62	£3,200	£1,500	—
P4 110	2625/6	1963-64	£3,250	£1,600	—
P5 3 litre	2995/6	1959-67	£3,500	£2,000	£550
P5 3 litre Coupé	2995/6	1959-67	£5,500	£3,500	£750
P5B (V8)	3528/8	1967-74	£6,000	£4,000	£900
P5B (V8) Coupé	3528/8	1967-73	£6,000	£4,250	£1,250
P6 2000 SC Series 1	1980/4	1963-65	£2,200	£800	—
P6 2000 SC Series 1	1980/4	1966-70	£2,000	£800	—
2000 SC Auto Series 1	1980/4	1966-70	£1,500	£600	—
P6 2000 TC Series 1	1980/4	1966-70	£2,000	£900	—
P6 2000 SC Series 2	1980/4	1970-73	£2,000	£900	—
P6 2000 SC Auto Series 2	1980/4	1970-73	£1,500	£800	—
P6 2000 TC Series 2	1980/4	1970-73	£1,750	£900	—
P6 3500 Series 1	3500/8	1968-70	£2,500	£1,400	—
P6 2200 SC	2200/4	1974-77	£1,750	£850	—
P6 2200 SC Auto	2200/4	1974-77	£2,250	£900	—
P6 2200 TC	2200/4	1974-77	£2,000	£950	—
P6 3500 Series 2	3500/8	1971-77	£2,800	£1,700	—
P6 3500 S Series 2	3500/8	1971-77	£20,000	£15,000	—

1966 Rover 3 Litre Saloon,
condition 2.
£2,500-2,850 *Mot*

The 3 litre MkIII is distinguishable by the larger badge on the front and the continuous chrome strip.

1966 Rover 3 Litre MkIII Coupé,
6 cylinder, inlet over exhaust valves, 2995cc engine, 125bhp, 4 speed synchromesh gearbox with overdrive, disc front, drum rear brakes, independent front suspension, semi-elliptic live rear axle, power assisted steering, right hand drive.
£350-450 *C*

1966 Rover 3 Litre Saloon.
£5,000-10,000 *S8*

1971 Rover 3.5 Litre V8 Saloon,
one owner, 40,000 miles recorded, in
very good condition.
£5,750-6,250 *MC*

1971 Rover 3.5 Litre P5B Saloon.
£5,000-5,500 *WCC*

Make: **Rover**
Model: P6
Type: Saloon
Years Manufactured: 2000,
1963-73; 2200, 1973-77; 3500,
1968-76
Quantity: 4 cyl, 243,959; V8,
80,100
Price when new: 2000, £1,264;
3500, £2,178
Engine Type: 2000, 2200
overhead camshaft 4 cyl; 3500,
overhead valve V8
Size: 2000, 1978; 2200, 2204cc;
3500, 3528cc
Max Power: 2000, 90 bhp @
5000 rpm; 2200, 98 bhp @ 5000
rpm; 3500, 143 bhp @ 5000 rpm
Transmission: 2000/2200, 4
speed or auto; 3500, auto
Performance: Max speed: 2000,
100+ mph; 2200, 104 mph;
3500, 115 mph; 0-60: 2000, 14.5
secs; 2200, 13.0 secs; 3500, 9.5
secs; Mpg: 2000/2200, 20-26;
3500, 18-25.

1967 Rover 2000, 4 cylinder, 1978cc engine, manual gearbox.
Est. **£2,000-2,500** *ADT*

1972 Rover 3500S, 8 cylinder, 3528cc engine,
in very good condition.
£3,300-3,500 *ADT*

Salmson

1971 Rover 3500 V8 Auto, in good
condition, engine and automatic
gearbox rebuilt.
£450-500 *Cen*

1936 British Salmson S4C
Drophead Coupé, twin
carburettor, 70bhp version of double
overhead camshaft engine,
mechanically rebuilt, restored body
frame panelled with aluminium.
£38,500-40,000 *PC*

1938 Salmson Coupé, 4 cylinder, 1300cc, twin camshaft engine.
£15,000-20,000   *Ree*

Scootacar

Scootacar MkII, modified.
£800-1,000   *PC*

950 Scootacars were produced in Leeds during the late 50s and early 60s and there are still 100 cars in existence. The Scootacar Register formed approximately 11 years ago has 60 members worldwide.

Simca

1955 Simca Aronde 'Grande Large' Two Door Coupé, 4 cylinder in line engine, 1221cc, overhead valve by pushrods, single camshaft, bore 72mm, stroke 75mm, compression ratio 7.8:1, 48bhp at 4,500rpm, Solex 32 carburettor, 4 speed synchromesh gearbox with steering column gearchange, hypoid bevel back axle, unit construction with steel 2 door, 4 seater coupé style bodywork, independent coil spring and wishbone front suspension, semi-elliptic leaf spring, live axle rear, 4 wheel hydraulic drum brakes with mechanical handbrake on rear wheels, 14in disc type wheels with 5.60 x 14in tyres, wheelbase 2,440mm, right hand drive.
£3,750-4,350   *C*

Did you know

MILLER'S Collectors Cars Price Guide builds up year by year to form the most comprehensive photo-reference system available

---

Singer

1938 Singer 9 Bantam, in excellent all round condition.
£4,000-5,500   *FCV*

MAKE Singer	ENGINE cc/cyl	DATES	CONDITION		
			1	2	3
10	1097/4	1918-24	£4,000	£2,000	£1,000
15	1991/6	1922-25	£6,000	£3,000	£1,500
14/34	1776/6	1926-27	£7,000	£4,000	£2,000
Junior	848/4	1927-32	£6,000	£3,000	£1,500
Senior	1571/4	1928-29	£7,000	£4,000	£2,000
Super 6	1776/6	1928-31	£7,000	£4,000	£2,000
9 Le Mans	972/4	1932-37	£12,000	£8,000	£5,000
Twelve	1476/6	1932-34	£10,000	£7,000	£6,000
1.5 litre	1493/6	1934-36	£3,000	£2,000	£1,000
2 litre	1991/6	1934-37	£4,000	£2,750	£1,000
11	1459/4	1935-36	£3,000	£2,000	£1,000
12	1525/4	1937-39	£3,000	£2,000	£1,000

1966 Singer Gazelle Saloon,
automatic.
£3,000-3,300 *WCC*

1955 Singer Roadster 4AD.
£10,000-12,000 *PC*

SS

1938 Singer 9 Bantam De Luxe,
overhead camshaft engine, 12 volt
electrics, 42,000 miles recorded,
2 owners from new.
£6,000-7,000 *PC*

1932 SSII Two Door Coupé,
4 cylinder, 1006cc engine, side
valve, stroke 88mm, 3 speed
manual gearbox, 4 wheel drum
brakes, half-elliptic springs front
and back suspension, right hand
drive, in good condition.
Est. **£18,000-22,000** *C*

1933 Standard Swallow SS, 1056cc engine, rear axle missing, in need of restoration. **£4,250-4,750** *LAR*

1938 SS Jaguar 1½ Litre Three Position Drophead Coupé, coachwork by SS Cars, 4 cylinder in line, water-cooled monobloc, 1775cc engine, overhead valve, bore 73mm, stroke 106mm, 4 speed synchromesh and reverse gearbox, single SU carburettor, single dry plate clutch, spiral bevel rear axle, wheelbase 112½in, 500 x 18in tyres, excellent restored condition. **£17,000-18,000** *S*

William Lyons was to announce a plan which was to transform the structure of SS completely in September 1935. The Swallow Coachbuilding Co. went into voluntary liquidation and a new concern, Swallow Coachbuilding Co. (1935) Ltd., was formed as a subsidiary of SS Cars Ltd. to continue sidecar manufacture.

> **Miller's is a price GUIDE not a price LIST**

Standard

1924 Standard 11.4hp Coleshill Two Seater with Dickey, 4 cylinder in line, water-cooled monobloc, 1307cc engine, overhead valve, bore 68mm, stroke 90mm, 3 speed gearbox, plate clutch, worm final drive, semi-elliptic leaf spring suspension front and rear, wheelbase 105in, in original condition. **Est. £7,000-9,000** *S*

1946 Standard 8 Drophead Coupé, condition 1. **£4,750-5,250** *CC*

1934 Standard 10, condition 1. **£4,500-5,500** *PA*

MAKE Standard	ENGINE cc/cyl	DATES	CONDITION 1	2	3
SLS	1328/4	1919-20	£5,000	£4,000	£1,000
VI	1307/4	1922	£5,000	£4,000	£1,000
SLO/V4	1944/4	1922-28	£5,000	£4,000	£1,000
6V	2230/6	1928	£10,000	£8,000	£5,000
V3	1307/4	1923-26	£4,000	£3,000	£1,000
Little 9	1006/4	1932-33	£4,000	£2,000	£1,000
9	1155/4	1928-29	£4,000	£3,000	£1,000
Big 9	1287/4	1932-33	£4,500	£3,250	£2,000
15	1930/6	1929-30	£6,000	£4,000	£2,000
12	1337/6	1933-34	£4,000	£3,000	£1,500
10hp	1343/4	1933-37	£4,000	£2,500	£1,000
9	1052/4	1934-36	£4,000	£2,500	£1,000
Flying 9	1131/4	1937-39	£3,000	£1,800	£750
Flying 10	1267/4	1937-39	£3,000	£1,800	£750
Flying 14	1776/4	1937-48	£4,000	£2,000	£1,000
Flying 8	1021/4	1939-48	£3,000	£1,800	£750

1934 Standard 10hp Saloon, 4 cylinder, water-cooled monobloc, 1343cc engine, side valve, bore 63.5mm, stroke 106mm, 4 speed gearbox, single dry plate clutch, coil ignition, spiral bevel rear axle, wheelbase 94in, 4.75/5.00 x 18in tyres. **£3,500-4,000** *S*

1958 Standard 8, excellent condition throughout, exceptionally low mileage. **£900-1,000** *LF*

Make: **Standard**
Model: Eight/Ten/Pennant
Type: Saloon
Years Manufactured: 1953-61
Price when new: Eight, £481; Ten, £624; Pennant, £729
Engine Type: Overhead valve 4 cyl
Size: Eight, 803cc; Ten 948cc
Max Power: Eight, 26 bhp @ 4500 rpm; Ten, 33 bhp @ 4500 rpm
Transmission: 4 speed, 2 pedal control or overdrive optional on Gold Star models from April 1957
Performance: Max speed: Eight, 65 mph; Ten, 68 mph; 0-60: Eight, 50.0+ secs; Ten, 38.0 secs; Mpg: 38-45.

Stanley

1907 Stanley H5, boiler rebuilt in 1987, excellent condition. **£39,000-45,000** *PMc*

Studebaker

1926 Studebaker Standard 6 27.3hp Sedan, 6 cylinder in line, water-cooled monobloc 241.6cu in engine, side valve, bore 3⅜in, stroke 4½in, 3 speed gearbox with reverse, single dry plate clutch, bevel rear axle, semi-elliptic leaf spring suspension front and rear, wheelbase 113in, 5.25 x 21in tyres. **£7,000-7,750** *S*

This 4 door passenger sedan sold for $1,595 in 1926.

Thomas Edison designed the first Studebaker car in 1902, an electric car which was to be produced in small numbers for 10 years or so. It was in 1904 that their first petrol driven car was built.

1912 Studebaker 15/20hp Four Seater Open Tourer, 4 cylinder, water-cooled monobloc, 3153cc engine, side valve, bore 92mm, stroke 96mm, 3 speed manual gearbox, leather lined cone clutch, shaft and bevel drive, leaf springs suspension front and rear, fixed wooden wheels with detachable rims, 30 x 3½in tyres, in good original condition. **£7,000-8,000** *S*

1950 Studebaker Champion Starlight Coupé, in excellent original condition throughout, 60,000 miles recorded, rebuilt 6,000 miles ago, left hand drive.   **£7,500-8,500**   *CGB*

Sunbeam

1904 Sunbeam 12/16hp Five Seater Phaeton, 4 cylinder, 4 speed chain drive.
£120,000-130,000   *SL*

This car has been driven on the Brighton run by Sir Malcolm Campbell, Sir Jack Brabham and Bruce McLaren.

1928 Sunbeam 20 Tourer.
£15,000-16,000   *DB*

> **Miller's is a price GUIDE not a price LIST**

MAKE	ENGINE	DATES	CONDITION		
Sunbeam	cc/cyl		1	2	3
12/16	2412/4	1909/11	£20,000	£14,000	£9,500
16/20	4070/4	1912-15	£32,000	£222,000	£15,000
24	4524/6	1919-22	£28,000	£18,000	£10,000
3 litre	2916/6	1925-30	£48,000	£30,000	£20,000
16	2040/6	1927-30	£16,000	£12,500	£10,000
20	2916/6	1927-30	£22,000	£15,000	£10,500
Speed 20	2916/6	1932-35	£15,000	£10,000	£8,000
Dawn	1627/4	1934-35	£8,000	£5,000	£3,500
25	3317/6	1934	£10,000	£8,000	£4,000

Prices can vary depending on replica bodies, provenance, coachbuilder, drop head, etc.

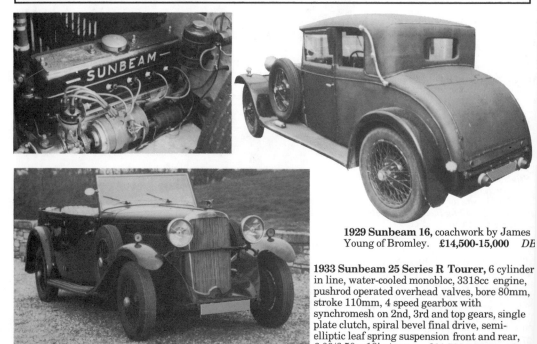

1929 Sunbeam 16, coachwork by James Young of Bromley. **£14,500-15,000**   *DB*

1933 Sunbeam 25 Series R Tourer, 6 cylinder in line, water-cooled monobloc, 3318cc engine, pushrod operated overhead valves, bore 80mm, stroke 110mm, 4 speed gearbox with synchromesh on 2nd, 3rd and top gears, single plate clutch, spiral bevel final drive, semi-elliptic leaf spring suspension front and rear, 6.00/6.50 x 18in tyres. **£11,500-12,500**   *S*

1952 Sunbeam Talbot 90 Convertible, 4 cylinder, 2267cc engine, good all round condition. £3,750-4,000 *ADT*

The Rootes Group bought up the remains of the Sunbeam Talbot concerns in 1935 and launched their own Sunbeam Talbot marque in 1938.

1951 Sunbeam Talbot 90 Sports Saloon, 4 cylinder, 2267cc engine. Est. £3,500-4,500 *ADT*

1953 Sunbeam Talbot Alpine Sports, in condition 1. £10,000-12,500 *PA*

1954 Sunbeam Talbot 90. £1,500-1,750 *LF*

These cars produce 77bhp and had a maximum speed of some 80mph.

1956 Sunbeam MkIII Sports Saloon, 4 cylinder, 2267cc engine. £2,000-2,500 *ADT*

About 19,000 of these cars were built before 1957 and each had a capacity of about 2 litres. In 1956 the car sold for £1,148. The final phase of the Sunbeam Talbot 90 was renamed Sunbeam MkIII in 1955. It is also interesting to note that to avoid confusion with Lago Talbots, Sunbeam Talbots were sold in France after the war as Sunbeams.

1956 Sunbeam MkIII. £600-700 *Cen*

1954 Sunbeam Talbot Alpine. £8,750-9,250 *WCC*

MAKE	ENGINE	DATES	CONDITION		
Sunbeam-Talbot/Sunbeam	cc/cyl		1	2	3
Talbot 80	1185/4	1948-50	£4,000	£2,250	£750
Talbot 80 DHC	1185/4	1948-50	£6,000	£4,500	£2,000
Talbot 90 Mk I	1944/4	1949-50	£4,000	£2,100	£750
Talbot 90 Mk I DHC	1944/4	1949-50	£7,000	£4,750	£2,000
Talbot 90 II/IIa/III	2267/4	1950-56	£5,000	£3,000	£1,500
Talbot 90 II/IIa/III DHC	2267/4	1950-56	£8,000	£4,500	£2,250
Talbot Alpine I/III	2267/4	1953-55	£9,000	£7,500	£3,750
Talbot Ten	1197/4	1946-48	£3,500	£2,000	£750
Talbot Ten Tourer	1197/4	1946-48	£7,000	£4,000	£2,000
Talbot Ten DHC	1197/4	1946-48	£6,500	£4,000	£2,000
Talbot 2 litre	1997/4	1946-48	£4,000	£2,500	£1,000
Talbot 2 litre Tourer	1997/4	1946-48	£7,500	£4,000	£2,250
Rapier I	1392/4	1955-57	£1,200	£700	£300
Rapier II	1494/4	1957-59	£1,800	£900	£300
Rapier II Conv	1494/4	1957-59	£3,000	£1,500	£450
Rapier III	1494/4	1959-61	£2,000	£1,200	£400
Rapier III Conv	1494/4	1959-61	£3,500	£1,600	£600
Rapier IIIA	1592/4	1961-63	£2,000	£1,200	£400
Rapier IIIA Conv	1592/4	1961-63	£3,600	£1,700	£650
Rapier IV/V	1592/				
	1725/4	1963-67	£2,000	£700	£250
Alpine I-II	1494/4	1959-62	£6,000	£3,500	£1,800
Alpine III	1592/4	1963	£6,500	£4,000	£1,250
Alpine IV	1592/4	1964	£6,500	£4,000	£1,250
Alpine V	1725/4	1965-68	£7,000	£4,000	£1,250
Harrington Alpine	1592/4	1961	£8,000	£4,750	—
Harrington Le Mans	1592/4	1962-63	£10,000	£6,500	—
Tiger Mk 1	4261/8	1964-67	£15,000	£10,000	£5,000
Tiger Mk 2	4700/8	1967	£18,000	£13,000	£5,000
Rapier Fastback	1725/4	1967-76	£1,100	£700	£250
Rapier H120	1725/4	1968-76	£1,500	£800	£300

1963 Sunbeam Alpine Convertible MkIII. £4,750-5,250 *Cen*

1961 Sunbeam Alpine Series II Roadster, S4 1592cc engine, overhead valve, 4 speed and overdrive, hard and soft tops, fully refurbished interior, new tyres. **£3,400-3,500** *SCC*

1964 Sunbeam Alpine MkIV GT, fully restored, condition 1/2. **£5,500-6,000** *Cen*

Introduced in August 1959 the Alpine MkI was fitted with the 1494cc Rapier engine. In 1964 the MkIV was introduced carrying on with the 1592cc engine introduced for the MkII.

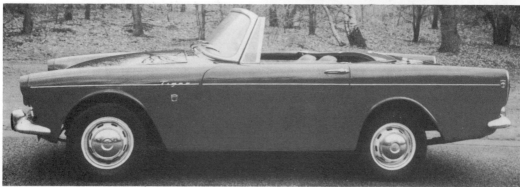

1965 Sunbeam Tiger MkI, 8 cylinder, 4700cc engine.   Est. **£17,000-20,000** *ADT*

1967 Sunbeam Alpine.
£3,400-3,700   *AUT*

1963 Sunbeam Alpine GT,
excellent original condition, low
mileage.
£5,750-6,000   *CCTC*

*By late 1965 production of the
Sunbeam Alpine had reached the
MkV stage. Since 1959 the model
range had been updated on a
number of occasions, the final
derivative having a 1725cc engine
which produced 92bhp.*

1966 Sunbeam Alpine MkV,
4 cylinder, 1725cc engine,
mechanically very good.
Est. £5,500-6,500   *ADT*

**1967 Sunbeam Alpine Series V
Convertible,** 4 cylinder, in line,
water-cooled monobloc, 1724cc
engine, overhead valves, bore 3.2in,
stroke 2.25in, 4 speed manual
gearbox with overdrive, single dry
plate clutch, shaft drive to live rear
axle, semi-floating hypoid rear axle,
semi-elliptic leaf spring suspension
front and rear, 4 wheel disc brakes,
wheelbase 86in, in excellent order,
new chrome wire wheels.
£6,000-8,500   *S*

1969 Sunbeam Rapier, 4 cylinder,
1750cc engine, manual gearbox
with overdrive, in rust free
condition.
Est. £4,000-4,500   *ADT*

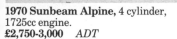

1970 Sunbeam Alpine, 4 cylinder,
1725cc engine.
£2,750-3,000   *ADT*

**1968 Sunbeam Alpine Series V
1725cc GT,** 4 cylinder, in line,
water-cooled monobloc, 1725cc
engine, overhead valves, 4 speed
manual gearbox with overdrive,
single dry plate clutch, shaft drive to
live rear axle, semi-floating hypoid
rear axle, semi-elliptic leaf spring
suspension front and rear, 4 wheel
disc brakes, wheelbase 86in.
Est. £5,500-6,500   *S*

1972 Sunbeam Rapier H120. £3,500-3,750 *WCC*

Talbot

Swift

1927 Swift 10hp P Type Tourer.
£9,500-10,000 *LF*

The Swift Cycle Company was formed in 1896 and in 1889 started to build both tricycles and motorcycles. Motor quads were introduced in 1900 and cars entered production in 1902. The company then became part of Harper Bean but ceased trading in 1931.

1936 Talbot 105 Speed Convertible, straight 6, 2969cc engine, pre-select gearbox, fully restored to original condition.
£80,000-120,000 *Ree*

The last of the proper Roesch Talbots and probably the most desirable.

1933 Talbot 75 Sportsman's Saloon, original and restored, engine/chassis rebuilt, new leather, resprayed.
£18,000-20,000 *BC*

1930 Talbot 14/45, 2 door saloon, very original. £7,500-8,500 *BC*

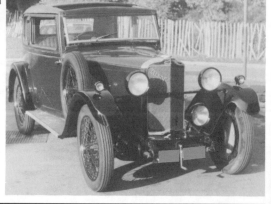

MAKE Talbot	ENGINE cc/cyl	DATES	CONDITION 1	2	3
25hp and 25/50	4155/4	1907-16	£35,000	£25,000	£15,000
12hp	2409/4	1909-15	£25,000	£15,000	£9,000
8/18	960/4	1922-25	£8,000	£5,000	£2,000
14/45	1666/6	1926-35	£16,000	£10,000	£5,000
75	2276/6	1930-37	£22,000	£12,000	£7,000
105	2969/6	1935-37	£28,000	£20,000	£15,000

Higher value for tourers and coachbuilt cars.

Talbot Darracq

1927 Talbot Darracq Type DUS 17/55hp Rolling Chassis,
6 cylinder, water-cooled monobloc, 2546cc engine, overhead valve, bore 70mm, stroke 110mm, 4 speed gearbox, single plate clutch, wheelbase 132in, 33 x 6in tyres, a restored chassis without bodywork.
Est. £9,000-9,500 *S*

Theophile Schneider

1912 Theophile Schneider 18/20hp Four Seat Tourer, 4 cylinder in line, water-cooled monobloc engine, side valve, 18/20hp, 4 speed gate change gearbox, cone clutch, shaft drive to bevel rear axle, semi-elliptic leaf springs front suspension, three-quarter elliptic rear, wheelbase 121½in, 4.40 x 23in tyres, major restoration. **£28,000-30,000** *S*

Although initially involved with Rochet Schneider, who built their first cars on Benz lines as early as 1894, Theophile Schneider built the first car to bear his own name at Boulogne-sur-Seine in 1910.

1926 Theophile Schneider 13/55hp Le Mans Tourer, 4 cylinder in line, water-cooled monobloc, 1954cc engine, overhead valve, bore 72mm, stroke 120mm, 4 speed centre change gearbox, cone clutch, bevel rear axle, semi-elliptic leaf springs front and rear, wheelbase 118¼in, 5.50 x 19in tyres.
Est. **£30,000-40,000** *S*

Thomas

1902 Thomas Runabout, single cylinder, water-cooled, 1743cc engine, bore 121mm, stroke 152mm, 3 speed gearbox, 2 rear wheel brakes, single chain drive.
Est. **£15,000-20,000** *CNY*

Toyota

1986 Toyota MR2. **£5,400-6,000** *CA*

Trojan

1961 Trojan Bubblecar.
£1,000-3,000 *PC*

Cross Reference
BMW Isetta
Messerschmitt

Trojan 198cc 200 Bubblecar, rear mounted engine, single cylinder, air-cooled, 4 stroke, 198cc, 4 speed gearbox, chain final drive.
£3,000-3,500 *S*

Triumph

Make: **Triumph**
Model: 1800/2000 Roadster
Type: Roadster
Years Manufactured: 1946-49
Quantity: 1800 (1946-48), 2,501;
2000 (1949), 2,000
Price when new: £799
Engine Type: Standard
overhead valve 4 cyl
Size: 1946-48, 1776cc; 1949,
2088cc
Max Power: 1776cc, 65 bhp @
4500 rpm; 2088cc, 68 bhp @
4200 rpm
Max Torque: 1776cc, 92 ft/lb @
2000 rpm; 2088cc, 108 ft/lb @
2000 rpm
Transmission: 1946-48, 4 speed
manual; 1949, 3 speed manual
Wheelbase: 108in
Performance: Max speed: 70-77
mph; 0-60: 27.9-34.4 secs.

**1948 Triumph Roadster 1800cc
Two Seater with Dickey,**
4 cylinder in line, water-cooled,
1776cc engine, pushrod operated
overhead valves, bore 73mm, stroke
106mm, 4 speed synchromesh
gearbox, single dry plate clutch,
bevel rear axle, transverse leaf
spring independent front
suspension, semi-elliptic leaf rear
springs, wheelbase 100in, 16in
tyres.
Est. **£18,000-20,000**   *S*

**1947 Triumph Roadster 1800.
£12,500-13,000**   *WCC*

1948 Triumph Roadster 1800,
4 cylinder, 1776cc engine.
£11,000-12,000   *ADT*

*In 2 years 2,500 1800cc Roadsters
were built.*

1955 Triumph TR3, fully restored
in June 1990.
£8,250-8,500   *LF*

1955 Triumph TR2, excellent condition, right hand drive.
£9,800-10,200   *AUT*

Make: **Triumph**	

Make: **Triumph**
Model: TR2
Type: Sports, optional lift-off hard top
Years Manufactured: 1953-55
Quantity: 8,628
Price when new: £887
Engine Type: Overhead valve 4 cyl
Size: 1991cc
Max Power: 90 bhp @ 4800 rpm
Max Torque: 117 ft/lb @ 3000 rpm
Transmission: 4 speed manual (overdrive optional)
Wheelbase: 88in
Performance: Max speed: 103 mph; 0-60: 11.9 secs.

1955 Triumph TR2 Sports, original condition 1/2, totally unrestored apart from a repaint in 1987.
£7,500-8,000 *Cen*

1960 Triumph TR3A.
£6,500-7,000 *WCC*

1960 Triumph TR3A, all original, US import, rust free, left hand drive.
£9,000-9,500 *FOR*

1961 Triumph TR3A, a fully restored American export, left hand drive.
£5,000-6,000 *PC*

1956 Triumph TR3A Roadster, right hand drive.
£7,000-7,500 *AUT*

1960 Triumph TR3A, requiring total restoration, left hand drive.
£2,750-3,000 *DB*

1965 Triumph TR4,
left hand drive.
£6,000-6,500   *AUT*

1963 TR4 Works Rally Replica.
£25,000-30,000   *CH*

Only 4 produced of which one remains in UK.

MAKE Triumph	ENGINE cc/cyl	DATES	CONDITION 1	2	3
1800/2000 Roadster	1776/ 2088/4	1946-49	£12,000	£7,500	£2,500
1800	1776/4	1946-49	£4,200	£2,000	£950
2000 Renown	2088/4	1949-54	£4,200	£2,000	£950
Mayflower	1247/4	1949-53	£1,700	£750	£350
TR2 long door	1247/4	1953	£14,000	£10,000	£8,000
TR2	1247/4	1953-55	£12,000	£9,000	£5,000
TR3	1991/4	1955-57	£9,000	£8,500	£3,500
TR3A	1991/4	1958-62	£9,000	£8,500	£3,500
TR4	2138/4	1961-65	£10,000	£7,000	£3,000
TR4A	2138/4	1965-67	£11,000	£6,500	£3,000
TR5	2498/6	1967-68	£14,500	£8,500	£4,000
TR6 P1	2498/6	1969-74	£12,500	£7,500	£3,500
Herald	948/4	1959-61	£800	£400	£150
Herald FHC	948/4	1959-61	£1,200	£550	£300
Herald DHC	948/4	1960-61	£2,000	£800	£350
Herald 'S'	948/4	1961-64	£800	£400	£150
Herald 1200	1147/4	1961-70	£1,100	£500	£200
Herald 1200 FHC	1147/4	1961-64	£1,400	£800	£300
Herald 1200 DHC	1147/4	1961-67	£2,000	£900	£350
Herald 1200 Est	1147/4	1961-67	£1,300	£700	£300
Herald 12/50	1147/4	1963-67	£1,250	£600	£250
Herald 13/60	1296/4	1967-71	£1,300	£600	£200
Herald 13/60 DHC	1296/4	1967-71	£2,000	£1,200	£400
Herald 13/60 Est	1296/4	1967-71	£1,500	£650	£300
Vitesse 1600	1596/6	1962-66	£2,000	£1,250	£550
Vitesse 1600 Conv	1596/6	1962-66	£2,800	£1,350	£600
Vitesse 2 litre Mk I	1998/6	1966-68	£1,800	£800	£300
Vitesse 2 litre Mk I Conv	1998/6	1966-68	£3,000	£1,500	£650
Vitesse 2 litre Mk II	1998/6	1968-71	£2,000	£1,500	£300
Vitesse 2 litre Mk II Conv	1998/6	1968-71	£4,000	£1,750	£650
Spitfire Mk I	1147/4	1962-64	£2,000	£1,750	£300
Spitfire Mk II	1147/4	1965-67	£2,500	£2,000	£350
Spitfire Mk III	1296/4	1967-70	£3,500	£2,500	£450
Spitfire Mk IV	1296/4	1970-74	£2,500	£2,000	£350
Spitfire 1500	1493/4	1975-78	£3,500	£2,500	£750
Spitfire 1500	1493/4	1979-81	£4,500	£3,000	£1,200
GT6 Mk I	1998/6	1966-68	£6,000	£4,000	£1,200
GT6 Mk II	1998/6	1968-70	£7,000	£4,500	£1,400
GT6 Mk III	1998/6	1970-73	£8,000	£5,000	£1,500
2000 Mk I	1998/6	1963-69	£2,000	£1,200	£400
2000 Mk III	1998/6	1969-77	£2,000	£1,200	£500
2.5 PI	2498/6	1968-75	£2,000	£1,500	£900
2500 TC/S	2498/6	1974-77	£1,750	£700	£150
2500S	2498/6	1975-77	£2,500	£1,000	£150
1300 (FWD)	1296/4	1965-70	£800	£400	£150
1300TC (FWD)	1296/4	1967-70	£900	£450	£150
1500 (FWD)	1493/4	1970-73	£700	£450	£125
1500TC (RWD)	1296/4	1973-76	£850	£500	£100
Toledo	1296/4	1970-76	£850	£450	£100
Dolomite 1500	1493/4	1976-80	£1,350	£750	£125
Dolomite 1850	1854/4	1972-80	£1,450	£850	£150
Dolomite Sprint	1998/4	1976-81	£8,000	£5,500	£1,000
Stag	2997/8	1970-77	£11,000	£6,000	£2,000
TR7	1998/4	1975-82	£3,000	£1,200	£500
TR7 DHC	1998/4	1980-82	£4,500	£3,500	£1,500

1967 Triumph TR4A.
Est. £8,000-9,000   *Cen*

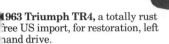

1963 Triumph TR4, a totally rust free US import, for restoration, left hand drive.
£3,000-3,500   *CCTC*

Make: **Triumph**
Model: TR4/4A
Type: Sports
Years Manufactured: 1961-67
Quantity: 68,718
Price when new: 1961-65, £1,106
Engine Type: Overhead valve 4 cyl
Size: 2138cc (1991cc optional)
Max Power: TR4, 100 bhp @ 4600 rpm; TR4A, 104 bhp @ 4700 rpm
Transmission: 4 speed, overdrive optional
Performance: Max speed: 109 mph; 0-60: 11.0 secs; Mpg: 24-26.

1966 Triumph TR4A, rebuilt.
£12,000-12,500   *FOR*

1967 Triumph TR4A, original.
£4,500-5,500   *PC*

1965 Triumph TR4A, 2 litre.
Est. £9,000-11,000   *HA*

1968 Triumph TR4A, independent rear suspension, right hand drive 'Surrey' top.
£10,000-10,500   *AUT*

1967 Triumph TR5, 6 cylinder, 2498cc engine, overhead valve fuel injection, extensively restored to original.
£16,000-16,500 *Ree*

1968 Triumph TR250, left hand drive.
£6,000-6,500 *AUT*

1968 TR5.
£10,500-11,000 *SC*

1968 Triumph TR250, American export, left hand drive.
£3,000-4,000 *PC*

1970 Triumph TR6, rust free California car, left hand drive, in usable condition but in need of some restoration.
£3,750-4,000 *CCTC*

1969 Triumph TR6, completely rebuilt.
£16,000-17,000 *FOR*

1971 Triumph TR6, 150bhp, original car with some restoration, in excellent condition.
£6,500-7,500 *FCV*

The 150bhp engine is more keenly sought.

1972 Triumph TR6, rust free US import, left hand drive, excellent condition.
£6,000-6,500 *CCTC*

Make: **Triumph**
Model: TR5/TR6
Type: Sports
Years Manufactured: 1967-75
Quantity: 106,050
Price when new: TR5, (1967-69), £1,321; TR6PI, £1,396
Engine Type: In line 6 cyl
Size: 2498cc
Max Power: TR5, 150 bhp @ 5500 rpm; TR6, 150 bhp @ 5500 rpm
Transmission: 4 speed, overdrive optional, overdrive standard from 1973
Performance: Max speed: 120 mph; 0-60: 8.8 secs; Mpg: 22-27.

1973 Triumph TR6 P1, 150bhp, low mileage, all original panels, repainted, new trim and soft top.
£7,500-8,000 *CCTC*

1971 Triumph TR6, 150bhp.
£7,000-7,500 *AUT*

1975 Triumph TR6, 4 cylinder, 2498cc engine, twin Stromberg carburettors as fitted to export models and not the injection equipment used on UK cars, good condition, left hand drive.
£5,750-6,250 *ADT*

1981 Triumph TR7 Convertible.
£2,500-3,500   *PC*

1980 Triumph TR7 (TR8 Conversion), 8 cylinder, 3500cc engine, complete restoration.
Est. £9,000-12,000   *ADT*

Using a TR7 as a donor car with the addition of a new bodyshell this car has been rebuilt to TR8 specification using technical information obtained from British Leyland.

1968 Triumph Spitfire MkIII, restored.
£4,000-4,500   *FOR*

1980 Triumph Spitfire, original condition, low mileage.
£1,500-2,500   *PC*

1970 Triumph Spitfire MkIII, 1300cc, excellent condition, all original panels including floor panels, recent respray after long storage.   **£2,500-3,500**   *FCV*

1968 Triumph GT6 MkI, 6 cylinder, 1998cc engine.
Est. £3,900-4,900   *ADT*

1973 Triumph GT6 MkIII.
£3,500-4,500   *PC*

1974 Triumph GT6 MkIII, 6 cylinder, 1998cc reconditioned engine.
£4,250-4,750   *ADT*

1974 Triumph Stag V8, manual.
€6,000-8,000   *AUT*

> *A rebuilt car is not necessarily of more value than a car in good original condition, even if the restoration has cost thousands of pounds.*

1972 Triumph Stag MkI, totally restored.
Manual £12,000-14,000
Automatic £11,000-13,000   *PC*

1972 Triumph Stag, 8 cylinder, 2997cc engine, good original condition.
£4,000-4,250   *ADT*

1976 Triumph Stag MkII, manual overdrive, totally original.
£12,000-14,000   *PC*

1978 Triumph Stag, in concours condition.
£12,500-13,500   *SC*

1978 Triumph Stag, 8 cylinder, 2997cc engine, one of the final cars manufactured, in very good condition.
£14,500-15,500   *ADT*

1977 Triumph Stag, 8 cylinder, 2997cc engine, totally restored.
£10,500-11,500   *ADT*

1976 Triumph Stag, automatic.
£4,500-5,500   *PC*

1971 Triumph Vitesse Convertible, 2 litre.
£4,000-5,000   *WCC*

1969 Triumph Vitesse, 6 cylinder, 1998cc engine.
Est. **£1,000-2,000**   *ADT*

1971 Triumph Herald Convertible.
£700-3,000   *PC*

1971 Triumph Herald Convertible.
Est. **£1,500-2,500**   *CMA*

1969 Triumph 1300, front wheel drive.   £750-850   *PC*

1973 Triumph MkII P1 Estate.
£2,500-2,750   *PC*

Make: **Triumph**
Model: 2000/2500
Type: Saloon
Years Manufactured: 1963-77
Price when new: 2500, £1,481
Engine Type: Overhead valve
6 cyl
Size: 1998cc/2498cc
Max Power: 2000, 90 bhp @
5000 rpm; 2.5PI, 132 bhp @
5450 rpm; 2500TC, 106 bhp @
4700 rpm
Transmission: 4 speed,
overdrive optional, standard on
2.5PI from Oct 1972, auto
optional
Performance: Max speed: 2000,
96 mph; 2.5PI, 111 mph;
2500TC, 103 mph; 0-60: 2000,
14.0 secs; 2.5PI, 9.8 secs;
2500TC, 11.2 secs; Mpg: 19-30.

1975 Triumph 2500S MkII Saloon.
£2,000-2,250   *PC*

TVR

1972 TVR 1600.
£4,500-5,500   *AUT*

1979 TVR 3000S.   **£10,000-12,000**   *CA*

Make: **TVR**
Model: Turbo
Type: Sports Car/Sports
Coupé/Sports Hatchback
Years Manufactured: 1976-80
Quantity: 63
Engine Type: V6 cyl
Size: 2994cc
Max Power: 230 bhp
Transmission: 4 speed, optional
overdrive
Performance: Max speed: 139
mph; 0-60: 5.8 secs; Mpg: 18.

| MAKE | ENGINE | DATES | CONDITION | | |
TVR	cc/cyl		1	2	3
Grantura I	1172/4	1957-62	£4,000	£3,000	£2,000
Grantura II	1558/4	1957-62	£4,300	£3,000	£2,000
Grantura III/1800S	1798/4	1963-67	£5,000	£3,000	£2,200
Vixen S2/3	1599/4	1968-72	£5,000	£3,000	£1,500

*The Blackpool built TVR is one of
the longest lived and most successful
of the small specialist sports cars.*

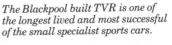

1987 TVR 420i.   **£16,000-18,000**   *CA*

**c1959 TVR Grantura Two Seater
Sports Coupé,** MGA 4 cylinder,
water-cooled monobloc, 1622cc
engine, overhead valve, bore
76.2mm, stroke 88.9mm, 4 speed
MGA twin cam gearbox, live rear
axle, wheelbase 84in, 5.60 x 15in
tyres, believed to have been built as
a factory race car.
Est. **£5,250-5,500**   *S*

UNIC

**1914 Unic 12/16hp Type G9 Two
Seater with Dickey,** 4 cylinder in
line, water-cooled engine, 4 speed
gearbox, shaft and bevel final drive,
semi-elliptic leaf front springs,
three-quarter elliptic leaf rear,
815 x 105mm tyres.
£12,000-15,000   *S*

Vanden Plas

1972 Vanden Plas Princess 1300.
£850-950   *LF*

> *Make:* **Vanden Plas**
> *Model:* Princess 4 litre R
> *Type:* Saloon
> *Years Manufactured:* 1964-68
> *Quantity:* 6,555
> *Price when new:* £1,995
> *Engine Type:* 6 cyl
> *Size:* 3909cc
> *Max Power:* 175 bhp @ 4800 rpm
> *Transmission:* Auto
> *Performance:* Max speed: 106 mph; 0-60: 12.7 secs; Mpg: 15.

The Austin or Morris 1300 luxuriously fitted by Vanden Plas in London and fitted with a smart grille and Vanden Plas badges.

1966 Vanden Plas Princess 4 Litre Limousine, 3993cc engine, bodywork and mechanics excellent, interior above average.
£4,750-5,250   *LF*

1973 Vanden Plas 1300 Princess.
£650-750   *LF*

MAKE	ENGINE	DATES	CONDITION		
Vanden Plas	cc/cyl		1	2	3
3 litre I/II	2912/6	1959-64	£4,000	£2,000	£700
4 litre R	3909/6	1964-67	£4,300	£2,500	£700
1100 Princess	1098/4	1964-67	£2,000	£1,000	—
1300 Princess	1275/4	1967-74	£2,200	£1,500	£500

Vauxhall

1924 Vauxhall 30/98 Velox, good condition.
£100,000-120,000   *DG*

VAUXHALL

1929 Vauxhall 20/60 Tourer, good condition.
£25,000-26,500   *Mot*

1935 Vauxhall 20 Big Six, restored condition.
Est. **£2,000-3,000**   *LF*

1935 Vauxhall Light Six, 1531cc, 6 cylinders.   Est. **£2,000-4,000**   *ADT*

Known as the 12/6 or Light Six the 6 cylinder engine had a capacity of 1531cc and has a designated treasury rating of 12.08hp. The original price tag of £195 was a full £20 above the Morris equivalent.

1956 Vauxhall Velox E Series.
£4,000-4,500   *WCC*

MAKE	ENGINE	DATES	CONDITION		
Vauxhall	cc/cyl		1	2	3
Wyvern LIX	1500/4	1948-51	£3,000	£1,000	£500
Velox LIP	2200/6	1948-51	£3,000	£1,000	£500
Wyvern EIX	1500/4	1951-57	£3,000	£1,320	£400
Velox EIPV	2200/6	1951-57	£3,000	£1,650	£400
Cresta EIPC	2200/6	1954-57	£3,000	£1,650	£400
Velox/Cresta PAS/PAD	2262/6	1957-59	£2,850	£1,300	£300
Velox/Cresta PASY/PADY	2262/6	1959-60	£2,700	£1,500	£300
Velox/Cresta PASX/PADX	2651/6	1960-62	£2,700	£1,300	£300
Velox/Cresta PASX/PADX Est	2651/6	1960-62	£2,700	£1,300	£300
Velox/Cresta PB	2651/6	1962-65	£1,600	£800	£100
Velox/Cresta PB Est	2651/6	1962-65	£1,600	£800	£100
Cresta/Deluxe PC	3294/6	1964-72	£1,500	£800	£100
Cresta PC Est	3294/6	1964-72	£1,500	£800	£100
Viscount	3294/6	1964-72	£1,700	£900	£100
Victor I/II	1507/4	1957-61	£2,000	£1,000	£250
Victor I/II Est	1507/4	1957-61	£2,100	£1,100	£300
Victor FB	1507/4	1961-64	£1,500	£900	£200
Victor FB Est	1507/4	1961-64	£1,600	£1,000	£300
VX4/90	1507/4	1961-64	£2,000	£900	£150
Victor FC101	1594/4	1964-67	£1,600	£900	£150
Victor FC101 Est	1594/4	1964-67	£1,800	£1,000	£200
101 VX4/90	1594/4	1964-67	£2,000	£1,500	£250
VX4/90	1975/4	1969-71	£700	£600	—
Ventora I/II	3294/6	1968-71	£500	£375	—
Viva HA	1057/4	1963-66	£500	£350	—
Viva SL90	1159/4	1966-70	£500	£350	—
Viva Brabham	1159/4	1967-70	£1,200	£500	—
Viva	1600/4	1968-70	£500	£350	—
Viva Est	1159/4	1967-70	£500	£400	—
D/OD	3969/4	1914-26	£35,000	£30,000	£25,000
E/OE	4224/4	1919-28	£40,000	£33,000	£25,000
Eighty	3317/6	1931-33	£10,000	£8,000	£5,000
Cadet	2048/6	1931-33	£7,000	£5,000	£3,000
Lt Six	1531/6	1934-38	£5,000	£4,000	£1,500
14	1781/6	1934-39	£4,000	£3,000	£1,500
25	3215/6	1937-39	£5,000	£4,000	£1,500
10	1203/4	1938-39	£4,000	£3,000	£1,500

1971 Vauxhall Cresta Automatic.
£250-750   *PC*

Volkswagen

1971 Volkswagen Beetle Cabriolet, by Karmann, left hand drive.
£4,500-5,000   *AUT*

Introduced in Germany during the 30s as the workers' 'strength through joy' car, the Volkswagen Beetle was evaluated by the British motor industry immediately following WWII, and pronounced a non-starter. It outsold Ford's Model T, which had previously held the production record at over 15 million units, and continued to be sold in Britain from the plant at Wolfsburg until 1978. It is still built in Mexico and Africa to this day in its original Beetle form but German built versions have not been made for the past 14 years.

1957 Vauxhall Victor Series I F Type.
£1,500-3,500   *PC*

This car is fitted with several optional accessories including spot lamps and rubber bumper buffers.

Vauxhall Victor F Type Series 1, 4 door saloons were introduced in 1957. The car was of unitary construction with a 1500cc engine and 3 speed, all synchromesh, column change gearbox. There were 2 models, Standard and Super. The car became very successful, especially in export markets, but was criticised in Britain for the amount of chrome work. Rust soon became a serious problem and today less than 100 are known to have survived in the UK.

1971 Volkswagen Beetle 1300 Convertible, completely restored, condition 1.
£5,000-5,250   *Cen*

Over 21 million Volkswagen Beetles were produced.

1973 Volkswagen Beetle 1300, requires restoration.   £350-500   *DB*

1977 Volkswagen Beetle Saloon, rear mounted, air-cooled, flat four engine, 1192cc, 4 speed gearbox, rear wheel drive, wheelbase 94in, excellent condition.
£6,000-6,500   *S*

1976 Volkswagen Convertible, by Karmann, 1598cc, 4 cylinders, excellent overall condition.
£8,250-8,750   *ADT*

VOLKSWAGEN

MAKE Volkswagen	ENGINE cc/cyl	DATES	CONDITION		
			1	2	3
Beetle (split)	1131/4	1945-53	£5,500	£3,500	£2,000
Beetle (oval)	1192/4	1953-57	£4,000	£2,000	£1,000
Beetle slope headlamps	1192/4	1957-68	£2,500	£1,000	£600
Beetle DHC	1192/4	1954-60	£7,000	£4,500	£2,000
Beetle 1500	1493/4	1966-70	£3,000	£2,000	£1,000
Beetle 1302 LS	1600/4	1970-72	£2,500	£1,850	£850
Beetle 1303 S	1600/4	1972-79	£3,000	£2,000	£1,500
1500 Variant/1600	1493/ 1584/4	1961-73	£2,000	£1,500	£650
1500/1600 notchback	1493/ 1584/4	1961-73	£3,000	£2,000	£800
Karmann Ghia/I	1192/4	1955-59	£4,000	£3,000	£1,000
Karmann Ghia/I DHC	1192/4	1957-59	£8,000	£5,000	£2,500
Karmann Ghia/I	1192/4	1960-74	£4,000	£3,000	£1,800
Karmann Ghia/I DHC	1192/4	1960-74	£6,000	£4,500	£2,000
Karmann Ghia/3	1493/4	1962-69	£3,000	£2,500	£1,250

1978 Volkswagen Beetle Saloon,
1192cc.
£6,000-7,000 *S*

**1973 Volkswagen Beetle
Convertible,** by Karmann.
£4,250-4,500 *Cen*

**1969 Volkswagen Karmann Ghia
Coupé,** right hand drive.
£6,000-7,000
Left hand drive.
£3,000-4000 *AUT*

Make: **Volkswagen**
Model: Karmann-Ghia 1500
Type: Coupé/Convertible
Years Manufactured: 1962-69
Engine Type: 4 cyl
Size: 1493cc
Max Power: 44 bhp @ 4200 rpm
Transmission: 4 speed
Performance: Max speed: 80+
mph; 0-60: 20.0 secs; Mpg: 26-32.

**1971 Volkswagen Karmann Ghia
Coupé.**
Est. **£4,000-5,000** *Cen*

1970 Volkswagen Karmann Convertible Type 1, 1600cc, right hand drive, rebuilt. **£10,000-11,000** *PC*

1965 Volkswagen Karmann Ghia Type 1 Coupé, 1200cc. **£3,000-3,500** *PC*

1972 Volkswagen Karmann Ghia Sports Coupé, 4 cylinder engine, horizontally opposed, air-cooled, pushrod operated overhead valves, bore 85.5mm, stroke 69mm, 1584cc, 4 speed gearbox, single dry plate clutch, bevel final drive, independent front and rear suspension, wheelbase 94½in, low mileage, unused for several years. **£10,500-11,500** *S*

Volvo

1968 Volvo 131 Coupé, 1780cc, 4 cylinders. **£3,500-4,000** *ADT*

1957 Volvo PV 444 Two Door Saloon, 4 cylinder in line engine, water-cooled monobloc, overhead valve, bore 79.37mm, stroke 80mm, 1583cc, 3 speed manual gearbox, bevel rear axle, independent front and rear suspension, wheelbase 2,600mm, 5.90 x 15in tyres, left hand drive. **£3,000-3,500** *S*

Volvo 1800 ES, condition 1. **£3,200-3,500** *CC*

Make: **Volvo**
Model: P1800
Type: Coupé/Sports Hatchback
Years Manufactured: 1963-68
Engine Type: Overhead valve 4 cyl
Size: 1778cc
Max Power: 103 bhp @ 5600 rpm
Transmission: 4 speed plus overdrive
Performance: Max speed: 107 mph; 0-60: 11.9 secs; Mpg: 22-28.

1972 Volvo P 1800 ES Shooting Brake. **£5,500-6,500** *AUT*

VOLVO

MAKE Volvo	ENGINE cc/cyl	DATES	CONDITION		
			1	2	3
PV444	1800/4	1958-67	£4,000	£1,750	£800
PV544	1800/4	1962-64	£4,000	£1,750	£800
120(B16)	1583/4	1956-59	£3,000	£1,000	£300
121	1780/4	1960-67	£3,500	£1,500	£350
122S	1780/4	1960-67	£4,500	£1,500	£250
131	1780/4	1962-69	£4,000	£1,500	£350
221/222	1780/4	1962-69	£2,500	£1,500	£300
123Gt	1986/4	1967-69	£3,000	£2,500	£750
P1800	1986/4	1960-70	£3,500	£2,000	£1,000
P1800E	1986/4	1970-71	£4,000	£2,500	£1,000
P1800ES	1986/4	1971-73	£5,000	£3,000	£1,000

1972 Volvo 1800 ES, 1986cc, 4 cylinders. **£1,500-1,750** *ADT*

1973 Volvo 1800 ES Estate, good condition. **£6,500-7,000** *CMA*

The P 1800 family of cars first came into production in 1961. Production ceased in 1973 after 47,585 cars had been made. The 1800 ES accounted for 8,000 of these and was a square backed estate fuel injected development of the original model. It was produced from 1971 to 1973.

1991 Westfield Seven, Lotus Seven derivative, built to exceptional standard with chromed suspension and wheels, trimmed in tan with matching weather equipment. **£6,000-7,000** *KSC*

Westfield

White

Willys-Knight

1903 White Model C 10hp Steam Open Drive Limousine, twin cylinder steam compound engine, cylinders 3in and 5in x 3.5in, semi-flash boiler, armoured wood frame, semi-elliptic leaf springs front and rear, wheel steering, shaft final drive, wheelbase 80in, 80 x 8.5in tyres, engine rebuilt, good mechanical condition. Est. **£35,000-38,000** *S*

1926/27 Willys-Knight Model 65 40hp Four Door Tourer, 4 cylinder, water-cooled, sleeve valve, 3 speed gearbox in unit with the engine, open shaft drive to rear axle, semi-elliptic front and rear springs, 6.00 x 20in tyres. **£6,800-7,200** *S*

Willys are known for their pioneer work in using pressed steel rather than hand beaten panels for their bodywork. The sleeve valve system had many proponents, not least the English Daimler Company, who also produced engines under a Knight licence from 1909 to 1936.

Willys-Overland

1916 Willys-Overland Five
Seater Tourer, 3818cc, 4 cylinders.
Est. £18,000-23,000 *ADT*

Did you know
*MILLER'S Collectors Cars
Price Guide builds up year
by year to form the most
comprehensive photo-
reference system
available*

Wolseley

**1923 Wolseley A9 15.6hp Open
Drive Landaulette**, 4 cylinder in
line engine, water-cooled monobloc,
overhead camshaft, bore 80mm,
stroke 130mm, 2614cc, 15.6hp,
4 speed right hand gate change
gearbox, multi-plate clutch, shaft
drive to rear axle, quarter-elliptic
leaf spring suspension front and
rear, wheelbase 129in, 20in tyres.
Est. £20,000-30,000 *S*

1934 Wolseley Hornet Special,
completely restored.
£15,000-20,000 *PC*

MAKE Wolseley (Veteran & Vintage)	ENGINE cc/cyl	DATES	CONDITION		
			1	2	3
10	987/2	1909-16	£16,000	£12,500	£9,000
CZ (30hp)	2887/4	1909	£18,000	£13,000	£9,000
10 and E3	1320/4	1920-24	—	—	—
7 and H7	840/2	1922-24	—	—	—
15hp and A9	2614/4	1920-27	£12,000	£10,000	£8,000
20 and C8	3921/				
	3862/6	1920-27			
E4 (10.5hp)	1267/				
	1542/4	1925-30	—	—	—
E6 and Viper and 16hp	2025/6	1927-34	£18,000	£15,000	£10,000
E8M	2700/8	1928-31	£22,000	£18,000	£14,000
Hornet	1271/4	1931-35	£10,000	£8,000	£4,500
Hornet Special	1271/				
	1604/6	1933-36	£12,000	£8,000	£5,000
Wasp	1069/4	1936	£7,000	£5,000	£3,500
Hornet	1378/6	1936	£8,000	£6,000	£4,000
21/60 and 21hp	2677/				
	2916/6	1932-39	£11,000	£6,000	£4,000
25	3485/6	1936-39	£11,000	£6,500	£4,000
12/48	1547/4	1937-39	£5,000	£3,000	£1,750
18/80	2322/6	1938-39	£11,000	£6,750	£4,000

Early Wolseley cars are well made and very British and when housing coachbuilt bodies command a
premium of at least + 25%.

1952 Wolseley 6/80, 6 cylinder in line engine, 2225cc, column gear change, 4 speed gearbox, torsion bar front suspension, semi-elliptic rear springs.
£3,500-4,000 *ESM*

1952 Wolseley 6/80.
£6,500-7,000 *WCC*

1969 Wolseley 16/60, 1622cc, 4 cylinders, 31,000 miles.
£1,800-2,000 *ADT*

1967 Wolseley Hornet.
£1,500-1,750 *WCC*

MAKE Wolseley	ENGINE cc/cyl	DATES	CONDITION 1	2	3
8	918/4	1939-48	£1,800	£1,000	£500
10	1140/4	1939-48	£2,500	£1,000	£500
12/48	1548/4	1939-48	£2,500	£1,000	£500
14/60	1818/6	1946-48	£2,500	£1,200	£500
18/85	2321/6	1946-48	£3,000	£1,200	£500
25	3485/6	1946-48	£2,500	£1,000	£500
4/50	1476/4	1948-53	£1,900	£600	£300
6/80	2215/6	1948-54	£2,000	£1,000	£400
4/44	1250/4	1952-56	£1,850	£850	£350
15/50	1489/4	1956-58	£1,850	£850	£350
1500	1489/4	1958-65	£2,000	£1,000	£500
15/60	1489/4	1958-61	£1,500	£700	£300
16/60	1622/4	1961-71	£1,600	£800	£300
6/90	2639/6	1954-57	£2,000	£1,000	£500
6/99	2912/6	1959-61	£2,000	£1,000	£500
6/110 Mk I/II	2912/6	1961-68	£1,500	£800	£400
Hornet (Mini)	848/4	1961-70	£1,250	£450	£250
1300	1275/4	1967-74	£1,250	£750	£200
18/85	1798/4	1967-72	£950	£400	£150

Zim

1956 Zim Gaz 12, 7 seat Russian limousine, totally original and unrestored apart from GAZ 24 engine fitted.
Est. **£1,500-2,000** *Cen*

This limited production government car is a rare example based on the ZIS which lasted until 1959. The design was heavily influenced by American vehicles of the time and in 1959 the ZIL 111 was introduced with very similar lines to the Cadillac even down to the 6 litre short stroke V8 engine of General Motors type.

Commercial Vehicles

1906 Cretors Popcorn Wagon on a 1914 Model T Ford Chassis, 4 cylinder in line, cast iron block, crankcase and cylinder heads, 2 side valves per cylinder, single camshaft, 2896cc, bore 95.2mm, stroke 101.6mm, epicyclic transmission, 2 forward 1 reverse speeds incorporating take-up clutches in unit with engine, steel chassis ladder frame, forged front axle beam, transverse leaf spring, handbrake on to rear brake drums, 30in artillery style wheels, wheelbase 100in.
£13,000-15,000 *CNY*

1922 Ford Model T Depot Hack.
£3,000-3,300 *DB*

> **Miller's is a price GUIDE not a price LIST**

c1914/1918 Daimler Platform Lorry, 4 cylinder in line engine, water-cooled and cast in pairs, side valves, 4 speed right hand gate change gearbox, shaft final drive, semi-elliptic leaf spring suspension front and rear, solid rubber tyres to all wheels, twin rear wheels 32in diam.
£17,000-17,500 *S*

1913 Ford Model T, ex-baker's van, good condition.
£8,000-10,000 *DG*

1928 Rosengart Light Van, 747cc, restored. **£5,250-5,750** *HA*

Very few of these vehicles survive today. Made at the Bellanger factory of Rosengarts, they were based on the current Austin Seven model and built under licence using the same 747cc power unit.

1928 Morris L-Type 12cwt Van, 1550cc, 4 cylinders.
£11,000-12,000 *ADT*

1928 Morris 10cwt Van,
condition 1.
£10,000-12,000 *PA*

1929 Peugeot 201 Pick-Up,
1100cc, 4 cylinders.
Est. **£4,800-5,200** *ADT*

1929 Morris Light Van, 1479cc.
Est. **£8,000-10,000** *HA*

**1930 Ford Model A Pick-Up
Truck,** converted saloon body.
Est. **£4,000-6,000** *LF*

1932 Morris Truck.
£2,250-2,500 *DB*

**1931 Ford Model A Closed Cab
Pick-Up,** 4 cylinder, side valve,
3 speed manual gearbox, left hand
drive, recently restored.
Est. **£6,000-8,000** *C*

1933 Austin 10/4 Pick-Up,
4 cylinder, side valve, 1125cc,
4 speed manual gearbox, right hand
drive, recent restoration.
Est. **£6,000-8,000** *C*

*This example left the factory as a
saloon but has been converted to a
pick-up.*

1934 Commer Six Woody, 16hp,
2107cc, 6 cylinder engine,
restoration project.
£300-350 *LF*

*Rootes took over Commer Cars
Limited in 1934.*

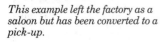

1935 Commer 8 cwt Van,
condition 2.
£5,500-6,500 *PA*

1935 Morris 5 cwt Van, 918cc,
4 cylinders.
£5,500-6,000 *ADT*

c1940 Austin Light Van, 1000cc,
4 cylinders.
Est. **£1,500-2,500** *ADT*

1940 Ford 5 cwt Van, 1172cc,
4 cylinders.
Est. **£500-750** *ADT*

1951 Ford 5 cwt Van, 800cc,
4 cylinders.
£2,750-3,000 *ADT*

1947 Morris 8 Series Z Van, good
condition.
£3,500-4,000 *WCC*

1960 Morris JB-Type Van,
1486cc, 4 cylinders.
Est. **£1,500-2,500** *ADT*

1951 Ford Step-Side Pick-Up,
6 litre, Cleveland Block, imported
from U.S.A.
£8,000-10,000 *RE*

1961 Ford Thames 15 cwt Pick-Up, reasonable condition.
£850-1,000   *LF*

1943 AEC Matador 4 x 4 Winch Tractor,
7700cc.   Est. **£5,000-7,000**   *LF*

Supplied new to the Army in 1943 this AEC has 6 cylinder diesel engine of the type used in London buses over the years.

Breakdown Trucks

c1939 Morris Breakdown Truck,
3990cc, 6 cylinders, manual gearbox.
Est. **£1,500-2,000**   *ADT*

Fire Engines

1946 Austin K2 Breakdown Wagon,
good condition.   **£2,000-2,500**   *Cen*

1921 Stutz Triple Combination Fire Engine, 6 cylinder in line, 2 cast iron blocks of 3 cylinders with single crankcase and 2 cast iron cylinder heads, side valve, 505cu in, maximum engine speed 2,600rpm, single Zenith downdraught carburettor, 2 plugs per cylinder with Bosch magneto and coil distributor ignition, multi-plate clutch with 3 speed and reverse gearbox, shaft drive with straight bevel differential, pressed steel ladder frame with 2 channel section side members, crossbraced with open type Fire Pumper bodywork, 600 gallon water tank, hoses, ladder, single rotary gear water pump, brass bell, red flashing light, 60mph, 6mpg, right hand drive.   **£10,000-12,000**   *CNY*

1956 Bedford Fire Tender,
4 cylinder in line petrol engine, water-cooled monobloc, 4 speed synchromesh gearbox, hypoid rear axle, leaf spring suspension front and rear, twin rear wheels, 7.00 x 20in tyres.
£2,500-3,000   *S*

One of the longest surviving independent commercial vehicle builders in Britain, Dennis of Guildford produced their first car as early as 1899 and continued in car manufacture until WWI before concentrating their efforts in the commercial vehicle sector.

1934 Dennis Fire Engine.   £7,500-8,000   *S*

Military Vehicles

1960 Alvis Ferret MkII Armoured Scout Car, Rolls-Royce RB60 3.9 litre engine, 4 cylinder, water-cooled, overhead valves, 5 speed pre-selector gearbox, 4 wheel drive, independent coil spring suspension front and rear, wheelbase 100in, 9.00 x 16in tyres. **£3,250-3,500** *S*

c1941 Willys 1/4 Ton MB General Purpose Jeep, 4 cylinder, side valve, water-cooled engine, 2200cc, 3 speed synchromesh gearbox, leaf spring suspension, live rear axle, good condition. **£5,000-5,500** *S*

Omnibuses

1962 Land Rover 'The Wader', 4 cylinder, modified 1 ton, 109in chassis, flotation gear, propeller on rear propshaft, fully sealed body. **£16,000-18,000** *DL*

Motor Caravans

1961 Leyland Atlantean PDR 1/1, Mk2 Double Decker Bus. **£1,900-2,100** *LF*

1936 Pontiac 27.4hp Motor Caravan, requires an overhaul. **£5,000-5,500** *S*

Taxis

c1939 Aero Bubble Trailer, built by Aero Products, Queen St Mills, Batley, Yorkshire, panelled in aluminium, double folding tailgate, swinging arm suspension, 60in overall length, 48in wide, 38½in high. **£125-150** *S*

1937 Austin Low Loader 12/4 Landaulette London Taxicab, coachwork by Jones of Westbourne Grove, 4 cylinder, side valve, water-cooled monobloc, bore 72mm, stroke 114.5mm, 1479cc, 4 speed gearbox, worm final drive, wheelbase 112in, good overall condition. **£13,000-14,000** *S*

Competition Cars

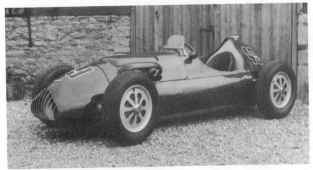

1952 Alta Formula II Grand Prix car.
Est. £80,000-100,000   C

The Alta Car and Engineering Co. of Tolworth, Surrey, under the guidance of engineer/designer Geoffrey Taylor, introduced their first sports racing car in 1929 which was followed by a series of supercharged cars of 1100cc, 1½ and 2 litre capacity that achieved some success before the war in Voiturette racing.

The Alfa Romeo GTAm was the racing version of the extraordinarily successful 1750 GT Veloce, the 'A' signifying 'Allegerita' or lightened and the small 'm' indicating 'maggiorata' or enlarged. The Chizzola brothers had set up Autodelta to build the famous TZ Alfas and they were responsible for building just 40 of the GTAm cars during 1970/71. The fuel injected engines developed some 220bhp at 7,200rpm.

1970 Alfa Romeo 1750 GTAm Competition Coupé, 4 cylinder in line engine, water-cooled, twin overhead camshaft, bore 84.5mm, stroke 88.5mm, 1985cc, 5 speed gearbox, plate clutch, hypoid bevel rear axle, independent coil spring front and rear suspension, wheelbase 93in, 13in tyres.
Est. £50,000-70,000   S(M)

1989 Arrows A10/B Grand Prix Car.
£60,000-75,000   DHA

1960 Bandini rear engine Formula Junior, 1100cc, Fiat engine and gearbox.
£25,000-27,500   SL

1929 Cagle Ford USAC Sprint Car, VS CC eligible.
£17,500-18,500   CA

This car is kept in a museum in USA and believed to have raced at Pike's Peak and Ascot Raceway.

1963 Austin Healey Lenham Le Mans body Sprite.
£6,500-7,000   CA

1973 Brabham BT410 Formula 3.
£8,000-9,000   *CA*

1970 Chevron B17 Formula 2.
£25,000-26,000   *CA*

1960 Cooper Formula Junior Type 52 MkI, 1100cc, BMC engine, Citroën Ersa gearbox.
£22,000-23,000   *SL*

This car won Helsinki and Roskilde Formula Junior races driven by Kurt Lincoln in 1960.

1953 Cooper Mk7 500cc Formula 3, for restoration. When restored.
£14,000-16,000 *CA*

1959 Elva Formula Junior.
£20,000-22,000   *CA*

This model is a fine example of one of the foremost front engine juniors with a BMC engine.

1972 Dulon MP15 Formula Ford.
£2,000-3,000   *CA*

1954 Ford Zephyr Zodiac MkI,
with roll cages, all rally prepared.
£8,500-9,500   *WCC*

*This car has competed in 2 Pirelli Classic Marathons and one Monte
Carlo rally.*

1965 Ginetta G4
Sports Racer.
£25,000-27,000
CA

1969 Hawk Formula Ford DL2.
£3,500-4,000   *CA*

Miller's is a price Guide not a price List

The price ranges given reflect the average price a purchaser should pay for similar vehicle. Condition, rarity, provenance, racing history, originality and any restoration are factors that must be taken into account when assessing values. When buying or selling, it must always be remembered that prices can be greatly affected by the condition of any vehicle. Unless otherwise stated, all cars shown in Miller's are of good merchantable quality, and the valuations given reflect this fact. Vehicles offered for sale in exceptionally fine condition or in poor condition may reasonably be expected to be priced considerably higher or lower respectively than the estimates given herein

1953 JLR 500 Cooper Copy, raced extensively in the 1950s.
£5,500-6,500   *CA*

1978 Lancia LC2.
£120,000-135,000   *DHA*

1955 Lister Bristol Competition Two Seater Sports, coachwork by Williams & Pritchard.
Est. £100,000-120,000   *C(M)*

1956 Lotus II Le Mans, fully restored.
£45,000-55,000   *CA*

1960 Lotus 19, fully restored, 2.5 litre Coventry Climax engine.
£150,000-200,000   *CA*

Use the Index!

Because certain items might fit easily into any of a number of categories, the quickest and surest method of locating any entry is by reference to the index at the back of the book.

This has been fully cross-referenced for absolute simplicity

1964 Lotus 23, fully restored.
£60,000-65,000   *CA*

1963 Lotus 23B Sports Racing Car.
£65,000-70,000   *CA*

1964 Lotus 23B, fully restored.
£65,000-70,000   *CA*

1964 Lotus 22 Formula Junior Single Seat Racing Car, 4 cylinder rear mounted, 1097cc engine, overhead valve modified Ford 105E by Cosworth, 100bhp, Hewland H6-827 gearbox, tubular space frame chassis, double wishbone and coil spring and damper units front suspension, reversed lower wishbones, parallel radius arms and coil and spring damped units rear, wheelbase 90in, 4.50 x 13in and 5.25 x 13in tyres. Est. **£22,000-25,000**   *S*

Lotus began in 1952 under the direction of Colin Chapman and Team Lotus commenced in 1954 under the parent company.

1969 Lotus 61 Formula Ford, fully restored.   **£10,000-11,000**   *CA*

1970 March 703 Formula 3.
£10,000-11,000   *CA*

1973 March 733 Formula 3.
£10,000-11,000 *CA*

Locate the source

*The source of each
illustration in Miller's can
be found by checking the
code letters below each
caption with the list of
contributors*

1969 Merlyn MkIIA Formula
Ford.
£10,000-11,000 *CA*

1970 Merlyn MkIIA.
£8,000-9,000 *CA*

1971 Merlyn Mk20.
£11,000-12,000 *CA*

1989 Metro 6R4 V6, 24 valve
Clubman's model new.
£19,000-20,000 *AUT*

1971 Nike Mk6 Formula Ford,
pre-74 club racer.
£3,000-4,000 *CA*

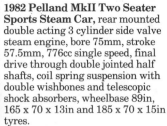

1982 Pelland MkII Two Seater Sports Steam Car, rear mounted double acting 3 cylinder side valve steam engine, bore 75mm, stroke 57.5mm, 776cc single speed, final drive through double jointed half shafts, coil spring suspension with double wishbones and telescopic shock absorbers, wheelbase 89in, 165 x 70 x 13in and 185 x 70 x 15in tyres.
£11,500-12,000 *S*

Peter Pellandine, the designer and builder of the Pelland MkII steam car, has had a remarkable career commencing as a junior draughtsman with coachbuilders H. J. Mulliner of Chiswick. He pioneered fibreglass bodies for Austin Sevens and was behind Ashley Laminates and Falcon Shells, Peregrine Cars, the Australian-built Pellandini and a steam car project for the State Government of South Australia. Back in the UK a VW-based Pelland sports car followed and work commenced on a MkII version of the steam car, the ambition being to beat the existing steam record of 127.66mph, set at Daytona early this century.

1966 Porsche 906 Carrera 6 Coupé, coachwork by Porsche KG Zuffenhausen-Stuttgart.
Est. **£380,000-420,000** *C(M)*

1988 Porsche 962.
£300,000-325,000 *DHA*

c1948 Ranger Sprint Car, built by Bob Helms, 6 cylinder Ranger aero engine, spring front suspension and torsion bar, restored to pristine condition.
£18,000-20,000 *PMc*

Miller's is a price GUIDE not a price LIST

335

1960 Rejo, 4 cylinder, 1100cc Ford
engine.
£25,000-26,000   *SL*

Ross Page Offenhauser Special,
183 c.i.d. Offenhauser engine,
Duray supercharger, Kurtis chassis.
Est. **£70,000-80,000**   *S(NY)*

1959 Taraschi Formula Junior,
Fiat front engine.
£12,500-13,500   *CA*

1960 Taraschi Formula Junior.
£15,000-16,000   *CA*

**1977 Triumph TR7 British
Leyland Works Rally Team Car,**
4 cylinder, 16 valve overhead
camshaft, water-cooled monobloc
engine, 2 litre, 5 speed close ratio
gearbox, Bilstein adjustable
independent suspension, 4HA rear
axle, 215 x 60 x 13in tyres.
Est. **£14,000-15,000**   *S*

1959 Volpini Formula Junior.
£20,000-22,000   *CA*

*Example of an early front engine
Fiat-based Formula Junior.*

1988 017 Tyrrell, rolling chassis only.
£55,00-60,000   *DHA*

A Dunlop tyre and wheel from Donald Campbell's Bluebird CN7 World Land Speed Record car, 1964.
£2,000-2,500 *S*

A Bugatti engine block, with enamel Bugatti badges, 1920s, 11 by 3½in (28 by 9.5cm).
£150-200 *S(M)*

A Briand nickel-plated Motormeter, c1925.
£175-200 *S(M)*

A driver's armband and plaque, 1935.
£80-100 *S(M)*

A Continental silver coloured metal hunter cased pocket watch, c1920.
£300-350 *S(M)*

A crash helmet used by the late Graham Hill, painted in his favourite London Rowing Club colours, 1964-66.
£4,000-5,000 *C(M)*

The Continental Tyre Company porcelain victory charger, c1937, repaired.
£675-775 *S(M)*

Five enamel signs, including Vacuum Motor Car Oils.
£200-250 *S*

A 9ct gold and enamel cigarette case, engraved C.B.B., August 7th 1930, hallmarked Birmingham 1930, 3½in (9.5cm) wide. **£2,000-3,000** *S*

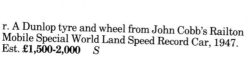

r. A Dunlop tyre and wheel from John Cobb's Railton Mobile Special World Land Speed Record Car, 1947.
Est. **£1,500-2,000** *S*

Nicholas Watts, signed gouache on paper.
Est. £1,200-1,500   S(NY)

Nicholas Watts, signed gouache, 30 by 36in (76 by 92cm). £2,500-3,500   C(M)

D. Maria, signed oil on canvas. Est. £1,200-1,500   S(NY)

Nicholas Watts, signed gouache on paper, 1938. £1,750-2,250   S(NY)

Ken Eberts, signed gouache, 16½ by 30½in (42 by 77cm). £1,500-2,000   CNY

Nicholas Watts, signed gouache on paper.
Est. £1,800-2,500   S(NY)

Nicholas Watts, signed gouache on paper, 23½ by 21in (60 by 55cm). £1,200-1,500   S(NY)

Nicholas Watts, signed gouache on paper, 1938 Mille Miglia, 29½ by 43in (75 by 109cm). £1,600-1,800   S(NY)

D. Maria, signed oil on canvas,
1967 Le Mans.
£2,500-3,000 *S(NY)*

F. Gordon Crosby, pencil, charcoal and watercolour on paper, framed
and glazed, 18 by 29in (46 by 73cm). Est. **£3,500-4,000** *S(M)*

Four motoring prints, c1905.
£500-600 *CNY*

Alan Fearnley, oil on canvas,
signed and dated '89, Ferrari
Duel, 1961 Le Mans.
£3,000-3,500 *CNY*

Nicholas Watts, signed gouache,
Mille Miglia, 1948, Tazio
Nuvolari driving the
Ferrari 166 in his last
great race.
£1,750-2,200 *C(M)*

Alan Fearnley, oil on canvas,
signed and dated '89, Winners
First Time Out, 1951 Le Mans.
£2,300-2,700 *CNY*

Michael Wright, watercolour
and gouache with charcoal,
signed and inscribed Culver
City Boards, 1927, Leon Duray,
Norman Batten with Harry Hartz
during the 1927 250 mile race.
£775-1,000 *CNY*

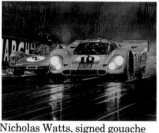

Nicholas Watts, signed gouache
on paper, Pedro's Victory,
29in (74cm) wide.
Est. **£2,000-2,500** *S(NY)*

Walter Montel, signed oil,
acrylic and paper on
canvas, 69 by 60in (175
by 152cm).
£1,200-1,500 *C(M)*

De La Maria, oil on canvas,
signed and dated 1989.
£2,200-2,500 *CNY*

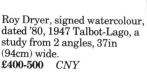

Roy Dryer, signed watercolour,
dated '80, 1947 Talbot-Lago, a
study from 2 angles, 37in
(94cm) wide.
£400-500 *CNY*

Nicholas Watts, signed gouache on paper, On The Ragged Edge. **£1,300-1,600**   *S(NY)*

Dion Pears, oil on canvas, QD 1342 Speed 6, framed. **£750-800**   *CNY*

Alan Fearnley, oil on canvas, signed and dated '89, Pit Stop at Le Mans, 1958. **£2,000-2,500** *CNY*

Dion Pears, signed oil on canvas, 1982 San Marino Grand Prix. **£775-1,000**   *CNY*

Dion Pears, signed oil on canvas, Le Mans 1930, 4½ litre Blower Bentley. **£650-750**   *C(M)*

Walter Gotschke, signed watercolour on paper. **£1,500-2,000**   *CNY*

Dion Pears, signed oil on canvas, 1957 German Grand Prix. **£1,000-1,500** *CNY*

Dion Pears, signed oil on canvas, Le Mans 1934. **£1,000-1,200**   *CNY*

Nicholas Watts, signed gouache on paper, Mercedes-Benz Garage Scene. **£2,000-2,500**   *S(NY)*

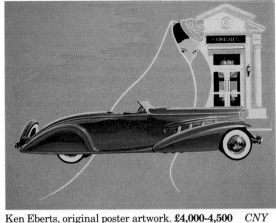

Ken Eberts, original poster artwork. **£4,000-4,500**   *CNY*

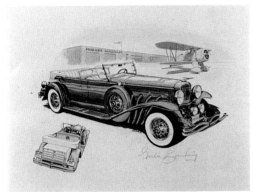

John Souder, Duesenberg Model SJ Tourister, 21½in (55cm) high. Est. **£2,000-3,000** *CNY*

John Souder, Duesenberg Model J Beverley Berline. Est. **£2,000-2,500** *CNY*

John Souder, 1937 Cord 812 Phaeton, 21½in (55cm) high. Est. **£2,000-2,500** *CNY*

A BARC Brooklands car badge, No. 1604, enamel and chromium plated brass, on a desk stand. **£2,000-2,500** *S(M)*

A Life Member's RAC badge, No. B1714, c1907, on marble base. **£1,600-2,000** *S*

A JRDC enamelled chromium plated badge, mounted on a desk stand. **£600-800** *S(M)*

A Brooklands Aero-Club badge, No. 153, mounted on a desk stand. **£3,500-4,500** *S(M)*

A chrome and enamel car badge, Les Vieux Du Volant, c1930. Est. **£180-220** *S(M)*

An AGACI enamelled car badge, c1950. Est. **£350-500** *S(M)*

A rare SS enamel car club badge, on display stand. Est. **£2,000-3,000** *S*

An AGACI enamel on brass car badge, c1950. **£350-450** *S(M)*

A BARC Brooklands enamel badge. Est. **£1,000-1,200** *S*

A patinated bronze model, by Stanley Wanlass, The Racers, 1987, 1/30 edition, 24in (61cm) long. Est. **£6,500-7,000** *S(NY)*

l. A limited edition cold painted bronze, by Stanley Wanlass. Est. **£7,500-8,500** *S(NY)*

r. No. 1 of a limited edition bronze model, by Benoit Jourdan. **£950-1,200**   *C(M)*

l. A limited edition bronze model, by Albert Guibara. **£4,000-4,500**   *S(NY)*

r. A limited edition cold painted bronze, by J. Paul Nesse. **£5,000-6,000**   *CNY*

The Trials Championship Trophy, a signed bronze by Frederick Gordon Crosby, mounted on a marble plinth, 1930, 12in (30.5cm) long. Est. **£15,000-20,000**   *S*

l. A bronze, Stanley Wanlass, 1984. **£5,500-6,000** *CNY*

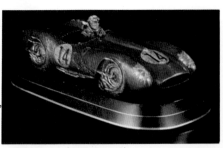

r. A|cold painted bronze, by Stanley Wanlass, on granite base, 1987. Est. **£7,000-8,000**   *S(NY)*

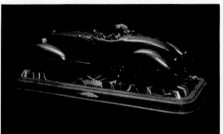

The Spirit of Mercedes, a patinated and gilt bronze model, by Stanley Wanlass, 1985, 25in (64cm) long, on mahogany base. Est. **£7,000-8,000**   *S(NY)*

High Gear, a limited edition patinated bronze model, by Stanley Wanlass, 1987, 29in (74cm) long, on marble plinth and teak base. Est. **£5,000-5,500**   *S(NY)*

c1927 Bugatti Type 52 'Electric' Child's Car, half scale type 35 Grand Prix car, top speed 12-15mph, right hand drive.
£8,000-10,000 *CNY*

A Rolls-Royce 8-day desk clock, in silver case, London 1929, 5½in (13.5cm).
£3,500-4,000 *S(M)*

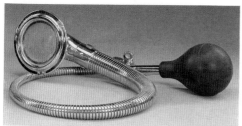

A boa constrictor trumpet horn, c1910, 50in (127cm) long. **£350-450** *S*

An Alfa Romeo P2 Pedal Car, metal chassis, hand finished livery, 70in (177.5cm) long.
£4,500-5,500 *S(M)*

A nickel-plated Cicca testaphone four-note horn.
£600-700 *CNY*

A pair of Lucas trumpet windtone horns, restored.
£600-700 *S*

An Elliott speed indicator.
£200-250 *S*

A Smith's brass dashboard clock.
£170-200 *S*

Morgan 4/4 Pedal Cars, with steel chassis and fibreglass bodies, with battery operated headlights and horns, c1991, 49in (124.5cm) long. **£600-800 each** *MM*

An Ansonia 8-day mantel clock, American, c1910.
£400-450 *S(M)*

A Bugatti child's car, by Westwood, gas powered by single cylinder.
£5,500-6,000 *CNY*

Morgan 4/4 Pedal Car, with steel chassis and fibreglass body, c1991, 49in (124.5cm) long.
£600-800 *MM*

Lucas Short Trumpet Horns, unused. **£500-550** *S*

Rushmore searchlight headlamps, each lens 11in (28cm) diam. **£725-825** *CNY*

A brass carbide generator, c1910, 19in (48cm) high. **£325-425** *CNY*

A pair of Scintilla double rear Bugatti lights, Swiss, 1930s, restored, correct lenses, chrome cases, Bakelite backs. **£800-1,200** *S*

A pair of Bosch pillar mounted head-lamps, with chromed bodies and ribbed glass lenses, 1920s. Est. **£1,500-1,800** *S*

A pair of Marchal fork mounted bull's-eye headlamps, with triple bulb carrier, restored, c1932, lens 10in (25cm) diam. Est. **£2,000-3,000** *S*

A pair of Lucas stainless steel P100s headlamps, c1935. Est. **£1,000-1,500** *S*

A pair of Marchal Striluxe electric headlamps, Type 292, 1930s, 11in (28cm) diam. Est. **£2,000-2,500** *S*

A pair of Lucas QK596/SS100 headlamps, restored and re-wired, 9in (23cm) diam. Est. **£1,500-2,500** *S*

A pair of Woods black painted prototype head-lamps, complete with carrying trunk and original sales document, 22in (57cm) high. **£720-800** *CNY*

A pair of Lucas self-generating acetylene head-lamps, each brass bodied with loop handle, dents and repairs, 7in (17.5cm) diam. **£1,650-1,750** *S*

A Bosch triple rear light, with original lenses, German, restored, 1930s, 7in (18cm) wide.
£780-850 *S*

A pair of Lucas P100DB bull's-eye headlamps, restored and re-wired, c1930, 10in (25.5cm) diam. **£1,200-1,500** *S*

A Phares Grebel hand spot-lamp, restored and re-wired, 1920-30s, 5½in (14cm) diam.
Est. **£2,000-2,400** *S*

A pair of Carl Zeiss stirrup mounted headlamps, suitable for a Speed 6 Bentley, 10½in (26cm) diam. **£2,400-2,600** *S*

A Phares Grebel hand/spot- lamp, 1920-30s.
Est. **£2,000-2,400** *S*

A Stephen Grebel bull's-eye hand spotlamp, with original swivel brackets, 3 bulb housings, restored, 1920-30s, convex lens, 9in (23cm) diam. **£2,000-2,500** *S*

A pair of Marchal sunburst bull's-eye headlamps, Type 67, restored and rewired, c1930.
£3,000-3,800 *S*

A Marchal pillar mounted spotlamp, 1930s, polished nickel plated casing with aluminium rims, restored.
£1,500-2,000 *S*

A pair of Marchal bull's-eye headlamps. **£2,000-2,500** and a pair of Marchal wing mounted side-lights. **£250-300** *S*

A pair of Lucas New Alto horns, complete with mounting brackets, restored and re-wired, c1937, 6½in (16.5cm) high.
£250-300 *S*

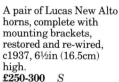

A Drew & Sons 'En Route' two person picnic set, 1920s. Est. **£2,200-2,500** *S*

A Drew & Sons six person picnic set, 1930s, in excellent condition, 21in (53cm) wide. Est. **£8,000-10,000** *S*

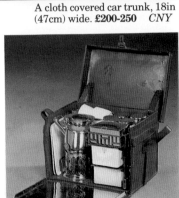

A cloth covered car trunk, 18in (47cm) wide. **£200-250** *CNY*

A Drew & Sons six person picnic set, c1910. Est. **£5,000-7,000** *S*

A Drew & Sons brass and leather bound two person picnic set, 1920s, 16in (41cm) wide. Est. **£4,000-5,000** *S*

A Drew & Sons 'En Route' two person picnic set, 1920s, 15in (38cm) wide. Est. **£2,000-2,800** *S*

An Oakland auto trunk and four small cases, 18½in (48cm) wide. **£650-750** *CNY*

A black canvas covered wicker basket two person picnic set, 1920s, 22in (56cm) wide. Est. **£1,000-1,800** *S*

A Brooks Bros. picnic hamper, c1915, 12½in (32.5cm) wide. **£550-700** *CNY*

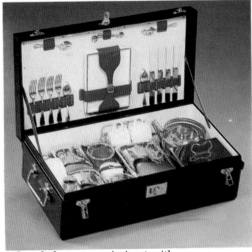

A Coracle four person picnic set, with black leathercloth exterior and chrome handles, 1920s-30s, 23½in (60cm) wide. Est. **£2,000-3,000** *S*

A travelling sandwich box
and flask, English, c1920.
Est. **£1,000-1,200**   *S(M)*

A Drew & Sons four person picnic set,
monogrammed CC, plated locks and
fittings, nickel plated Thermos flask,
sandwich container, tea kettle and
burner, milk jug, various preserve
containers. **£2,000-3,000**   *S(M)*

A Drew four person picnic set,
wicker basket, plated brass
locks, enamel plates,
Thermos flask, c1915, 12in
(30cm) sq. **£650-700**   *S(M)*

A Drew & Sons gentleman's
fitted suitcase, leather with
plated fittings, all contents
monogrammed H.R.
£1,300-1,500   *S(M)*

A leather and impregnated canvas bound
wicker travelling trunk, with leather
straps, monogrammed Ettore Bugatti,
c1920. Est. **£3,000-4,000**   *S(M)*

Ettore Bugatti's personal case
with brushes, bottles and
manicure set.
£5,000-7,000   *CNY*

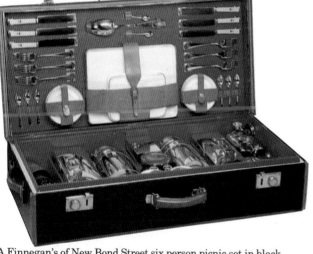

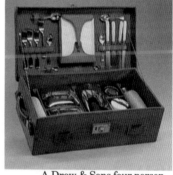

A Finnegan's of New Bond Street six person picnic set in black
leather covered case, brass locks, handles and fittings, all
contents monogrammed V with a coronet, possibly for James Walter,
3rd Earl of Verulam, c1910, 33in (83cm) wide. **£16,000-18,000**   *S(M)*

A Drew & Sons four person
picnic set, in leather covered
case, with plated locks,
handles and fittings, three
food containers, two cane
covered flasks and glasses,
1920s. **£1,500-1,800**   *S(M)*

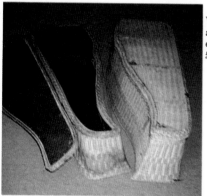

Wicker baskets shaped to fit
around the sides of a rear
entrance tonneau car, c1903.
£460-560   *CNY*

r. A Drew & Sons four
person picnic set, in
rexine covered case
with hinged lid, cane
covered interior, two
Thermos flasks, cane
covered bottle and
glasses, preserve
containers, c1920, 14in
(35cm) wide.
£1,600-1,800   *S(M)*

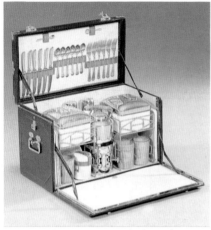

A Drew & Sons wicker two person drinks set, some pieces aged and worn, c1910, basket 12½in (32cm) wide. Est. **£450-600** *S*

A Brexton four person picnic set, in black leathercloth case, c1930, 22in (56cm) wide. **£550-850** *S*

A Drew & Sons six person picnic set, in black leather cloth covered case, 1920s, 21in (53.5cm) wide. Est. **£6,000-8,000** *S*

A Coracle four person picnic set, 1920s. Est. **£1,600-2,000** *S*

A child's picnic case, cloth lined interior, with 'Pip, Squeak and Wilfred' pattern, 1930s. Est. **£320-400** *S*

A four person wicker picnic basket, containing cutlery, food boxes, kettle and burner, plates, cups, saucers, butter container, wicker covered bottles and glasses, slight worm, 1920s, 28in (71cm) wide. Est. **£2,000-3,000** *S*

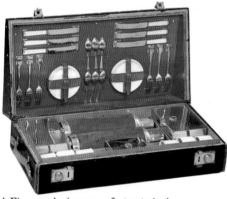

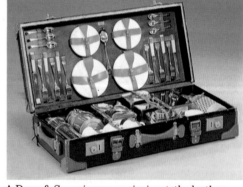

A Finnegan's six person footrest picnic set, containing 2 Thermos flasks, 1920s. **£1,200-1,500** *S*

A Drew & Sons six person picnic set, the leather cloth bound case with tan leather reinforcers, c1912, 33in (84cm) wide. Est. **£6,000-8,000** *S*

A two person tea set, possibly French, c1920. Est. **£700-900** *S*

Two Asprey picnic sets:
l. six person, c1920,
r. four person, c1936,
believed to have been the property of King Edward VIII.
Est. **£15,000-20,000** *S*

A Lalique ram's head car mascot, signed R. Lalique, France, 1930s, 4in (10cm). **£5,000-6,000** *S(M)*

A 'Safety First' car mascot, the cold enamelled metal policeman coloured blue and white, English, marked, c1920, on wooden display base, 4½in (11cm). **£160-180** *S(M)*

A Bofil serpent mascot, with a reptile perched on a rocky outcrop, mounted on a radiator cap, c1930, 4in (10cm). **£560-660** *S(M)*

A Ballot speed nymph car mascot, the nickel plated bronze figure standing astride a Ballot engine, French, c1925, 5½in (13.5cm). **£400-500** *S(M)*

An F. Bazin Latil elephant's head car mascot, base marked Latil and signed F. Bazin, French, 1925, on marble desk stand, 7in (17.5cm). **£220-240** *S(M)*

A Desmo Schneider Trophies S5 Supermarine Napier seaplane brass car mascot, c1930, 5½in (14cm). **£500-600** *S(M)*

A Michelin Bibendum aero mascot, partly painted orange, white and black, French, 1920, 5in (12cm). **£120-150** *S(M)*

A Lalique Tête de Coq Nain rooster's head car mascot, French, c1926, 7in (18cm). **£170-200** *S(M)*

A Lalique archer mascot, French, c1927, 4½in (12cm). **£160-200** *S(M)*

A Red Indian riding a snail mascot, French, c1920, 5in (12.5cm). **£170-180** *S(M)*

A Rolls-Royce 20hp mascot,
on display plinth, 4in
(10cm) high.
Est. **£300-400** *S*

A banking supermarine S6.B Schneider
trophy seaplane mascot, English,
c1930, 6in (15cm).
Est. **£2,000-3,000** *S*

A St. Christopher car mascot, French,
c1920, signed H. Fugère, 7in (18cm).
Est. **£800-1,200** *S(M)*

A Lejeune brass Girl
Guide mascot,
English, c1930.
Est. **£500-600** *S*

A Lalique Tête d'Aigle
glass mascot, French,
c1930, 4in (11cm) high,
on metal display base.
£2,600-2,800 *S*

A Lalique archer
mascot, French, c1930,
5in (12cm).
Est. **£1,200-1,800** *S*

An Egyptian slave girl
mascot, English, c1930,
plated brass figure
in enamelled decorative
dress, 7in (17cm) high,
mounted on radiator cap.
Est. **£500-600** *S*

An Isotta-Fraschini
Spirit of Triumph mascot,
c1930, designed by
F. Bazin, 6in (15cm)
high, on metal base.
Est. **£550-700** *S*

A Rolls-Royce Phantom II
Spirit of Ecstasy mascot.
Est. **£320-400** *S*

A Charlie Chaplin car mascot, English,
c1930, signed Veyrard, mounted on
wooden display plinth, 5in (13cm)
high. Est. **£600-900** *S(M)*

An engineer's model of the Bugatti Royal Chassis, German, commissioned by Miodraj Jelesijevic, exquisitely detailed with working suspension, steering and braking, lamps battery operated, fitted in a transportable case.
Est. **£1,000-1,400**　*S(M)*

A model Bentley Speed Six by Fulgurex. **£970-1,300**　*CNY*

A model 1924 Bugatti Type 35 G. P. de Lyon, 23in (60cm) long. **£3,250-3,750**　*CNY*

A model 1973 Matra 670B by Jean-Claude Chesnel. **£300-400**　*C(M)*

A model Mercedes Benz SSKL by Fulgurex, 1976, 14½in (37cm) long. Est. **£180-220**　*S(M)*

Detail of engine of model 1973 Matra 670B.

A model 1913 Raceabout by Manuel Olive Sans, 14in (36cm) long. Est. **£1,800-2,000**　*S(M)*

Detail of model 1898 Benz.

1951 Indianapolis 500 winner. Est. **£3,300-3,600**　*S(NY)*

An Edwardian Renault Taxi, wooden model, English, c1970. Est. **£500-700**　*S(M)*

A Pocher kit model of a Zagato-bodied Alfa Romeo, 19in (48cm) long. **£1,000-1,200**　*S(M)*

A model 1929 Bugatti Type 41 Royale Chassis, by Mischko Jelesijevic in Germany, 28in (75cm) long. Est. **£8,000-10,000**　*C(M)*

A 1:8 scale model of the 1967 Ferrari 412P. **£8,500-9,000**　*C(M)*

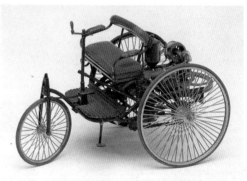

A detailed scratch built model of a 1898 Benz, by Charles Morat, scale 1:12, French, c1965, 7½in (19cm). **£1,400-1,500**　*S(M)*

An Auto Rally
Souvenir plaque,
c1934.
£180-200 *S(M)*

A pair of shagreen covered motor car interior vanity sets,
French, c1925, one with an eight-day top winding timepiece
with oval face and black Roman numerals, fitted with brush,
powder bottle, note pad, vesta case, the matching
covered case with applied enamel medallion, each 9½in (24cm)
wide. **£2,500-3,000** *S(M)*

An FNCAF Ancien de L'Auto
Rally plaque, mounted on
a wooden plaque.
£100-150 *S(M)*

A 1932 Monte Carlo Rally
plaque, in presentation
case. **£1,000-3,000** *S(M)*

A vanity set, probably French,
c1920, Swiss timepiece mounted
in front, 9½in (24cm) wide.
Est. **£2,000-2,500** *S*

A motor car interior vanity set,
English, c1910, domed mahogany
surround with sliding tambour cover,
8in (20cm) wide.
Est. **£2,000-2,500** *S(M)*

A G. Keller motor car interior vanity set,
French, with an eight-day keyless clock
inset in shaped walnut surround, 10½in (26cm)
wide. Est. **£3,000-5,000** *S(M)*

A G. Keller interior vanity
set, French, c1910, the
mahogany case inset with
eight-day Swiss made clock,
10in (26cm) wide.
Est. **£1,000-1,500** *S*

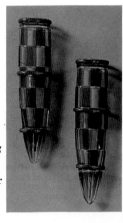

A silver and
glass interior
flower vase,
hallmarked,
7in (18cm).
Est. **£300-400** *S*

A motoring interior vanity set, c1925,
bow fronted with walnut inlay, containing silver
topped bottles marked London 1925, the front
inset with Swiss made clock, 9in (23cm) wide.
Est. **£2,000-3,000** *S*

A pair of cut glass interior
flower vases, c1910.
£400-450 *S*

ABC

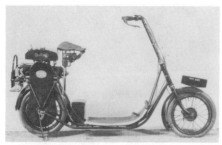

1919 ABC Skootamota Model 1 B Solo Motorcycle, engine No. 3464, rear mounted horizontal single cylinder, pushrod-operated overhead valve, 4 stroke engine, 125cc, chain drive, rigid frame, 14 x 2 x 1¾ tyres.
£900-1,000 *S*

Aermacchi

1952 Aermacchi Model N 125cc Deluxe Scooter, engine No. 12505976-1031B, frame No. 12505976, inclined single cylinder, air-cooled, 2 stroke, bore 52mm, stroke 58mm, 125cc, 3 speed gearbox with twist change, chain final drive, swinging arm front and rear suspension, 16in tyres.
Est. **£900-1,200** *S*

c1968 Aermacchi 350cc Solo Racing Motorcycle, frame No. 01 31056, single cylinder engine, air-cooled, overhead valve, 4 stroke, 350cc, 5 speed gearbox, chain final drive, telescopic front forks, swinging arm rear suspension.
£4,750-8,250 *S*

This motorcycle is a 248cc racer and was ridden by Italian ace Pasolini. Some 10 years or so ago the bike was converted to its present form with a 350cc engine, and substantially rebuilt with the original frame remaining.

1959 Aermacchi 175 Ala Rosso/Ala D'Oro, frame No. 175-111375, with a Dell Orto SSF 25 D carburettor, a TZ Marmitta exhaust, a racing seat and a Smith's 0-10,000rpm rev-counter, in excellent condition and ready to race.
£3,000-3,250 *C(M)*

AJS

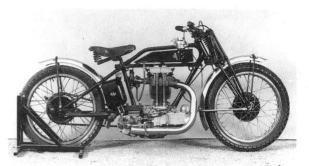

1928 AJS Big Port 500cc Solo Racing Motorcycle, engine No. M 212, single vertical cylinder, air-cooled, overhead valve, 4 stroke engine, 500cc, Sturmey Archer gearbox, missing gear change lever, girder forks with coil spring front suspension, rigid frame at rear, chain final drive, 360 H 19 tyres front and rear.
Est. **£3,600-5,400** *S*

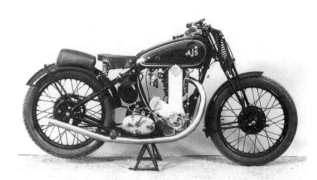

1931 AJS 500cc Solo Motorcycle, engine No. 33/10 519.
Est. **£4,500-5,400** *S*

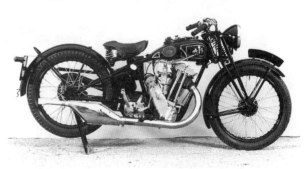

1933 AJS Big Port 350cc Solo Motorcycle, engine No. 33 B 6 153931, inclined single cylinder, overhead valve, 4 stroke engine, 4 speed gearbox, girder forks with coil spring front suspension, rigid frame at rear, chain final drive, 3.00 x 19 tyres front and rear.
Est. **£3,400-3,500** *S*

1926 AJS 7.99hp Motorcycle Combination, frame/engine No. G60136, V-twin cylinder engine, air-cooled, side valve, 4 stroke, bore 74mm, stroke 93mm, 799cc, 3 speed hand change gearbox, chain final drive, girder forks and coil spring front suspension, rigid rear with sprung sidecar frame, bulb horn, electric lighting, luggage carrier and leather tool pannier.
£3,300-3,800 *S*

The first A. J. Stevens motorcycles appeared in 1909 and the company was seen to offer a comprehensive range of machines with the big V-twin bikes at the top of the range. The machines excelled in Reliability Trials and the 7.99hp machines proved well suited to sidecar work.

c1928-29 AJS 500cc Solo Sprint Special Motorcycle, engine No S 7/145271, single vertical cylinder, air-cooled, overhead camshaft, 4 stroke engine, 500cc, 4 speed hand change gearbox, girder forks with Andre dampers, rigid frame at rear, chain final drive, Avon Speedmaster 2.75 x 19 front tyres, 3.25/2.50 x 19 rear.
£4,000-4,300 *S*

1932 AJS S3 498cc Solo Motorcycle, engine No. 53150015, frame No. 150015, 50° transverse, air-cooled, side valve, 4 stroke, twin cylinder, bore 65mm, stroke 75mm, 498cc, 3 speed hand change gearbox, chain final drive, central spring girder forks, rigid rear end.
£2,600-3,000 *S*

c1934 AJS Model R10 Special 500cc Racing Motorcycle, engine No. 1003, single vertical cylinder engine, air-cooled, overhead valve, overhead camshaft, 500cc, 4 speed gearbox, chain final drive, girder fork and coil spring front suspension, rigid rear.
£4,500-4,800 *S*

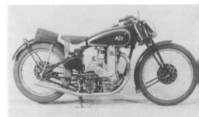

1930s AJS 500cc Solo Motorcycle, engine No. 35/10 1041, single vertical cylinder, single port, overhead camshaft, air-cooled, 4 stroke engine, 4 speed gearbox, girder forks with coil spring front suspension, rigid frame at rear, chain final drive, 3.00 x 21 front tyres, 3.25 x 19 rear.
Est. **£1,800-2,500** *S*

1961 AJS CSR 646cc Solo Motorcycle, engine No. 61/31 CSX 7160, vertical twin cylinder, overhead valve, air-cooled, 4 stroke engine, 4 speed gearbox, telescopic forks with sprung frame at rear, chain final drive, 3.25 x 19 tyres front, 410 H19 rear.
£2,500-2,750 *S*

c1956 AJS 498cc Trials Solo Motorcycle, engine No. 56/18 M 17920, single vertical cylinder, overhead valve, air-cooled, 4 stroke engine, 498cc, 4 speed gearbox, telescopic forks, sprung frame at rear, chain final drive, 3.00 x 21 front tyres, 3.50 x 19 rear.   **£1,700-2,000** *S*

1955/56 AJS 18S 500cc Solo Motorcycle, engine No. 55/185-28851, frame No. A34887, single vertical cylinder, air-cooled, overhead valve, 4 stroke, bore 82.5mm, stroke 93mm, 497cc, 4 speed foot operated gearbox, telescopic front forks, pivoted fork rear suspension.
£2,400-2,700 *S*

Matchless and AJS singles were essentially identical, having been introduced in the 1930s, and were continuously updated to enable them to remain competitive in the market place.

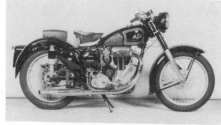

1952 AJS Model 18S 500cc Solo Motorcycle, engine No. 52/18S 21796, frame No. 88148, single vertical cylinder engine, air-cooled, overhead valve, 4 stroke, bore 82.5mm, stroke 93mm, 497cc, 4 speed gearbox, chain final drive, telescopic front forks, swinging arm rear suspension, 19in tyres, rebuilt and restored.
£3,750-4,000 *S*

c1931 AJS 350cc Special Solo Motorcycle, engine No. 14520.S, single vertical cylinder, air-cooled, overhead camshaft, 4 stroke engine, possibly 350cc, Albion 3 speed gearbox, girder forks with coil spring front suspension, modified McCandless sprung frame at rear, chain final drive, 3.25 x 19 tyres front and rear.
£1,650-1,850 *S*

c1949 AJS 7R 348cc Solo Racing Motorcycle, engine No. 49 7R 676, single vertical cylinder, overhead camshaft, bronze head air-cooled, 4 stroke engine, 348cc, 4 speed gearbox, telescopic forks, plunger suspension, chain final drive.
£7,250-7,750 *S*

The ultimate 'Boy's Racer', the AJS 7R was introduced in 1948 and examples were also used by the works team.

1961/1955 AJS Matchless 350cc Trials Solo Motorcycle, engine No. 55/G3LS 1675C, single vertical cylinder, air-cooled, overhead valve, 4 stroke, bore 69mm, stroke 93mm, 348cc, 4 speed positive stop gearbox, telescopic front forks, pivoted rear fork.
£1,750-1,850 *S*

1954 AJS 350cc Solo Racing Motorcycle, engine No. 54 7R 1070, single vertical cylinder engine, air-cooled, overhead valve, overhead camshaft, 4 stroke, bore 74mm, stroke 81mm, 348cc, 4 speed gearbox, chain final drive, telescopic front forks, swinging arm rear suspension.
Est. **£12,000-14,000** *S*

The 7R appeared in February 1948, a production model which was very successful on the circuits, particularly at club level, it was a 7R which took Nilsson to victory in the World Moto-Cross Championships of 1957.

1961 AJS 650cc Model 31 CSR Solo Motorcycle, engine No. G12LX3911, frame No. 79737, vertical air-cooled, overhead valve, parallel twin cylinder, 4 stroke, bore 72mm, stroke 79.3mm, 4 speed foot operated gearbox, chain primary and final drive, swinging arm rear suspension, telescopic front forks.
£3,000-3,250 *S*

Ariel

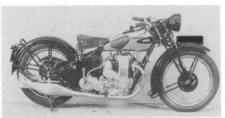

1932 Ariel Square Four 600cc Solo Motorcycle, engine No. P 689, vertical square 4, air-cooled, 4 stroke, with overhead camshaft engine, bore 56mm, stroke 61mm, 597cc, 4 speed counter-shaft gearbox, girder forks with coil spring front suspension, rigid frame at rear, 3.25 x 19 front tyres, 3.25/2.50 x 19 rear.
£3,500-3,750 *S*

Locate the source

The source of each illustration in Miller's can be found by checking the code letters below each caption with the list of contributors

1934 Ariel Red Hunter 500cc Solo Motorcycle, engine No. GA 844, single vertical cylinder, twin port air-cooled, overhead valve, 4 stroke engine, 4 speed gearbox with foot change, girder forks with coil springs front suspension, rigid frame at rear, chain final drive, 3.00 x 20 front tyres, 3.50 x 19 rear.
£3,750-4,000 *S*

1929 Ariel 500cc Solo Motorcycle, engine No. H 5775T, frame No. 6183, single vertical cylinder engine, air-cooled, overhead valve, 4 stroke, 497cc, 3 speed hand change gearbox, chain final drive, girder fork and coil spring front suspension with adjustable dampers, rigid rear suspension, 3.25 x 19in tyres.
£2,650-2,850 *S*

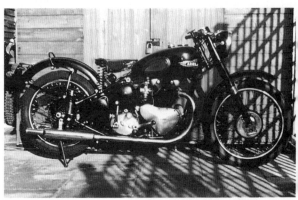

1953 Ariel KH 500cc Solo Motorcycle, engine No. TE2208, frame No. SE1833, vertical, twin cylinder, air-cooled, overhead valve, 4 stroke, bore 63mm, stroke 80mm, 499cc, 4 speed positive stop gearbox, telescopic front forks, Ariel link rear suspension.
£1,750-2,000 *S*

1949 Ariel VG 500cc Solo Motorcycle, engine No. EJ 1956, frame No. RF 2813, single vertical cylinder engine, air-cooled, overhead valve, 4 stroke, bore 81.8mm, stroke 95mm, 499cc, 4 speed foot change gearbox, chain final drive, telescopic front forks, rigid rear suspension, 3.25 x 19in tyres.
£2,000-2,100 *S*

1947 Ariel Square Four 1000cc Solo Motorcycle, engine No. DK 946, frame No. AX 941.
£2,400-2,600 *S*

c1946 Ariel Model VCH 500cc Ex-Works Trials Solo Motorcycle, engine No. CO 125, frame No. BP 10 877, single cylinder, 5 stud overhead valve, air-cooled, 4 stroke engine, 4 speed foot change gearbox, telescopic front forks, rigid frame at rear, chain final drive, 3.00 x 20 Dunlop Sport front tyres, 4.00 x 19 Trials rear.
£3,500-3,750 *S*

1953 Ariel KH 500cc Solo Motorcycle, engine No. TE2208, frame No. SE1833, vertical twin cylinder, air-cooled, overhead valve, 4 stroke, bore 63mm, stroke 80mm, 499cc, 4 speed positive stop gearbox, telescopic front forks, Ariel Link rear suspension.
£1,800-2,000   *S*

1962 Ariel Leader 250cc Solo Motorcycle, engine No. T 33938 B, frame No. T 33938 B, inclined parallel twin cylinder engine, 2 stroke, bore 54mm, stroke 54mm, 249cc, 4 speed gearbox, chain final drive, trailing link front forks with coil springs and hydraulic dampers, swinging arm rear suspension, 3.25 x 16in tyres.   **£825-1,000**   *S*

1956 Ariel NH 350cc Motorcycle, single vertical cylinder, air-cooled, overhead valve, 347cc, 4 speed gearbox, telescopic forks front and rear suspension, chain final drive.
£1,500-1,650   *S*

1964 Ariel Leader 250cc Solo Motorcycle, engine No. T 34220 B, frame No. T 34220 B, inclined parallel twin cylinder engine, 2 stroke, bore 54mm, stroke 54mm, 249cc, 4 speed gearbox, chain final drive, trailing link front forks with coil springs and hydraulic dampers, swinging arm rear suspension, 3.25 x 18in tyres.
£800-1,000   *S*

1957 Ariel Square Four 997cc Solo Motorcycle, engine No. MML868, frame No. GM868, 4 cylinder, air-cooled, overhead valve, 4 stroke, bore 65mm, stroke 75mm, 4 speed foot operated gearbox, chain primary and final drive, telescopic front forks, Ariel link rear suspension.
£2,750-3,000   *S*

Autoped

Ascot-Pullin

1930 Ascot-Pullin 498cc Solo Motorcycle, horizontal single cylinder, air-cooled, overhead valve, 4 stroke engine, bore 82mm, stroke 94mm, 3 speed gearbox with multi-plate clutch and hand change, semi-dry sump lubrication, pressed steel frame, hydraulic braking, chain final drive, 3.50 x 21in front and rear tyres.   **£4,000-4,250**   *S*

1922 Autoped 123cc Solo Motor Scooter, engine No. D 2158, frame No. D 2158, front mounted single cylinder, overhead inlet, side exhaust valve, air-cooled, 4 stroke engine over front wheel, with folding steering control of clutch, brake, throttle, and chain drive.
£2,500-2,800   *S*

BAT

1914 BAT 1000cc Solo Motorcycle, engine No. 123, frame No. 612, air-cooled JAP, overhead valve, V-twin, belt final drive, leading link fork (primitive), rigid rear end.
£7,000-7,500 *S*

Built between 1902 and 1926 the Tusier family's company, BAT (or Best After Test), produced a series of sporting machines, ranging in size from singles of 492cc to V-twins of 980cc. All of their products were of a high quality, and all possessed a good turn of speed.

Beardmore

1923 Beardmore Precision, engine No. 317, frame No. 649, single vertical, air-cooled, side valve, 4 stroke, bore 70mm, stroke 90mm, 347cc, chain final drive, girder front forks, rigid rear, front wheel missing, heavily corroded and in need of restoration.
£2,600-2,800 *S*

Produced between 1921 and 1924 Beardmore were active in all fields of transport from motorcycles through to locomotives as a result of which all their machines displayed sound engineering principles, coupled with some technical innovation.

1924 2¾hp Beardmore Precision Solo Motorcycle, engine No. 658, frame No. 968, single vertical cylinder, air-cooled, side valve, 4 stroke, 650cc, chain final drive, girder front forks, rigid rear, dry plate clutch, 3 speed box, with major components of the engine and Sturmey Archer gearbox, requires restoration. **£600-650** *S*

Benelli

c1978 Benelli 750 SE1 Solo Motorcycle, engine No. 9840, frame No. 7932, inclined transverse 6 cylinder in-line engine, overhead valve, overhead camshaft, 750cc, 5 speed gearbox, chain final drive, telescopic front forks, swinging arm rear suspension.
Est. **£3,000-3,500** *S*

1936 Benelli 250cc Solo Motorcycle, engine No. 25-10352, frame No. 25-10352, single vertical cylinder engine, air-cooled, overhead valve, overhead camshaft, 4 stroke, 4 speed foot change gearbox, chain final drive, girder fork and coil spring front suspension, plunger rear, concours standard, good mechanical condition. Est. **£4,700-5,200** *S*

BMW

Major restoration in 1990 and since then it has been museum displayed.

1931 BMW RII 350cc Solo Motorcycle, engine No. F1761, frame No. F1761, horizontally opposed twin cylinder engine, air-cooled, 4 stroke, 4 speed hand change gearbox, shaft final drive, friction damped trailing link front forks, rigid rear suspension, 19in tyres. **£2,450-2,600** *S*

Introduced in 1935 the R12 was BMW's best selling bike of the inter-war years and was the solo motorcycle 'work-horse' of the Wehrmacht.

c1942 BMW R12 745cc Solo Military Motorcycle, engine No. 661326, frame No. 30464, horizontally opposed flat twin cylinder engine, air-cooled, 4 stroke, 745cc, 4 speed gearbox, shaft final drive, telescopic front forks, rigid rear suspension.
£1,800-2,000 *S*

c1938/41 BMW R66 600cc Solo Military Motorcycle, horizontally opposed twin cylinder engine, air-cooled, overhead valve, 4-stroke, bore 69.8mm, stroke 78mm, 597cc, 4 speed gearbox, shaft final drive, telescopic front forks, plunger rear suspension, 19in tyres, original and unrestored.
£1,600-1,850 *S*

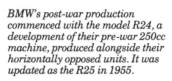

BMW's post-war production commenced with the model R24, a development of their pre-war 250cc machine, produced alongside their horizontally opposed units. It was updated as the R25 in 1955.

c1955 BMW R25 250cc Solo Military Motorcycle, engine No. 329418, frame No. 329418, single vertical cylinder engine, air-cooled, overhead valve, 4 stroke, bore 68mm, stroke 68mm, 247cc, 4 speed foot change gearbox, unit construction, shaft final drive, telescopic front forks, plunger rear suspension, 18in tyres.
£900-1,000 *S*

c1943 BMW Model R75 Military Motorcycle Combination, engine No. 7549309, frame No. 7671895, transverse horizontally opposed twin cylinder engine, air-cooled, overhead valve, 4 stroke, bore 78mm, stroke 78mm, 745cc, 8 forward gears, 4 reverse gears, dual ratio hand change gearbox, shaft final drive with side car drive, telescopic front forks, rigid rear suspension, following major restoration this machine has been museum stored.
£5,000-5,500 *S*

1981 BMW R80 GS Solo Motorcycle, engine No. 625 1678, frame No. 625 1678, twin cylinder, horizontally opposed, air-cooled, 4 stroke, bore 84.8mm, stroke 7.06mm, 797cc, 5 speed foot operated gearbox, shaft final drive, telescopic front forks, monolever rear suspension. **£2,500-2,800** *S*

Brough Superior

1932 Brough Superior 680cc Solo Motorcycle, engine No. 13692/S, frame No. 1179, V-twin cylinder engine, air-cooled, overhead valve, 4 stroke, 680cc, 3 speed gearbox, chain final drive, girder fork and coil spring front suspension, rigid rear, 19in wheels, restored to concours standard.
Est. **£15,000-18,000** *S*

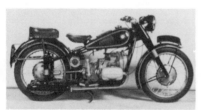

1940 BMW R51 500cc Solo Motorcycle, engine No. 505632, frame No. 511256, transverse horizontally opposed twin cylinder engine, pushrod operated overhead valves, bore 68mm, stroke 68mm, 494cc, 4 speed foot and hand change gearbox, shaft drive, telescopic front forks, plunger rear suspension, 3.00 x 19in front, 3.25 x 19in rear tyres, museum stored since 1986.
£4,800-5,200 *S*

The outbreak of war in 1939 prevented the R51 from achieving the international acclaim which it deserved, however post-war production was to continue until 1954.

1930 Brough Superior SS80 988cc Solo Motorcycle, engine No. KTCV/1/70463/SX, JAP V-twin side valve, air-cooled, 4 stroke engine, 988cc, 3 speed hand change gearbox, Castle forks, sprung frame at rear, chain final drive, 3.25 x 19in front and rear tyres.
Est. **£10,800-11,500** *S*

1937 Brough Superior SS80 1000cc Combination Motorcycle, engine No. BS/X44507, frame No. P8 1723, Matchless V-twin cylinder, air-cooled, side valve, 4 stroke, 996cc, 4 speed gearbox with posi-stop foot change, sprung front forks, rigid frame at rear, chain final drive, 3.50 x 18in front, 4.00 x 19in rear tyres.
Est. **£9,000-12,000** *S*

Brough machines achieved an enviable record on the track in the hands of noted riders such as Eric Fernihough, Freddie Dixon and Harold 'Oily' Karslake. T. E. Lawrence of Arabia owned no less than 7 Brough machines over the years.

1929 Brough Superior 680 Model 680cc Solo Motorcycle, engine No. GTO Y/5/56429/S, frame No. J.920, JAP V-twin, air-cooled, overhead valve, 4 stroke engine, bore 70mm, stroke 88mm, 680cc, Sturmey Archer 3 speed gearbox, girder forks with coil spring front suspension, rigid frame at rear, chain final drive, 26 x 3 tyres. **£13,500-14,000** *S*

BSA

1929 Brough Superior SS100 and Sidecar, engine No. 6281, frame No. 1027, V-twin cylinder, air-cooled, overhead valve, 4 stroke, bore 80mm, stroke 99mm, 998cc, 3 speed hand operated gearbox, chain final drive, Brampton front forks, cantilever sprung rear frame, fitted with a sporting launch sidecar, with a folding hood and screen.
£21,000-22,000 *S*

BSA offered their 350cc bike in either side valve or overhead valve form in 1924. It sold for £45.3s.0d. or over 12 months on BSA's hire purchase scheme for £46.17s.0d.

1924 BSA 350cc Solo Motorcycle, engine No. 10929 AP, frame No. D 9368, single vertical cylinder engine, air-cooled, side valve, bore 72mm, stroke 85.5mm, 349cc, 3 speed hand change gearbox, chain final drive, girder forks and coil spring front suspension, rigid rear, 26 x 2½in tyres.
£2,100-2,300 *S*

1914 BSA Model H 557cc Motorcycle Combination, engine No. 8736, frame No. 8689, single vertical cylinder, air-cooled, side valve, 4 stroke, 557cc, 3 speed countershaft gearbox, girder fork and coil spring fork suspension, rigid rear, leaf springing to sidecar, with acetylene lamps and bulb horn, original purchase receipt from 1914, original guarantee and sale catalogue.
£7,250-7,500 *S*

The bike remained in the hands of its first owner until the early 1950s, subsequently being sold, it was then carefully laid up for about 20 years.

1927 Brough Superior 680cc Solo Motorcycle, engine No. GTO/I/73397/SD, frame No. 518, V-twin cylinder engine, air-cooled, overhead valve, 4 stroke, 680cc, 3 speed gearbox, chain final drive, girder forks and coil spring front suspension, rigid rear suspension, 19in wheels.
£19,000-20,000 *S*

1924 BSA Model L 2¾hp Solo Motorcycle, engine No. 17674, frame No. 17000, single vertical cylinder, air-cooled, side valve, 4 stroke engine, 2¾hp, 3 speed hand change gearbox, girder forks with coil spring suspension, rigid frame at rear, chain final drive. Est. **£1,350-1,500** *S*

This machine was first registered on 1 July 1924 to Theophilus Jones of Alltygrug Road, Ystalyfera, Swansea, who later moved to Penlan, Upper Chaple, Breconshire. Mr Jones fell off the machine in 1927 and never rode it or taxed it again, although he retained it until 1966. It was then acquired by the present owner and has thus had but two owners from new.

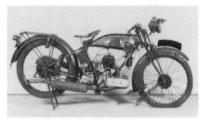

1927 BSA Model L27 350cc Solo Motorcycle, engine No. 36567, frame No. 9154, single vertical cylinder engine, air-cooled, side valve, bore 72mm, stroke 85.5mm, 349cc, 3 speed hand change gearbox, chain final drive, girder forks and coil spring front suspension, rigid rear, 2.75 x 21in tyres. **£1,850-2,000** *S*

1939 BSA B21 250cc Solo Motorcycle, engine No. KB 21 463, frame No. KB 20 734, single vertical cylinder engine, air-cooled, overhead valve, 4 stroke, bore 63mm, stroke 80mm, 249cc, 4 speed foot change gearbox, chain final drive, girder forks and coil spring front suspension, rigid rear, 3.25 x 19in tyres. **£1,700-1,900** *S*

1931 BSA Model G31-12 986cc Motorcycle Combination, engine No. Y-12208, frame No. Y-12409, V-twin side valve, air-cooled, 4 stroke engine, bore 80mm, stroke 98mm, 986cc, 3 speed hand change gearbox, girder forks with coil spring front suspension, rigid frame at rear, chain final drive. Est. **£5,000-5,500** *S*

c1928 BSA 175cc Ladies Solo Motorcycle, engine No. N 2438, frame No. SE 2793, single vertical cylinder, air-cooled, 2 stroke, 175cc, 3 speed hand change gearbox, chain final drive, girder forks and coil spring front suspension, rigid rear. Est. **£650-950** *S*

Sold in 1928 for just £39.15s.0d., the B28 'De Luxe' was the second cheapest in Small Heath's range.

1928 BSA Model B28 249cc Solo Motorcycle, engine No. B25368, single vertical cylinder, air-cooled, side valve, 4 stroke engine, 249cc, 3 speed gearbox, girder forks with coil spring front suspension, rigid frame at rear, chain final drive, 2.75 x 19 front tyres, 3.00 x 19 rear. **£1,000-1,200** *S*

1934 BSA Blue Star 350cc Solo Motorcycle, engine No. E7340, frame No. E51447, vertical, air-cooled, overhead valve, single cylinder, 4 stroke, bore 71mm, stroke 88mm, 348cc, foot operated gearbox, chain primary and final drive, girder front forks, rigid rear end. **£4,500-4,750** *S*

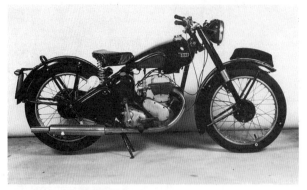

**1955 BSA C11G 250cc Solo
Motorcycle,** engine No. BC11G
22940, frame No. BC 11S4 8661,
single vertical cylinder engine,
air-cooled, overhead valve, 4 stroke,
bore 63mm, stroke 80mm, 249cc,
4 speed gearbox, chain final drive,
telescopic front suspension, plunger
rear, 19in tyres, recent restoration
to original specification.
£600-650   *S*

**1947 BSA C10 250cc Solo
Motorcycle,** engine No.
XC 10T 329, frame No.
YC 10T 4773, single vertical
cylinder engine, air-cooled, side
valve, bore 63mm, stroke 80mm,
249cc, 3 speed foot change gearbox,
chain final drive, telescopic front
forks, rigid rear suspension, 3.00 x
19in front, 3.25 x 19in rear tyres.
£1,800-2,000   *S*

*The C10 first appeared in
January 1938.*

> **Miller's is a price
> GUIDE not a price
> LIST**

*The C11G appeared for 2 years, 1954
and 1955, and was derived from the
earlier C11 lightweights. The 250cc
engine developed 11bhp at 5400rpm
giving the bike a top speed in excess
of 60mph.*

**1949 BSA Gold Star 350cc Trials
Motorcycle,** engine No.
ZB 32GS 459, frame No.
ZB 31-6282, single vertical cylinder
engine, overhead valve, air-cooled,
4 stroke, bore 71mm, stroke 88mm,
348cc, 4 speed gearbox, chain final
drive, telescopic front fork
suspension, rigid rear.
Est. **£3,900-4,500**   *S*

*The Earls Court Show of 1948 saw
the introduction of the Gold Star
range of BSA bikes, were
available in either 350cc or 500cc
form and were offered in either
racing, scrambling, touring or trials
specification.*

1950 BSA 650cc A10 Motorcycle,
fitted with Watsonian Monaco
sidecar.
£1,750-1,850   *LAR*

**c1950 BSA Gold Star Scrambler
348cc Solo Motorcycle,**
engine No. ZB32A 3162, single
cylinder overhead valve,
air-cooled, 4 stroke engine,
348cc, 4 speed gearbox,
telescopic front forks with rigid
frame at rear, chain final drive,
3.00 x 21in front, 4.00 x 19in
rear tyres.
£2,600-2,800   *S*

1949 BSA C11 De Luxe 250cc Solo Motorcycle,
single vertical cylinder, air-cooled, overhead valve, 4 stroke, bore
63mm, stroke 80mm, 249cc, 3 speed posi-stop gearbox, chain final drive,
telescopic front forks, rigid rear suspension, 20in tyres. **£850-950**   *S*

1951 BSA 650cc A10 Motorcycle,
and Monza sidecar.
£1,250-1,350 *LAR*

1952 BSA 600cc M21 Motorcycle,
with box sidecar.
£700-750 *LAR*

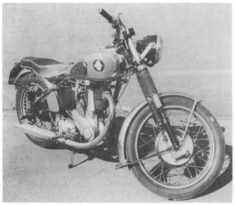

1956 BSA 350cc B31 Motorcycle.
£850-900 *LAR*

*BSA's B 31 was
introduced in 1945
and remained in
production until
1959.*

**1956 BSA B 31 350cc Solo
Motorcycle,** engine No. BB 31
22142, frame No. CB 31 13877,
single vertical cylinder engine,
air-cooled, overhead valve, bore
71mm, stroke 88mm, 348cc, 4 speed
posi-stop gearbox, chain final drive,
telescopic front forks, swinging arm
rear suspension, 3.25 x 19in tyres.
£1,300-1,500 *S*

**1957 BSA Gold Star 500cc Solo
Motorcycle,** engine No. DB661B,
frame No. EB316891, single vertical
cylinder, air-cooled, overhead valve,
4 stroke, bore 85mm, stroke 88mm,
499cc, 4 speed foot change gearbox,
telescopic front forks, swinging arm
rear suspension.
Est. **£6,000-7,000** *S*

*c1960 BSA D7
Bantam 175cc
Motorcycle.*
£120-150 *LAR*

**1959 BSA A10 R Super Rocket
Cafe Racer 650cc Solo
Motorcycle,** engine No.
DA10R9663, frame No. CA7-1047,
vertical, air-cooled, twin cylinder,
overhead valve, 4 stroke, bore
70mm, stroke 84mm, 646cc, 4 speed
foot operated gearbox, swinging
arm rear suspension, telescopic
front forks.
£3,100-3,500 *S*

*BSA's series of pre-unit 500cc and
650cc machines were noted for
performance and fine handling, and
many were customised in the cafe
racer style.*

1960 BSA C15 250cc Solo Motorcycle, engine No. C15 12472, frame No. C15 12601, single vertical cylinder engine, air-cooled, overhead valve, bore 67mm, stroke 70mm, 250cc, 4 speed gearbox, chain final drive, telescopic front forks, swinging arm rear suspension, 17in tyres.
Est. **£600-650** *S*

The lightweight C15 had a ten-year production run from 1958 to 1967 with only minor updating modifications.
The overhead valve engine developed 15bhp @ 7000rpm and the bike was both nimble and economical.

1956 BSA Gold Star 350cc Solo Motorcycle, engine No. DB32GS587, frame No. CB323003, single vertical, air-cooled cylinder, overhead valve, 4 stroke, bore 71mm, stroke 88mm, 348cc, 4 speed foot change gearbox, telescopic front forks, rear pivoted fork.
Est. **£5,000-6,000** *S*

1960 BSA Super Rocket 650cc Sprint Racer Solo Motorcycle, engine No. DA 10R 2961 HC, frame No. DA7 12029, vertical twin cylinder engine, air-cooled, overhead valve, bore 70mm, stroke 84mm, 646cc, 4 speed gearbox, chain final drive, telescopic front forks, swinging arm rear suspension, 19in front, 18in rear tyre.
Est. **£1,600-2,000** *S*

c1960 BSA Shooting Star 497cc Solo Motorcycle, engine No. A7 SS 7297, vertical twin cylinder, overhead valve, air-cooled, 4 stroke engine, 497cc, 4 speed gearbox, telescopic forks, sprung frame at rear, chain final drive, 3.25 x 19in front, 3.50 x 19in rear tyre.
£2,100-2,350 *S*

Did you know

MILLER'S Collectors Cars Price Guide builds up year by year to form the most comprehensive photo-reference system available

---

1961 BSA DBD 34 Gold Star Catalina 500cc Solo Motorcycle, engine No. DBD345830, frame No. CB32C607, single vertical, air-cooled cylinder, overhead valve, 4 stroke, bore 85mm, stroke 88mm, 499cc, 4 speed posi-stop gearbox, pivoted for rear suspension, telescopic front forks.
£3,900-4,250 *S*

1960 BSA Gold Star 348cc Solo Motorcycle, engine No. DB 32 GS 582, single vertical cylinder, overhead valve, air-cooled, 4 stroke engine, 348cc, 4 speed gearbox, telescopic forks, sprung frame at rear, chain final drive, 3.60 x 19in front, 410 H 19 rear tyre.
£4,000-4,500 *S*

1969 BSA Bantam/Triumph Tiger Cub Trials Motorcycle, 200cc.
£500-550 *LAR*

Bultaco

Mid-1970s Bultaco Sherpa Trials Bike, engine No. PM 9101465, frame No. SN 360, single vertical cylinder, air-cooled, 2 stroke, foot operated gearbox, telescopic front forks, pivoted rear fork.
£350-400 *S*

1963 BSA Rocket Gold Star 646cc Solo Motorcycle, engine No. DA 10 R 10017, vertical twin cylinder, overhead valve, air-cooled, 4 stroke engine, 646cc, 4 speed foot change gearbox, telescopic forks, sprung frame at rear, chain final drive, 3.60 x 19 front, 410 H 19 rear tyres.
£4,500-4,800 *S*

Second only in price to the Gold Star Clubman, at £323 8s. 0d. in the 1963 BSA range, this example appears to be in original and tidy order.

1961 BSA A7 Solo Motorcycle, engine No. CA755 9032, frame No. CA7 19422, twin vertical cylinder, air-cooled, overhead valve, 4 stroke, bore 66mm, stroke 72.6mm, 497cc, 4 speed posi-stop gearbox, telescopic front forks, swinging rear arm suspension.
£1,250-1,400 *S*

Bultaco Sherpa 250cc Trials Solo Motorcycle, engine No. RM 19800835, frame No. RB 19800835, single inclined cylinder, air-cooled, 2 stroke, bore 71mm, stroke 60mm, 237cc, 5 speed posi-stop gearbox, telescopic front forks, pivoted rear fork suspension.
£850-950 *S*

Developed by Sammy Miller towards the end of the 1960s, Bultaco's trials machine, known as the Sherpa, along with Montesa, became a major force in international trials during the 1970s and 80s, before succumbing to the challenge of rival European companies such as Fantic, and to the Japanese, who were uncharacteristically late in challenging in this market.

Calthorpe

1970 BSA Lightning 650cc Special Devimede Conversion Solo Motorcycle, engine No. JD 11173 A 65 L, vertical twin cylinder, twin carburettor, air-cooled, overhead valve, 4 stroke Devimede engine conversion, 4 speed gearbox, telescopic forks, sprung frame at rear, chain final drive. **£2,250-2,500** *S*

c1915 Calthorpe – JAP 2¾hp Solo Motorcycle, single vertical cylinder engine, air-cooled, side valve, 4 stroke, 2 speed with coffee grinder gearchange, belt final drive, girder forks with twin coil spring front suspension, rigid rear, 26 x 2in tyres.
£2,400-2,500 *S*

1917 Calthorpe JAP 245cc Solo Motorcycle, engine No. A 1279, JAP single vertical cylinder, air-cooled, side valve, 4 stroke engine, Enfield 2 speed gearbox with coffee grinder change, girder forks with coil spring front suspension, rigid frame at rear, chain-cum-belt drive, 26 x 2½in tyres front and rear.
£2,500-2,700   *S*

George Hands' Calthorpe company were builders of light cars and motorcycles through the early part of this century with motorcycle production continuing, albeit on a small scale, as late as 1939. Early machines in 1911 used 2 stroke engines and 4 stroke JAP and Precision engines were options offered.

Cheney

c1969 Cheney BSA 500cc Scrambler Motorcycle, engine No. 1547, BSA single cylinder, overhead valve, air-cooled, 4 stroke engine believed with Westlake 4 valve conversion, 4 speed gearbox, telescopic forks, sprung frame at rear, chain final drive, requires restoration.
Est. **£400-600**   *S*

Carfield

1923 Carfield 147cc Solo Motorcycle, engine No. 185C-VI, single vertical cylinder, air-cooled, 2 stroke, bore 55mm, stroke 62mm, Albion 2 speed gearbox with hand change, chain primary drive, belt final drive, patent Carfield quadruple spring girder front suspension, rigid rear, 24 x 2in tyres.
£1,900-2,200   *S*

Condor

The Model A-580 Condor was introduced primarily for military use in 1948 and remained in production for almost 30 years during which time over 4,400 machines had been built.

1953 Condor Model A-580-I 580cc Solo Military Motorcycle, frame/engine No. 205668, horizontally-opposed transverse twin cylinder engine, air-cooled, side valve, 4 stroke, bore 70mm, stroke 75.2mm, 578cc, 4 speed foot change gearbox, shaft final drive, telescopic front forks, plunger rear suspension, 19in tyres.
£1,000-1,100   *S*

Chater-Lea

c1903 Chater-Lea 350cc Solo Motorcycle, engine No. 4411, frame No. 4411, single vertical cylinder, air-cooled, side valve, 2 speed gearbox with coffee grinder lever, belt drive with pedal assistance, girder forks, rigid rear end.
£4,000-4,250   *S*

Connaught

1914 Connaught 2¾hp Solo Motorcycle, engine No. HB149, frame No. 210, single vertical cylinder, air-cooled, 293cc, 2 speed Albion gearbox with hand change, clutchless, belt final drive, girder fork suspension front, rigid rear, EIC magneto, Amac carburettor.
Est. **£4,000-4,500**   *S*

Corgi

1921 Connaught 2¾hp Solo Motorcycle, engine No. K 172, frame No. 600, single vertical cylinder, air-cooled, 2 stroke engine, bore 73mm, stroke 70mm, 2 speed Albion countershaft gearbox with hand change, girder forks with twin coil spring front suspension, rigid frame at rear, chain-cum-belt drive, 26 x 2½in front and rear tyres.
£2,000-2,250 *S*

c1948 Corgi 98cc Folding Motor Scooter, Excelsior Spryt horizontal, air-cooled, 2 stroke engine, single plate clutch, chain final drive, 12½ x 2¼in tyres. **£850-950** *S*

Cotton

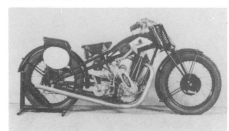

1929 Cotton-Blackburne 496cc Solo Racing Motorcycle, engine No. GCA 752, Blackburne inclined single cylinder, twin-port pushrod operated overhead valve, air-cooled, 4 stroke, 3 speed gearbox, girder forks with coil spring front suspension, rigid frame at rear, chain final drive, 3.25 x 19in front and rear tyres.
£3,300-3,600 *S*

Originally designed and built as a paratrooper's bike for use during WWII, the Spryt engined Corgi was adapted for civilian use by Brockhouse Engineering of Southport and sold between 1945 and 1948. Acclaimed as 'Britain's pocket prodigy', it weighed only 95lb and provided 30mph with a thrifty 120 miles per gallon.

> **Miller's is a price GUIDE not a price LIST**

1935 Cotton-JAP 350cc Solo Motorcycle, engine No. 10 S/R 65274/S, JAP inclined single cylinder engine with pushrod operated overhead valves and twin ports, air-cooled, 4 stroke, Burman 3 speed gearbox with hand change, Druid forks, rigid frame at rear, chain final drive, 3.00 x 19in front, 3.25 x 19in rear tyres.
£2,800-3,000 *S*

Coventry-Eagle

1916 Coventry-Eagle 269cc Solo Motorcycle, single vertical cylinder, air-cooled, 2 stroke engine, 269cc, single speed belt drive, girder forks with coil spring front suspension, rigid frame at rear, 24 x 2½in tyres front and rear.
£2,000-2,300 *S*

The old established bicycle makers Coventry-Eagle commenced making motorcycles as early as 1901, and by the 20s covered the whole range from lightweights to 1000cc V-twins.

1924 Cotton-Blackburne 350cc Solo Motorcycle, engine No. FD542, frame No. 1781, single inclined, air-cooled, overhead valve, 4 stroke, bore 71mm, stroke 88mm, 348cc, 3 speed hand change gearbox, chain primary and final drives, girder type forks, rigid rear end. **£2,500-2,800** *S*

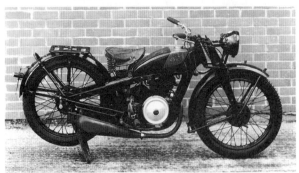

c1930 Coventry-Eagle 150cc Solo Motorcycle, engine No. 1501, single vertical cylinder, air-cooled, twin exhaust port, 2 stroke, bore 55mm, stroke 62mm, 147cc, 3 speed hand operated gearbox, rigid rear end, girder front forks.
Est. **£800-1,000**   *S*

Douglas

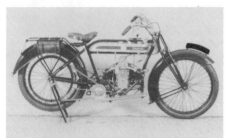

1922 Douglas 2¾hp Solo Motorcycle, horizontally opposed twin cylinder, air-cooled, 4 stroke engine, 2¾hp, 3 speed quadrant change gearbox, girder forks with coil spring front suspension, rigid frame at rear, chain-cum-belt final drive, 26 x 2½in front and rear tyres.
£2,650-2,800   *S*

DKW

c1939 DKW NZ 350cc Solo Motorcycle, inclined single cylinder engine, air-cooled, 2 stroke, 3 speed gearbox, chain final drive, girder fork and coil spring front suspension, rigid rear suspension.
£1,200-1,300   *S*

1914 Douglas 348cc Solo Motorcycle, engine No. 7874, frame No. 15563, longitudinally-mounted horizontally-opposed twin cylinder, side valve, air-cooled, 4 stroke engine, 2 speed gearing with P & M type coffee grinder clutch and change speed mechanism, girder forks with coil spring front suspension, rigid frame at rear, belt final drive.
£6,000-6,500   *S*

c1939 DKW NZ 350cc Solo Military Motorcycle, single cylinder engine, air-cooled, 2 stroke, 3 speed gearbox, chain final drive, parallelogram front forks, rigid rear suspension.
£1,500-1,650   *S*

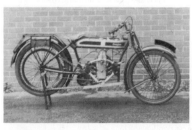

1923 Douglas 2¾hp Solo Motorcycle, engine No. LG46900/60991, frame No. 62635.
£1,900-2,100   *S*

1914 Douglas 2¾hp Solo Motorcycle, engine No. 13707, frame No. 13452, horizontally opposed twin cylinder engine, air-cooled, side valve, 4 stroke, 348cc, 2 speed hand change gearbox, belt final drive, girder fork and coil spring front suspension, rigid rear, 26 x 2½in tyres.
£9,000-10,000   *S*

Cheney

1917 Calthorpe JAP 245cc Solo Motorcycle, engine No. A 1279, JAP single vertical cylinder, air-cooled, side valve, 4 stroke engine, Enfield 2 speed gearbox with coffee grinder change, girder forks with coil spring front suspension, rigid frame at rear, chain-cum-belt drive, 26 x 2½in tyres front and rear.
£2,500-2,700 *S*

George Hands' Calthorpe company were builders of light cars and motorcycles through the early part of this century with motorcycle production continuing, albeit on a small scale, as late as 1939. Early machines in 1911 used 2 stroke engines and 4 stroke JAP and Precision engines were options offered.

c1969 Cheney BSA 500cc Scrambler Motorcycle, engine No. 1547, BSA single cylinder, overhead valve, air-cooled, 4 stroke engine believed with Westlake 4 valve conversion, 4 speed gearbox, telescopic forks, sprung frame at rear, chain final drive, requires restoration.
Est. **£400-600** *S*

Condor

Carfield

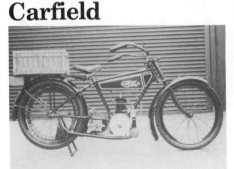

1923 Carfield 147cc Solo Motorcycle, engine No. 185C-VI, single vertical cylinder, air-cooled, 2 stroke, bore 55mm, stroke 62mm, Albion 2 speed gearbox with hand change, chain primary drive, belt final drive, patent Carfield quadruple spring girder front suspension, rigid rear, 24 x 2in tyres.
£1,900-2,200 *S*

The Model A-580 Condor was introduced primarily for military use in 1948 and remained in production for almost 30 years during which time over 4,400 machines had been built.

1953 Condor Model A-580-I 580cc Solo Military Motorcycle, frame/engine No. 205668, horizontally-opposed transverse twin cylinder engine, air-cooled, side valve, 4 stroke, bore 70mm, stroke 75.2mm, 578cc, 4 speed foot change gearbox, shaft final drive, telescopic front forks, plunger rear suspension, 19in tyres.
£1,000-1,100 *S*

Chater-Lea

Connaught

c1903 Chater-Lea 350cc Solo Motorcycle, engine No. 4411, frame No. 4411, single vertical cylinder, air-cooled, side valve, 2 speed gearbox with coffee grinder lever, belt drive with pedal assistance, girder forks, rigid rear end.
£4,000-4,250 *S*

1914 Connaught 2¾hp Solo Motorcycle, engine No. HB149, frame No. 210, single vertical cylinder, air-cooled, 293cc, 2 speed Albion gearbox with hand change, clutchless, belt final drive, girder fork suspension front, rigid rear, EIC magneto, Amac carburettor.
Est. **£4,000-4,500** *S*

Bultaco

**1963 BSA Rocket Gold Star
646cc Solo Motorcycle,** engine
No. DA 10 R 10017, vertical twin
cylinder, overhead valve, air-cooled,
4 stroke engine, 646cc, 4 speed foot
change gearbox, telescopic forks,
sprung frame at rear, chain final
drive, 3.60 x 19 front, 410 H 19 rear
tyres.
£4,500-4,800 *S*

*Second only in price to the Gold
Star Clubman, at £323 8s. 0d. in the
1963 BSA range, this example
appears to be in original and tidy
order.*

1961 BSA A7 Solo Motorcycle,
engine No. CA755 9032, frame No.
CA7 19422, twin vertical cylinder,
air-cooled, overhead valve, 4 stroke,
bore 66mm, stroke 72.6mm, 497cc,
4 speed posi-stop gearbox, telescopic
front forks, swinging rear arm
suspension.
£1,250-1,400 *S*

**Mid-1970s Bultaco Sherpa Trials
Bike,** engine No. PM 9101465,
frame No. SN 360, single vertical
cylinder, air-cooled, 2 stroke, foot
operated gearbox, telescopic front
forks, pivoted rear fork.
£350-400 *S*

Bultaco Sherpa 250cc Trials Solo Motorcycle, engine
No. RM 19800835, frame No. RB 19800835, single inclined
cylinder, air-cooled, 2 stroke, bore 71mm, stroke 60mm,
237cc, 5 speed posi-stop gearbox, telescopic front forks,
pivoted rear fork suspension.
£850-950 *S*

*Developed by Sammy Miller towards the end of the
1960s, Bultaco's trials machine, known as the Sherpa,
along with Montesa, became a major force in
international trials during the 1970s and 80s, before
succumbing to the challenge of rival European
companies such as Fantic, and to the Japanese, who
were uncharacteristically late in challenging in this
market.*

Calthorpe

**1970 BSA Lightning 650cc
Special Devimede Conversion
Solo Motorcycle,** engine No.
JD 11173 A 65 L, vertical twin
cylinder, twin carburettor,
air-cooled, overhead valve, 4 stroke
Devimede engine conversion,
4 speed gearbox, telescopic forks,
sprung frame at rear, chain final
drive.　　**£2,250-2,500** *S*

**c1915 Calthorpe – JAP 2¾hp
Solo Motorcycle,** single vertical
cylinder engine, air-cooled, side
valve, 4 stroke, 2 speed with coffee
grinder gearchange, belt final drive,
girder forks with twin coil spring
front suspension, rigid rear, 26 x 2in
tyres.
£2,400-2,500 *S*

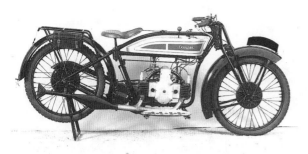

c1926 Douglas 2¾hp Solo Motorcycle, engine No. YE 6963, frame No. IF 6976, horizontally opposed twin cylinder, air-cooled, 4 stroke engine, rating 2¾hp, 3 speed hand change gearbox, girder forks with coil spring suspension, rigid frame at rear, chain final drive, 24 x 2½in front and rear tyres. **£2,000-2,200** *S*

1923 Douglas 2¾hp Solo Motorcycle, engine No. 57993, frame No. 59630. **£2,100-2,250** *S*

1923 Douglas 2¾hp Solo Motorcycle, engine No. 59671, frame No. 61930, horizontally opposed twin cylinder, air-cooled, side valve, 4 stroke, bore 60.8mm, stroke 60mm, 348cc, 2 speed gearbox, belt final drive, girder fork and coil spring suspension, rigid rear, 26 x 2½in tyres. **£2,750-3,000** *S*

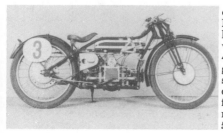

c1935 Douglas 596cc Solo Racing Motorcycle, engine No. EL 827, horizontally opposed, overhead valve, air-cooled, twin cylinder, 4 stroke engine, 596cc, 3 speed gearbox, girder forks with coil spring suspension and Andre dampers, rigid frame at rear, chain final drive, 2.75 x 21 front, 3.00 x 21 racing rear tyres. **£6,800-7,000** *S*

c1950 Douglas 90 Plus 348cc Solo Racing Motorcycle, engine No. 138, transverse horizontally opposed, twin cylinder, overhead valve, air-cooled, 4 stroke engine, 4 speed gearbox, torsion bar suspension front and rear, chain final drive, 3.00 x 21 front, 3.25 x 19 rear tyres. **£3,250-3,500** *S*

1949 Douglas 350cc Competition Solo Motorcycle, engine No. 7898/4, frame No. 7898/4B, horizontally opposed twin cylinder engine, air-cooled, overhead valve, 4 stroke, 4 speed gearbox, chain final drive, Douglas front forks, rigid rear suspension. Est. **£3,300-3,600** *S*

1951 Douglas Trials 350cc Solo Motorcycle, engine No. T35/S/2131, frame No. 9086C, horizontal, air-cooled, overhead valve, 4 stroke twin, bore 60.8mm, stroke 60mm, 348cc, 4 speed foot operated gearbox, chain final drive, leading link front forks, rigid rear end. **£1,500-1,600** *S*

1956 Douglas Dragonfly 350cc Solo Motorcycle, frame/engine No. 1885-6, flat twin cylinder, air-cooled, overhead valve, 348cc, 4 speed gearbox, telescopic front and rear fork suspension, chain final drive. Est. **£2,000-3,000** *S*

Ducati

1963 Ducati Daytona 250cc Solo Motorcycle, engine No. DM25082627, frame No. DM25085969, inclined air-cooled, single overhead cam, 4 stroke, single cylinder, bore 74mm, stroke 57.8mm, 248cc, 4 speed positive stop gearbox, chain final drive, telescopic front forks, pivoted fork rear suspension.
£1,600-1,700 S

c1970 Ducati Mk III 350cc Racing Solo Motorcycle, engine No. DM 350 18506, inclined single cylinder, air-cooled, overhead valve, 4 stroke, bore 76mm, stroke 75mm, 340cc, 4 speed positive stop gearbox, chain final drive, telescopic front forks, swing arm rear suspension.
£1,250-1,400 S

1974 Ducati 750 Sports Solo Motorcycle, engine No. 755818, frame No. 7505 755988, 90° V-twin, air-cooled, bevel driven, overhead camshaft, 4 stroke, bore 80mm, stroke 74.4mm, 747.96cc, 5 speed posi-stop gearbox, chain final drive, pivoted fork rear suspension, telescopic front forks.
Est. **£5,000-6,000** S

Excelsior

c1937 Excelsior Manxman 250cc Solo Racing Motorcycle, engine No. BRR 257, frame No. MVF 129, single vertical cylinder, air-cooled, overhead valve, overhead camshaft, 4 stroke, 250cc, 4 speed foot change gearbox, chain final drive, girder fork and coil spring front suspension, rigid rear, restored about five years and presented in racing trim.
£4,800-5,000 S

Excelsior's Manxman range of the mid-1930s was offered in 250cc, 350cc and 500cc versions and were immortalised in competition, particularly on the island from which they derive their name. Famous riders were to include 'Ginger' Wood and Tyrell-Smith, building on racing successes already achieved for the marque by Eric Fernihough, Chris Staniland and Syd Gleave.

1934 Excelsior Manxman 350cc Solo Racing Motorcycle, engine No. BRA 118, frame No. 169 GM, single vertical cylinder, air-cooled, overhead camshaft, 4 stroke engine, 348cc, 4 speed Albion gearbox, girder Webb forks with coil spring front suspension, rigid frame at rear, chain final drive, 2.75 x 21in front, 3.00 x 20in rear tyres. **£5,400-5,600** S

c1937 Excelsior Manxman 500cc Sports Solo Motorcycle, engine No. GJA 127, single cylinder, overhead camshaft, air-cooled, 4 stroke engine, 498cc, 4 speed gearbox, Webb girder forks with coil spring front suspension, rigid frame at rear, chain final drive, 3.00 x 21 front, 3.00 x 19 rear tyres. **£6,500-7,000** S

Federation

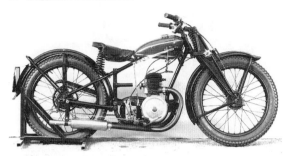

1936 Federation 150cc Solo Motorcycle, engine No. GY 4200, Villiers single vertical cylinder, twin port, air-cooled, 2 stroke engine, Albion gearbox, Webb pressed steel forks with coil spring front suspension, rigid frame at rear, chain final drive, 3.00 x 19 front and rear tyres.
£900-950   *S*

Francis-Barnett

1940 Francis-Barnett Plover 148cc Solo Motorcycle, single vertical cylinder, twin port, air-cooled, 2 stroke engine, 3 speed Albion gearbox, girder forks with coil spring front suspension, rigid frame at rear, chain final drive, 3.00 x 19 front, 2.75 x 19 rear tyres.
£1,100-1,300   *S*

Introduced for the 1935 season, and continuing Francis-Barnett's bird name theme of the 30s, the Plover was the cheapest machine in the range when first announced at £25 10s. 0d.

FN

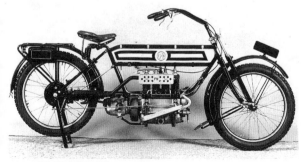

1914 FN 7hp Solo Motorcycle, engine No. 400, 4 vertical cylinders in-line, side valve, air-cooled, 4 stroke engine, 746cc, 2 speed gearbox, girder forks and rigid frame at rear, shaft and bevel final drive, 26 x 3 front and rear tyres.
£10,000-10,500   *S*

Gilera

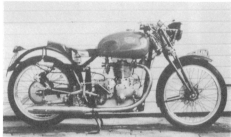

1946 Gilera Saturno Competizione Sport, engine No. 265854, frame No. 269094, narrow front and rear wings, large capacity tank, Webb fork, Gilera special rear suspension, compass shock absorbers, 21in alloy wheels with black spokes, original alloy cylinder head, Dell Orto RDF 28 carburettor, Lucas magneto, Veglia-Gilera 0-12000rpm, later rev-counter, right side remote gear-shift.
Est. **£7,000-8,000**   *C(M)*

Gnome et Rhone

c1937/38 Gnome et Rhone Model AX2 800 Military Combination, engine No. 164789, frame No. 164789, horizontally opposed twin cylinder engine, air-cooled, side valve, 4 stroke, 804cc, 4 speed gearbox, shaft drive to rear and sidecar wheels, girder fork and coil spring front suspension, rigid rear.
£2,500-2,750   *S*

The Gnome et Rhone AX2 was the superbike of the French Army very much in the idiom of the German BMW and Zundapp machines.

c1934 Gnome et Rhone 800cc Solo Motorcycle, engine No. AX2 30490, frame No. AX2 30490, inclined twin cylinder engine, air-cooled, side valve, 4 stroke, 804cc, 4 speed gearbox, chain final drive, girder fork and coil spring front suspension, rigid rear, 19in tyres.
£1,750-1,875   *S*

Greeves

1960 Greeves Scottish 250cc Trials Motorcycle, engine No. 863B-1856, frame No. 61-1604, single cylinder engine, air-cooled, 2 stroke, 246cc, 4 speed gearbox, chain final drive, telescopic front forks, swinging arm rear suspension.
£575-625 *S*

1960s Greeves Scottish 250cc Trials Solo Motorcycle, engine No. 787B 16364, frame No. 60-2969, Villiers single cylinder, air-cooled, 2 stroke engine, 4 speed gearbox, Earles leading links forks with sprung frame at rear, chain final drive, 3.25 x 19 front, 4.00 x 18 trials rear tyres. **£900-1,000** *S*

c1966 Greeves 250cc Solo Racing Motorcycle, frame No. 24 RBS 115, single vertical cylinder, air-cooled, 2 stroke engine, 4 speed gearbox, telescopic forks, sprung frame at rear, chain final drive, Dunlop Racing KR 73 3.00 x 18 front, Dunlop Racing KR 76 3.00/3.25 x 18 rear tyres.
£1,500-1,750 *S*

1968 Greeves 250cc Solo Trials Motorcycle, frame No. 24T JSB 286, single cylinder, air-cooled, 2 stroke, 4 speed gearbox with foot change, chain final drive, telescopic fork front suspension, telescopic rear suspension with hydraulic plungers and coil springs, wheelbase 52in, 2.75 x 21in front, 4.00 x 18in rear tyres.
£1,000-1,250 *S*

Hagon

Alf Hagon – JAP V-twin Supercharged Spring Racing Special, JAP V-twin overhead valve, air-cooled, 4 stroke racing engine, 1000cc, countershaft posi-stop racing gearbox No. 2263, Roots type supercharger, telescopic forks, sprung frame, chain final drive, 2.50 x 18in front, 400 x 18 Racemaster slick rear tyres, full fairing at front with fuel tank in nascelle.
£3,600-4,000 *S*

Alf Hagon is well-known in the world of sprints, grass track and long track events. His work with JAP engined spring specials post-dates the cessation of production of JAP engines at Tottenham.

Harley Davidson

c1944 Harley Davidson Model WLA 740cc Solo Military Motorcycle, engine No. WLA 419, frame No. 42035, V-twin cylinder engine, air-cooled, side valve, 4 stroke, bore 69.85mm, stroke 96.83mm, 742cc, 3 speed left hand change gearbox, chain final drive, leading link girder fork and coil spring front suspension, rigid rear, 18in tyres, front mudguard mounted tool box and supplies box on front forks, finished in US Army livery though also used by the Allied Forces.
£3,600-3,850 *S*

1926 Harley Davidson 1200cc Motorcycle Combination, engine No. 25 JDCB 3905, frame No. 25F 4009, V-twin cylinder engine, air-cooled, inlet over exhaust valves, bore 86.9mm, stroke 106.6mm, 1205cc, 3 speed left hand change gearbox, chain final drive, girder fork and coil spring front suspension, rigid rear with leaf C springs on sidecar, 3.50 x 18in front, 710 x 90mm rear tyres, 710 x 90mm on sidecar. **£10,000-11,000** *S*

Harris

1984 Harris/Kawasaki Magnum 1260cc Solo Motorcycle, engine No. KZT00AE037691, frame No. HP527, inclined air-cooled, overhead cam, 4 stroke, transverse 4, posi-stop gearbox, chain final drive, Marzocchi telescopic front forks with mechanical anti-dive, monoshock rear suspension. **£2,300-2,600** *S*

Henderson

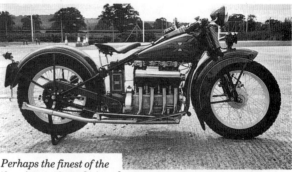

Perhaps the finest of the 'fours' were those designed by William 'Bill' Henderson, bearing his name, which were later developed by Arthur Lemon after the firm had been acquired by the Schwinn factory, before production ceased in 1931.

1929 Henderson 1303cc Solo Motorcycle, engine No. KJ30451, frame No. 3006, in-line, air-cooled, side valve, 4 cylinder, 4 stroke, bore 68.3mm, stroke 88.9mm, 3 speed hand operated gearbox, chain final drive, rigid rear end, girder front forks. **£7,750-8,250** *S*

Hesketh

1982 Hesketh V1000 Solo Motorcycle, engine No. 092, frame No. 051, V-twin, air-cooled, overhead cam, 4 stroke, bore 95mm, stroke 70mm, 992.3cc, 5 speed foot operated gearbox, chain final drive, rear pivoted fork suspension, Marzocchi telescopic front forks. **£5,750-6,250** *S*

Lord Hesketh introduced the V1000 in 1982, with the machine being clearly aimed at the luxury end of the market.

Hesketh Vampire 1000cc Solo Motorcycle, engine No. 0056, frame No. 0056, 90° V-twin, air-cooled, overhead cam, 4 stroke, bore 95mm, stroke 70mm, 992cc, 5 speed foot operated gearbox, chain final drive, pivoted fork rear suspension, telescopic front forks. **£8,100-8,500** *S*

Honda

1964 Honda CB 77 305cc Solo Motorcycle, engine No. CB 77 102479, frame No. CB 77 102477, inclined twin cylinder engine, air-cooled, overhead camshaft, 4 stroke, bore 60mm, stroke 54mm, 4 speed gearbox, chain final drive, telescopic front forks, swinging arm rear suspension, 18in tyres.
Est. **£1,800-2,200**   *S*

1981 Honda CBX 1000 Solo Motorcycle, engine No. 2015470, frame No. 2014553, inclined, air-cooled, twin overhead cam, 4 stroke, transverse 6 cylinder, bore 64.5mm, stroke 63.4mm, 1047cc, 5 speed posi-stop gearbox chain final drive, telescopic front forks, pivoted fork rear suspension.
£4,250-4,500   *S*

1974 Honda CB 750 Solo Motorcycle, engine No. CB750 2310363, frame No. CB750 2310363, 4 cylinder, air-cooled, overhead cam, 4 stroke, bore 61mm, stroke 63mm, 736.5cc, 5 speed foot operated gearbox, chain final drive, telescopic front forks, pivoted rear forks.
£1,600-1,750   *S*

c1982 Honda CR125R Motocross Solo Motorcycle, frame No. JH2 JE0103 EC500 116, single vertical cylinder, liquid cooled, 2 stroke, 125cc, foot operated positive stop gearbox, monoshock rising rate rear suspension.
£950-1,000   *S*

Humber

1922 Humber 4½hp Flat Twin Solo Motorcycle, horizontally opposed twin cylinder, air-cooled engine, bore 75mm, stroke 68mm, 600cc, 3 speed hand change countershaft gearbox, multiple disc clutch, chain final drive, girder fork and coil spring front suspension, rigid rear, 26 x 3in tyres, restored 15 years ago, having been discovered in original condition in a garage where it had lain untouched since 1931.
£9,000-11,000   *S*

1978 Honda CB400/4 Solo Motorcycle, engine No. CB400FE1073364, frame No. CB400F1077563, vertical, 4 cylinder, air-cooled, single overhead cam, 4 stroke, bore 51mm, stroke 50mm, 408.6cc, 6 speed posi-stop gearbox, telescopic front forks, pivoted fork rear suspension.
Est. **£800-1,000**   *S*

Honda's CB400/4 is now becoming regarded as one of the classic machines of its era. Producing approximately 37bhp, the machine will comfortably exceed 105mph, whilst its lightweight, fine road holding and good brakes combine to produce a machine that is easy to handle, stylish and responds quickly.

Indian

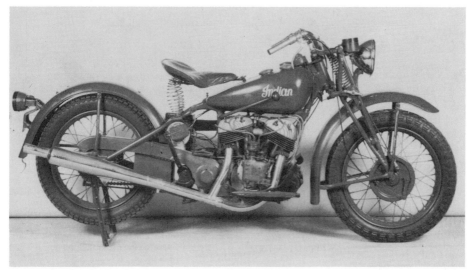

1939 Indian Model 741 Scout Solo Motorcycle, V-twin cylinder engine, air-cooled, side valve, bore 2.5in, stroke 3.062cu in, 3 speed hand change gearbox, chain final drive, girder fork and coil spring front suspension with adjustable dampers, rigid rear suspension, 3.50 x 18in tyres.
£3,250-3,500 *S*

The Springfield factory of Indian Motorcycle Co produced their first motorcycle in 1901 and took an active part in competition in their early days with Freddie Dixon and Bert Le Vack, among others, riding their machines with some success. The V-twin of 1939 was clearly produced with military service in mind and the Junior and the Scout were to give sterling service in World War II. The contracts from armed forces throughout the world for supply of Indian bikes enabled the company to remain in business into the post-war years.

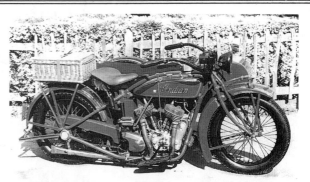

1925 Indian Super-Chief 1220cc Goulding Combination, engine No. 91Y748, frame No. 105, V-twin cylinder with fixed heads, air-cooled, side valve, bore 83mm, stroke 113mm, 1222cc, 74cu in, 3 speed gearbox with hand change, foot operated clutch, helical gear primary drive, chain final drive, leaf spring and girder fork suspension front, rigid rear, Goulding 3 point mounting sidecar chassis with full elliptic and coil spring suspension, fully floating body mounts, expanding shoe drum brake on rear wheel, 20 x 3.00 tyres.
Est. £9,000-12,000 *S*

c1944 Indian 741 B 30.60cu in Solo Military Motorcycle, engine No. 25325, frame No. 25325, V-twin cylinder engine, air-cooled, side valve, 4 stroke, bore 2.5in, stroke 3.062in, 3 speed gearbox, chain final drive, girder fork and coil spring front suspension, rigid rear, 18in tyres.
£2,500-2,750 *S*

Locate the source

The source of each illustration in Miller's can be found by checking the code letters below each caption with the list of contributors

c1968 Indian Velo Thruxton 500cc Solo Motorcycle, engine/frame No. VMT 828C, single vertical cylinder engine, air-cooled, overhead valve, 4 stroke, 4 speed foot change gearbox, chain final drive, telescopic front forks, swinging arm rear suspension.
Est. £3,200-3,800 *S*

Jackson-Rotrax

c1952 Jackson-Rotrax Speedway JAP Solo Motorcycle, single vertical cylinder, overhead valve, air-cooled, 4 stroke engine, rigid frame, chain final drive, 2.75 x 23 front, 2.75 x 22 rear tyres. Est. **£1,800-2,700** *S*

The Jackson-Rotrax company's machines, dominated Speedway tracks in the early 50s.

JES

1914 JES 102cc Motor Assisted Pedal Cycle, engine No. 1124, single inclined cylinder, overhead inlet side exhaust valve, air-cooled, 4 stroke engine, single speed direct belt drive, rigid frame, 28 x 1½ front and rear tyres. **£1,750-2,000** *S*

JC

1964 JC Special 350cc Solo Trials Motorcycle. Est. **£2,000-2,500** *S*

John Catchpole's Sidcup garage provided the means and facilities for this clever engineer to exercise his fertile brain, first with Scott Specials, later with an Austin/Scott/Berkeley/Norton hybrid trials car and in 1964 the JC Special Trials bike developed for the 1965 season.

Kawasaki

c1978 Kawasaki Z400 Solo Motorcycle, vertical twin cylinder, air-cooled, single overhead cam, 4 stroke, bore 64mm, stroke 62mm, 398cc, 5 speed foot operated gearbox, telescopic front forks, pivoted fork rear suspension. **£300-350** *S*

Lambretta

1948 Lambretta Model A 125cc Motor Scooter, engine No. 44936, frame No. 44936, single cylinder engine, air-cooled, 2 stroke, 3 speed gearbox, multi-plate clutch, chain final drive, 8in tyres. **£750-850** *S*

The arrival of Innocenti's Model A scooter in 1948 met a desperate need for cheap transport at the end of World War II. As well as practical and utilitarian the new scooters were fun and much loved by the younger generation.

This machine, produced under licence granted to Lyons in France, is unusual in having rubber seats with hand grip and carries a spare wheel.

1959 Lambretta Model LD 125cc Motor Scooter (French Built), engine No. 198956, frame No. 198715, single cylinder engine, air-cooled, 2 stroke, 123cc, 3 speed twist grip gear change, chain final drive, rocker arm and coil spring front suspension, 8in tyres. **£650-750** *S*

1964 Lambretta Model LI 125cc Motor Scooter (Italian Built), engine No. 082148, frame No. 082650, single cylinder engine, air-cooled, 2 stroke, 123cc, 3 speed gearbox, chain final drive, rocker arm and coil spring front suspension, 8in tyres.
£800-875 *S*

This example of Model LI was built by Innocenti of Milan.

c1969/70 Lambretta Grand Prix 200cc Motor Scooter, engine No. 200 259349, frame No. 2212 259145, single cylinder engine, air-cooled, 2 stroke, 198cc, 4 speed gearbox, chain final drive, trailing link, helical springs and hydraulic shock absorber front suspension, swinging arm rear suspension, 10in tyres.
£2,000-2,250 *S*

This example, from a major museum collection, is brand new, has never been registered or run, and is missing only its original petrol tap.

Levis

1921 Levis 2¼hp Solo Motorcycle, single inclined, air-cooled cylinder, 2 stroke, bore 62mm, stroke 70mm, 211cc, 2 speed hand operated gearbox, belt drive, rigid rear end, girder forks.
£2,500-2,750 *S*

Levis' early machines were predominantly 2 strokes of their own manufacture, which earned a considerable reputation for longevity and reliability.

L'Rallier

c1940s L'Rallier Tricycle. **£675-725** *S*

This three-wheeled, two seater motorcycle, was one of numerous economical means of transport produced in France during times of economic stress. Propelled by a single cylinder petrol engine, with electric starting and lighting, and the 4 speed hand change gearbox delivers a speed of up to 40mph. The rear facing passenger has a folding footrest. Since restoration it has been museum stored.

Martinsyde

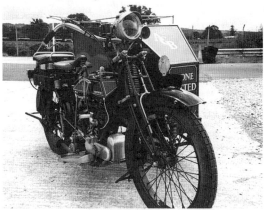

c1920 Martinsyde 680cc Motorcycle and Commercial Sidecar, engine No. 109, frame No. 1044, V-twin, air-cooled, exhaust over inlet, 4 stroke, bore 70mm, stroke 88mm, 676cc, 3 speed hand operated gearbox, rigid rear end, girder front forks, comprehensive restoration, and now fitted with 'baker's box' sidecar.
£6,200-6,500 *S*

Matchless

1930 Matchless Silver Arrow 397cc Solo Motorcycle, engine No. A1558, frame No. 1554, 26° V-twin cylinder, side valve, 4 stroke, bore 54mm, stroke 88mm, 3 speed hand change gearbox, pivoted fork rear suspension, girder front forks. **Est. £5,500-6,000** *S*

1921 Matchless Model H and Sidecar 996cc, engine No. 269V 6121, frame No. H 1376, V-twin cylinder, air-cooled, inlet over exhaust, 4 stroke, 3 speed hand change gearbox, chain final drive, girder front forks, coil sprung pivoted fork rear suspension.
£8,500-9,000 *S*

The Collier brothers' Matchless company produced a series of successful machines using a number of different engine makes, one of their most impressive machines being the Model H specifically designed with sidecar haulage in mind. The machines had some innovative design features such as the coil sprung controlled pivoted fork, chain final drive and a drum front brake, at a time when many machines still had no front brakes.

1936 Matchless 250cc Solo Motorcycle, engine No. 36 G/2 2433, single cylinder, overhead valve, air-cooled, 4 stroke engine, 4 speed foot change gearbox, girder forks with coil spring front suspension, rigid frame at rear, chain final drive, 3.00 x 19 tyres.
£1,900-2,250 *S*

Miller's is a price GUIDE not a price LIST

c1930 Matchless Silver Arrow 394cc Solo Motorcycle, engine No. A1448, frame No. 588, 26°, air-cooled, side valve, 4 stroke, V-twin, bore 54mm, stroke 86mm, 3 speed hand operated gearbox, chain final drive, girder front forks, pivoted fork rear suspension.
£3,000-3,250 *S*

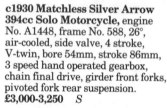

c1931 Matchless Silver Hawk 593cc Solo Motorcycle, engine No. B824, narrow angle V4 cylinder, air-cooled, overhead camshaft, 4 stroke engine, 4 speed gearbox, girder forks with coil spring front suspension, sprung frame at rear, chain final drive, 3.25 x 19 front, 4.00 x 19 rear tyres.
£5,750-6,000 *S*

c1944 Matchless Model G3L 350cc Solo Military Motorcycle, single vertical cylinder engine, air-cooled, overhead valve, bore 69mm, stroke 93mm, 347cc, 4 speed foot change gearbox, chain final drive, telescopic front forks, hydraulically damped, rigid rear suspension, 19in tyres.
£1,500-1,750 *S*

At the outbreak of World War II Matchless received a lucrative contract to supply their civilian Model G3 to the War Department for dispatch rider use. In 1941 they introduced the G3L, the first British bike to be offered with hydraulically damped telescopic front forks.

c1958 Matchless G3L 347cc Scrambler Solo Motorcycle, engine No. 58/G3L 19350, single vertical cylinder, air-cooled, overhead valve, 4 stroke engine, 4 speed gearbox, telescopic forks, sprung frame at rear, chain final drive, 2.75 x 21 front, 4.00 x 19 rear tyres.
£1,800-1,900 *S*

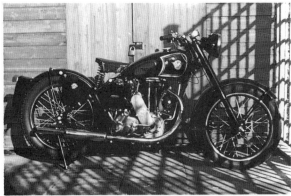

1948 Matchless G3L 350cc Solo Motorcycle.
£1,500-1,750 *S*

1959 Matchless G12 650cc Solo Motorcycle, engine No. 59/G12X1959, frame No. A72157, vertical twin cylinder, air-cooled, overhead valve, 4 stroke, bore 72mm, stroke 79.3mm, 646cc, 4 speed foot operated gearbox, swinging arm rear suspension, telescopic front forks.
£1,900-2,100 *S*

1965/67 Matchless G50/Rickman Metisse 500cc Solo Motorcycle, single vertical cylinder engine, air-cooled, overhead valve, overhead camshaft, bore 90mm, stroke 78mm, 496cc, 5 speed gearbox, chain final drive, telescopic front forks, swinging arm rear suspension. **£11,500-12,500** *S*

A well executed special clubman bike adopting the Matchless overhead camshaft engine in a Rickman frame and fitted with a Petty 5 speed gearbox. The engine was rebuilt and raced in Europe in 1989-90.

Montesa

Motobi

1977 Montesa 348 Cota Trials Motorcycle, engine No. 5TM 8770, frame No. 5TM 8770, single inclined cylinder, air-cooled, 2 stroke, bore 78mm, stroke 64mm, 305.8cc, 6 speed gearbox, telescopic front forks, exceptional condition.
£1,350-1,450 *S*

The Italian built Motobi was the brainchild of Giovanni Benelli and built in the Benelli factory at Pesaro. Both 2 stroke and overhead valve engines were built, the largest capacity being 250cc, and the bikes were variously badged as either Benelli or Motobi.

1965-67 Motobi 175 Sport, engine No. 9850, frame No. 441519, restored competition motorcycle, fitted with 18in alloy wheels, vertical Dell Orto UB 24 S2 carburettor and a Veglia 0-10000rpm competition rev-counter.
Est. **£3,500-4,500** *C(M)*

Cross Reference
Benelli

Moto Guzzi

c1945 Moto Guzzi Alce 500cc Solo Military Motorcycle, engine No. 104551, frame No. 104551, horizontal single cylinder engine, air-cooled, inlet over exhaust valve, 4 stroke, bore 88mm, stroke 82mm, 498cc, 4 speed hand change gearbox, unit construction, chain final drive, girder fork and coil spring front suspension, rigid rear, 19in tyres, restored and finished in military police livery. **£1,950-2,000** *S*

Introduced in 1939 and developed from the Moto Guzzi GT-20, the Alce (or Elk) was Italian built and designed specifically for that country's armed forces.

1952 Moto Guzzi Falcone Sport 500, engine No. F.97991, frame No. F.31161, restored to Concours standard, fitted with a Dell Orto SS 29A carburettor and an original Veglia speedometer calibrated to 160mph, CEV electrics and original fishtail exhaust.
£5,000-5,500 *C(M)*

c1955 Moto Guzzi Airone 250cc Solo Motorcycle, engine No. M83758, frame No. 16668, single horizontal cylinder, air-cooled, overhead valve, 4 stroke, bore 70mm, stroke 64mm, 247cc, 4 speed foot operated gearbox, telescopic front forks, spring and friction controlled rear suspension.
Est. **£1,500-2,000** *S*

1952 Moto Guzzi Airone Sport 250cc Solo Motorcycle, engine No. M 100071, frame No. 23955, single horizontal cylinder engine, air-cooled, overhead valve, 4 speed gearbox, chain final drive, telescopic front forks, friction dampers at rear.
Est. **£3,300-3,600** *S*

c1957 Moto Guzzi Superalce 500cc Solo Motorcycle, engine No. AV 92399, frame No. 28932, horizontal, air-cooled, overhead valve, 4 stroke single, bore 88mm, stroke 82mm, 498cc, foot operated 4 speed gearbox, helical gear primary drive, chain final drive, girder front forks, pivoted fork rear suspension.
Est. **£1,800-2,200** *S*

Introduced in 1946 as a replacement for Moto Guzzi's Ake, the Superalce adopted a 4 speed gearbox and a new horizontal single cylinder engine offering significantly improved performance, 18.5hp against its predecessor's 13.2hp, and remained in production until 1957.

1956 Moto Guzzi Falcone 500cc Solo Motorcycle, engine/frame No. FAH 87, single horizontal cylinder engine, air-cooled, overhead valve, 4 stroke, bore 88mm, stroke 82mm, 498cc, 4 speed foot change gearbox, chain final drive, telescopic front forks, swinging arm rear suspension with friction dampers. Est. **£5,600-6,200** *S*

MV Augusta

c1973/74 MV Augusta 750 S America Solo Motorcycle, engine No. 2210199, frame No. 2210225, inclined 4 cylinder engine, air-cooled, overhead valve, double overhead camshaft, 4 stroke, 743cc, 5 speed gearbox, shaft final drive, telescopic front forks, swinging arm rear suspension. Est. **£15,000-18,000** *S*

Such all-time greats as Surtees, Agostini, Read and Hailwood were to prove the outstanding performance of Augusta's in-line 4 cylinder bikes and were to keep the name well to the fore in the minds of the keen biker. The MV Augusta 750 model was to find a worldwide market to appreciate its qualities of performance and handling.

New Hudson

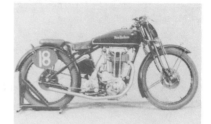

1927 New Hudson 500cc TT Racing Solo Motorcycle, engine No. DSF 46, frame No. 3869, single vertical cylinder, overhead valve, air-cooled, 4 stroke engine, 3 speed Albion gearbox, girder forks with coil spring front suspension, rigid frame at rear, chain final drive, 3.00 x 21 tyres. **£5,500-6,000** *S*

1973 MV Augusta 750cc Solo Motorcycle, engine No. 2140422, frame No. MV 750 2210599, inclined 4 cylinder engine, air-cooled, double overhead camshaft, overhead valve, 4 stroke, 743cc, 5 speed gearbox, shaft final drive, telescopic front forks, swinging arm rear suspension. Est. **£13,000-15,000** *S*

New Imperial

Norman

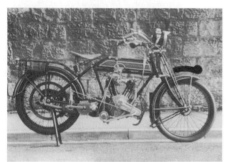

1917/21 New Imperial 770cc Solo Motorcycle, engine No. KTE/7489, frame No. A7299, V-twin cylinder, air-cooled, side valve, 4 stroke, bore 71mm, stroke 85.5mm, Burman 3 speed hand change gearbox, chain final drive, rigid rear end, Brampton Bi-Flex girder front forks, restored to 1921 specification. **£5,100-5,500** *S*

1961 Norman Nippy 49cc Moped, engine No. 909B/1886, Villiers inclined single cylinder, air-cooled, 2 stroke engine, sprung frame, chain drive, 23 x 2 tyres, original condition. **£550-600** *S*

Norton

1915 Norton 16 H 500cc Solo Record Holding Motorcycle, engine No. T. 1108, single cylinder side valve, air-cooled, 4 stroke engine, 490cc, single speed belt drive (missing belt), girder forks with coil spring front suspension, rigid frame at rear, 26 x 2½ x 2¼ tyres. **£5,750-6,500** *S*

c1921 New Imperial 2¾hp Solo Motorcycle, engine No. F/E 200943/D, JAP single vertical cylinder, air-cooled, side valve, 4 stroke engine, rating 2¾hp, 3 speed Albion gearbox, girder forks with coil spring front suspension, rigid frame at rear, chain-cum-belt drive, 26 x 2 tyres. **£1,450-1,600** *S*

1924 Norton Type 16H 490cc Solo Motorcycle, single vertical cylinder, side valve, air-cooled, 2 speed gearbox, girder fork front suspension, rigid rear, chain primary drive, belt final drive. **£4,000-4,500** *S*

A **Norton Overhead Valve Motorcycle,** possibly an ES2, in extremely distressed condition.
£400-450 *S*

1933 Norton International 490cc Solo Motorcycle, engine No. 49253, frame No. 55177, single vertical cylinder, air-cooled, overhead valve, bore 79mm, stroke 100mm, 3 speed gearbox, girder fork front suspension, rigid rear, wheelbase 54.75in, 3.25 x 26in tyres.
Est. **£5,000-7,000** *S*

Norton's Inter of the early 1930s found a steady following amongst British bike enthusiasts, and the model became one of the Company's most successful. The model saw active use in competition and is today considered by many to be the best of the pre-war Norton machines.

1935 Norton International 350cc Solo Racing Motorcycle, engine No. 6729, frame No. 106635, vertical cylinder, air-cooled, single overhead cam, 4 stroke, bore 71mm, stroke 88mm, 348cc, 4 speed foot operated gearbox, chain primary and final drives, rigid rear end, girder front forks.
£4,100-4,600 *S*

c1930 Norton CS1 490cc Solo Motorcycle, engine No. CS 39986, frame No. 40582, single vertical cylinder, overhead camshaft, air-cooled, 4 stroke engine, 3 speed Sturmey Archer gearbox, Webb girder forks with coil spring front suspension, rigid frame at rear, chain final drive, 3.25 x 19 front, 3.50 x 19 rear tyres.
£3,750-4,500 *S*

1931 Norton CS1 490cc Solo Motorcycle, engine No. CS 67157, single vertical cylinder, overhead camshaft, air-cooled, 4 stroke engine, 3 speed gearbox, girder forks with coil spring front suspension, rigid frame at rear, chain final drive, 3.50 x 19 front, 3.25 x 19 rear tyres.
£1,700-1,800 *S*

James Lansdowne Norton established the Norton company in 1901. The earliest machines used improved engines, including Moto-Reve and Peugeot, and early successes at the Isle of Man TT races were on these machines. A variety of overhead valve and side valve machines were built during the post WWI years.

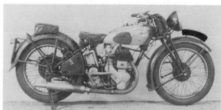

1937 Norton 16H 490cc Solo Motorcycle, engine No. 82134, single vertical cylinder, air-cooled, side valve, 4 stroke engine, 4 speed foot change gearbox, girder forks with coil spring front suspension, rigid frame at rear, chain final drive, 3.25 x 19in front, 3.50 x 19in rear tyres.
£2,350-2,600 *S*

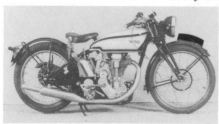

1935 Norton International Model 40 348cc Solo Motorcycle, engine No. 4027, single vertical cylinder, overhead camshaft, air-cooled, 4 stroke, bore 71mm, stroke 88mm, 4 speed gearbox, girder forks with coil spring front suspension and Andre dampers, rigid frame at rear, chain final drive, 3.00 x 21 front, 3.25 x 30 rear tyres.
£4,800-5,000 *S*

1934 Norton CSI 490cc Solo Motorcycle, single cylinder bronze head, overhead camshaft, air-cooled, 4 stroke engine, 4 speed Sturmey Archer gearbox, girder forks with coil spring front suspension, rigid frame at rear, chain final drive, 3.00 x 21in front, 410 H 19in rear tyres.
£3,750-4,250   *S*

1948 Norton ES2 490cc Solo Motorcycle, engine No. 18066, frame No. 18649, single vertical, air-cooled, overhead valve, 4 stroke, bore 79mm, stroke 100mm, 4 speed posi-stop gearbox, chain final drive and primary drives, Norton Roadholder telescopic front forks, plunger rear suspension.   **£2,100-2,300**   *S*

c1948 Norton International Model 30 490cc Solo Motorcycle, engine No. C11 1605, frame No. 10.439.13776, single vertical cylinder, overhead camshaft, air-cooled, 4 stroke, bore 79mm, stroke 100mm, 4 speed positive stop gearbox, chain primary and final drives, telescopic front forks, plunger rear suspension.   **Est. £6,000-7,000**   *S*

1949 Norton 500T Solo Trials Motorcycle, engine/frame No. D3T 21333, single cylinder, vertical engine, overhead valve, air-cooled, bore 79mm, stroke 100mm, 490cc, 3 speed gearbox, chain final drive, telescopic front forks, rigid rear suspension, 21in front, 19in rear tyres, original condition.
£2,900-3,200   *S*

1946 Norton Model 16H 500cc Solo Motorcycle, frame/engine No. A 26295, single vertical cylinder engine, air-cooled, side valve, 4 stroke, bore 79mm, stroke 100mm, 4 speed foot change gearbox, chain final drive, girder fork and coil spring front suspension, rigid rear, 3.25 x 19in tyres, original specification.
£1,800-2,000   *S*

1950 Norton International 500cc Solo Motorcycle, engine/frame No. E1129034, vertical, air-cooled, overhead cam, 4 stroke, single cylinder, bore 79mm, stroke 100mm, 490cc, 4 speed posi-stop gearbox, chain primary and final drives, telescopic front forks, plunger rear suspension.
£4,700-5,000   *S*

c1949 Norton 500cc Racing Special, engine No. CS 54023, frame No. D4 22975, single vertical cylinder engine, air-cooled, overhead camshaft, overhead valve, bore 79mm, stroke 100mm, 490cc, 4 speed foot change gearbox, chain final drive, Norton Roadholder front forks, plunger rear suspension, 3.50 x 19in front, 3.25 x 19in rear tyres.   **£5,000-5,500**   *S*

1951 Norton 500T 490cc Trials Solo Motorcycle, engine No. 47203 3T, single vertical cylinder, air-cooled, overhead valve, 4 stroke engine, 4 speed gearbox, telescopic forks with sprung frame at rear, chain final drive, 2.75 x 21in front, 4.00 x 19in Trials rear tyres.
£3,500-3,750 *S*

Norton's 500T was current from 1949 until 1954, and cost £182.4s.11d.

1953 Norton ES2 500cc Solo Motorcycle, engine/frame No. H448707, vertical, air-cooled, overhead valve, single cylinder, 4 stroke, bore 79mm, stroke 100mm, 490cc, 4 speed foot operated gearbox, chain primary and final drives, pivoted fork rear suspension, telescopic front forks.
£2,700-2,800 *S*

1954 Norton Manx 350cc Solo Racing Motorcycle, engine No. IOM 77283, single vertical cylinder, double overhead camshaft, air-cooled, 4 stroke, 4 speed foot change gearbox, Norton roadholder forks, sprung frame at rear, chain final drive, 3.00 x 19in racing front, 3.50 x 19in racing rear tyres. **£11,250-11,750** *S*

1952 Norton International Model 30 500cc Solo Motorcycle, engine No. 45607, frame No. 44820, single vertical cylinder engine, air-cooled, overhead camshaft, bore 79mm, stroke 100mm, 490cc, 4 speed gearbox, chain final drive, telescopic front forks, plunger rear suspension.
Est. **£7,500-8,000** *S*

c1955 Norton 350cc Model 40M Manx Solo Racing Motorcycle, vertical, air-cooled, double overhead cam, single cylinder, 4 stroke, bore 76mm, stroke 76.85mm, 349cc, 4 speed gearbox, chain final and primary drives, telescopic front forks, swinging arm rear suspension.
£4,750-5,000 *S*

c1955 Norton Model 40M 350cc Solo Racing Motorcycle, vertical, air-cooled, double overhead cam, single cylinder, 4 stroke, bore 76mm, stroke 76.85mm, 349cc, 4 speed gearbox, chain primary and final drives, pivoted fork rear suspension, telescopic front forks. **£8,000-8,500** *S*

1953 Norton Dominator Model 7 500cc Solo Motorcycle, engine/frame No. J 12 53686, vertical parallel twin cylinder engine, air-cooled, overhead valve, bore 66mm, stroke 72.6mm, 497cc, 4 speed posi-stop gearbox, chain final drive, telescopic front forks, swinging arm rear suspension, 3.25 x 19in front, 3.50 x 19in rear tyres.
£4,100-4,400 *S*

With the introduction of the Rex McCandlers designed 'Featherbed' frame, the already successful Norton Manx became one of the hardest machines to beat in both the 350cc and 500cc classes.

384

1962 Norton Model R14 99 Deluxe 650cc Solo Motorcycle, engine/frame No. 89478, vertical twin cylinder engine, air-cooled, overhead valve, 4 stroke, bore 68mm, stroke 89mm, 646cc, 4 speed foot change gearbox, chain final drive, telescopic front forks, swinging arm rear suspension. Est. **£2,000-2,250** *S*

1976 Norton Commando Mk III 745cc Solo Motorcycle, engine No. 330203, vertical twin cylinder overhead valve, air-cooled, 4 stroke engine, 4 speed foot change gearbox, telescopic forks with sprung frame at rear, chain final drive, 410 H 19in front and rear tyres, in good original condition. **£2,600-2,800** *S*

1973 John Player Norton 750cc Solo Motorcycle, engine/frame No. 210232, inclined, air-cooled, overhead valve, twin cylinder, 4 stroke, bore 73mm, stroke 89mm, 745cc, 4 speed foot operated gearbox, chain final drive, telescopic front forks, pivoted fork rear suspension. **£2,000-2,200** *S*

NSU

1973 Norton Commando 750cc Solo Motorcycle, engine/frame No. 303265, inclined twin cylinder, air-cooled, overhead valve, 4 stroke, bore 73mm, stroke 89mm, 745cc, 4 speed positive stop gearbox, chain final drive, telescopic front forks, pivoted for rear suspension, full restoration. **£2,700-2,900** *S*

1955 NSU 250cc Solo Motorcycle, frame No. 1295631, inclined single cylinder, air-cooled engine, 4 speed gearbox, chain final drive, NSU front suspension. **£500-575** *S*

NUT

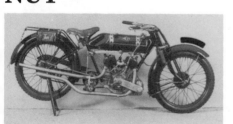

1923 NUT 700cc Motorcycle, engine No. 0524, frame No. E.904, V-twin, side valve, air-cooled, 4 stroke engine, Sturmey Archer 3 speed countershaft gearbox with hand change, girder forks with coil spring suspension, rigid frame at rear, all chain drive, 26 x 3in front and rear tyres. **£4,600-5,000** *S*

OK Supreme

1935 OK Supreme 248cc Solo Motorcycle, engine No. 67HS178, frame No. 23087, single vertical, air-cooled, overhead cam, 4 stroke, bore 66mm, stroke 72.5mm, 4 speed positive stop foot operated gearbox, Webb girder forks, rigid rear end. **£2,875-3,000** *S*

Panther

1939 Panther Model 100 600cc Solo Motorcycle, engine No. M 9090, frame No. 14084, inclined single cylinder engine, air-cooled, overhead valve, 4 stroke, 598cc, 4 speed foot change gearbox, chain final drive, girder fork and coil spring front suspension, rigid rear.
£2,350-2,550 *S*

Phelon & Moore

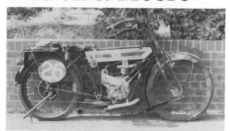

1912 Phelon & Moore 465cc Solo Motorcycle, engine No. S1422, single, air-cooled, vertical side valve, 4 stroke engine, bore 82mm, stroke 88mm, 464cc, 2 speed transmission with chain drive, some restoration.
£3,250-3,500 *S*

Joah Phelon and Richard Moore produced the first machine to bear their name in 1901 in Cleckheaton, and from the outset the P & M (and later Panther) trade mark, the inclined, 4 stroke single being used as a stressed frame member was apparent. By 1906 P & M were also equipping their machines with a 2 speed variable gearbox, employing an expanding clutch and 2 primary drive chains with different gear ratios.

1922 Phelon & Moore 499cc 3½hp Solo Motorcycle, engine No. 021202, inclined single cylinder, side valve, air-cooled, 4 stroke engine, 2 speed expanding pulley gear with hand control, girder forks with coil spring front suspension, rigid frame at rear, enclosed chain final drive, 26 x 2½in tyres, old restoration.
£2,700-3,000 *S*

Peugeot

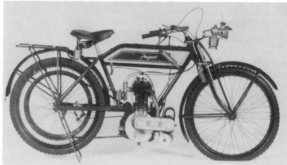

c1914 Peugeot 3½hp Solo Motorcycle, engine No. 20383, frame No. 7047, single vertical cylinder engine, air-cooled, side valve, maker's horsepower 3½hp, single speed, belt final drive, girder fork and coil spring front suspension, rigid rear, 26 x 2½in tyres, old restoration.
£3,600-3,850 *S*

Quadrant

Quadrant was one of the earliest British motorcycle companies, under the direction of L. Lloyd, also of L.M.C., from 1901-27.

1924 Quadrant 3½hp Solo Motorcycle, engine/frame No. 5290, single vertical cylinder, air-cooled, side valve, 4 stroke engine, 490cc, Burman 3 speed gearbox with hand change, girder forks with coil spring front suspension, rigid frame at rear, chain final drive, 26 x 2½in tyres.
£3,000-3,250 *S*

Quasar

1981 Quasar Series RMA 850cc Solo Motorcycle, engine No. 1C/85/63053, frame No. 1-11-81, 4 cylinder in line, water-cooled engine, overhead valve, 848cc, 4 speed gearbox, shaft final drive, wheelbase 78in, 4.25 x 18in tyres.
Est. **£5,000-7,000** *S*

Raleigh

1922 Raleigh 350cc Solo Motorcycle, engine No. 7006, single vertical cylinder, air-cooled, side valve, 4 stroke engine, Sturmey Archer 2 speed gearbox, girder forks with coil spring front suspension, rigid frame at rear, chain-cum-belt drive, 26 x 2½in front, 27 x 2.75in rear tyres.
£1,800-2,000   *S*

Made in Nottingham by the famous cycle makers, Raleigh motorcycles were made from 1899 until 1906 and from 1919 until the early 30s. The company also controlled the Sturmey Archer gearbox and engine company.

c1926 Raleigh 2¾hp Solo Motorcycle, frame No. 6525, single vertical cylinder engine, air-cooled, side valve, 4 stroke, bore 71mm, stroke 88mm, 348cc, 3 speed hand change gearbox, chain final drive, girder fork and coil spring front suspension, rigid rear, 26 x 2½in tyres, museum displayed.
£1,600-1,750   *S*

Revere

1919 Revere 2½hp Solo Motorcycle, engine No. C 529, frame No. 3988, Villiers single vertical cylinder, air-cooled, 2 stroke engine, 269cc, 2 speed countershaft gearbox with hand change, girder forks with twin coil spring front suspension, rigid frame at rear, chain-cum-belt final drive, 26 x 2¼in tyres.
£1,750-1,800   *S*

Revere machines were built by W. H. Whitehouse & Co. Ltd., of Friars Road, Coventry from 1915 until 1922, and survivors are now very rare.

Rollifix

c1950 Rollifix (Göricke) 97cc Trade Tricycle, engine No. 3193062, frame No. PS 49, Fichtel & Sachs single cylinder, air-cooled, 2 stroke engine, with in-unit gearbox and chain final drive.
£2,250-2,500   *S*

Miller's is a price GUIDE not a price LIST

Rotrax

c1950 Rotrax JAP 500cc Speedway Motorcycle, single cylinder, air-cooled, vertical overhead valve, 4 stroke.
£2,300-2,500   *S*

During the post-war years, speedway machines relied heavily on JAP engines, with a number of manufacturers fitting them to frames of their own manufacture.

Rex

1905 Rex 3¼hp Solo Motorcycle, engine No. 9, single vertical cylinder, air-cooled, side valve, 4 stroke engine, single speed belt drive, battery and coil ignition, rigid frame front and rear, 26 x 2¼in Avon Stonehenge front, 26 x 2½ x 2¼in Clincher original rear tyres.
£3,750-4,000   *S*

Rover

1916 Rover Imperial 3½hp Motorcycle Combination, engine No. 6708, frame No. 42771, single vertical cylinder, air-cooled, side valve, 4 stroke engine, 3 speed countershaft gearbox, girder forks with coil spring front suspension, rigid frame at rear, chain-cum-belt final drive, 26 x 3in tyres.
Est. **£4,000-6,000** *S*

Rover motorcycles were made by the same company which produced Rover cars from 1902.

1921 Rover TT 500cc Solo Motorcycle, single cylinder, air-cooled, side valve, 4 stroke engine, single speed belt drive, girder forks with coil spring suspension, rigid frame at rear, 26 x 3in tyres.
£2,800-2,900 *S*

Royal Enfield

c1921 Royal Enfield 223cc Solo Motorcycle, single vertical cylinder, air-cooled, 2 stroke, chain final drive, girder fork front suspension, rigid rear.
£575-600 *S*

Royal Enfield built a range of three-wheeled machines from 1898, using De Dion engines, progressing afterwards to two-wheeled motorcycles with Minerva engines, and then, after WWI, motorcycles of their own make with their own single cylinder and V-twin motors. Later JAP engines were also fitted. The company earned a wide reputation for high quality products of traditional design, and the factories survived in production until 1971.

1924 Royal Enfield Model 201 225cc Solo Motorcycle, single vertical cylinder, air-cooled, 2 stroke, bore 64mm, stroke 70mm, 2 speed foot operated gearbox, chain final drive, rigid rear end, girder front forks. **£1,600-1,800** *S*

1924 Royal Enfield 8hp Solo Motorcycle, V-twin side valve, air-cooled, 4 stroke engine, 986cc, 2 speed gearbox with hand change, girder forks with coil spring front suspension, rigid frame at rear, chain final drive, 26 x 3in front, 710 x 90 rear tyres. **£3,400-3,800** *S*

1923 Royal Enfield 976cc Solo Motorcycle, engine No. 1856/2675 W, Wolseley V-twin, air-cooled, side valve, 4 stroke engine, Enfield 2 speed expanding gear with coffee grinder control, girder forks with coil spring front suspension, rigid frame at rear, chain final drive, 26 x 3in tyres. **£3,600-3,800** *S*

1946 Royal Enfield Flying Flea Rickshaw, engine/frame No. 14265, inclined, single cylinder, air-cooled, 2 stroke, bore 54mm, stroke 55mm, 126cc, chain final drive, 3 speed hand change gearbox, blade type girder forks, sprung rear suspension. **£2,300-2,500** *S*

1939 Royal Enfield 250cc Solo Motorcycle, engine No. D 317, frame No. 1113, single vertical cylinder engine, air-cooled, 4 stroke, side valve, 4 speed hand change gearbox, chain final drive, girder fork and coil spring front suspension, rigid rear.
£500-550 *S*

1960 Royal Enfield Constellation 700cc Solo Motorcycle, engine No. SB 10385, frame No. 9682, vertical twin cylinder engine, air-cooled, overhead valve, 4 stroke, bore 70mm, stroke 90mm, 693cc, 4 speed gearbox, chain final drive, telescopic front forks, swinging arm rear suspension, 3.50 x 19in rear, 3.25 x 19in front tyres.
£2,900-3,100 *S*

Royal Enfield Series/Interceptor 738cc Solo Motorcycle, engine No. 15051, frame No. 11189, vertical twin cylinder, air-cooled, overhead valve, bore 71mm, stroke 93mm, 4 speed, foot operated gearbox, chain final drive, dual 6in drum brakes at front, 7in single at rear, swinging arm rear, telescopic front forks.
Est. **£4,000-4,500** *S*

Developed from Royal Enfield's 700cc Constellation, the Interceptor, introduced in 1962, further refined what many considered to be the ultimate twin.

1967 Royal Enfield 350cc Continental GT Solo Motorcycle, engine No. GT18439, frame No. 73074, single vertical cylinder, air-cooled, overhead valve, 4 stroke, bore 70mm, stroke 90mm, 346cc, 4 speed, foot operated gearbox, chain final drive, telescopic front forks, pivoted fork rear suspension. **£2,000-2,400** *S*

1965 Royal Enfield 250cc Continental GT Solo Motorcycle, engine No. 15691, single vertical cylinder, overhead valve, air-cooled, 4 stroke engine, 4 speed posi-stop gearbox, telescopic forks with sprung frame at rear, chain final drive.
£1,800-1,900 *S*

1976 Indian Enfield 350cc Solo Motorcycle, engine No. 147259, frame No. 8/147259/SKX, single vertical cylinder, air-cooled, overhead valve, 4 stroke, bore 70mm, stroke 90mm, 346cc, 4 speed foot operated gearbox, telescopic front forks, pivoted fork rear suspension. **£275-300** *S*

c1966 Royal Enfield Cafe Racer 250cc Solo Motorcycle, single vertical cylinder, air-cooled, 4 stroke, overhead valve, bore 70mm, stroke 64.5mm, 248cc, foot operated posi-stop gearbox, telescopic front forks, pivoted fork rear suspension.
Est. **£1,000-1,800** *S*

Rudge-Whitworth

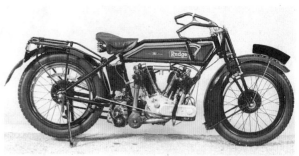

1922 Rudge Multi 3½hp Solo Motorcycle, single vertical cylinder, overhead inlet, side exhaust valve, air-cooled, 4 stroke engine, variable pulley gearing, girder forks with coil spring front suspension, rigid frame at rear, belt final drive with chain driven pedal starting, 26 x 3in tyres.
£4,000-4,250   *S*

1920s Rudge 998cc 7/9hp Solo Motorcycle, engine No. 26637, V-twin, overhead inlet, side exhaust valve, air-cooled, 4 stroke engine, 4 speed countershaft gearbox, girder forks with coil spring front suspension, rigid frame at rear, chain final drive, 26 x 3in tyres.   **£4,250-4,500**   *S*

1927 Rudge - Whitworth 500cc Solo Motorcycle, engine No. 43209, frame No. 22541, single vertical cylinder, air-cooled, side valve, 498cc, 4 speed gearbox with hand change, girder fork front suspension, rigid rear, chain final drive, wheelbase 60in, 3.25 x 19in tyres.
Est. **£3,800-4,000**   *S*

Rudge was established in the 19thC as bicycle manufacturers, and progressed to motorcycle production before the Great War. A 499cc inlet-over-exhaust valve single cylinder machine was available together with a 998cc V-twin. Rudge constructed a famous multi-gearing system at this time which allowed up to 21 gear positions. Chain drive machines appeared in 1920, and the models were constantly upgraded and improved until the end of production in 1940.

1934 Rudge Radial 250 Sports Motorcycle, engine No. 87, frame No. 52530, single vertical cylinder, air-cooled, overhead valve, 4 valve, 4 stroke, 4 speed gearbox, girder forks with coil spring front suspension, rigid frame at rear, rebuilt.
£2,000-2,250   *S*

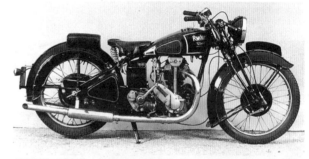

1936 Rudge Ulster GP 499cc Solo Motorcycle, engine No. U.1412, single cylinder, bronze head, overhead valve, twin-port, air-cooled, 4 stroke engine, 4 speed foot change gearbox, girder forks with coil spring front suspension, rigid frame at rear, chain final drive, 2.75 x 21in front, 3.00 x 20in rear tyres.
£3,600-3,800   *S*

1929 Rudge-Whitworth 350cc Roadster Solo Motorcycle, engine No. 55511, frame No. 36029, single vertical cylinder, air-cooled, overhead valve, 4 stroke, bore 70mm, stroke 88mm, 5 speed hand change gearbox, chain final drive, rigid rear end, girder front forks, drum brakes front and rear.
Est. **£3,000-3,500**   *S*

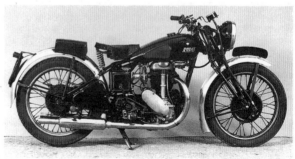

1937 Rudge 495cc Solo Motorcycle, engine No. 3748, frame No. 59001, single vertical cylinder, twin-port overhead valve, air-cooled, 4 stroke, 4 speed gearbox with foot change, girder forks with coil spring front suspension, rigid frame at rear, chain final drive, 3.25 x 19in tyres.
£2,500-2,750   *S*

Scott

1922 Scott Squirrel Two-Speed Solo Motorcycle, engine No. 4898, frame No. 1601, inclined twin cylinder engine, water-cooled, 2 stroke, bore 70mm, stroke 63.5mm, 487cc, 2 speed gearbox, chain final drive, girder fork and coil spring front suspension, rigid rear. Est. £3,500-4,500   *S*

This machine has been converted to coil ignition but the original mag/dyno unit is available.

1928 Scott 500cc Motorcycle, with contemporary aluminium bodied sidecar. £2,500-2,600   *LAR*

1925 Scott Two-Speed 498cc Solo Motorcycle, engine No. Z.7987, frame No. 934, inclined siamesed, water-cooled, twin cylinder, 2 stroke, 2 speed gearbox, open frame with girder forks and coil spring front suspension, rigid frame at rear, chain final drive, 3.00 x 26in tyres. £3,750-4,000   *S*

Scott introduced the Super Squirrel, available in either 498cc or 596cc forms with either a 2 or 3 speed gearbox, in 1924 and it was to remain in production until 1931.

1930 Scott Super Squirrel 500cc Solo Motorcycle, engine No. 2794A, inclined siamesed, twin cylinder, water-cooled, 2 stroke, 498cc, bore 68.25mm, stroke 68.25mm, 2 speed gearbox, rigid rear end, girder front forks. £3,450-3,650   *S*

1923/1928 Scott Spring 'Special' 620cc Solo Motorcycle, engine No. RZ1207, inclined twin cylinder, water-cooled, 2 stroke, 3 speed gearbox, chain final drive, girder forks, rigid rear ends.   £5,000-5,250   *S*

1930s Scott Flying Squirrel 498cc Solo Motorcycle, engine No. FY 1845 A, inclined siamesed, water-cooled, twin cylinder, 2 stroke, 3 speed foot change gearbox, girder forks with coil spring front suspension, rigid frame at rear, chain final drive, 3.00 x 20in front, 3.50 x 19in rear tyres. £3,250-3,500   *S*

Use the Index!

Because certain items might fit easily into any of a number of categories, the quickest and surest method of locating any entry is by reference to the index at the back of the book.

This has been fully cross-referenced for absolute simplicity

1926 Scott Super Squirrel 500cc Solo Motorcycle, engine No. 9043, frame No. 1413, inclined twin cylinder, water-cooled, 2 stroke, 498cc, 2 speed gearbox, chain final drive, Scott front suspension, rigid rear, dismantled. £2,250-2,500   *S*

1939 Scott Clubman Special 600cc Solo Motorcycle, engine No. DPY 4720 CS, frame No. 4266 M, inclined twin cylinder, water-cooled, 2 stroke, 596cc, 3 speed gearbox, chain final drive, telescopic front forks, rigid rear suspension.
£2,150-2,350 *S*

1948 Scott Flying Squirrel 600cc Solo Motorcycle, engine No. DPY 5062, frame No. 4966, inclined twin cylinder, water-cooled, 2 stroke, 596cc, 3 speed gearbox, chain final drive, telescopic front forks, rigid rear suspension.
£1,500-1,600 *S*

Simplex

1939 Scott 600cc Clubman Special Solo Motorcycle, engine No. DPY 4811, frame No. 49M, twin cylinder, 2 stroke, water-cooled, bore 73mm, stroke 71.4mm, 596cc, detachable alloy head, Amal downdraught carburettor, magdyno, duplex triangulated frame, girder pattern central type front forks with twin adjustable shock absorbers, 3 speed gearbox, 27 x 3.25in tyres.
Est. £4,000-5,000 *S*

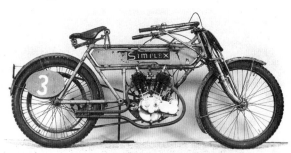

c1907 Simplex 560cc Solo Racing Motorcycle, engine/frame No.17054, Fafnir V-twin cylinder, side valve, air-cooled, 4 stroke girder forks with coil spring front suspension, rigid frame at rear, single speed belt final drive, 26 x 2½in tyres.
£5,250-5,500 *S*

Singer

1901 Singer Single Seat Powered Cycle, engine No. 181, frame No. 393, single vertical cylinder, air-cooled, 208cc, rigid rear end, cycle front forks, fair condition, largely complete, but the motor wheel is not currently installed in the frame.
£5,000-5,250 *S*

1913 Singer 499cc Solo Motorcycle, engine No. 3342, frame No. 3658.2, single vertical cylinder, air-cooled, side valve, 4 stroke, 2 speed gearbox, belt final drive.
£3,500-3,750 *S*

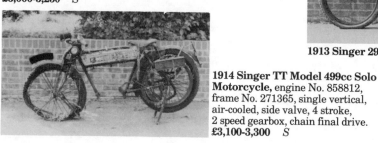

1913 Singer 299cc Solo Motorcycle, engine No. 103.28/R128, frame No. 274029, single vertical cylinder, air-cooled, side valve, 4 stroke, 2 speed gearbox.
£2,900-3,100 *S*

1914 Singer TT Model 499cc Solo Motorcycle, engine No. 858812, frame No. 271365, single vertical, air-cooled, side valve, 4 stroke, 2 speed gearbox, chain final drive.
£3,100-3,300 *S*

Socovel

1946 Socovel 2.6/1.2hp Solo Electric Motorcycle, engine No. 481684, frame No. 972, electric motor, chain final drive, rigid rear end, girder forks, drum front and rear brakes, 3.25 x 14in tyres.
£2,300-2,500 *S*

This machine would appear to have been produced in Belgium directly after WWII by Socovel, who are probably better known for their equally unorthodox lightweights with fully enclosed Villiers engine.

Solex

c1974 Solex S3800 Autocycle, with forward mounted, single cylinder, air-cooled, 2 stroke engine, driving by friction roller to the front wheel, pedal-assisted and complete with luggage carrier and 0-40mph speedometer.
£425-475 *S*

Sparkbrook-Villiers

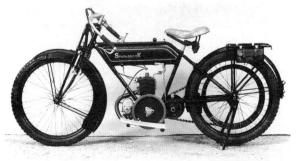

1920s Sparkbrook-Villiers 250cc Solo Racing Motorcycle, engine No. A.4724, frame No. 1562, Villiers single vertical cylinder, air-cooled, 2 stroke engine, 2 speed countershaft gearbox with hand change, chain-cum-belt final drive, girder forks with rigid frame at rear, 26 x 2½in tyres.
£1,400-1,600 *S*

Sunbeam

1924 Sunbeam 350cc 2¾hp Solo Motorcycle, engine No. 188/21232, frame No. P20250, single vertical cylinder, air-cooled, side valve, 4 stroke, bore 70mm, stroke 90mm, 347cc, 3 speed hand change gearbox, chain final drive, girder front forks, rigid rear end.
£3,000-3,300 *S*

1919 Sunbeam 3½hp Solo Motorcycle, engine No. 6286, frame No. 5282, single vertical cylinder, air-cooled, side valve, 499cc, 3 speed gearbox, chain final drive, girder fork and coil spring front suspension, rigid rear, 26 x 2½in tyres.   Est. **£3,700-4,200** *S*

1926 Sunbeam Model 5, 3½hp Solo Motorcycle, engine No. 112/5001 GS, frame No. S/09073, single vertical cylinder, air-cooled, side valve, 4 stroke engine, 499cc, 3 speed hand change gearbox, girder forks with coil spring front suspension, rigid frame at rear, chain final drive, 26 x 3in tyres.
£2,600-2,800 *S*

1931 Sunbeam Model 9, 493cc Solo Motorcycle, engine No. PP 1017, single vertical cylinder, overhead valve, air-cooled, 4 stroke, 3 speed gearbox, girder forks with rigid frame at rear, chain final drive, 3.50 x 19in tyres.
£2,750-3,000 *S*

1932 Sunbeam Model 9 500cc Solo Motorcycle, engine No. 9L51902680, frame No. BA12475, single vertical cylinder, air-cooled, overhead valve, 4 stroke, bore 80mm, stroke 98mm, 493cc, 3 speed hand change gearbox, chain final and primary drives, rigid rear end, girder front forks.
£2,600-2,800 *S*

> **Miller's is a price GUIDE not a price LIST**

c1950 Sunbeam S8 487cc Solo Motorcycle, engine No. S.8 8733, vertical in-line twin cylinder, overhead valve, air-cooled, 4 stroke engine, 4 speed gearbox, telescopic forks, sprung frame at rear, shaft final drive, 4.50 x 16in front, 5.00 x 16in rear tyres.
£1,500-1,700 *S*

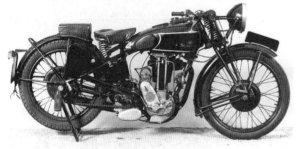

c1934 Sunbeam Model 95 L 493cc Solo Motorcycle, engine No. 95L 495.4.1431, single vertical cylinder, overhead valve, air-cooled, 4 stroke engine, 4 speed gearbox, girder forks with coil spring front suspension, rigid frame at rear, chain final drive, 3.00 x 21in front, 3.25 x 20in rear tyres, unrestored and requiring full renovation.
£2,600-2,800 *S*

1950 Sunbeam S8 500cc Solo Motorcycle, engine No. S82797, frame No. S81856, vertical, air-cooled, overhead cam, in-line twin cylinder, 4 stroke, bore 70mm, stroke 63.5mm, 489cc, 4 speed foot operated gearbox, shaft final drive, telescopic front forks, plunger rear suspension.
£2,400-2,500 *S*

Suzuki

1972 Suzuki T250J Solo Motorcycle, engine No. 58884, frame No. 59752, inclined, twin cylinder, air-cooled, 2 stroke, bore 54mm, stroke 54mm, 247cc, 6 speed foot operated gearbox, chain final drive, telescopic front forks, pivoted fork rear suspension.
£1,400-1,500 *S*

Introduced in 1969 the T250 twin was derived from the T20, but with changes to the gear ratios and primary drive ratio, the oil pump now sat on the top of the crankcase, shielded from road dirt by a cover. The later J model differed cosmetically, although not mechanically, from its predecessors.

1974 Suzuki GT380 Solo Motorcycle, engine No. 59983, frame No. 53754, 3 cylinder, air-cooled, 2 stroke, bore 54mm, stroke 54mm, 371cc, 6 speed foot controlled gearbox, chain final drive, telescopic front forks, swinging arm rear suspension.
£425-475 *S*

1976 Suzuki RE5 Solo Motorcycle, engine No. RE515662, frame No. RE516005, rotary Wankel engine, liquid-cooled, 497cc, 5 speed foot operated gearbox, telescopic front forks, pivoted fork rear suspension.
Est. **£1,500-1,800** *S*

1976 Suzuki GT500 Solo Motorcycle, engine No. 92890, frame No. 92754, 2 cylinder, air-cooled, 2 stroke, bore 70mm, stroke 64mm, 493cc, 5 speed foot operated gearbox, chain final drive, swinging arm rear suspension, telescopic front forks.
£525-575 *S*

The 1975/76 Suzuki TR 750 Works Racing Motorcycle, frame No. 6286, 3 cylinder in-line engine, water-cooled, bore 70mm, stroke 64mm, 738cc, developing 110bhp @ 7700rpm, 6 speed gearbox, multi-plate clutch, chain final drive, Kayaba front fork suspension, swinging arm rear suspension with Kayaba gas springs.
Est. **£30,000-35,000** *S*

The 1979 Suzuki RGB 500 Works Racing Motorcycle, ridden by Barry Sheene during the 1979 season, frame No. 1005, square 4 cylinder engine, water-cooled, 2 stroke, bore 54mm, stroke 54mm, 494cc, side loading 6 speed gearbox, multi-plate clutch, chain final drive, Kayaba fork front suspension, swinging arm rear with Kayaba Air shocker units.
£11,500-12,500 *S*

This was one of two works bikes prepared for Barry Sheene for the 1979 season – his last with Heron Suzuki GB – and with this machine he won both the Venezuelan and the French Grand Prix.

The machine enjoyed a number of other successes in European International races and, after it was taken out of commission, it was completely rebuilt in the works at Heron Suzuki and has remained in that state and is now running and ready to race.

Triton

Tritons are 'special' motorcycles, consisting of a Triumph engine and a Norton frame.

c1965 Triton Weslake Road Racer, vertical twin air-cooled cylinders, 8 overhead valve head, 4 stroke, 700cc, telescopic front forks, swinging arm rear suspension.
£1,500-1,600 *S*

c1969 Triton 650cc Solo Motorcycle, engine No. T120 D7460, frame No. 8050P, twin cylinder, vertical, air-cooled, 4 stroke, overhead valve, 4 speed foot operated gearbox, telescopic front forks, pivoted fork rear suspension.
Est. **£1,800-2,200** *S*

Triumph

1915 Triumph Junior 225cc Solo Motorcycle, engine No. 24662/13 2429213, frame No. 257144, single vertical cylinder, air-cooled, 2 stroke, bore 64mm, stroke 70mm, 2 speed gearbox, belt final drive, girder front forks, rigid rear suspension.
£1,375-1,450 *S*

1911/12 Triumph TT Model 499cc Solo Motorcycle, engine/frame No. 67702, single cylinder, side valve, air-cooled, 4 stroke, variable pulley gearing with belt drive, girder forks with coil spring front suspension, rigid frame at rear, 26 x 2½in tyres.
£4,000-4,200 *S*

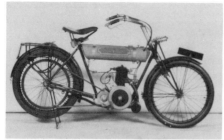

1915 Triumph Junior 2¼hp Solo Motorcycle, engine No. 1221, frame No. 257359, single vertical cylinder, air-cooled, 2 stroke, bore 64mm, stroke 70mm, 225cc, 2 speed gearbox, belt final drive, girder fork with coil spring front suspension, rigid rear, 600 x 55mm front, 24 x 2in rear tyres.
£1,600-1,750 *S*

The 2¼hp Triumph Junior was introduced in 1913 and continued in production until 1922.

1921 Baby Triumph 225cc Solo Motorcycle, engine No. M 98/6778/12, single vertical cylinder, air-cooled, 2 stroke, 2 speed countershaft gearbox, girder forks with coil spring front suspension, rigid frame at rear, chain-cum-belt drive with push starting, 24 x 2¼in tyres. **£2,150-2,350** *S*

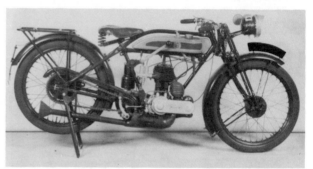

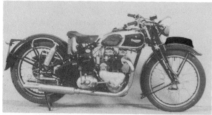

c1939 Triumph 5 T 500cc Solo Motorcycle, engine No. 9/5T 17673, vertical twin cylinder, air-cooled, overhead valve, 4 stroke, 4 speed posi-stop gearbox, girder forks with coil spring front suspension, rigid frame at rear, chain final drive, 3.00 x 20in front, 3.50 x 19in rear tyres.
£3,600-3,800 *S*

The Model P Triumph was in production from 1925 to 1927 and shared many of the characteristics of the SD and the H models. The Model P found favour as a dispatch rider's bike as well as an economical civilian machine.

1927 Triumph Model P 500cc Solo Motorcycle, engine No. 246727, frame No. 1004533, single vertical cylinder, air-cooled, side valve, bore 84mm, stroke 89mm, 494cc, 3 speed hand change gearbox, chain final drive, girder fork and coil spring front suspension, rigid rear, 27 x 2.75in tyres, older restoration.
£3,000-3,400 *S*

c1948 Triumph T100 498cc Solo Competition Motorcycle, engine No. 48.T.100 88844, vertical twin overhead valve, air-cooled, 4 stroke, 4 speed gearbox, telescopic front forks, rigid frame at rear, chain final drive, 300 H 20 Avon Speedmaster front, 3.50 H 19 57 H Avon GR rear tyres.
£6,000-6,250 *S*

c1940 Triumph 3HW 350cc Solo Motorcycle, engine No. 3HW 57640, frame No. TL7731, single vertical cylinder, air-cooled, overhead valve, 4 stroke, foot change gearbox, chain final drive, girder fork and coil spring front suspension, rigid rear, 19in tyres.
£400-450 *S*

The 3HW was built primarily for military use and although production ceased with the war, many 3HWs found their way into civilian hands and gave sterling service both on and off the road.

1950s Triumph 500cc Trials Special Solo Motorcycle, vertical twin cylinder, air-cooled, overhead valve, 4 stroke, bore 63mm, stroke 80mm, 499cc, 4 speed, posi-stop gearbox, chain primary and final drives, telescopic front forks, rigid rear end.
£1,400-1,600 *S*

1955 Triumph T110 650cc Solo Motorcycle, engine No. 71129, frame No. S.71129, vertical twin cylinder, air-cooled, 4 stroke, 4 speed posi-stop gearbox, telescopic front forks, swinging arm rear suspension, chain final drive.
£4,250-4,750 *S*

Triumph introduced the Tiger Cub in 1954, having developed it using the 149cc Terrier as its basis, and over the years gradually updated and revised the machine to improve its reliability.

1959 Triumph Tiger Cub T20 200cc Solo Motorcycle, engine No. T20 M3721, frame No. T92578, single inclined cylinder, air-cooled, overhead valve, 4 stroke, bore 63mm, stroke 64mm, 199cc, 4 speed positive stop gearbox, swinging arm rear suspension, telescopic front forks.
£625-675 *S*

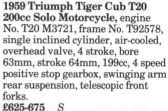

1956 Triumph 6T Thunderbird 650cc Solo Motorcycle, engine/frame No. 81965, vertical twin cylinder, air-cooled, overhead valve, 4 stroke, bore 71mm, stroke 82mm, 649cc, 4 speed gearbox, chain final and primary drives, telescopic front forks, swinging arm rear suspension.
£3,250-3,500 *S*

Locate the source

The source of each illustration in Miller's can be found by checking the code letters below each caption with the list of contributors

c1960 Triumph Tiger Cub 200cc Solo Motorcycle, single inclined cylinder, air-cooled, overhead valve, 4 stroke, bore 66mm, stroke 64mm, 199cc, 4 speed posi-stop gearbox, telescopic front forks, pivoted fork rear suspension.
£575-625 *S*

1959 Triumph Tiger T100 Solo Motorcycle, engine No. T10028439, frame No. 028439, vertical twin cylinder, air-cooled, overhead valve, 4 stroke, bore 63mm, stroke 80mm, 499cc, 4 speed positive stop gearbox, chain final drive, telescopic forks, swinging arm rear suspension.
£2,600-2,800 *S*

Introduced in 1939, the Tiger 100 was developed from Triumph's Speed Twin to offer greater performance for the sporting rider. The machines were developed to incorporate improvements like telescopic forks and sprung frames.

1961 Triumph Tiger Cub 200cc Trials Motorcycle, engine No. T20 67007, frame No. T20 71514, single inclined cylinder, air-cooled, overhead valve, 4 stroke, bore 63mm, stroke 64mm, 199.5cc, 4 speed gearbox, chain final drive, telescopic front forks, swinging arm rear suspension, 21in front, 18in rear tyres. **£675-725** *S*

1961 Triumph TRW 500cc Solo Motorcycle, engine No. 27796 NA, frame No. 26743 NA, vertical twin cylinder, air-cooled, side valve, 4 stroke, bore 63mm, stroke 80mm, 499cc, 4 speed foot change gearbox, chain final drive, telescopic front suspension, rigid rear.
£475-525 *S*

1961 Triumph 5TA Speed Twin 500cc Solo Motorcycle,
engine/frame No. H20884, vertical twin cylinder, air-cooled,
overhead valve, 4 stroke, bore 69mm, stroke 65.5mm, 490cc,
4 speed foot operated gearbox, primary drive by duplex chain,
final drive by chain, telescopic front forks, swinging arm
rear suspension, drum brakes front and rear.
Est. **£2,750-3,000**   *S*

**1969 Triumph T150 Trident
750cc Solo Motorcycle,**
engine/frame No. X001259T150T,
triple vertical cylinder, air-cooled,
overhead valve, 4 stroke, bore
67mm, stroke 70mm, 740cc, 4 speed
gearbox, chain final drive, telescopic
front forks, pivoted fork rear
suspension controlled by hydraulic
dampers.
£2,900-3,100   *S*

**1965 Triumph T20 Tiger Cub
Solo Motorcycle,** engine No.
T20 74823, frame No. 175582,
single inclined cylinder, air-cooled,
overhead valve, bore 63mm, stroke
64mm, 199.5cc, 4 speed gearbox,
chain final drive, telescopic front
forks, swinging arm rear
suspension, 17/18in tyres.
£800-850   *S*

Did you know

*MILLER'S Collectors Cars
Price Guide builds up year
by year to form the most
comprehensive photo-
reference system
available*

**1969 Triumph Trophy TR6C
650cc Solo Motorcycle,**
engine/frame No. TR6C PCO5060,
vertical twin cylinder, air-cooled,
overhead valve, 4 stroke, bore
71mm, stroke 82mm, 649cc, 4 speed
posi-stop gearbox, telescopic front
forks, pivoted fork rear suspension.
£3,650-3,850   *S*

**1965 Triumph 5TA 500cc Solo
Motorcycle,** engine No. H 39837,
vertical twin cylinder, air-cooled,
overhead valve, bore 69mm, stroke
65.5mm, 490cc, 4 speed foot change
gearbox, chain final drive, telescopic
front forks, swinging arm rear
suspension, 17in tyres.
£250-275   *S*

1974 Triumph X75 Hurricane 750cc Solo Motorcycle,
engine/frame No. TRX75 PH01146, inclined, air-cooled,
overhead valve, 4 stroke, triple cylinder, bore 67mm,
stroke 70mm, 740cc, 5 speed posi-stop gearbox,
chain final drive, telescopic front forks,
pivoted fork rear suspension.
£3,800-4,000   *S*

**1968 Triumph T 20 Tiger Cub
199cc Solo Motorcycle,** engine
No. 120 B 8053, single inclined
cylinder, overhead valve, air-cooled,
4 stroke, 4 speed gearbox, telescopic
forks, sprung frame at rear, chain
final drive, 3.00 x 18in tyres.
£675-750   *S*

1975 Triumph Slippery Sam 741cc Solo Motorcycle, engine No. T.160. CK02755, frame No. 160 CK02755, vertical triple cylinder, overhead valve, air-cooled, 4 stroke, triple carburettors, 4 speed gearbox, telescopic forks, sprung frame at rear, chain final drive. Est. £3,200-3,600 *S*

Racing versions of the Trident took their name 'Slippery Sam' from the original Ray Pickrell machine which won the production TT 5 times, commencing in 1970. The name derived from the 1970 Bol D'Or race, in which the machine drenched its riders in oil. The 'Sam' part of the name may derive from the fact that Percy Tait was known at Meriden as 'Sam the transport man' and this name eventually was adopted for his bike.

1975 Triumph Trident T160 750cc Solo Motorcycle, engine/frame No. T160GK04903, inclined 3 cylinder, air-cooled, overhead valve, 4 stroke, bore 67mm, stroke 70mm, 740cc, 5 speed positive stop gearbox, chain final drive, telescopic front forks, swinging arm rear suspension. £3,000-3,350 *S*

1977 Triumph Bonneville Silver Jubilee Limited Edition 744cc Solo Motorcycle, engine No. T 140 OV CP 81638, vertical twin cylinder, overhead valve, air-cooled, 4 stroke engine, 4 speed gearbox, telescopic forks, sprung frame at rear, chain final drive, 410 V19 and 410 VB 18 tyres. £3,000-3,500 *S*

Velocette

1981 Triumph 500cc Solo Motorcycle, engine No. TR5 1096 NA, vertical twin cylinder, overhead valve, air-cooled, 4 stroke, 4 speed gearbox, chain final drive, 3.00 x 20in and 4.00 x 19in tyres. £3,000-3,200 *S*

Tusroke

1925 Velocette Lady's Model EL 250cc Solo Motorcycle, engine No. 2415, frame No. 4141, single vertical, air-cooled, 2 stroke, bore 63mm, stroke 80mm, 2 speed gearbox, chain final drive. £2,000-2,200 *S*

Produced during the early 1920s the Lady's model Velocette featured open frames, special aluminium cowls over the cylinder to protect the rider's clothes, and leg shields. The resultant machine was built to the usual high Velocette standards.

1919 Tusroke 350cc 2¾hp Solo Motorcycle, engine/frame No. 19168, vertical single cylinder, air-cooled, 2 stroke, single speed direct drive by belt to V-rim on rear wheel, girder forks with coil spring front suspension, rigid frame at rear, 26 x 2in tyres. £2,300-2,400 *S*

Miller's is a price GUIDE not a price LIST

1937 Velocette KSS 350cc Solo Motorcycle, engine No. 8011, frame No. 3638, single vertical cylinder, air-cooled, overhead camshaft, 4 stroke engine, 4 speed gearbox, girder forks, with coil spring front suspension, rigid frame at rear, chain final drive.
£2,350-2,600 *S*

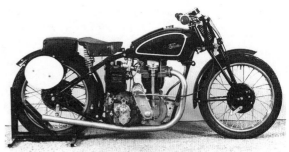

Velocette KSS Mk I 348cc Solo Racing Motorcycle, engine No. KSS 10094, single vertical cylinder, air-cooled, overhead camshaft, 4 stroke, 3 speed gearbox, girder forks with coil spring front suspension, rigid frame at rear, chain final drive, 27 x 3in tyres.
£4,500-4,750 *S*

1932 Velocette KTT Mk IV 348cc Solo Racing Motorcycle, engine No. KTT 412, single vertical cylinder, overhead camshaft, bronze head, air-cooled, 4 stroke engine, 4 speed gearbox with foot change, girder forks with coil spring suspension and Andre dampers, rigid frame at rear, chain final drive, 3.00 x 21in Speedmaster front, 400 H 19in Roadmaster rear tyres.
£8,400-8,500 *S*

c1940 Velocette MDD-WD 350cc Solo Motorcycle, engine No. MDD 11053, frame No. MDD 11872, vertical single cylinder engine, air-cooled, overhead valve, 4 stroke, **bore 68mm,** stroke 96mm, 349cc, 4 speed foot change gearbox, chain final drive, girder fork and coil spring front suspension, rigid rear, 19in tyres.
£1,800-1,900 *S*

1936 Velocette MOV 250cc Solo Motorcycle, engine No. 1819, frame No. 3683, single vertical cylinder, air-cooled, overhead valve, 4 stroke engine, 4 speed gearbox, girder forks with coil spring suspension, rigid frame at rear, chain final drive.
£1,000-1,250 *S*

This is a rare model, in original condition, but not complete.

1938 Velocette KTT Mk VII 348cc Solo Racing Motorcycle, engine No. KTT 707, single vertical cylinder, overhead camshaft, air-cooled, 4 stroke engine, 4 speed gearbox with foot change, girder forks with coil spring front suspension and Andre damper, rigid frame at rear, chain final drive, 3.00 x 21in and 3.50 x 19in tyres.
£17,000-18,000 *S*

1939 Velocette GTP 250cc Solo Motorcycle, engine No. GB7314, frame No. GB7390T, vertical single cylinder, twin port, 2 stroke, bore 63mm, stroke 80mm, 249cc, 4 speed positive stop gearbox, chain final and primary drives, girder forks, rigid rear end.
£2,000-2,100 *S*

1947 Velocette MAC 350cc Solo Motorcycle, engine No. 11349, frame No. 4527, single vertical cylinder, overhead valve, air-cooled, 4 stroke engine, 4 speed gearbox, Dowty forks with rigid frame at rear, chain final drive.
£900-1,000 *S*

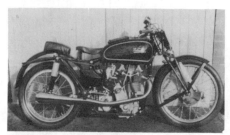

1949 Velocette Model KTT Mk VIII 350cc Solo Racing Motorcycle, engine No. 1001, frame No. 174, vertical single cylinder engine, air-cooled, overhead valve, overhead camshaft, 4 stroke, 4 speed gearbox, chain final drive, girder fork and coil spring front suspension with adjustable dampers, swinging arm rear suspension.
Est. £17,000-20,000 *S*

1949 Velocette KTT Mk VIII 348cc Solo Racing Motorcycle, engine No. KTT 1028F, frame No. SF83, vertical single cylinder, air-cooled, single overhead cam, 4 stroke, bore 74mm, stroke 81mm, 4 speed foot operated gearbox, chain primary and final drives, girder front forks, pivoted fork rear suspension.
£11,250-11,500 *S*

1950s Velocette KSS 349cc Solo Motorcycle, engine No. 9215, frame No. 6229, single vertical cylinder, overhead camshaft, air-cooled, 4 stroke engine, 4 speed gearbox, telescopic forks, sprung frame, chain final drive, 3.25 x 19in and 3.50 x 19in tyres.
£4,000-4,500 *S*

1950 Velocette KTT 350cc Solo Motorcycle, engine No. 1078, frame No. 241, single vertical cylinder, overhead camshaft, air-cooled, 4 stroke engine, 4 speed gearbox, Dowty forks and sprung rear suspension, chain final drive, with some racing history.
£16,000-17,000 *S*

1953 Velocette MAC 350cc Solo Motorcycle, engine No. 20840, frame No. 1945, single vertical cylinder, overhead valve, air-cooled, 4 stroke engine, 4 speed gearbox, telescopic forks, Spring rear suspension, chain final drive.
£2,000-2,100 *S*

1954 Velocette MSS 500cc Solo Motorcycle, engine No. 10592, frame No. 3297, single vertical cylinder, air-cooled, overhead valve, 4 stroke engine, telescopic forks, Springer rear suspension, chain final drive.
£1,800-2,000 *S*

1960 Velocette LE 200cc Solo Motorcycle, horizontally opposed flat twin cylinder, water-cooled, side valve, 4 stroke engine, bore 50mm, stroke 49mm, 192cc, 4 speed gearbox, telescopic front forks, swinging arm rear suspension, shaft final drive, 3.00 x 18in and 3.25 x 18in tyres, in original condition, requiring restoration.
£500-550   *S*

The Velocette LE (Little Engine), known as 'The Policeman's Friend' because of its adoption by many police forces, was announced in October 1948. It featured a hand operated starter, all enclosed mechanics, and a remarkably quiet engine. It remained in production until 1971.

1966 Velocette Thruxton 500cc Solo Motorcycle, engine No. VMT431, frame No. RS18931, vertical single cylinder, air-cooled, overhead valve, 4 stroke, bore 86mm, stroke 86mm, 499cc, 4 speed posi-stop gearbox, chain final drive, telescopic front forks, pivoted rear fork suspension.
£5,500-6,000   *S*

Verus-Blackburne

1921 Verus-Blackburne 2¾hp Solo Motorcycle, engine No. L.1061, Blackburne single cylinder, air-cooled, side valve, 4 stroke engine, 2 speed hand change countershaft gearbox, chain-cum-belt drive, girder forks with rigid frame at rear, 26 x 2½in tyres.
£1,850-2,000   *S*

c1965 Velocette MSS 499cc Scrambler Solo Motorcycle, engine No. MSS 12599, single cylinder, air-cooled, overhead valve, 4 stroke engine, 4 speed gearbox, telescopic forks, sprung frame at rear, chain final drive, 3.00 x 21in and 4.00 x 19in tyres.
£2,900-3,250   *S*

1971/1973 Velocette Venom Clubman Special 500cc Solo Motorcycle, engine No. VM5836, frame No. MH1, single vertical cylinder, air-cooled, 4 stroke, overhead valve engine, bore 86mm, stroke 86mm, 499cc, 4 speed gearbox, telescopic forks, pivoted fork rear suspension.
£3,300-3,700   *S*

Vincent

1930s Vincent HRD 500cc Solo Motorcycle, engine No. BD 601/C 977, frame No. 11738, single vertical cylinder, air-cooled, overhead valve, with hairpin valve spring, 4 stroke engine, 4 speed gearbox, girder forks with sprung frame at rear, chain final drive, 3.00 x 20in and 3.50 x 19in tyres.
£4,500-5,000   *S*

Founded by the famous racing rider H. R. Davis in Wolverhampton in 1924, the HRD company was taken over by Philip Vincent in 1928 and production moved to Stevenage.
Thereafter until 1950 the machines were known as the Vincent HRD, and this is a rare pre-war example of the 500cc single.

Miller's is a price GUIDE not a price LIST

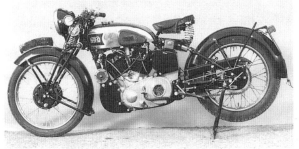

c1937 Vincent HRD Series A Rapide 998cc Solo Motorcycle, engine No. V.1046, frame No. DV 1614, V-twin, overhead valve, air-cooled, 4 stroke engine, 4 speed gearbox, girder forks with sprung frame at rear, chain final drive.
£10,000-11,000 *S*

1938 HRD Vincent 500cc Series 'A' Comet, engine No. C838, frame No. D1492, single cylinder, inclined overhead valve, air-cooled, 4 stroke engine, bore 84mm, stroke 90mm, 497cc, Burman 4 speed gearbox, Ferodo multi-plate clutch, girder forks, sprung frame, chain final drive, 26 x 3.00in tyres.
Est. **£6,000-7,000** *S*

Introduced by Vincent in 1934, the high camshaft single cylinder engines powered both the Comet and the Meteor models. Another feature was the unusual rear suspension design and these models were produced alongside the new V-twin Rapide.

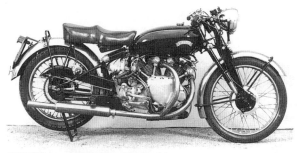

1950 Vincent HRD Rapide Series 'C' 998cc Solo Motorcycle, frame No. RC5375, rear frame RC/1/11092/C, V-twin, overhead valve, air-cooled, 4 stroke engine, 4 speed foot change gearbox, girdraulic forks, sprung frame at rear, chain final drive, 3.00 x 20in and 410 H 19in tyres.
£8,000-8,500 *S*

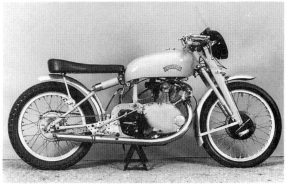

1950s Vincent Grey Flash 500cc Replica Solo Motorcycle, engine No. 15/AB/2A 6535, frame No. RC/1/6919, rear frame RC 10871, single vertical cylinder, overhead valve, air-cooled, 4 stroke, 4 speed gearbox, girdraulic forks, sprung frame, chain final drive, 3.00 x 20in and 410 H 19in tyres. **£4,000-4,500** *S*

1950 Vincent Grey Flash 500cc Solo Motorcycle, engine No. F5AB/2B/3697, frame No. 5597, inclined single cylinder engine, air-cooled, overhead valve, 4 stroke engine, bore 84mm, stroke 90mm, 499cc, 4 speed gearbox, chain final drive, girdraulic front forks, cantilever rear suspension with hydraulic dampers. Est. **£14,000-16,000** *S*

Make the Most of Miller's

CONDITION is absolutely vital when assessing the value of a vehicle. Top class vehicles on the whole appreciate much more than less perfect examples. However a rare, desirable car may command a high price even when in need of restoration

c1952 Vincent Black Shadow Series B 998cc Solo Motorcycle, engine No. F10AB/1/B/28257, frame No. C 10157 B/C, V-twin, air-cooled, overhead valve, 4 stroke engine, 4 speed gearbox, girdraulic forks with sprung frame at rear, chain final drive, 3.50 x 19in tyres.
Est. **£6,000-8,000** *S*

1955 Vincent Black Knight 1000cc Solo Motorcycle, V-twin cylinder engine, air-cooled, overhead valve, 4 stroke, bore 84mm, stroke 90mm, 998cc, 4 speed foot change gearbox, chain final drive, girdraulic oil damped front suspension, cantilever monoshock rear.
Est. **£18,000-21,000** *S*

Vincent Grey Flash Replica 500cc Solo Motorcycle, inclined single cylinder, air-cooled, overhead valve, 4 stroke engine, bore 84mm, stroke 90mm, 499cc, girdraulic oil damped front suspension with twin spring boxes and hydraulic dampers, 4 speed gearbox, chain final drive.
Est. **£5,000-7,000** *S*

The Series C Grey Flash appeared in 1949 as Vincent's first post-war entry into the road racing scene. It was based around the Comet and with tuning from the Brown brothers the 500cc unit was capable of developing 35bhp @ 6200rpm and had a top speed of 115mph. Factory apprentice John Surtees enjoyed a successful period on the circuits astride a Grey Flash.

c1955 Vincent Series D 1000cc Solo Motorcycle, in Black Shadow trim, engine No. 10AB/2B/10689, frame No. RD12589B, V-twin, air-cooled, overhead valve, bore 84mm, stroke 90mm, 998cc, 4 speed foot operated gearbox, chain final drive, girdraulic front forks, cantilever, pivoted fork rear suspension. **£10,500-11,500** *S*

Wall

1914 Wall Autowheel 119cc attached to a Sunbeam Gentleman's Bicycle, engine No. 9846, frame No. 89353, single vertical cylinder engine, air-cooled, 4 stroke, external flywheel, mounted in independent detachable frame, 28 x 1½in cycle wheel tyres.
£1,775-1,850 *S*

Designed specifically for attachment to a bicycle, the first Wall Autowheels offered a horizontally opposed 2 stroke engine. However by 1912 the new single cylinder 4 stroke engine appeared. They were used for invalid chairs as well as bicycles and despite appearances they were capable of propelling lightweight cyclists alarmingly quickly.

Yamaha

1972 Yamaha DS7 250cc Solo Motorcycle, engine No. 127819, frame No. 111515, twin cylinder, air-cooled, 2 stroke engine, bore 54mm, stroke 54mm, 247cc, 5 speed foot change gearbox, swinging arm rear suspension, telescopic front forks. **£450-500** *S*

1974 Yamaha FSIE 50cc Solo Sports Moped, engine/frame No. 19168, inclined single cylinder, air-cooled, 2 stroke, bore 40mm, stroke 39.7mm, 49cc, 4 speed foot change gearbox, telescopic front forks, pivoted fork rear suspension. **£200-250** *S*

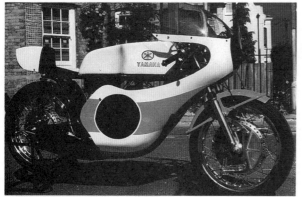

c1973 Yamaha TZ 350cc Racing Motorcycle, engine No. TZ 350, frame No. 992094, inclined twin cylinder, water-cooled, 2 stroke engine, bore 64mm, stroke 54mm, 347cc, 6 speed gearbox, chain final drive, telescopic front forks, swinging arm rear suspension, 18in tyres.
£3,500-4,000   *S*

The production TZ 350s differed little from the racing machines prepared by the Yamaha works for Agostini and Braun and the water-cooled engines developed some 62bhp at 10000rpm. The TZ 350s were favourites on the club racing circuits and spares were not only readily available but were relatively inexpensive.

c1977 Yamaha RD400 Cafe Racer Solo Motorcycle, engine/frame No. 1A800217, twin cylinder, inclined, air-cooled, 2 stroke, bore 64mm, stroke 62mm, 398cc, 6 speed posi-stop gearbox, telescopic front forks, swinging fork rear suspension.
£650-700   *S*

1977 Yamaha TY 175cc Trials Motorcycle, engine/frame No. 525 120544, single inclined cylinder, 2 stroke, air-cooled, 171cc, 5 speed gearbox, telescopic front forks, swinging arm rear suspension.
£825-875   *S*

1980 Yamaha XS 500 Solo Motorcycle, engine/frame No. 1H 2210549, inclined twin cylinder, air-cooled engine, double overhead camshaft, 4 valves per cylinder, 498cc, 5 speed gearbox, chain final drive, telescopic front forks, swinging arm rear suspension.
£2,000-2,500   *S*

1984 Yamaha RD 125 LC Solo Motorcycle, engine/frame No. 12A 101006, single inclined cylinder, water-cooled, 2 stroke, 123cc, 6 speed foot operated gearbox, cantilever rear suspension, telescopic front forks.
£700-775   *S*

Yamaha produced during the 1970s a series of high performance 2 stroke twins known as RDs, of which the largest was the 400.

1984 Yamaha RD 500 LC Solo Motorcycle, frame No. 47X001334, V-4 cylinder, liquid cooled, 2 stroke, foot operated positive stop gearbox, chain final drive, telescopic front forks, rising rate, monoshock rear suspension.
£4,000-4,500   *S*

Zedel

1907 Zedel 2hp Solo Motorcycle, engine No. 20770, frame No. 20195, inclined single cylinder, overhead inlet, side exhaust valve, air-cooled, 4 stroke engine, single speed belt drive with chain driven pedal assistance and starting, girder forks, rigid frame, 24 x 2¼in tyres.
£3,500-4,000 *S*

The French-built Zedel motorcycle took its name from the founders of the Swiss parent company, Ernest Zurcher and Hermann Luthi, ZL.

Make the Most of Miller's

Price ranges in this book reflect what one should expect to pay for a similar example. When selling, however, one should expect to receive a lower figure. This will fluctuate according to a dealer's stock, saleability at a particular time, etc. It is always advisable, when selling, to approach a reputable specialist dealer or an auction house which has specialist sales

c1938 Zündapp K800 Solo Military Motorcycle, transverse opposed 4 cylinder, air-cooled, side valve engine, bore 62mm, stroke 66.6mm, 804cc, 4 speed unit construction gearbox, shaft final drive, friction damped parallelogram front forks, rigid rear suspension, 19in tyres.
£2,650-2,850 *S*

Zündapp's K Series bikes were announced in 1933 and the following year were adopted for use by the German army, the military versions being designated W indicating Wehrmacht.

Zündapp

c1945 Zündapp KS-750-W 750cc Military Combination, transverse horizontally opposed twin cylinder, air-cooled, overhead valve, 4 stroke engine, bore 75mm, stroke 85mm, 751cc, 8 forward gears, 4 reverse gears, dual ratio hand change gearbox, shaft final drive with sidecar drive, telescopic front forks, rigid rear suspension, 16in tyres.
£5,250-5,750 *S*

Like the German-built BMW R75 the Zündapp had been designed to tow light guns, but over heavy ground the front wheel had a tendency to lift off the ground and the bike was therefore developed as a purposeful all-terrain vehicle. The KS-750-W featured the distinctive pressed steel frame and, as with the BMW, the sidecar was designed by Steib.

Sidecars

c1950 Steib Model S501 Sports Single Seat Sidecar, produced in West Germany.
£800-850 *S*

1927 Sandum Sidecar and Chassis.
£450-500 *S*

Sandum was one of a host of British sidecar manufacturers producing accessories for motorcyclists during the 1920s.

Pedal Cars

A Mercedes-Type Single Seat Racing Pedal Car, Post-War, simple steering mechanism, 69in (175cm) long.
£850-950 *S*

An Austin Pathfinder Pedal Car, 1949-50, repainted, badge damaged, replaced windscreen, 65in (165cm) long.
£1,100-1,200 *S*

A Lines Bros. Vauxhall Pedal Car, c1935, fully restored.
Est. **£2,250-2,750** *ADT*

A pressed-steel Austin J40 Pedal Car, late 1960s, 62in (157cm) long.
£1,250-1,350 *CSK*

An Austin J40 Pedal Car, c1950, 60in (152cm) long.
£1,250-1,350 *C.A.R.S.*

A Tri-ang Child's Pedal Car, veteran type, c1950s, restored, in its original cardboard carton.
£250-300 *C.A.R.S.*

See page 448

A Vanwall Racing Car Replica Child's Pedal Car by Tri-ang, 1960s, windscreen missing, restored.
£200-250 *C.A.R.S.*

**A Vanwall Racing Car Replica
Child's Pedal Car,** c1960, by
Tri-ang, fully restored.
£200-250   *C.A.R.S.*

**A Jaguar XK 120 Sports Car
Replica Pedal Car,** c1980, by
Touchwood Models Ltd., fibreglass
moulded body with working lights
and horn.
£1,000-1,500   *C.A.R.S.*

**A Child's Motorised 4½ Litre
Blower Bentley Toy Car,** English,
fibreglass moulded body, 77in
(196cm) long.
£2,500-2,750   *S*

**A Mercedes 500 S E C Child's
Pedal Car, c1970,** by Tri-ang,
original condition.
£100-125   *C.A.R.S.*

A Morgan 4/4 Pedal Car, c1991, to
⅓ scale, in two-tone fibreglass,
opening bonnet, folding windscreen,
electric headlamps, rear lamps,
indicators, horn, authentic Morgan
badges, English, 49in (124.5cm)
long.
£700-800   *MM*

AN INTRODUCTION TO AUTOMOBILIA

The automobilia collector falls into two camps. The first is someone who owns a vintage or classic vehicle and would like to enhance that vehicle by collecting items of interest associated with it. The other type of collector, and the writer certainly falls into this category, is someone who collects all the various forms of automobilia which is a much less expensive, but equally enjoyable, hobby

In times past, the majority of automobilia collectors started their hobby in a simple way. The most common method was for schoolboys to collect company hand-outs at motor shows and the like, and once smitten to continue collecting. For the person with a little money to spend, asking at small bookshops for anything motoring or making a pilgrimage to scrap yards looking for old lighting components or badges was an admirable and enjoyable pastime. Today, however, the sources of supply have changed dramatically. All but gone are the scrap yards and car breakers and the antique bookshop seldom turns up any little gems. On the other hand, there is the Auto Jumble, a cross between a jumble sale and an antiques fair. Although these events are frequently seen advertised across the country, the biggest and first such event is the annual Beaulieu Auto Jumble which attracts enormous crowds during the first weekend of September. There also now exist professional motor book dealers, most of whom seem to be fair and honest, who regularly send out book lists to collectors worldwide offering a much needed service. Thirdly, of course, is the 1980s phenomenon: the boot sale.

For the purposes of this introduction, I thought it would be an idea to give a few tips about the purchase of motor car mascots and the storage of printed literature.

MASCOTS

Since the earliest days of motoring, man has sought to embellish and personalise his vehicle. Mascots started to be offered to the public in accessory catalogues from c1905, but it was the introduction of the Rolls-Royce mascot in 1910 that heralded the vast selection of designs that were to be manufactured between the wars and that, today, offer the collector a varied choice. Mascots fall into two main categories: those APPROVED by the vehicle manufacturers themselves and those that were offered simply as an embellishment for the vehicle. Vauxhall's Wyvern mascot is still used as a company logo today and Rolls-Royce's Spirit of Ecstasy, created with the artistry of Charles Sykes, are excellent examples of the approved type. Conversely such diverse subjects as mechanical propellers, glass mascots and flying birds of every description are the more popular ACCESSORY types.

Because the value of some of the more rare mascots has increased in recent years, modern reproductions are being manufactured in a deliberate attempt to deceive both the new and mature collector. However, if enthusiasts follow two golden rules when purchasing an item, they will probably avoid being cheated.

Firstly, most metal mascots can be purchased with a choice of finishes. Chromium and nickel plate were the most common, but these will oxidise with time and, after a few years, will show their age. Beware, therefore, mascots that have been re-plated and look as good as new.

Secondly, is the mascot being supplied by a bona-fide dealer? Will he stake his reputation on the item's authenticity and provenance? If not, then purchase from somebody who will.

PRINTED LITERATURE

This category is so very large and diverse that we can only scratch the surface with this resumé. Encompassing such diverse subjects as cased books, pamphlets, brochures and magazines, it must not be forgotten that the photograph also has a place in motoring history. As well as being inexpensive at auction or in the retail market, the photograph offers an opportunity for the enthusiast to acquire a good collection of motoring based ephemera at modest cost. Grandad standing by the family car in the 1930s may be of interest to the family concerned but is not of any real use; however, photographs of cars at a speed event, hill climb or rally will be of interest, particularly if their entry number can be identified and in consequence many hours of pleasure can be obtained not only in identifying the venue, but also the event and the owner. A good street scene showing period cars will also give many hours of pleasure.

When collecting and storing paperwork, like magazines, brochures and photographs, it is important to store them safely and in such a way as to avoid further deterioration and possibly permanent damage. Exposure to sunlight is the worst possible thing that can happen to paper. The rays from the sun will change the consistency of paper, together with some drying, and the eventual result will be flaking paper that will disintegrate on touch. The handling of paper will also play a part in destroying it. The salt from your hands attacks the paper fibre, so always wash your hands, or better still use cotton gloves. Remember that the paper used in the production of magazines and catalogues was often the cheapest available, and in consequence is little better than tissue paper. Like tissue paper, magazines will soak up water from the atmosphere with alarming ease and subsequently attract dust and dirt. The resultant cocktail then hastens the activity of fungus and bacteria which further breaks the paper fibre and very soon all that is left is a white, mildewy, sticky mess.

All paperwork should be kept in a dry, well ventilated environment and should not be exposed to long periods of sunlight.

Remember collecting should be fun, but if you also apply common sense, your collection should be a worthy investment and give continued pleasure.

Peter W. Card

Automobile Art

Gordon Horner, Isle of Man Side Car TT, monochrome watercolour, mounted, framed and glazed, 11 x 19in (28 x 48cm).
£225-250   *S*

G. Richardson, Prince Bira in his ERA, signed and dated '37 by the artist and Bira, watercolour, mounted, framed and glazed, 8½ x 10in (21.5 x 25.5cm).
£350-375   *S*

Michael Wright, Marquis Antonio Brivio in the Alfa Romeo P3, watercolour and gouache, signed and inscribed, 28 x 21in (73 x 55cm).
£2,500-2,600   *C(M)*

Four F. Wood cartoons, 1950s, pen and ink, signed, 3 with blue wash, all framed and glazed.
£70-80   *S*

Michael Turner, Fittipaldi at Monaco, 1975, watercolour and gouache, signed and dated '75, mounted, framed and glazed, 18 x 24in (46 x 61cm).
£2,000-2,500   *S*

Phil May, Clive on the Barnato 8 litre Bentley, Brooklands 1932, signed watercolour, mounted, framed and glazed, 14 x 17in (35.5 x 43cm).
£375-425   *S*

Roy Nockolds, Richard Seaman Works Mercedes Grand Prix Driver, c1938, pencil portrait, mounted, framed and glazed, 5½in (14cm) square.
£90-100   *S*

This work was commissioned by the Mercedes Factory for use as a commemorative plaque after the death of Richard Seaman.

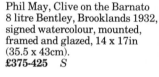

E. Montaut, Le Dirigeable 'Republique', Moteur Panhard et Levassor, original polychrome lithographic print, good condition, 18 x 35½in (45 x 90cm).
£600-650   *S*

Michael Wright, Dignity and Impudence, watercolour and gouache depicting Sir Henry Birkin in his Bentley and Archie Fraser-Nash in his Austin 7 crossing Conway Square, Newtownards, signed, lettered 1930 ARDS TT, mounted, framed and glazed, 17 x 23½in (43 x 59.5cm).
£700-775   *S*

Unknown, Automobiles Delage, oil on canvas, advertising original artwork, c1910, damaged, unframed, 41 x 33½in (104 x 85cm).
£400-450   *S*

Four 'Mac' Strip Cartoons by HRH, 1950s, pen and ink, initialled, mounted, framed and glazed, 17in (43cm) wide.
£50-60   *S*

E. Montaut, Raid Paris-Verdun, original polychrome lithographic print, good condition, 18 x 35½in (45 x 90cm).
£425-475 *S*

Michael Wright, 1936 Monaco Grand Prix, signed watercolour and gouache, Etancelin in a Maserati crossing Casino Square, mounted, framed and glazed, 24 x 20in (60 x 50cm).
£880-920 *S*

The Monaco Grand Prix of 1936 was held on 13 April, after heavy rain and mistral winds on the practice day and the morning of the race, the street course was still awash when the 1.30pm start approached. Infamous for the chicane pile-up on the first lap, and the heavy rains pouring down again after the 20th lap, this race was one of the slowest Monaco Grand Prix of the 1930s. Carracciola eventually won, completing 100 laps in 3:49:20.4 with an average speed of 51.96mph, Stuck came 3rd behind Varzi completing 99 laps with the lap record speed of 2min 07.4secs, an average speed of 55.86mph. For once Etancelin in the Maserati was hardly in the race, never higher than 9th, delayed when a bent wheel was changed after hitting a curb, and eventually forced to retire in the 37th lap with a split tank damaged at the same time.

Dion Pears, Graham Hill B.R.M. Zandvoort, 1962, signed watercolour, framed and glazed, 20 x 24½in (50 x 62cm).
Est. **£500-800** *S*

Bob Murray, Short Finals, watercolour depicting a type 35 Bugatti racing against a Hawker Hector, signed, mounted, framed and glazed, 17½ x 15in (44.5 x 38cm).
£475-525 *S*

Bob Murray, Race for Home, Birkin 'Blower' Bentley versus Hawker Fury, signed watercolour, framed and glazed, 18 x 14in (46 x 36cm).
£650-675 *S*

Gamy (Marguerite Montaut), untitled, original polychrome lithographic print depicting Bedelia racing cars, display mounted, good condition, 18 x 35½in (45 x 90cm).
Est. **£400-500** *S*

Bob Murray, Crew Change, Invicta low chassis 4½ litre and Spitfire Mk VB, signed watercolour, framed and glazed, 18 x 14in (46 x 36cm).
£500-550 *S*

Bob Murray, 1919 Rolls-Royce Silver Ghost Alpine Eagle and Bristol Fighter of 139 Sqdn, signed watercolour and gouache, framed and glazed, 18 x 14in (46 x 36cm).
£600-650 *S*

Automobilia

Bob Murray, Aston Martin DB4 GT Zagato 1 VEV with a pair of Hawker Hunters of 43 Squadron, c1963, signed watercolour, mounted, framed and glazed, 18 x 13in (46 x 33cm).
£375-425 *S*

A selection of key rings, 2½in (6cm) long.
50p-£5 each *PC*

A Mickey Mouse radiator grille decoration, American, painted flat brass figure, some damage, 1930s, 5½in (14cm) high.
Est. **£700-900** *S*

A bronze cigarette lighter modelled as a Renault, on marble base, 8in (20cm) long. **£200-300** *C(M)*

BARC blazer badges, 1950s.
£5-8 each *PC*

A pair of bronzed resin busts of Charles Stewart Rolls and Frederick Henry Royce, 8½in (22cm) high. **£700-1,000** *CNY*

These were commissioned by Rolls-Royce Motors Ltd. to commemorate the 75th Anniversary of the meeting of C. S. Rolls and F. H. Royce at the Midland Hotel, Manchester, on 4th May 1904. Possibly reproduction.

A Firestone Tyre ashtray, 6in (15cm) diam.
£2-10 *PC*

A silver radiator shaped cigarette case, probably French, marked 51 900 G St, maker's badge missing, 4in (10cm) high.
Est. **£320-400** *S*

Two tax discs, 1954 and 1955.
£1-10 each *PC*

Two Thoroughbreds, by Stanley Wanlass, signed, edition FC/50 gold painted bronze of Phil Hill driving a Ferrari, 21in (53cm) long.
Est. **£4,000-6,000** *S*

A glass model of a Mercedes 300SL Gullwing, by Daum of Nancy, c1958, 13in (32.5cm) long.
Est. **£380-450** *S*

A model of VMF 65, the 1950 Aston Martin DB2 Saloon Flt. Lt. J. Bloomfield raced between 1950 and 1954, by Henri C. Baigent, on mirrored floor with glazed case, 20½in (52cm) long.
£2,000-2,250 *C(M)*

The nose cone from the 1990 Formula I Ferrari driven by Alain Prost, carrying the champion's number I and identifying yellow flashes on the front wing, 51in (133cm) long.
£5,750-6,250 *C(M)*

A motoring bronze, believed to be a Thompson Museum Trophy, Austrian, signed and marked AR C Philipp on the base, c1904, 17in (43cm) long.   **£16,000-17,000** *S*

A Breitling miniature clock in the form of the radiator grille of a Rolls-Royce, 3½in (8.5cm) high.
£1,500-1,600 *HSS*

A brass vehicle licence holder, 3in (7.5cm) diam.
£38-40 *BS*

A silver cigarette lighter, in the shape of an oil lamp, hallmarked Birmingham 1909, 4in (10cm) high.
£550-575 *S*

An AA ashtray, given as a trade gift, c1920-30, 4½in (11cm) high.
£15-40 *PC*

A rare Hispano Suiza bronze commemorative medal, signed F. Bazin, in original presentation box, hinge damaged, 1953, 2½in (6.5cm) diam.
£275-300 *S*

A Thrills of Brooklands Totalisator Fruit Machine, repainted blue, 24in (61cm) high.
£650-700 *S*

A JAP V-Twin engine, No. 12101, Bosch magneto, carburettor and manifold, c1912.
£625-650   *S*

A letter from the Vintage Motor Cycle Club with the engine suggests that this engine is of pre-1914 manufacture.

A Napier radiator shaped silver vesta case, probably English, indistinctly hallmarked, 2in (5cm) high.
Est. **£400-500**   *S*

Badges

An Austin Cooper badge, 5½in (14cm) wide.
£2-5   *PC*

British racing flags badge, 5in (12.5cm) wide.
£8-15   *PC*

Two Ford badges, 3 to 3½in (7.5 to 9cm) wide.   **£2-5**   *PC*

A German badge, 2½in (6.5cm) diam.
£5-15   *PC*

A dashboard St Christopher emblem.
£2-10   *PC*

An Austin Cooper S badge.
£2-5   *PC*

A Greeves motorcycle badge, 5in (12.5cm) wide.
£3-5   *PC*

A Morris Cooper badge.
£2-5   *PC*

An early BARC Brooklands enamel badge, No. 96, enamel chipped, 3½in (9.5cm) high.
Est. **£700-900**   *S*

A BSA motorcycle badge, 5in (12.5cm) wide.
£2-4   *PC*

A selection of RAC and AA badges, including a rare AA Committee Member's badge.
£500-575 *S*

A Duple Coachwork's badge, 2in (5cm) high.
£5-20 *PC*

A GB badge, 3in (7.5cm) wide.
£1-3 *PC*

An RAC Club badge, 1920-30, mounted, 8½ in (21cm) high.
£150-350 *PC*
BEWARE REPRODUCTIONS.

Four motorcycle lapel badges, c1960.
£2-3 each *COB*

Wolseley badges, 9½in (24cm) and 6½in (16cm) wide. **£1-5 each** *PC*

Two RAC badges: l. pre-1953, r. post-1953, 4in (10cm) high.
£5-15 each *PC*

Two Associate Member RAC badges, l. 4½in (11cm) high, r. 5in (12.5cm) high.
£5-15 *PC*

Four AA badges, 4 to 5½in (10 to 13.5cm) high.
£10-30 each   *PC*

An AA Committee Member's badge, No. OC30, 6in (16cm) high.   **£650-675**   *S*

An AA Committee Member's badge, No. OC96, 6in (16cm) high. Est. **£300-400**   *S*

A Jaguar Drivers' Club badge, 5in (12.5cm) high.
£5-15   *PC*

Two BARC badges for bar and grille fixing, 3½ to 4½in (8.5 to 11.5cm) high.   **£5-15 each**   *PC*

Two Civil Service motoring badges with different crowns, l. Queen's crown, post-1953, r. pre-1953, 10in (25cm) high.
£5-15 each   *PC*

A St Christopher badge, 5in (12.5cm) high.
£10-15   *PC*

A Cote d'Azur badge, with Arms of Monaco, 3in (7.5cm) diam.   **£5-10**   *PC*

A selection of car badges. **£5-15 each**   *RE*

The Order of the Road Club badge (without 'Member Not Driving' tag).
£15-30   *PC*

A British Racing & Sports Car Club badge, enamel worn, 4½in (11.5cm) high.
£10-20   *PC*

A JRDC enamel badge in 5 colours, depicting a racing car at speed on a shield shaped badge, 3½in (9cm) high.
£400-425   *S*

An Edinburgh badge, 4½in (11.5cm) high.
£2-5   *PC*

An Indonesia car badge, 3½in (9cm) high.   **£5-15**   *PC*

An English Lakes car badge, 3½in (8.5cm).   **£5-15**   *PC*

Car Mascots

A Spirit of Ecstasy Rolls-Royce mascot, post-1929, 5½in (14cm) high.   **£100-200**   *PC*
Beware of modern reproductions.

An F. Bazin Triumph Mascot, French, Designed, stamped 42, 1930s, 8½in (21cm) high.
£1,700-1,900   *S(M)*

A Spirit of Ecstasy Rolls-Royce Silver Ghost mascot, 1918-25, 6in (15cm) high, mounted on radiator cap.
£350-375   *S*

A Wee Jamie mascot,
1930s, 5in
(12cm) high.
£300-350 *S*

A 'Libellule' plated bronze mascot,
probably by M. Bertin, French,
damaged, 1920s, 6in (15cm) high.
Est. **£350-450** *S*

A Supermarine S.6B Schneider
Trophy Seaplane mascot, English,
engraved Rolls-Royce Motors Ltd.,
mounted on a radiator cap, repaired,
1930s, 7in (18cm) long.
£1,200-1,500 *S*

A running fox nickel plated mascot,
on display stand, 6½in (16cm) long.
£100-125 *S*

A bulldog on a chain mascot,
French, marked CG 639, mounted
on a radiator cap, c1924, 4½in
(11.5cm) high.
Est. **£950-1,100** *S*

A biplane car mascot by Art Medal
Works, New Jersey, with cast metal
body, c1913, wingspan 7½in (19cm).
Est. **£600-700** *S*

An Et. Mercier cat in the moon
plated brass mascot, French, signed,
1920s, 4½in (11.5cm) high.
£900-950 *S*

A Bleriot type monoplane nickel
plated mascot, probably French,
mounted on radiator cap, c1914, 8in
(20cm) long. **£680-720** *S*

A L'Oeuf du Elephant mascot,
French, 1920s, nickel plated bronze,
5in (13cm) high, worn.
£1,750-2,000 *S*

An E. Bregeon golfer mascot,
French, c1920, the bronze figure
mounted on a wooden base, 6in
(15cm) high.
£375-400 *S*

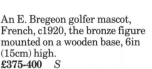

A Clement Bayard Crusader
mascot, French, some paint missing,
1920s, 4in (10cm) high.
£1,100-1,250 *S*

A rotary aircraft engine and propeller mascot, c1914, mounted on a radiator cap, 8in (20cm) wide. Est. **£575-600** *S*

A Bofill monkey and grapes mascot, French, signed with MMA mark, on marble base, pre-1914, 5in (13cm) high. **£900-1,100** *S*

A champagne bottle mascot, French, engraved Louis Clerc Vins Mousseux à Mantry (Jura), 5½in (14cm) high. **£325-350** *S*

A Charlie Chaplin nickelled bronze mascot, attributed to L. Veyrard, French, mounted on wooden base, plating rubbed and worn, 1920s, 5in (12.5cm) high. Est. **£700-900** *S*

A Vauxhall wyvern polished bronze mascot, English, c1929, 4in (9.5cm) high. **£475-500** *S*

A Maurice Guiraud Rivière bronze boxer mascot, French, signed around base, plating rubbed, 1920s, 5½in (14cm) high. Est. **£1,000-1,500** *S*

The boxer used as the model for this mascot was the great French Heavyweight Champion in the late 1920s, George Carpentier.

A Gordon Crosby Icarus chromed metal mascot, English, signed, 1930s, wingspan 7in (17cm). **£475-500** *S*

A horse and jockey cold painted mascot, on a wooden base, 5in (13cm) high. **£150-175** *S*

Current issue.

A Bofill mandarin mascot, French, with pre-Great War foundry MMA mark, signed, pre-1914, 5in (13.5cm) high. Est. **£1,000-1,200** *S*

A Pierce Arrow car nickel plated brass mascot, American, c1928, 4in (10cm) high. Est. **£500-600** *S*

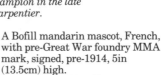

A huntsman and fox silver plated bronze mascot, probably French, 1920s, mounted on a radiator cap, 6½in (14cm) high. **£250-275** *S*

A Lalique Tête de Bélier glass mascot, French, moulded R. Lalique, France, on radiator cap mount, 1930s, 4in (10cm) high.
£3,500-4,500 *S*

A Telcote pup plated brass mascot, English, rubbed, 1930s, 6in (15cm) long.
£225-250 *S*

A Hudson cast zinc mascot, American, designed by F. C. Ruppel, cast as one with radiator cap, 1928, 8in (20cm) high.   **£300-350** *S*

A Buick goddess mascot, nickel plated die cast zinc, American, by William Schnell, some damage, 1927, 4½in (11.5cm) long.
£175-200 each *S*

Note slight difference in casting.

An F. Bazin Latil elephant's head mascot, French, marked Latil and F. Bazin on the base, mounted on a marble stand, c1920s, 4in (10cm) high.
£2,000-2,500 *S*

A cock-a-snoot nickel plated bronze mascot, English, on a radiator cap, worn, 1920s, 5½in (14cm) high.
£420-460 *S*

An early Lalique Petite Libellule glass mascot, French, moulded Lalique, chipped, c1928, 6½in (16.5cm) long.
£2,000-2,500 *S*

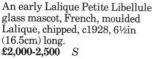

A Marmon 16 cylinder die cast chrome and plated zinc car mascot, American, 1931-33, 5in (12.5cm) long.
£525-550 *S*

An Essex cast zinc mascot, American, designed by F. C. Ruppel, cast as one with radiator cap, some damage, 1928, 5in (13cm) high.
£250-300 *S*

An E. Seago St. George and the Dragon mascot, signed on base, screw shank mounting, 7in (17.5cm) high.
Est. **£1,700-2,300** *S(M)*

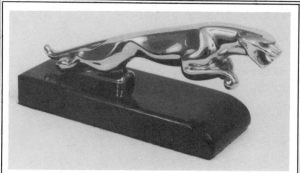

A Jaguar mascot, mounted, designed by F. Gordon Crosby, 9in (22cm) wide.
£10-40 *PC*

A cross-legged Pierrot car mascot, mounted on a radiator cap, 4½in (12cm) high.
£800-1,000 *CNY*

A rare Bofill Naiad nickel plated bronze mascot, French, signed, c1920, 6in (16cm) high.
Est. **£600-800** *S*

An A. Begas nude dancer plated brass mascot, French, signed, 1930s, rubbed, 7in (18cm) high.
£300-325 *S*

A Vickers Wellington bomber aeroplane silver plated mascot, probably by A. E. Lejeune, English, mounted on a radiator cap, 1940s, 9½in (24cm) wingspan.
£500-550 *S*

A bizarre winged insect-golfer chromium plated mascot, probably English, 1930s, 6in (15cm) high.
£475-500 *S*

An Austin winged wheel nickel plated bronze mascot, English, marked Rd 286069 and AUSTIN MOTOR CO. around the radiator cap, plating rubbed, 5in (13cm) wingspan.
£450-475 *S*

The registered design number, 286069, first appeared on Austin mascots in 1923. This design of mascot was no longer used by Austin on their vehicles after 1927.

A souvenir of Brussels anvil mascot, marked Bovy, Bruxelles, mounted on a radiator cap, bronze discoloured, 1930s, 3½in (9cm) wide.
£350-375 *S*

A North Eastern Automobile Association mascot, No. 233, marked NEAA, base stamped Grant & Sons, South Shields, c1920, 5½in (13.5cm) high.
£350-375 *S*

Ephemera

Braunbeck (Gustav): Offizieller Fuhrer Zum Gordon Bennett Rennen 17 Juni 1904 und Damit Verbunden Offiziellen Festlichkeiten, Munich 1904, mounted frontispiece, plates, some coloured, folding map, original embossed cloth.
£340-380 *CNY*

166 Sport, Inter, Formula 2, Mille Miglia, Italian text, 1949.
£1,200-1,500 *C(M)*

> **Miller's is a price GUIDE not a price LIST**

Garage Equipment

A garage flag for Guaranteed Shell From The Pump, damaged, 1920s, 95 by 57in (243 by 145cm).
£225-250 *S*

A Ruston-Hornsbury Shellmex petrol pump, type No. 4, slight damage to globe, repainted, 1920s, 115in (292cm) high.
Est. **£1,400-1,600** *S*

A Bowser hand operated petrol pump, American, painted red and black body, wired for illumination, restored and repaired, 116in (294cm) high.
£2,100-2,600 *S*

A Pneumatic Components Ltd. (PCL) Airmeter Mk III forecourt air tower, restored, 70in (178cm) high.
£350-375 *S*

A Bowser hand operated petrol pump, restored and repainted, 1920s, 100in (254cm) high.
Est. **£800-1,000** *S*

A Kismet forecourt air tower, red with beige lettering at base, English, restored, 74in (188cm) high. **£900-1,000** *S*

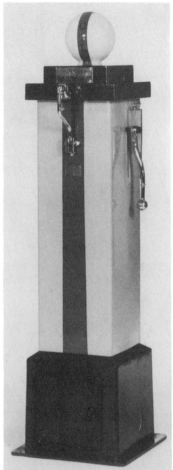

A Wayne petrol pump and a Shell blue glass globe, c1950. **£300-350 each** *MSMP*

A Redline-Glico Ltd. heavy motor oil pump, light and dark green with red line, English, restored, c1930, 65in (265cm) high. **£575-625** *S*

A Boa Constrictor brass horn, with 3½in (9cm) trumpet, 80in (203cm) long. **£250-275** *S*

This is believed to be from a Rolls-Royce Silver Ghost.

Horns

A Boa Constrictor snake's head horn, c1915, 78in (198cm) long. **£1,600-1,700** *S*

The Boa Constrictor Horn Company operated in England from 1909, producing a wide range of effective reed horns for bicycles, motorcycles and cars. The large version of the snake's head horn was available in cast or pressed brass prior to 1914, and in a smaller and lighter version after 1918. The company continued until 1939.

Recently a number of poorly sand cast copies of the snake's head horn have been seen on the market. These were reproduced in India in the 1970s and early 80s, and many are deliberately aged in an attempt to deceive.

Two Boa Constrictor motoring horns, c1915, straight tube, 30in (75cm) long, and a flexible brass tube 76in (190cm) long. **£1,100-1,200** *CNY*

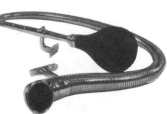

A Boa Constrictor motor horn, with mounting brackets, 57in (145cm) long. **£500-550** *S*

A Lucas car horn with original paintwork, c1920, 11in (28cm) long. **£70-75** *BS*

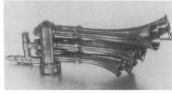

A 6 note brass horn. **£1,150-1,200** *CNY*

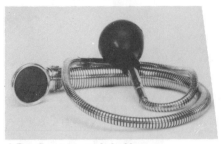

A Boa Constrictor polished brass motor horn, c1925, 70in (178cm) long.
Est. **£650-750** *S*

A Smith & Sons brass angle mounted dashboard clock, No. 258-1396, Swiss made.
£225-250 *S*

An Elliott Brothers speed indicator, Young's Patent No. 2933, in original leather case.
£250-275 *S*

Instruments

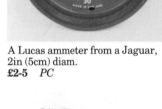

A Lucas ammeter from a Jaguar, 2in (5cm) diam.
£2-5 *PC*

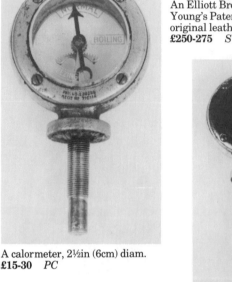

A calormeter, 2½in (6cm) diam.
£15-30 *PC*

A car radiator temperature gauge, c1920, 7½in (18.5cm) long.
£70-75 *BS*

Four assorted Jaeger dashboard instruments: a black faced eight-day clock, a black faced speedometer in kilometres and 2 silver faced speedometers, one in mph, the other in kph.
£475-500 *S*

A Smith's combined lighting switch and ammeter, an Alba petrol indicator, and a dashboard timepiece. Est. **£250-320** *S*

Lighting

A Lucas oil illuminated rear lamp, No. 432, polished brass body.
£300-325 *S*

A pair of Marchal Aerolux headlamps type 347, pillar mounted, 8in (21cm) diam ribbed glass lenses.
Est. **£350-450** *S*

A pair of quality brass fork mounting electric headlamps, probably English, 8in (20cm) diam.
£130-150 *S*

Three Lucas King of the Road
oil illuminated side lamps,
English, No. 742, two left and one
right sided, all in original boxes,
c1910, and a Lucas No. 432 tail
lamp in original box, good condition.
£1,400-1,500   *S*

A Lucas King of the Road oil
illuminated brass rear light,
English, No. 432, c1910, 3½in
(8.5cm) diam.
£450-500   *S*

A pair of Bleriot illuminated
brass opera lamps, French, and one
red sight lens, c1908, 12in (30.5cm)
high, damaged, and a pair of
Ducellier opera lamps converted to
electric, without side glasses,
damaged.
£800-900   *S*

A pair of Powell & Hanmer oil
illuminated lamps, English,
No. 540, c1920s, 4in (10cm) diam.
£400-450   *S*

An A. J. Wilson Browne & Son Orto
oil illuminated rear number plate
lamp, with black painted brass
body, damaged.
£125-150   *S*

A Lucas Duplex self contained
acetylene headlamp, English,
No. 794, twin generators, cracked,
polished brass body, c1910, 6in
(15cm) diam glass lens.
£200-225   *S*

A pair of large Ducellier brass opera
lamps, French, converted to
electricity, restored, c1910, 14in
(35.5cm) high.
£800-900   *S*

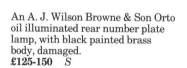

A Lucas Lorlite self contained
acetylene headlamp, English,
No. CM 52, with single generator,
black painted body, c1915, 6in
(15cm) glass lens.
£240-280   *S*

A Lucas oil illuminated rear
numberplate lamp, No. 634, with
polished brass body, clear 3in
(7.5cm) diam side numberplate lens,
one 2in (5cm) diam red rear lens and
small clear sight lens, damaged.
£350-375   *S*

A pair of Marchal Striluxe electric
headlamps, French, type 292, 1930s,
11in (28cm) diam clear glass lens.
£950-1,000   *S*

A pair of Rosen & Co.
'Rosco' small opera
sidelights, American,
electrically illuminated,
1920s, 4½in (12cm) high,
on mounting arm.
Est. **£140-200**   *S*

A large Lucas King of the Road oil
illuminated brass side lamp,
English, type No. 764, 5in (14cm)
outer lens and a 3in (7.5cm)
bull's-eye lens, 14in (35cm) high,
restored.
£460-500   *S*

A pair of Bosch JG240 type
headlights, brass bodied with black
painted cases, 9½in (24cm) diam
lens, with fork mounts.
Est. **£600-800**   *S*

A pair of Autoroche oil illuminated
sidelamps, French, with plated
brass body, c1919, 3in (7.5cm) diam
lens, and faceted red sight glass.
Est. **£200-280**   *S*

A pair of Marchal Aerolux
headlamps type 397, pillar
mounted, weathered, 7in (18cm)
diam.
Est. **£300-400**   *S*

A Lucidus pillar mounted spotlamp,
French, with 8in (20cm) diam
convex lens, mounted on running
board adjustable support, 41in
(104cm) high.
£460-490   *S*

A pair of Lucas divers helmet rear
lights, black japanned cases, 2in
(5cm) diam red lens and clear lenses.
£450-475   *S*

A pair of CAV brass opera style
sidelights, c1912, 9½in (24cm) high.
£500-550   *S*

A pair of English CAV style stirrup
mounting electric headlamps, with
removable hinged lenses, 10in
(25cm) diam.
£140-160   *S*

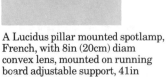

A pair of Marchal Aerolux
headlamps type 314, pillar
mounted, 9in (22.5cm) diam glass
lenses, one replaced.
Est. **£600-800**   *S*

A pair of Scintilla double rear (Bugatti) lights, Swiss, Bakelite backs, restored, 1930s, 4½in (11.5cm) wide.
£1,000-1,200 *S*

A Scintilla (Bugatti) rear light, Swiss, casing painted black with original lenses and black Bakelite back, 1930s, 4½in (11.5cm) wide.
£450-500 *S*

A Lucas magnetic parking light, 1920s, 3in (8cm) long.
£5-8 *PC*

A pair of Marchal streamlined sidelights, French, 1930s, with original lenses, cases restored, 6in (15cm) long.
£225-250 *S*

These are suitable for a Bugatti.

A pair of Bosch triple rear lights, German, with original lenses, restored, 1930s, 7in (18cm) long.
£1,000-1,200 *S*

A pair of Marchal bull's-eye side rear lights, French, 1930s, each case 4in (10cm) wide.
£225-250 *S*

Luggage

A Coracle wicker two-person picnic set, English, 1920s, 15in (38cm) wide.
£325-350 *S*

A Drew & Sons motoring picnic set, English, the black leather covered case with fitted interior, including kettle and heater, 1920s.
Est. **£2,000-3,000** *S*

Petrol Pump Globes

A Standard Oil Company flame globe, red and white celluloid, 1930s, 20½in (52cm) high.
Est. **£360-420** *S*

A Shell fat glass petrol pump globe, slightly faded, 20in (51cm) high.
£175-200 *S*

A BP glass petrol pump globe, c1955.
£285-325 *MSMP*

A Shell glass petrol pump globe, with base rubber, lettering faded, 17½in (44.5cm) high.
£125-140 *S*

A Shell Diesoline glass petrol pump globe, with base rubber, in red and black, 17½in (44.5cm) high.
£90-120 *S*

A Guaranteed No. 1 petrol globe, probably English, 2 convex glass plates lettered black on white, in American style metal globe housing, paint worn, 19½in (50cm) high.
Est. **£600-800** *S*

A Shell Economy glass petrol pump globe, with base rubber, lettering faded, 17½in (44.5cm) high.
£100-125 *S*

A Super Shell white glass petrol pump globe, with red and blue letters, slight damage, 17½in (44.5cm) high.
£175-200 *S*

A VIP glass petrol pump globe, c1960.
£165-185 *MSMP*

A Shellmex fat glass petrol pump globe, red lettering faded, 20in (51cm) high.
£200-225 *S*

A Dominion three-sided glass petrol pump globe, lettered in black with blue, slightly faded, 17in (43cm) high.
£300-350 *S*

A Dominion three-sided glass petrol pump globe, c1950.
£300-350 *MSMP*

A National Benzole Mixture three-sided glass petrol pump globe, lettered in black and yellow, faded, 17in (43cm) high.
£300-350 *S*

A Regent Benzole glass petrol globe, c1936.
£300-350 *MSMP*

Petrol globes are often not as old as they seem. They are usually coded in red on the foot with the month and year, i.e. 9.60 = September 1960.

They are very susceptible to cracking due to changes in temperature.

Photographs

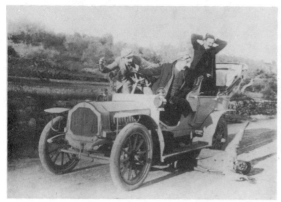

Thirteen early motoring photographs, 8 drivers portraits, c1906, 2 photographs of vehicles and a humorous series of 3 photographs.
£300-325 *S*

A collection of photographic negatives and original photographs, 1947-50, approx 144 negatives with contact sheets.
£250-275 *S*

Coupe Gordon Bennett Circuit d'Auvergne, 1905, a collection of 28 silver gelatin prints in a green cloth display album.
£1,000-1,100 *CNY*

Posters

A collection of photographic negatives and original photographs, c1929, approx 186 negatives with contact sheets.
£230-250 *S*

Grand Prix de Monaco, a collection of 24 original posters from 1963 to 1990, by various artists including Pierre Beligond and Michael Turner.
£2,200-2,500 *C(M)*

Rene Vincent, Peugeot, c1928, full colour.
Est. **£50-100** *ADT*

Bay State Automobile Ass'n, Races at Readville, May 30 1906, chromolithograph poster, 22in (56.5cm) wide.
£780-1,000 *S(NY)*

Caspary, Alfa Romeo, offset lithograph in colours, printed by Sauberlin & Pfeiffer, damaged, 50 by 35½in (127 by 90cm).
£260-300 *CSK*

Clincher non-skid tyres, colour lithographic poster, on original board, 13½ by 10in (35 by 25cm).
£1,400-1,500 *ONS*

Hans Liska, 1954 Grand Prix of Italy, Switzerland, France and Berlin.
£575-600 *ONS*

Robert Falcucci, Huile Energol, lithograph in colours, printed by Bedos & Cie, Paris, damaged, 1938, 63 by 46½in (160 by 118cm).
£680-720 *CSK*

24 heures du Mans, a collection of 32 original posters from 1959 to 1990, by various artists including Pierre Beligond and Guy Leygnac.
£2,800-3,000 *C(M)*

Locate the source

The source of each illustration in Miller's can be found by checking the code letters below each caption with the list of contributors

A Shellubrication Takes Out The Squeak!, an original advertising poster, late 1930s, polychrome lithograph, damaged, 33½ by 57in (85 by 148cm).
Est. **£380-450** *S*

A Shell Winter Grade original advertising poster, polychrome lithograph, display mounted, late 1930s, 33 by 57½in (84 by 146cm).
£350-375 *S*

Radiators

A copper Panhard et Levassor radiator, French, polished copper body, with cap and French St Christopher mascot, c1905, 24½in (62cm).
£475-500 *S*

A Rolls-Royce Phantom II radiator core and grille, c1929, polished, 32½in (82.5cm) high.
Est. **£1,500-2,200** *S*

A Rolls-Royce Silver Cloud radiator shell with Flying Lady, 30in (75cm) high.
£580-620 *CNY*

Signs

A Dunlop double-sided advertising sign, in black, green and yellow, 1930s, 24in (61cm) diam.
£85-100   *S*

A Rolls-Royce illuminated glass showroom display sign, etched glass inlaid with gold leaf lettering, c1920, 48in (121cm) long.
£1,300-1,400   *S*

An Automobile Club of Great Britain & Ireland enamel sign, c1902, 28in (71cm) high.
£575-650   *S*

The Automobile Club of Great Britain & Ireland was founded in December 1897. Upon receiving Royal patronage in 1907 it changed its name to The Royal Automobile Club (RAC).

A Bedford Drivers Club double-sided enamel hanging sign.
£200-250   *MSMP*

A Studebaker enamel sign, c1930.
£185-200   *MSMP*

A Shell enamel sign, damaged, 48in (122cm) wide.
£50-80   *PC*

A Dunlop Stock enamel sign, 24in (61cm) diam.   **£75-95**   *ONS*

A National Benzole enamel garage sign, in mounting bracket, the other side reading OPEN or CLOSED.
£115-135   *MSMP*

A Michelin reproduction enamel sign, 8in (20cm) diam.
£5-8   *PC*

A Look for Motors enamel sign, brown on white, some rust and chips, 28in (71cm) high.   **£225-250**   *S*

A Royal Insurance Company Limited enamel sign, 30in (76cm) wide.   **£25-45**   *PC*

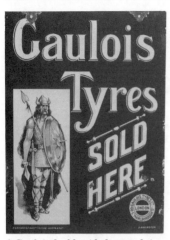

A Gaulois double-sided enamel sign, white lettering on black ground.
£360-380 *S*

An AA hanging cast metal sign, paint worn, 27in (68.5cm) high.
£850-900 *S*

A Delahaye enamel sign, 43in (111cm) high.
£1,450-1,550 *CNY*

Tins & Packaging

A Gamages 5 gallon oil can, with a speedboat and Brooklands car on the other sides, c1930.
£100-150 *MSMP*

An unopened tin of Schrader Valve Caps, 1½in (3.5cm) wide.
£2-5 *PC*

A Zero anti-freeze tin with contents, c1925.
£100-125 *MSMP*

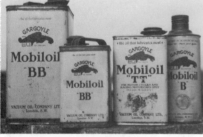

Four Mobil oil tins, 1920-30.
£20-30 each *MSMP*

A Russian Oil Products 1 gallon oil can.
£125-150 *MSMP*

A Castrol oil can, c1930s.
£35-55 *MSMP*

Two pre-war oil cans.
£25-35 each *MSMP*

Three Shell oil cans, c1930.
Large **£75-95**
Medium **£55-75**
Small **£40-60**
MSMP

Two sparking plug enamel tins, 3½in (8.5cm) wide.
£10-15 each *PC*

A Shell lighter fuel miniature petrol can, 4½in (11.5cm) high.
£5-15 *PC*

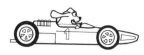

Glossary

We have attempted here to define some of the terms that you will come across in this book. Many of them, notably the bodywork terms, are open to interpretation and where there is a different meaning in America we have tried to explain it. If there are any terms or technicalities you would like explained or you feel that should be included in future please let us know.

Berline – See Sedanca de Ville.

Brake – A term from the days of horse drawn vehicles for any form of open carriage, sometimes used for shooting parties, hence shooting brake. If a shooting brake, or estate car was used to ferry passengers to the railway station it became known as a station wagon. Originally the seating was fore and aft, with the passengers facing inwards.

Brougham – A limousine with some or all of its rear windows blanked out to ensure extra privacy.

Cabriolet – A two-door four-seater body with a folding soft top, usually with wind-up windows. A commonly mis-used term.

Chassis – A framework to which the car body, engine, gearbox, and axles are attached.

Chummy – An open top two-door body just about covered by a folding hood.

Cloverleaf – A three-seater open body style usually with a single door, two seats in the front and one at the rear.

Coachbuilt – A car body which is built separately from the rest of the vehicle and attached to the chassis. Usually an aluminium or fabric covering over a wooden frame.

Convertible – A general term (post-war) for any car with a soft top.

Dickey Seat – A passenger seat, usually for two people contained in the boot of the car without a folding hood (the boot lid forms the backrest). Known in America as a rumble seat.

Doctors Coupé – A much abused term; strictly speaking a fixed or folding head coupé without a dickey seat and the passenger seat slightly staggered back from the driver's to accommodate the famous black bag.

Coupé – Before the war it was a general term applied to a two-door two-seater with a folding hood. There are a number of versions some of which were applied or created at the whim of the manufacturer, see Doctors Coupé, Golfers Coupé, Fixed Head Coupé.

1926 Ford Model T, condition 1. £9,000-9,500 *CC*

Coupé de Ville – Body type with the rear passenger compartment enclosed and the driver either in the open or with a sliding or folding canvas roof.

Dog Cart – A horse drawn dog cart was originally used to transport beaters and their dogs to a shoot (the dogs were contained in louvred boxes under the seats, the louvres were kept for decoration long after the dogs had gone).

Dos-a-dos – Literally back-to-back, i.e. the passenger seating arrangement.

Drop Head Coupé – Originally a two-door two-seater with a folding roof, see Roadster.

Engine – Engine sizes are given in cubic centimetres (cc) in Europe and cubic inches (cu in) in the USA. 1 cubic inch equals 16.38cc (1 litre = 61.02cu in).

Estate Car – See brake.

1970 Lotus Europa SII, Renault engine, alloy wheels. £6,000-7,000 *KSC*

1974 Triumph TR6, condition 1. £9,500-10,000   CC

Fixed Head Coupé – FHC a coupé with a solid fixed roof.

Golfers Coupé – Usually an open two-seater with a square-doored locker behind the driver's seat to accommodate golf clubs.

Hansom – As with the famous horse drawn cab, an enclosed two-seater with the driver out in the elements either behind or in front.

Landau – An open carriage with a folding hood at each end which would meet in the middle when erected.

Landaulette – Half a Landau, i.e. the rear passenger compartment would fold down.

Limousine – A large enclosed car, usually with a glass sliding door between the passengers and the driver, often with pull down occasional seats, sometimes called a pullman.

Monocoque – A type of construction of car bodies without a chassis as such, the strength being in the stressed panels. Most modern mass produced cars are built this way.

Phaeton – A term from the days of horse drawn vehicles for an open body. If there are two rows of seats it is a double phaeton. Replaced by the term Tourer or Touring in the USA. Normally a folding hood would be provided.

Post Vintage Thoroughbred (PVT) – A British term drawn up by the Vintage Sports Car Club (VSCC) for selected models made in the vintage tradition between 1931 and 1942.

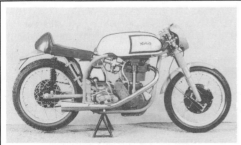

Norton Manx 500cc Solo Motorcycle, engine No. FB 5261, single vertical cylinder, air-cooled, overhead camshaft, 4 stroke engine, 4 speed gearbox, telescopic forks, sprung frame at rear, chain final drive, 3.00 x 19in racing front, 3.50 x 19in racing rear tyres.   **£11,250-11,750   S**

Roadster – An American term for a two-seater sports car. The hood should be able to be removed totally rather than folded down as a drop head coupé.

Runabout – Light open two-seaters from the 1900s

Roi des Belges – A very elaborate open touring car named after King Leopold II of Belgium.

Saloon – A two- or four-door car with four or more seats and a fixed roof.

Sedan – See Saloon.

Sedanca de Ville – Generally a version of a limousine body with the driving compartment covered with a folding or sliding roof section. Sometimes known in America as a Town Car.

Sociable – A cycle car term meaning that the passenger and driver sat side-by-side.

Spider/Spyder – An open two-seater sports car, sometimes a 2+2 (a 2+2 means there are two small occasional seats behind the two front seats).

Station Wagon – See Brake.

Surrey – An early 20thC open four-seater with a fringed canopy. A term from the days of horse drawn vehicles.

Stanhope – Originally a term from the days of horse drawn vehicles for a single seat two-wheel carriage with a hook. Later, a four-wheeled two-seater, sometimes with an underfloor engine.

Tandem – A cycle car term, the passengers sat in tadem, with the driver at the front or at the rear.

Targa – A coupé with a removable centre roof section.

Tonneau – A rear entrance tonneau is a four-seater with access through a centrally placed door at the rear. A detachable tonneau meant that the rear seats could be removed to make a two-seater. Tonneau nowadays usually means a waterproof cover over an open car used when the roof is detached.

Torpedo – An open tourer with an unbroken line from the bonnet to the rear of the body.

Tourer – An open four- or five-seater with three or four doors, folding hood, with or without sidescreens, generally replaced the term torpedo.

Veteran – All vehicles manufactured before 31st December 1918, only cars built before 31st March 1904 are eligible for the London to Brighton Commemorative Run.

Victoria – Generally an American term for a two- or four-seater with a very large folding hood, if a four-seater, the hood would only cover the rear seats.

Vintage – Any vehicles manufactured between the end of the veteran period and 31st December 1930. See Post Vintage Thoroughbred.

Vis-a-Vis – Face-to-face, an open car where one or two passengers sit opposite each other.

Voiturette – A French term meaning a very light car, originally used by Léon Bollée.

Weyman – A system of construction employing Rexine fabric panels over a Kapok filling to prevent noise and provide insulation.

MOTOR BOOKS

Leading specialists in automotive books for enthusiasts throughout the world.
All these books and thousands more at our branches:

MOTOR BOOKS, 33 St Martins Court, St Martins Lane, London WC2N 4AL   Tel: 071-836 5376/6728/3800   Fax: 071-497 2539
MOTOR BOOKS, 8 The Roundway, Headington, Oxford OX3 8DH   Tel: (0865) 66215   Fax: (0865) 63555
MOTOR BOOKS, 241 Holdenhurst Road, Bournemouth BH8 8DA   Tel: (0202) 396469   Fax: (0202) 391572
MOTOR BOOKS, 10 Theatre Square, Swindon SN1 1QN   Tel: (0793) 523170   Fax: (0793) 432070

MAIL ORDER: *Inland:* add 10% of order value, minimum £1.50, maximum £3.00. Orders over £50.00 post free.
Overseas: add 15% of order value on orders up to £150.00, minimum £5.00. Add 10% of order value
on orders over £150.00. For large orders we prefer insured parcel post (usually by air) which we will quote for.
CREDIT CARDS: Visa and Access welcome. Please quote full card number and expiry date.

Illustrated Abarth Buyer's Guide. Vack. Model-by-model assessments, plus specifications and photos. 128 pages, 150 illustrations **£10.95**

AC Cobra: The Complete Story. Laban. A colourful history of these awesome cars, including track endeavours, personalities, buying, etc. 208 pages, 200 mono & colour illustrations .   **£19.95**

Alfa Romeo Giulia History & Restoration. Braden. Packed with information for both enthusiasts and owners of these classic Alfas. 192 pages, 300 illustrations **£17.95**

Alfa Romeo Giulietta Gold Portfolio 1954-1965. Road tests, model introductions and other articles. 172 pages, 300 illustrations **£10.95**

Armstrong-Siddeley Gold Portfolio 1945-1960. Useful collection of road tests, appraisals, photos and data. 172 pages 300 illustrations **£10.95**

Aston Martin: The Postwar Competition Cars. Pritchard. The complete illustrated history. 200 pages, 190 illustrations . **£21.95**

Aston Martin Heritage. Nixon & Newton. All-colour album, including racing and restoration photos. 128 pages, 120 colour illustrations **£10.99**

Sprites & Midgets: The Complete Story. Clausager. Authoritative book by BL archivist. 224 pages, 200 illustrations, 126 colour **£19.95**

Bentley Specials And Special Bentleys. Roberts. Seventy years of works and privately built specials. 440 pages, over 750 illustrations, 24 pages in colour **£75.00**

Bentley Continental R. Lewandowski. High-quality "Art & Car" series book. 2500 numbered copies only. German/English text. 160 pages, 200 illustrations **£125.00**

Bentley Heritage. Bird. All-colour book on the great 1920s models. 128 pages, 120 colour illustrations **£10.99**

The British Citroën. Bobbitt. Full story of the Slough-built cars. 144 pages, illustrated **£23.95**

Daimler SP250/V8250 Saloon Gold Portfolio 1959-1969. Collected road tests, new model reviews and other contemporary material. 172 pages, 300 illustrations **£10.95**

Daimler & Lanchester: An Illustrated History. Long. The only history currently available. 144 pages, 200 illustrations . **£19.95**

Illustrated De Tomaso Buyer's Guide. Box. Full explanation of each model's good and bad points, investment rating, etc. 128 pages, 150 illustrations **£10.95**

Enzo Ferrari. Yates. Detailed, definitive biography of the man and his exploits. 466 pages, 16 pages of illustrations **£16.99**

Illustrated Ferrari Buyer's Guide. Batchelor. Third edition of respected historian's guide. 150 pages, 200 illustrations . **£10.96**

Inside Ferrari. Dregni. Unique look at Ferrari design, building and testing. 176 pages, 125 mono illustrations, 100 colour **£18.95**

Complete Catalogue Of Ford Cars In Britain. Burgess Wise. Illustrated history, Model T to Fiesta. 96 pages, 250 illustrations **£13.95**

Ford Escort. Foy. Penetrating account of Ford's efforts to make the Escort a car for the world marketplace. 192 pages, 200 illustrations **£18.99**

RS Fords In Colour. Foy (editor). All models from Lotus Cortina to Fiesta RS Turbo. 112 pages, 160 illustrations, 55 colour **£12.95**

Choice, Purchase & Performance 1: Ford Capri High Performance Models 1969-1987. Horton. Key information for buyers on all 100mph-plus Capris. 64 pages, 85 illustrations **£8.95**

Apex: The Inside Story Of The Hillman Imp. Henshaw. Second edition (1991) of much-acclaimed history. 190 pages, illustrated £15.95

Classics In Colour 2: Jaguar XJ-Series. Buckley & Mann. Superlative colour profile of the XJ range. Also includes specifications and other data. 96 pages, 121 colour illustrations £11.95

Jaguar: Performance And Pride. Lyons. A lavishly illustrated history from origins to present. 256 pages, 58 mono illustrations, 398 colour £14.99

Jaguar XJ: The Complete Companion. Thorley. Excellent combination of history and practical guidance for owners. 168 pages, 120 mono illustrations, 20 colour £17.95

Jaguar XJ-S. Wherrett. Colour photo-album with many striking pictures. 128 pages, 120 colour illustrations £10.99

E-Type Jaguar. Morland. All-colour album, same format as XJ-S book £10.99

Jaguar Saloons: Grace, Space And Pace. Harvey. Complete coverage of all saloon models, in Harvey's popular "Clasic Car" series format. 256 pages, 250 illustrations including colour £18.50

Jaguar E-Type 6-Cylinder Restoration & Originality Guide. Haddock. The definitive practical guide to authenticity and how to restore. 224 pages, over 500 illustrations £18.99

Jaguar V12 E-Type: A Guide To Authenticity. Russ. A work of exhaustive research detailing absolutely every feature and component. 103 pages, 8 pages of decal illustrations, 80 exploded views £29.95

Jaguar: An Illustrated History. Mennem. 304 pages, 288 mono illustrations, 16 pages in colour £39.95

Practical Classics On XK Jaguar. Complete restoration project, illustrated with step-by-step photos. 80 pages, 300 illustrations £7.95

Jensen Interceptor: The Complete Story. Tipler. Includes development history, personalities, ownership, etc. 200 pages, 200 mono & colour illustrations £19.95

The Complete Jowett History. Clark & Nankivell. Definitive chronicle of the company, the people, the cars. 224 pages, 196 mono illustrations, 27 colour £29.95

Famous Car Factories: Lamborghini. Pasini. A behind-the-scenes look at Lamborghini production. 128 pages, 100 colour illustrations £14.95

La Lancia. Weemink. Second edition (1991) of the truly definitive history of the company and the cars. 416 pages, 500 illustrations including colour £49.95

Lancia Beta: A Collector's Guide. Long. Coverage of Coupé, Spyder, HPE, Montecarlo. 128 pages, 130 illustrations . £12.95

Classics In Colour 4: Land Rover. Taylor. Superb colour history of civilian, military and special Land Rovers, with much technical data. 96 pages, 130 colour illustrations (June 1992) £11.95

Land-Rover Series I, II, & III: Guide To Purchase & DIY Restoration. Porter. How to restore and maintain all components. 208 pages, 1,107 illustrations £16.99

Lotus Elan. Hughes. The inside story of the exciting Elan for the 1990s. 200 mono illustrations, 16 colour £25.00

Lotus Europa Gold Portfolio 1966-1975. Collected road tests and other press articles. First-rate reference material. 172 pages, 300 illustrations £10.95

Lotus Esprit: The Complete Story. Walton. History, personalities, comparisons, etc. by a high-performance expert. 200 pages, 200 mono & colour illustrations **£19.95**

Lotus Seven: Restoration, Preparation, Maintenance. Weale. Most complete practical guide, company-approved. 240 pages, over 300 illustrations **£19.99**

Miata MX-5 Guide: Mazda Recreates The Sports Car. Lamm. Concept, creation and production history. 128 pages, 100 mono & colour illustrations **£10.95**

MGB: Restoration, Preparation, Maintenance. Tyler. Authoritative practical guidance for owners and restorers. 240 pages, over 300 illustrations **£19.99**

MG By McComb. Reissue of Wilson McComb's famous history. 320 pages, 300 illustrations **£20.00**

Choice, Purchase & Performance 2: MGB, MGC & MGB GT V8. Horton. Expert buyer's guide including what to look for, model comparisons, specifications, bargaining points etc. 64 pages, 85 illustrations **£8.95**

Famous Car Factories: Morgan. Holm. A "guided tour" of Morgan's legendary Malvern workshop. 128 pages, 100 colour illustrations **£14.95**

Practical Classics On Morgan Buying & Restoration. An informative series of articles on a Morgan restoration, with many step-by-step pictures. 80 pages, over 200 illustrations .. **£10.95**

Panther Gold Portfolio 1972-1990. Compilation of road tests, model reviews and other reference material. 172 pages, 300 illustrations **£10.95**

Classics In Colour 1: Porsche 924 & 944. Edwards. Colour photos – nearly all new – plus text and technical data. Also includes the new 968. 96 pages, 131 colour illustrations **£11.95**

Porsche Story. Weitmann. Fourth edition (1991) of famous illustrated history. 448 pages, 700 mono illustrations, 8 pages in colour **£25.00**

Porsche Catalogues: A Visual History From 1948 To The Present Day. Toogood. A colourful history of Porsche through the media of brochures, advertising and other literature. 128 pages, colour throughout **£12.95**

Porsche 914 "Caught By Camera". Reef & Mastenbroek. Large-format book with many detail shots of the 914 range plus specifications and statistics. German/English text. 76 pages, 144 illustrations, 19 colour **£19.95**

Royal Rolls-Royce Motor Cars. Pastouna. A detailed look at the cars used by royalty, including special features, blueprint drawings and Royal archive material. 240 pages, over 200 illustrations, some colour **£25.00**

The Postwar Rover P4 & P5. Taylor. First-rate appraisal and buyer's guide. 157 pages, illustrated **£10.95**

Rover 3- & 3.5-Litre Gold Portfolio 1985-1973. Collected tests and other magazine articles. Excellent reference material. 172 pages, 300 illustrations **£10.95**

Tiger: The Making Of A Sports Car. Taylor. Second edition (1990). 240 pages, 182 illustrations **£14.95**

Triumph Spitfire & GT6: A Collector's Guide. Robson. A reliable history and facts-and-figures book by a Triumph expert. 128 pages, 150 illustrations **£12.95**

Triumph Spitfire Gold Portfolio 1963-1980. Large collection of press reports, road tests and other valuable reference articles. 172 pages, 300 illustrations **£10.95**

Triumph Stag. Morland. All-colour album, with many detail and "whole car" shots. 128 pages, 120 colour illustrations ... **£10.99**

Original Triumph TR. Piggott. A complete "authenticity guide" with new colour photos of all details. 112 pages, 160 colour illustrations **£17.95**

Triumph TRs: The Complete Story. Robson. Full history of the range with numerous fine photos. 192 pages, 190 colour & mono illustrations **£19.95**

TVR Gold Portfolio 1959-1990. Compendium of road tests, new model introductions and other features. 172 pages, 300 illustrations **£10.95**

Vauxhall: The Postwar Years. Alder. All models documented, plus the company story. 184 pages, 200 mono illustrations, 39 colour **£19.99**

Volkswagen Golf GTI: First And Finest Of The Hot Hatchbacks. Wagstaff. Full story from inception to 1992 model and VR6. 144 pages, 170 illustrations, 18 colour **£14.95**

Classics In Colour 3: Volkswagen Golf GTI. Wagstaff. Colour photos with extensive captions trace the story from pre-production to present. 96 pages, 130 colour illustrations (June 1992) **£11.95**

VW Power & Style. Kuah. Depicts a huge variety of bodywork and engineering modifications. 192 pages, over 300 mono & colour illustrations **£19.95**

Mon Ami Mate. Nixon. A "double-biography" of Mike Hawthorn and Peter Collins. Rapturously reviewed, one of the most remarkable motorsport books ever published. 378 large pages, over 200 illustrations **£55.00**

Autocourse 1991-92. Full and spectacular coverage of the 1991 season, in the familiar *Autocourse* style. 288 pages, colour throughout **£24.99**

Automobile Year 39, 1991/92. Comprehensive annual covering both industry and sport. 280 pages, colour throughout **£27.95**

A-Z Of Sports Cars Since 1945. Lawrence. Massive make-by-make reference guide. 336 pages, 1,000 illustrations, 35 colour **£24.95**

Alf Francis, Racing Mechanic. Lewis. Reissue of a classic motor racing biography. 368 pages, 30 illustrations **£25.00**

Anatomy & Development Of The Sports Prototype Racing Car. Bamsey. 232 pages, 160 photos and drawings **£19.99**

Chevron: The Derek Bennett Story. Gordon. The first account of this small company and its big achievements. 272 pages, 100 illustrations **£18.50**

Classic Racing Cars: The Postwar Front-Engined GP Cars. Nye & Goddard. Memorable collaboration between a noted writer and photographer. 160 pages, 140 illustrations **£16.99**

Cooper Cars. Nye. Second edition (1991) of award-winning book. 376 pages, over 350 illustrations. 16 pages in colour **£30.00**

Cosworth: The Search For Power. Robson. Second edition (1990) of complete company history. 288 pages, 200 illustrations **£17.50**

Fangio: A Pirelli Album. Moss. A tribute to the *maestro*, with many period photos and magnificent new colour shots . **£25.00**

Grand Prix Racing: The Enthusiast's Companion. Pritchard (editor). Uses past and present writings to provide a highly readable history. 256 pages, 180 mono illustrations, 16 pages in colour **£17.95**

Jim Clark. Nye. A penetrating profile of the great driver, from the publishers of *Autocourse*. 112 pages, illustrated in mono and colour **£12.95**

John Surtees. Surtees & Henry. Full life and career story of the only man to win World Championship titles on two and four wheels. 256 pages, 100 mono illustrations, 20 colour **£18.99**

More Motor Racing. Rivers Fletcher. Memories of racing exploits in the postwar era. 224 pages, 315 illustrations . **£24.99**

Racers Apart. Tremayne. Thought-provoking studies of drivers memorable for strength of character, as well as achievement. 272 pages, 100 illustrations **£24.95**

Racing At Crystal Palace. Parfitt. An affectionate account of two- and four-wheel racing at the London circuit. 128 pages, 170 illustrations **£12.95**

Rosemeyer! Rosemeyer & Nixon. Biography written by Rosemeyer's widow and enlarged by Chris Nixon. 192 pages, 75 illustrations **£7.95**

Scarab: Race Log Of The All-American Specials 1957-1965. The amazing story of Lance Reventlow and his cars. 160 pages, 200 mono illustrations, 24 colour **£29.99**

Touch Wood. Enlarged new edition of Duncan Hamilton's lively and often hilarious autobiography. 168 pages, illustrated . **£19.95**

Uphill Racers: The History Of British Speed Hill Climbing. Mason. Massive history, researched over a period of many years. 416 pages, 300 illustrations **£39.95**

Vintage Auto Racing. Lepp. Marvellous colour photos of Alfas, Ferraris, Cobras and others in historic racing. 128 pages, 80 colour illustrations **£12.95**

CAR CLUBS DIRECTORY

If you wish to be included in next year's directory or if you have a change of address or telephone number, please could you inform us by December 31st 1992. Entries will be repeated in subsequent editions unless we are requested otherwise.

ABC Owners Club, D. A. Hales, Registrar, ABC Owners Club, 20 Langbourne Way, Claygate, Esher, Surrey

A.C. Owners Club, Brian Gilbert-Smith, The Coach House, Waltham St Lawrence, Berks. Tel: (0734) 343479

Alexis Racing and Trials Car Register, Duncan Rabagliati, 4 Wool Road, Wimbledon, London SW20

Alfa Romeo Section (VSCC Ltd), Allan & Angela Cherrett, Old Forge, Quarr, Nr Gillingham, Dorset

Alfa Romeo 1900 Register, Peter Marshall, Mariners, Courtlands Avenue, Esher, Surrey. Tel: (0223) 894300

Alfa Romeo 2600/2000 Register, Roger Monk, Knighton, Church Close, West Runton, Cromer, Norfolk

Alfa Romeo Owners Club, Michael Lindsay, 97 High Street, Linton, Cambs

Allard Owners Club, Miss P. Hulse, 1 Dalmeny Avenue, Tufnell Park, London N7

The Alvis 12/50 Register, Mr J. Willis, The Vinery, Wanborough Manor, Nr Guildford, Surrey. Tel: (0483) 810308

Alvis Owners Club, 1 Forge, Cottages, Bayham Road, Little Bayham, Nr Lamberhurst, Kent

American Auto Club, G. Harris, PO Box 56, Redditch

Pre '50 American Auto Club, Alan Murphy, 41 Eastham Rake, Eastham, S. Wirral. Tel: 051-327 1392

The Amilcar Salmson Register, R. A. F. King, The Apple House, Wilmoor Lane, Sherfield on Lodden, Hants

Armstrong Siddeley Owners Club Ltd, Peter Sheppard, 57 Berberry Close, Bournville, Birmingham

Aston Martin Owners Club Ltd, Jim Whyman, AMOC Ltd, 1A High Street, Sutton, Nr Ely, Cambs. Tel: (0353) 777353

Atlas Register, 38 Ridgeway, Southwell, Notts

Austin J40 Car Club, B. G. Swann, 19 Lavender Avenue, Coudon, Coventry CV6 1DA

Austin Atlantic Owners Club, Den Barlow, 10 Jennings Way, Diss, Norfolk. Tel: (0379) 642460

A40 Farina Club, Membership Secretary, 113 Chastilian Road, Dartford, Kent

The 1100 Club, Paul Vincent, 32 Medgbury Road, Swindon, Wilts

Austin Cambridge/Westminster Car Club, Mr J. Curtis, 4 Russell Close, East Budleigh, Budleigh Salterton, Devon

Austin Big 7 Register, R. E. Taylor, 101 Derby Road, Chellaston, Derby

Austin Counties Car Club, David Stoves, 32 Vernolds Common, Craven Arms, Shropshire. Tel: (058 47) 7459

Austin Gipsy Register 1958-1968, Mike Gilbert, 24 Green Close, Rixon, Sturminster Newton, Dorset

Austin Healey Club, Mrs P. C. Marks, 171 Coldharbour Road, Bristol

750 Motor Club, 16 Woodstock Road, Witney, Oxon. Tel: (0993) 702285

Austin Seven Mulliner Register, Mike Tebbett, Little Wyche, Walwyn Road, Upper Colwall, Nr Malvern, Worcs

Austin Seven Owners Club (London), Mr and Mrs Simpkins, 5 Brook Cottages, Riding Lane, Hildenborough, Kent

The Austin Seven Sports Register, C. J. Taylor, 222 Prescot Road, Aughton, Ormskirk, Lancs

Austin Seven Van Register, 1923-29, N. B. Baldry, 32 Wentborough Road, Maidenhead, Berks

Austin Swallow Register, G. L. Walker, School House, Great Haseley, Oxford

Austin Healey Club, Midland Centre, Mike Ward, 9 Stag Walk, Sutton Coldfield. Tel: 021-382 3223

Austin A30-35 Owners Club, Andy Levis, 26 White Barn Lane, Dagenham, Essex. Tel: 081-517 0198

Austin Maxi Club, Mr I. Botting, 144 Village Way, Beckenham, Kent

Pre-War Austin Seven Club Ltd, Mr J. Tantum, 90 Dovedale Avenue, Long Eaton, Nottingham. Tel: (0602) 727626

Austin Ten Drivers Club Ltd, Mrs Patricia East, Brambledene, 53 Oxted Green, Milford, Godalming, Surrey

Bristol Austin Seven Club Ltd, 1 Silsbury Cottages, West Kennett, Marlborough, Wilts

Vintage Austin Register, Frank Smith, The Briars, Four Lane Ends, Oakerthorpe, Alfreton, Derbyshire. Tel: (0773) 831646

Scottish Austin Seven Club, 16 Victoria Gardens, Victoria Park, Kilmalcolm, Renfrew

Solent Austin Seven Club Ltd, F. Claxton, 185 Warsash Road, Warsash, Hants

South Wales Austin Seven Club, Mr and Mrs J. Neill, 302 Peniel Green Road, Llansamlet, Swansea

The Wanderers (Pre-War Austin Sevens), D. Tedham, Newhouse Farm, Baveney Wood, Cleobury, Mortimer, Kidderminster, Worcs

Autovia Car Club, Alan Williams, Birchanger Hall, Birchanger, Nr Bishops Stortford, Herts

Battery Vehicle Society, Keith Roberts, 29 Ambergate Drive, North Pentwyn, Cardiff

Bean Car Club, G. Harris, Villa Rosa, Templewood Lane, Farnham Common, Bucks

Old Bean Society, P. P. Cole, 165 Denbigh Drive, Hately Heath, West Bromwich, W. Midlands

Bentley Drivers Club, 16 Chearsley Road, Long Crendon, Aylesbury, Bucks

Berkeley Enthusiasts Club, Paul Fitness, 9 Hellards Road, Stevenage, Herts. Tel: (0438) 724164

Biggin Hill Car Club, Peter Adams, Jasmine House, Jasmine Grove, Anerley, London SE20. Tel: 081-778 3537

The BMW Car Club (Club Office), 'Dracaena', Old Road, Shotover Hill, Headington, Oxford. Tel: (0865) 741229

BMW Drivers Club, Sue Hicks, Bavaria House, PO Box 8, Dereham, Norfolk. Tel: (0362) 694459

Bond Owners Club, Stan Cornock, 42 Beaufort Avenue, Hodge Hill, Birmingham

Borgward Drivers Club, David Stride, 81 Stanway Road, Earlsdon, Coventry

Brabham Register, E. D. Walker, The Old Bull, 5 Woodmancote, Dursley, Glos. Tel: (0453) 543243

Bristol Owners Club, John Emery, Uesutor, Marringden Road, Billingshurst, West Sussex

British Ambulance Preservation Society, Roger Leonard, 21 Victoria Road, Horley, Surrey

British Automobile Racing Club Ltd, Miss T. Milton, Thruxton Circuit, Andover, Hants

British Racing and Sports Car Club Ltd, Brands Hatch, Fawkham, Dartford, Kent

The Brooklands Society Ltd, 38 Windmill Way, Reigate, Surrey

Brough Superior Club, P. Staughton (Secretary), 4 Summerfields, Northampton

Bugatti Owners Club Ltd, Sue Ward, Prescott Hill, Gotherington, Cheltenham, Glos

U.K. Buick Club, Alf Gascoine, 47 Higham Road, Woodford Green, Essex. Tel: 081-505 7347

Buckler Car Register, Stan Hibberd, 52 Greenacres, Woolton Hill, Newbury, Berks. Tel: (0635) 254162

Bullnose Morris Club, Richard Harris, PO Box 383, Hove, East Sussex

C.A. Bedford Owners Club, G. W. Seller, 7 Grasmere Road, Benfleet, Essex

Cambridge-Oxford Owners Club, COOC Membership, 6 Hurst Road, Slough

Citroën Car Club, D. C. Saville, 49 Mungo Park Way, Orpington, Kent. Tel: (0689) 823639

Traction Owners Club, Peter Riggs, 2 Appleby Gardens, Dunstable, Beds

Traction Enthusiasts Club, Preston House Studio, Preston, Canterbury, Kent

2CVGB Deux Chevaux Club of GB, PO Box 602, Crick, Northampton

(Citroën) The Traction Owners Club, Steve Reed, 1 Terwick Cottage, Rogate, Nr Petersfield, Hants

Clan Owners Club, Chris Clay, 48 Valley Road, Littleover, Derby. Tel: (0332) 767410

Classic Corvette Club (UK), Ashley Pickering, The Gables, Christchurch Road, Tring, Herts

The Classic Crossbred Club, 29 Parry Close, Stanford Le Hope, Essex. Tel: (0375) 671843

Classic and Historic Motor Club Ltd, Tricia Burridge, The Smithy, High Street, Ston Easton, Bath

Classic Saloon Car Club, 7 Dunstable Road, Caddington, Luton. Tel: (0582) 31642

Classic Z Register, Lynne Godber, Thistledown, Old Stockbridge Road, Kentsboro, Wallop, Stockbridge, Hants. Tel: (0264) 781979

Clyno Register, J. J. Salt, New Farm, Startley, Chippenham, Wilts. Tel: (0249) 720271

Friends of The British Commercial Vehicle Museum, c/o B.C.V.M., King Street, Leyland, Preston

Commercial Vehicle and Road Transport Club, Steven Wimbush, 8 Tachbrook Road, Uxbridge, Middx

Connaught Register, Duncan Rabagliati, 4 Wool Road, Wimbledon, London SW20

The Crayford Convertible Car Club, Rory Cronin, 68 Manor Road, Worthing, West Sussex. Tel: (0903) 212828

Cougar Club of America, Barrie S. Dixon, 11 Dean Close, Partington, Manchester

Crossley Climax Register, Mr G. Harvey, 7 Meadow Road, Basingstoke, Hants

Crossley Register, Geoff Lee, 'Arlyn', Brickwall Lane, Ruislip, Middx, and M. Jenner, 244 Odessa Road, Forest Gate, London E7

DAF Owners Club, S. K. Bidwell (Club Secretary), 56 Ridgedate Road, Bolsover, Chesterfield, Derbyshire

Datsun Z Club, Mark or Margaret Bukowska. Tel: 081-998 9616

The Daimler and Lanchester Owners Club, John Ridley, The Manor House, Trewyn, Abergavenny, Gwent. Tel: (0873) 890737

Delage Section VSCC Ltd, Douglas Macmillan, Brook Farm, Broadway-on-Teme, Worcs

Delahaye Club GB, A. F. Harrison, 34 Marine Parade, Hythe, Kent. Tel: (0303) 261016

Dellow Register, Douglas Temple Design Group, 4 Roumella Lane, Bournemouth, Dorset. Tel: (0202) 304641

De Tomaso Drivers Club, Chris Statham, 2-4 Bank Road, Bredbury, Stockport. Tel: 061-430 5052

The Diva Register, Steve Pethybridge, 8 Wait End Road, Waterlooville, Hants. Tel: (0705) 251485

DKW Owners Club, C. P. Nixon, Rose Cottage, Rodford, Westerleigh, Bristol

Dutton Owners Club, Rob Powell, 20 Burford Road, Baswich, Stafford, Staffs. Tel: (0785) 56835

Elva Owners Club, R. A. Dunbar, Mapel Tree Lodge, The Hawthorns, Smock Alley, West Alley, West Chiltington, West Sussex

E.R.A. Club, Guy Spollon, Arden Grange, Tanworth-in-Arden, Warks

Facel Vega Owners Club, Roy Scandrett, 'Windrush', 16 Paddock Gardens, East Grinstead, Sussex

Fairthorpe Sports Car Club, Tony Hill, 9 Lynhurst Crescent, Hillingdon, Middx

Ferrari Owners Club, 231 Station Road, Balsall Common, Warks. Tel: (0676) 34862

Fiat 130 Owners Club, Michael Reid, 28 Warwick Mansions, Cromwell Crescent, London SW5. Tel: 071-373 9740

Fiat Dino Register, Mr Morris, 59 Sandown Park, Tunbridge Wells, Kent

Fiat Motor Club (GB), H. A. Collyer, Barnside, Chikwell Street, Glastonbury, Somerset. Tel: (0458) 31443

Fiat Osca Register, Mr M. Elliott, 36 Maypole Drive, Chigwell, Essex. Tel: 081-500 7127

Fiat Twin-Cam Register, Graham Morrish, 19 Oakley Wood Road, Bishops Tachbrook, Leamington Spa, Warks

X/19 Owners club, Sally Shearman, 86 Mill Lane, Dorridge, Solihull

Fire Service Preservation Group, Andrew Scott, 50 Old Slade Lane, Iver, Bucks

Pre-67 Ford Owners Club, Mrs A. Miller, 100 Main Street, Cairneyhill, Fife

Five Hundred Owners Club Association, David Docherty, 'Oakley', 68 Upton Park, Upton-by-Chester, Chester, Cheshire. Tel: (0244) 382789

Ford 105E Owners Club, Sally Harris, 30 Gower Road, Sedgley, Dudley. Tel: (0902) 671071

Ford Mk III Zephyr and Zodiac Owners Club, John Wilding, 10 Waltondale, Woodside, Telford, Salop. Tel: (0952) 580746

The Zephyr and Zodiac Mk IV Owners Club, Richard Cordle, 29 Ruskin Drive, Worcester Park, Surrey. Tel: 081-330 2159

Model A Ford Club of Great Britain, R. Phillippo, The Bakehouse, Church Street, Harston, Cambs

Ford Avo Owners Club, D. Hibbin, 53 Hallsfield Road, Bridgewood, Chatham, Kent

Ford Classic and Capri Owners Club, Roy Lawrence, 15 Tom Davies House, Coronation Avenue, Braintree, Essex. Tel: (0376) 43934

Ford Corsair Owners Club, Mrs E. Checkley, 7 Barnfield, New Malden, Surrey

Capri Club International, Field House, Redditch, Worcs. Tel: (0527) 502066

Ford Capri Enthusiasts Register, Liz Barnes, 46 Manningtree Road, South Ruislip, Middx. Tel: 081-842 0102

Capri Drivers Association, Mrs Moria Farrelly (Secretary), 9 Lyndhurst Road, Coulsdon, Surrey

Mk I Consul Zephyr and Zodiac Club, 180 Gipsy Road, Welling, Kent. Tel: 081-301 3709

Mk II Consul, Zephyr, Zodiac Club, 170 Conisborough Crescent, Catford

Mk I Cortina Owners Club, R. J. Raisey, 51 Studley Rise, Trowbridge, Wilts

The Cortina Mk II Register, Mark Blows, 78 Church Avenue, Broomfield, Chelmsford, Essex

Ford GT Owners, c/o Riverside School, Ferry Road, Hullbridge, Hockley, Essex

Ford Cortina 1600E Owners Club, Dave Marson, 23 Cumberland Road, Bilston, West Midlands. Tel: Bilston 405055

Ford Cortina 1600E Enthusiasts Club, D. Wright, 32 St Leonards Avenue, Hove

The Savage Register, Trevor Smith, Hillcrest, Top Road, Little Cawthorpe, Louth, Lincs

The Sporting Escort Owners Club, 26 Huntingdon Crescent, off Madresfield Drive, Halesowen, West Midlands

Ford Escort 1300E Owners Club, Robert Watt, 55 Lindley Road, Walton-on-Thames, Surrey

Ford Executive Owners Register, Mr Jenny Whitehouse, 3 Shanklin Road, Stonehouse Estate, Coventry

Ford Granada Mk I Owners Club, Paul Bussey, Bay Tree House, 15 Thornbera Road, Bishops Stortford, Herts

Granada Mk II Enthusiasts' Club (incorporating A Mk III Register), P. Gupwell, 515A Bristol Road, Selly Oak, Birmingham B29 6AU

The Ford RS Owners Club, Ford RSOC, 18 Downsview Road, Sevenoaks, Kent. Tel: (0732) 450539

Ford Sidevalve Owners Club, Membership Secretary, 30 Earls Close, Bishopstoke, Eastleigh, Hants

Ford Model 'T' Ford Register of G.B., Mrs Julia Armer, 3 Riverside, Strong Close, Keighley, W. Yorks. Tel: (0535) 607978

Mk II Independent O/C, 173 Sparrow Farm Drive, Feltham, Middx

XR Owners Club, Paul Townend, 50 Wood Street, Castleford, W. Yorks

The Ford Y and C Model Register, Bob Wilkinson, Castle Farm, Main Street, Pollington, Nr Goole, Humberside. Tel: (0405) 860836

Frazer-Nash Section of the VSCC, Mrs J. Blake, Daisy Head Farm, Caulcott, Oxford

The Gentry Register, Frank Tuck, 1 Kinross Avenue, South Ascot, Berks. Tel: (0990) 24637

Gilbern Owners Club, P. C. Fawkes, 24 Mayfield, Buckden, Huntingdon, Cambs. Tel: (0480) 812066

Ginetta Owners Club, Dave Baker, 24 Wallace Mill Gardens, Mid Calder, West Lothian. Tel: (0506) 8883129

Gordon Keeble Owners Club, Ann Knott, Westminster Road, Brackley, Northants. Tel: (0280) 702311

The Gwynne Register, K. Good, 9 Lancaster Avenue, Hadley Wood, Barnet, Herts

The Association of Healey Owners, Don Griffiths, The White House, Hill Pound, Swan More, Hants. Tel: (0489) 895813

Heinkel Trojan Owners and Enthusiasts Club, Y. Luty, Carisbrooke, Wood End Lane, Fillongley, Coventry

Hillman Commer Karrier Club, A. Freakes, 3 Kingfisher Court, East Molesey, Surrey KT8 9HL. Tel: 081-941 0604

Historic Commercial Vehicle Society, H.C.V.S., Iden Grange, Cranbrook Road, Staplehurst, Kent

Historic Sports Car Club, Cold Harbour, Kington Langley, Wiltshire

Historic Rally Car Register RAC, Alison Woolley, Tibberton Court, Tibberton, Glos. Tel: (0452) 79648

HRG Association, I. J. Dussek, Little Allens, Allens Lane, Plaxtol, Sevenoaks, Kent

The Holden U.K. Register, G. R. C. Hardy, Clun Felin, Woll's Castle, Haverfordwest, Pembrokeshire, Dyfed, Wales

Honda S800 Sports Car Club, Chris Wallwork, 23a High Street, Steeton, W. Yorks. Tel: (0535) 53845

Humber Register, Hugh Gregory, 176 London Road, St Albans, Herts

Post Vintage Humber Car Club, T. Bayliss, 30 Norbury Road, Fallings Park, Wolverhampton

The Imp Club, Jackie Clark, Cossington Field Farm, Bell Lane, Boxley, Kent. Tel: (0634) 201807

Isetta Owners Club, Brian Orriss, 30 Durham Road, Sidcup, Kent

Jaguar Car Club, R. Pugh, 19 Eldorado Crescent, Cheltenham, Glos

Jaguar Drivers Club, JDC, Jaguar House, 18 Stuart Street, Luton, Beds. Tel: (0582) 419332

Jaguar Enthusiasts Club, G. G. Searle, Sherborne, Mead Road, Stoke Gifford, Bristol. Tel: (0272) 698186

The Jensen Owners Club, Florence, 45 Station Road, Stoke Mandeville, Bucks. Tel: (0296) 614072

Jowett Car Club, Frank Cooke, 152 Leicester Road, Loughborough, Leics. Tel: (0509) 212473

Jupiter Owners Auto Club, Steve Keil, 16 Empress Avenue, Woodford Green, Essex. Tel: 081-505 2215

Karmann Ghia Owners Club (GB), Eliza Conway, 269 Woodborough Road, Nottingham

Kieft Racing and Sports Car Club, Duncan Rabagliati, 4 Wool Road, Wimbledon, London SW20

The Lagonda Club, Mrs Valerie May, 68 Saville Road, Lindfield, Haywards Heath, Sussex

Landcrab Owners Club International, Bill Frazer, PO Box 218, Cardiff

Land Rover Register (1947-1951), Membership Secretary, High House, Ladbrooke, Nr Leamington Spa

The Land Rover Series One Club, David Bowyer, East Foldhay, Zeal Monachorum, Crediton, Devon. Tel: (0363) 82666

Land Rover Series Two Club, PO Box 1609, Yatton, Bristol

Lancia Motor Club, The Old Shire House, Aylton, Ledbury, Herefordshire

Lea Francis Owners Club, R. Sawers, French's, Long Wittenham, Abingdon, Oxon

Lincoln-Zephyr Owners Club, Colin Spong, 22 New North Road, Hainault, Ilford, Essex

London Bus Preservation Trust, Cobham Bus Museum, Redhill Road, Cobham, Surrey

London Vintage Taxi Association, Keith White, 6 Alterton Close, Woking, Surrey

Lotus Cortina Register, 'Fernleigh', Homash Lane, Shadoxhurst, Ashford, Kent

Lotus Drivers Club, Lee Barton, 15 Pleasant Way, Leamington Spa. Tel: (0926) 313514

Lotus Seven Owners Club, David Miryless, 18 St James, Beaminster, Dorset

Club Lotus, PO Box 8, Dereham, Norfolk. Tel: (0362) 694459

Historic Lotus Register, Mike Marsden, Orchard House, Wotton Road, Rangeworthy, Bristol

Marcos Owners Club, 62 Culverley Road, Catford, London SE6. Tel: 081-697 2988

Club Marcos International, Mrs I. Chivers, Membership Secretary, 8 Ludmead Road, Corsham, Wilts. Tel: (0249) 713769

Marendaz Special Car Register, John Shaw, 107 Old Bath Road, Cheltenham. Tel: (0242) 526310

The Marina/Ital Drivers Club, Mr J. G. Lawson, 12 Nithsdale Road, Liverpool

Marlin Owners Club, Mrs J. Cordrey, 14 Farthings West, Capel St Mary, Ipswich

Maserati Club, Michael Miles, The Paddock, Old Salisbury Road, Abbotts Ann, Andover, Hants. Tel: (0264) 710312

Masters Club, Barry Knight, 2 Ranmore Avenue, East Croydon

Matra Enthusiasts Club, M.E.C., 19 Abbotsbury, Orton Goldhay, Peterborough, Cambs. Tel: (0733) 234555

The Mercedes-Benz Club Ltd, P. Bellamy, 75 Theydon Grove, Epping, Essex. Tel: Epping 73304

The Messerschmitt Owners Club, Mrs Eileen Hallam, The Birches, Ashmores Lane, Rusper, West Sussex

Messerchmitt Enthusiasts Club, Graham Taylor, 5 The Green, Highworth, Swindon, Wiltshire

Metropolitan Owners Club, Mr N. Savage, Goat Cottage, Nutbourne Common, Pulborough, Sussex. Tel: (07981) 3921

Club Peugeot UK, Dick Kitchingman, Pelham, Chideock, Bridport, Dorset

The Piper (Sports and Racing Car) Club, Clive Davies, Pipers Oak, Lopham Road, East Harling, Norfolk. Tel: (0953) 717813

Porsche Club Great Britain, Ayton House, West End, Northleach, Glos. Tel: (0451) 60792

Post Office Vehicle Club, 7 Bignal Rand Drive, Wells, Somerset

Post 45 Group, Mr R. Cox, 6 Nile Street, Norwich, Norfolk

Potteries Vintage and Classic Car Club, B. Theobold, 78 Reeves Avenue, Cross Heath, Newcastle, Staffs

The Post-War Thoroughbred Car Club, 87 London Street, Chertsey, Surrey

The Radford Register, Chris Gow, 108 Potters Lane, Burgess Hill, West Sussex. Tel: (0444) 248439

Railton Owners Club, 'Fairmiles', Barnes Hall Road, Burncross, Sheffield. Tel: (0742) 468357

Raleigh Safety Seven and Early Reliant Owners Club, Mick Sleap, 17 Courtland Avenue, London E4

Range Rover Register, Chris Tomley, Cwm/Cochen, Bettws, Newtown, Powys

Rapier Register, D. C. H. Williams, 'Smithy', Tregynon, Newton, Powys. Tel: (068687) 396

Reliant Owners Club, Graham Close, 19 Smithey Close, High Green, Sheffield

Reliant Rebel Register, M. Bentley, 70 Woodhall Lane, Calverley, Pudsey, West Yorks. Tel: (0532) 570512

Reliant Sabre and Scimitar Owners Club, RSSOC, PO Box 67, Northampton NN2 6EE. Tel: (0604) 791148

Rear Engine Renault Club, R. Woodall, 346 Crewe Road, Cresty, Crewe

Renault Frères, J. G. Kemsley, Yew Tree House, Jubilee Road, Chelsfield, Kent

Renault Owners Club, C. Marsden, Chevin House, Main Street, Burley-in-Wharfedale, Ilkley, West Yorks. Tel: (0943) 862700

Riley Motor Club Ltd, A. J. Draper, 99 Farmer Ward Road, Kenilworth, Warks. Tel: (0926) 57275

Riley R.M. Club, Bill Harris, 57 Cluny Gardens, Edinburgh

Riley Register, J. A. Clarke, 56 Cheltenham Road, Bishops Cleeve, Cheltenham, Glos

Ro80 Club GB, Simon Kremer, Mill Stone Cottage, Woodside Road, Windsor Forest, Windsor, Berks. Tel: (0344) 890411

Rochdale Owners Club, Brian Tomlinson, 57 West Avenue, Birmingham

Rolls-Royce Enthusiasts, Lt-Col Eric Barrass, The Hunt House, Paulersbury, Northants

Rootes Easidrive Register, M. Molley, 35 Glenesk Road, London SE9

Rover P4 Drivers Guild, Colin Blowers (PC), 32 Arundel Road, Luton, Beds

Rover P5 Owners Club, G. Moorshead, 13 Glen Avenue, Ashford, Middx. Tel: (0784) 258166

P6 Rover Owners Club, PO Box 11, Heanor, Derbyshire

Rover Sports Register, A. Mitchell, 42 Cecil Road, Ilford, Essex

British Saab Enthusiasts, Mr M. Hodges, 75 Upper Road, Parkstone, Poole, Dorset

The Saab Owners Club of GB Ltd, Mrs K. E. Piper, 16 Denewood Close, Watford, Herts. Tel: (0923) 229945

British Salmson Owners Club, John Maddison, 86 Broadway North, Walsall, West Midlands. Tel: (0922) 29677

The MG Car Club, PO Box 251, Abingdon, Oxon. Tel: (0235) 555552

MG Octagon Car Club, Harry Crutchley, 36 Queensville Avenue, Stafford. Tel: (0785) 51014

MG Owners Club, R. S. Bentley, 2/4 Station Road, Swavesey, Cambs. Tel: (0954) 31125

The MG 'Y' Type Register, Mr J. G. Lawson, 12 Nithsdale Road, Liverpool

Register of Unusual Micro-Cars, Jean Hammond, School House Farm, Hawkenbury, Staplehurst, Kent

Midget and Sprite Club, Nigel Williams, 15 Foxcote, Kingswood, Bristol. Tel: (0272) 612759

The Military Vehicle Trust, Nigel Gudfrey, 8 Selborne Close, Blackwater, Camberley, Surrey

Mini Cooper Club, Joyce Holman, 1 Weavers Cottages, Church Hill, West Hoathly, Sussex

Mini Cooper Register, Lisa Thornton, 1 Rich Close, Warwick. Tel: (0926) 496934

Mini Marcos Owners Club, Roger Garland, 28 Meadow Road, Claines, Worcester. Tel: (0905) 58533

Mini Moke Club, Paul Beard, 13 Ashdene Close, Hartlebury, Worcs

Mini Owners Club, 15 Birchwood Road, Lichfield

Morgan Sports Car Club, Mrs Christin Healey, 41 Cordwell Close, Castle Donington, Derby

Morgan Three-Wheeler Club Ltd, K. Robinson, Correction Farm, Middlewood, Poynton, Cheshire

Morris Cowley and Oxford Club, Derek Andrews, 202 Chantry Gardens, Southwick, Trowbridge, Wilts

Morris 12 Club, D. Hedge, Crossways, Potton Road, Hilton, Huntingdon

Morris Marina Owners Club, Nigel Butler, 'Llys-Aled', 63 Junction Road, Stourbridge, West Midlands

Morris Minor Owners Club, Jane White, 127-129 Green Lane, Derbyshire

Morris Register, Arther Peeling, 171 Levita House, Chalton Street, London

Moss Owners Club, David Pegler, Pinewood, Weston Lane, Bath. Tel: (0225) 331509

Norton Owners Club, Shirley Fenner, 18 Wren Crescent, Addlestone, Surrey

Nova Owners Club, Ray Nicholls, 19 Bute Avenue, Hathershaw, Oldham, Lancs

NSU Owners Club, Rosemarie Crowley, 58 Tadorne Road, Tadworth, Surrey. Tel: (073781) 2412

The Ogle Register, Chris Gow, 108 Potters Lane, Burgess Hill. Tel: (0444) 248439

Opel GT UK Owners Club, Martyn and Karen, PO Box 171, Derby. Tel: (0773) 45086

The Opel Manta Club, 14 Rockstowes Way, Westbury-on-Trym, Bristol

The Opel Vauxhall Drivers Club, The Old Mill, Borrow Hall, Dereham, Norfolk. Tel: (0362) 694459

Manta A Series Register, Mark Kinnon, 87 Village Way, Beckenham, Kent

Les Amis de Panhard et Levassor GB, Denise Polley, 11 Arterial Avenue, Rainham, Essex. Tel: (04027) 24425

Panther Car Club Ltd, 35 York Road, Farnborough, Hants. Tel: (0252) 540217

Salmons Tickford Enthusiasts Club, Keith Griggs, 40 Duffins Orchard, Ottershaw, Surrey

Scootacar Register, Stephen Boyd, 'Pamanste', 18 Holman Close, Aylsham, Norwich, Norfolk

Simca Owners Register, David Chapman, 18 Cavendish Gardens, Redhill, Surrey

Scimitar Drivers Club, c/o Mick Frost, Pegasus, Main Road, Woodham Ferrers, Essex. Tel: (0245) 320734

Singer O.C., Martyn Wray, 11 Ermine Rise, Great Casterton, Stamford, Lincs. Tel: (0780) 62740

Association of Singer Car Owners (A.S.C.O.), Paul Stockwell, 119 Camelot Close, King Arthurs Way, Andover, Hants

Skoda Owners Club of Great Britain, Ray White, 78 Montague Road, Leytonstone E11

South Devon Commercial Vehicle Club, Bob Gale, Avonwick Station, Diptford, Totnes, Devon. Tel: (0364) 73130

South Hants Model Auto Club, C. Derbyshire, 21 Aintree Road, Calmore, Southampton

Spartan Owners Club, Steve Andrews, 28 Ashford Drive, Ravenhead, Notts. Tel: (0623) 793742

Stag Owners Club, Mr H. Vesey, 53 Cyprus Road, Faversham, Kent ME13 8HD. Tel: (0795) 534376

Standard Motor Club, Tony Pingriff, 57 Main Road, Meriden, Coventry. Tel: (0675) 22181

Star, Starling, Stuart and Briton Register, D. E. A. Evans, New Woodlodge, Hyperion Road, Stourton, Stourbridge

Sunbeam Rapier Owners Club, Peter Meech, 12 Greenacres, Downton, Salisbury, Wilts. Tel: (0725) 21140

Sunbeam Alpine Owners Club, Pauline Leese, 53 Wood Street, Mow Cop, Stoke-on-Trent. Tel: (0782) 519865

Sunbeam Talbot Alpine Register, Peter Shimmell, 183 Needlers End Lane, Balsall Common, West Midlands. Tel: (0676) 33304

Sunbeam Talbot Darracq Register, R. Lawson, West Emlett Cottage, Black Dog, Crediton

Sunbeam Tigers Owners Club, Brian Postle, Beechwood, 8 Villa Real Estate, Consett, Co Durham

The Swift Club and Swift Register, John Harrison, 70 Eastwick Drive, Great Bookham, Leatherhead, Surrey. Tel: (0372) 52120

Tornado Register, Dave Malins, 48 St Monicas Avenue, Luton, Beds. Tel: (0582) 37641

TR Drivers Club, Bryan Harber, 19 Irene Road, Orpington, Kent. Tel: (0689) 73776

The TR Register, Rosy Good, 271 High Street, Berkhampstead, Herts. Tel: (0442) 870471

Trident Car Club, Ken Morgan, Rose Cottage, 45 Newtown Road, Verwood, Nr Wimborne, Dorset. Tel: (0202) 822697

Triumph 1300 Register, 39 Winding Way, Leeds

Club Triumph Eastern, Mrs S. Hurrell, 7 Weavers Drive, Glemsford, Suffolk. Tel: (0787) 282176

Club Triumph North London, D. Pollock, 86 Waggon Road, Hadley Wood, Herts

Triumph Mayflower Club, T. Gordon, 12 Manor Close, Hoghton, Preston, Lancs

Pre-1940 Triumph Owners Club, Alan Davis, 33 Blenheim Place, Aylesbury, Bucks

Triumph Razoredge Owners Club, Stewart Langton, 62 Seaward Avenue, Barton-on-Sea, Hants. Tel: (0425) 618074

The Triumph Roadster Club, Paul Hawkins, 186 Mawney Road, Romford, Essex. Tel: (0708) 760745

Triumph Spitfire Club, Johan Hendricksen, Begijnenakker 49, 4241 CK Prinsenbeek, The Netherlands

Triumph Sports Six Club Ltd, 121B St Mary's Road, Market Harborough, Leics. Tel: (0858) 34424

Triumph Sporting Owners Club, G. R. King, 16 Windsor Road, Hazel Grove, Stockport, Cheshire

Triumph 2000/2500/2.5 Register, G. Aldous, 42 Hall Orchards, Middleton, Kings Lynn. Tel: (0553) 841700

Dolomite Sprint Register, DSR, 39 Mill Lane, Arncott, Bicester, Oxon. Tel: (0869) 242847

Turner Register, Dave Scott, 21 Ellsworth Road, High Wycombe, Bucks

The Trojan Owners Club, Mrs Christine Potter (Secretary), 64 Old Turnpike, Fareham, Hants. Tel: (0329) 231073

TVR Car Club, c/o David Gerald, TVR Sports Cars, The Green, Inkberrow, Worcs. Tel: (0386) 793239

United States Army Vehicle Club, Dave Boocock, 31 Valley View Close, Bogthorn, Oakworth Road, Keighley, Yorkshire

Vanden Plas Owners Club, Nigel Stephens, The Briars, Lawson Leas, Barrowby, Grantham, Lincs

Vanguard 1 and 2 Owners Club, R. Jones, The Villa, 11 The Down, Alviston, Avon. Tel: (0454) 419232

Droop Snoot Group, 41 Horsham Avenue, Finchley, London N12. Tel: 081-368 1884

'F' and 'F.B' Victor Owners Club, Wayne Parkhouse, 5 Farnell Road, Staines, Middx

Victor 101 FC (1964-1967), 12 Cliff Crescent, Ellerdine, Telford, Shropshire

The F-Victor Owners Club, Alan Victor Pope, 34 Hawkesbury Drive, Mill Lane, Calcot, Reading, Berks. Tel: (0635) 43532

Vauxhall Cavalier Convertible Club, Ron Goddard, 47 Brooklands Close, Luton, Beds

Vauxhall Owners Club, Brian J. Mundell, 2 Flaxton Court, St Leonards Road, Ayr

Vauxhall PA/PB/PC/E Owners Club, G. Lonsdale, 77 Pilling Lane, Preesall, Lancs. Tel: (0253) 810866

Vauxhall VX4/90 Drivers Club, c/o 43 Stroudwater Park, Weybridge, Surrey

The Viva Owners Club, Adrian Miller, The Thatches, Snetterton North End, Snetterton, Norwich

Veteran Car Club of Great Britain, Jessamine House, High Street, Ashwell, Herts

Vintage Sports Car Club Ltd, The Secretary, 121 Russell Road, Newbury, Berks. Tel: (0635) 44411

The Association of British Volkswagen Clubs, Dept PC, 66 Pinewood Green, Iver Heath, Bucks

Volkswagen Cabriolet Owners Club (GB), Emma Palfreyman (Secretary), Dishley Mill, Derby Road, Loughborough

Historic Volkswagen Clubs, 11A Thornbury Lane, Church Hill, Redditch, Worcs. Tel: (0527) 591883

Volkswagen Owners Club GB, R. Houghton, 49 Addington Road, Irthlingborough, Northants

Volkswagen Owners Caravan Club (GB), Mrs Shirley Oxley, 18 Willow Walk, Hockley, Essex

Volkswagen Split Screen Van Club, Brian Hobson, 12 Kirkfield Crescent, Thorner, Leeds

Volkswagen '50-67' Transporter Club, Peter Nicholson, 11 Lowton Road, Lytham St Annes, Lancs. Tel: (0253) 720023

VW Type 3 and 4 Club, Jane Terry, Pear Tree Bungalow, Exted, Elham, Canterbury, Kent

Volvo Enthusiasts Club, Kevin Price, 4 Goonbell, St Agnes, Cornwall

Volvo Owners Club, Mrs Suzanne Groves, 90 Down Road, Merrow, Guildford, Surrey. Tel: (0483) 37624

Vulcan Register, D. Hales, 20 Langbourne Way, Claygate, Esher, Surrey

The Wartburg Owners Club, Bernard Trevena, 56 Spiceall Estate, Compton, Guildford. Tel: (0483) 810493

Wolseley 6/80 and Morris Oxford Club, John Billinger, 67 Fleetgate, Barton-on-Humber, North Lincs. Tel: (0652) 635138

The Wolseley Hornet-Special Club, Mrs P. Eames, Jasmin Cottage, Weston, Nr Sidmouth, Devon

Wolseley Register, B. Eley, 60 Garfield Avenue, Dorchester, Dorset

XR Owners Club, 20A Swithland Lane, Rothley, Leics

DIRECTORY OF AUCTIONEERS

United Kingdom

ADT Auction Centre, Blackbushe Airport, Blackwater, Camberley, Surrey. Tel: (0252) 878555

Bonhams, 65-69 Lots Road, Chelsea, London SW10. Tel: 071-351 7111

Brooks, 81 Westside, London SW4. Tel: 071-228 8000

Central Motor Auctions PLC, Central House, Pontefract Road, Rothwell, Leeds. Tel: (0532) 820707

Christie's, 8 King Street, St James, London SW1. Tel: 071-839 9060

Classic Motor Auctions, PO Box 20, Fishponds, Bristol. Tel: (0272) 701370

Coys of Kensington, 2-4 Queens Gate Mews, London SW7. Tel: 071-584 7444

Hampson Ltd, Road 4, Winsford Industrial Estate, Winsford, Cheshire. Tel: (0606) 559054

Hamptons Collectors Cars, 71 Church Street, Malvern, Worcs. Tel: (0684) 893110

Holloways, 49 Parsons Street, Banbury, Oxon. Tel: (0295) 253197

Husseys, Matford Park Road, Marsh Barton, Exeter. Tel: (0392) 425481

James Auctioneers, 33 Timberhill, Norwich. Tel: (0603) 625369

Lambert & Foster, 97 Commercial Road, Paddock Wood, Tonbridge, Kent. Tel: (0892) 832325

Phillips, West Two, 10 Salem Road, London W2. Tel: 071-229 9090

RTS Auctions Ltd, 11 Telford Close, Sweet Briar Industrial Estate, Norwich. Tel: (0603) 505718

Sentries Auctions, Huntworth Manor, Huntworth, Somerset. Tel: (0278) 663263

Shoreham Car Auctions, 5-6 Brighton Road, Kingston Wharf, Shoreham-by-Sea, West Sussex. Tel: (0273) 871871

Sotheby's, 34-35 New Bond Street, London W1. Tel: 071-493 8080

Sotheby's, Summers Place, Billingshurst, West Sussex. Te: (0403) 783933

Walton & Hipkiss, 111 Worcester Road, Hagley, West Midlands. Tel: (0562) 885555

International

'The Auction', 3535 Las Vegas Boulevard, South Las Vegas, Nevada 89101, USA. Tel: (0101) 702 794 3174

C. Boisgirard, 2 Rue de Provence, 75009 Paris, France. Tel: (010 33) 147708136

Carlisle Productions, The Flea Marketeers, 1000 Bryn Mawr Road, Carlisle, PA 17013-1588, USA

Christie's Australia Pty Ltd, 1 Darling Street, South Yarra, Melbourne, Victoria 3141. Tel: (03) 820 4311

Christie's (Monaco), S.A.M., Park Palace, 98000 Monte Carlo. Tel: (010 339) 325 1933

Christie, Manson & Woods International Inc, 502 Park Avenue, New York, NY 10022. Tel: (0101) 212 546 1000

Classic Automobile Auctions B.V., Goethestrasse 10, 6000 Frankfurt 1. Tel: (010 49) 69 28666/8

Kruse International Inc, PO Box 190-Co.Rd. 11-A, Auburn, Indiana, USA 46706. Tel: (0101) 219 925 5600

Paul McInnis Inc, Auction Gallery, Route 88, 356 Exeter Road, Hampton Falls, New Hampshire 03844, USA. Tel: (0101) 603 778 8989

Orion Auction House, Victoria Bldg-13, Bd Princess Charlotte, Monte Carlo, MC 98000 Monaco. Tel: (010 3393) 301669

Silver Collector Car Auctions, E204, Spokane, Washington 99207, USA. Tel: (0101) 509 326 4485

Sotheby's, 1334 York Avenue, New York, NY 10021. Tel: (0101) 212 606 7000

Sotheby's, B.P. 45, Le Sporting d'Hiver, Place du Casino, MC 98001 Monaco/Cedex. Tel: (0101) 3393 30 88 80

DIRECTORY OF MUSEUMS

Avon
Bristol Industrial Museum, Princes Wharf, City Docks, Bristol 1. Tel: (0272) 251470

Bedfordshire
Shuttleworth Collection, Old Warden Aerodrome, Nr Biggleswade. Tel: (096 727) 288

Buckinghamshire
West Wycombe Motor Museum, Cockshoot Farm, Chorley Road, West Wycombe

Cambridgeshire
Vintage M/C Museum, South Witham, Nr Peterborough

Cheshire
Mouldsworth Motor Museum, Smithy Lane, Mouldsworth. Tel: (0928) 31781

Cornwall
Automobilia Motor Museum, The Old Mill, St Stephen, St Austell

Co Durham
North of England Open Air Museum, Beamish

Cumbria
Lakeland Motor Museum, Holker Hall, Cark-in-Cartmel, Nr Grange-over-Sands. Tel: (0448) 53314

Cars of the Stars Motor Museum, Standish Street, Keswick. Tel: (07687) 73757

Derbyshire
The Donington Collection, Donington Park, Castle Donington. Tel: (0332) 810048

Devon
Totnes Motor Museum, Steamer Quay, Totnes. Tel: (0803) 862777

Essex
Ford Historic Car Collection, Ford Motor Co, Eagle Way, Brentwood

Gloucestershire
The Bugatti Trust, Prescott, Gotherington, Cheltenham. Tel: (0242) 677201

Cotswold Motor Museum, Old Mill, Bourton-on-the-Water, Nr Cheltenham. Tel: (0451) 821255

Hampshire
Gangbridge Collection, Gangbridge House, St Mary Bourne, Andover

The National Motor Museum, Beaulieu. Tel: (0590) 612345

Humberside
Peter Black Collection, Lawkholme Lane, Keighley

Bradford Industrial Museum, Moorside Mills, Moorside Road, Bradford. Tel: (0274) 631756

Hull Transport Museum, 36 High Street, Kingston upon Hull. Tel: (0482) 22311

Museum of Army Transport, Flemingate, Beverley. Tel: (0482) 860445

Sandtoft Transport Centre, Sandtoft, Nr Doncaster

Kent
Historic Vehicles Collection of C. M. Booth, Falstaff Antiques, High Street, Rolvenden

The Motor Museum, Dargate, Nr Faversham

Ramsgate Motor Museum, West Cliff Hall, Ramsgate. Tel: (0843) 581948

Lancashire
The British Commercial Vehicles Museum, King Street, Leyland, Preston. Tel: (0772) 451011

Bury Transport Museum, Castlecroft Road, off Bolton Street, Bury

Manchester Museum of Transport, Boyle Street, Manchester

Tameside Transport Collection, Warlow Brook, Frietland, Greenfield, Oldham

Leicestershire
Stanford Hall Motorcycle Museum, Stanford Hall, Lutterworth. Tel: (0788) 860250

Lincolnshire
Geeson Brothers Motorcycle Museum and Workshop, South Witham, Grantham. Tel: (057 283) 280/386

London
British Motor Industry, Heritage Trust, Syon Park, Brentford. Tel: 081-560 1378

Science Museum, South Kensington SW7. Tel: 071-938 8000

Norfolk
Caister Castle Car Collection, Caister-on-Sea, Nr Great Yarmouth. Tel: (0572) 84251/84202

Sandringham Museum, Sandringham. Tel: (0553) 772675

Nottinghamshire
Nottingham Industrial Museum, Courtyard Buildings, Wallaton Park

Shropshire
Midland Motor Museum, Stourbridge Road, Bridgnorth. Tel: (0746) 761761

Somerset
Haynes Sparkford Motor Museum, Sparkford, Nr Yeovil. Tel: (0963) 40804

Surrey
Brooklands Museum, Brooklands Road, Weybridge. Tel: (0932) 859000

Dunsfold Land Rover Museum, Alfold Road, Dunsfold. Tel: (0483) 200567

Sussex
Bentley Motor Museum, Bentley Wildfowl Trust, Halland. Tel: (082 584) 711

Effingham Motor Museum, Effingham Park, Copthorne

Filching Manor Museum, Filching Manor, Jevington Road, Wannock, Polegate. Tel: (0323) 487838/487933/487124

Tyne and Wear
Newburn Hall Motor Museum, 35 Townfield Garden, Newburn

West Midlands
Birmingham Museum of Science and Industry, Newhall Street, Birmingham. Tel: 021-235 1661

Black Country Museum, Tipton Road, Dudley

Museum of British Road Transport, St Agnes Lane, Hales Street, Coventry. Tel: (0203) 832425

Autoworld at The Patrick Collection, 180 Lifford Lane, Kings Norton, Birmingham. Tel: 021-459 9111

West Yorkshire
Automobilia Transport Museum, Billy Lane, Old Town, Hebden Bridge. Tel: (0422) 844775

Wiltshire
Science Museum, Red Barn Gate, Wroughton, Nr Swindon. Tel: (0793) 814466

Eire
The National Museum of Irish Transport, Scotts Garden, Killarney, Co Kerry

Isle of Man
Manx Motor Museum, Crosby. Tel: (0624) 851236

Port Erin Motor Museum, High Street, Port Erin. Tel: (0624) 832964

Jersey
Jersey Motor Museum, St Peter's Village

Northern Ireland
Ulster Folk and Transport Museum, Cultra Manor, Holywood, Co Down. Tel: (0232) 428428

Scotland
Doune Motor Museum, Carse of Cambus, Doune, Perthshire. Tel: (078 684) 203

Grampian Transport Museum, Alford, Aberdeenshire. Tel: (0336) 2292

Highland Motor Heritage, Bankford, Perthshire

Melrose Motor Museum, Annay Road, Melrose. Tel: (089 6822) 2624

Moray Motor Museum, Bridge Street, Elgin. Tel: (0343) 544933

Museum of Transport, Kelvin Hall, Bunhouse Road, Glasgow. Tel: 041-357 3929

Myreton Motor Museum, Aberlady, East Lothian. Tel: (087) 57288

Royal Museum of Scotland, Chambers Street, Edinburgh. Tel: 031-225 7534

Wales
Conwy Valley Railway Museum Ltd, The Old Goods Yard, Betws-y-Coed, Gwynedd. Tel: (0690) 710568

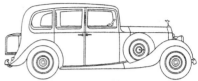

INDEX